Junius and Joseph

Joseph Smith as general in the Nauvoo Legion. Engraving after the 1842 portrait by Sutcliffe Maudsley. Courtesy of the Church Archives, the Church of Jesus Christ of Latter-day Saints.

Junius and Joseph

Presidential Politics and the Assassination of the First Mormon Prophet

Robert S. Wicks and Fred R. Foister

UTAH STATE UNIVERSITY PRESS
Logan, Utah

Utah State University Press
Logan, Utah 84322-7800
www.usu.edu/usupress

Manufactured in the United States of America
Printed on acid-free paper

Library of Congress Cataloging-in-Publication Data

Wicks, Robert Sigfrid, 1954-
        Junius and Joseph : presidential politics and the assassination of the first Mormon prophet /
Robert S. Wicks and Fred R. Foister.
            p. cm.
        Includes bibliographical references (p.) and index.
        ISBN 0-87421-607-9 (hardcover : alk. paper) -- ISBN 0-87421-608-7 (pbk. : alk. paper)
1. Smith, Joseph, 1805-1844. 2. Smith, Joseph, 1805-1844--Assassination. 3. Presidential candidates--
United States--Biography. 4. Mormons--United States--Biography. 5. Presidents--United States--Elec-
tion--1844. 6. United States--Politics and government--1841-1845. 7. Whig Party (U.S.)--History--19th
century. 8. Mormon Church--United States--Political activity--History--19th century. 9. Mormonism--
Political aspects--United States--History--19th century. 10. Illinois--Politics and government--To 1865. I.
Foister, Fred R., 1947- II. Title.
        BX8695.S6W49 2005
        289.3'73'09034--dc22

                                                                                        2005004399

to
the memory of
Mervin B. Hogan
(1906–1998)

and to
Ed Michaels

Contents

Illustrations

Acknowledgments

THE ORIGINS OF THIS STUDY can be traced to a 1980 local history piece written for the Hamilton, Ohio *Journal-News* by historian Jim Blount. Ed Michaels brought the article to our attention in early 1995; he had kept the clipping tucked away with his genealogical research notes and only unearthed it in 1994, the 150th anniversary of the murder of the founding prophet of the Church of Jesus Christ of Latter-day Saints. Blount's account, "Hamilton Marshal Killed Mormon's Joseph Smith," provided us with the first suggestion that the assassination of the Prophet Joseph was driven more by national political interests than disagreement over Mormon theology, economics, or even polygamy. As practicing Latter-day Saints, we intend this work to assist in a re-evaluation of the final months in the life of the first Mormon prophet.

This study would not have been possible without the generous assistance of countless individuals. First and foremost we must thank our wives and families for their forbearance as well as encouragement during numerous research trips to consult court records, historical society files, and church archives in Ohio, Kentucky, Illinois, Missouri, and Utah.

At times we were almost overwhelmed by the difficulties of navigating the complicated terrain of early Mormonism. Our journey was made easier by the insightful writings of Mervin D. Hogan, D. Michael Quinn, Scott H. Faulring, Lyndon Cook, and Will Bagley, each of whom unknowingly provided the catalyst for some critical breakthrough moments during the various phases of this project. Numerous colleagues and friends also offered assistance along the way. Chief among them were Gordon C. Thomasson, Carl Pletsch and Ryan J. Barilleaux. They willingly read early drafts of the manuscript and provided thought-provoking commentary. Gordon, in particular, always found time for late-night reflection and was generous with much needed moral support and practical advice.

Several institutions and individuals deserve special mention. The Chicago Historical Society's John J. Hardin Papers are an unheralded treasure of early Whig correspondence, without which this story could never have been told, much less imagined. Elder Dallin H. Oaks generously provided access to his research files for the classic 1975 study, *The Carthage Conspiracy: The Trial of the Accused Assassins of Joseph Smith, Jr.,* now housed at the L. Tom Perry Special Collections of the Harold B. Lee Library, Brigham Young University, Provo, UT. Ron Romig, archivist, Community of Christ, Independence, MO, allowed us to publish grand jury testimony during the fall of 1844 together with a rare contemporary sketch of the vicinity of Carthage jail used by defense attorneys at the 1845 trial. Ronald G. Watt, Church Archives and Library, Church of Jesus Christ of Latter-day Saints, Salt Lake City, UT, supplied transcripts of manuscript materials related to the death of Joseph Smith, Jr.; Bill Slaughter assisted in the selection of images. Rachel Hoover, Brigham Young University Museum of Art, Provo, UT, generously supplied transparencies of C. C. A. Christenen's paintings of Carthage jail. Sally McPherson, formerly of the Center for Hancock County History, Western Illinois University, Macomb, IL, provided an ideal setting for research and consultation during our visits. Stan Larson, Manuscripts Division, J. Willard Marriott Library, University of Utah Libraries, Salt Lake City, UT, guided us through the labyrinth of Mervin Hogan's self-published monographs and papers. Ed Via, of Miami's Interlibrary Loan department, located many hard-to-find sources. Duncan R. Oliver assisted in the early Ohio research. Beth Oliver ably rendered the maps and reconstruction of Carthage jail. Sue Gambrell proofread the manuscript. Pamela Fox, former dean of the School of Fine Arts at Miami University, and Jerry Morris, former chair of the Department of Art at Miami, provided much-needed research and travel support.

John Alley and his staff at the Utah State University Press were incredibly accommodating throughout the time this manuscript was under review as well as during the editing and production process. We are grateful as well for the care with which anonymous readers evaluated the preliminary manuscript and suggested improvements along the way. These have been incorporated whenever possible. We are especially indebted to Roger Launius, who made critical recommendations about the structure of the text and highlighted the importance of understanding "persecuted innocence" in the early Mormon worldview, and to Jan Shipps, whose generous appraisal of the manuscript proved vital to the success of this project. Any remaining shortcomings are our own.

The advent of the Internet and publications on CD-ROM has eased access to many previously obscure and rare resources. Fortunately, these research tools have not yet replaced the need for hands-on examination of primary source material. In addition to the repositories mentioned above, the following institutions also provided generous assistance throughout the course of this project:

Alton Area Historical Society and Research Library, Alton, IL
American Jewish Archives, Hebrew Union College, Cincinnati, OH
Ball State University Libraries, Muncie, IN
Beinecke Rare Book and Manuscript Library, Yale University, New Haven, CT
Butler County Historical Society, Hamilton, OH
Butler County Records Center, Hamilton, OH
Cincinnati Historical Society, Cincinnati, OH
Cincinnati Public Library, Cincinnati, OH
Family History Library, Salt Lake City, UT
Grand Lodges of Illinois, Iowa, Kentucky, and Ohio
Grant County Public Library, Williamstown, KY
Grant County Courthouse, Williamstown, KY
Hancock County Courthouse, Carthage, IL
Illinois Historical Survey, Urbana, IL
Illinois State Archives, Springfield, IL
Illinois State Historical Library, Springfield, IL

Iowa Masonic Library and Museum, Cedar Rapids, IA
Lane Public Library, Hamilton, OH
Library of Congress, Washington, D.C.
Miami University Archives, Oxford, OH
National Archives and Records Administration, Washington, D.C. and Chicago, IL
Ohio Historical Society, Columbus, OH
Quincy Public Library, Quincy, IL
Smith History Room, Oxford Branch, Lane Public Library, Oxford, OH
Southern Illinois University Library, Edwardsville, IL
University of North Texas Libraries, Denton, TX
Warren County Historical Society, Lebanon, OH

Last of all, we must thank our friends and acquaintances who, with much tolerance and endless patience, withstood years of seemingly incessant talk, of Nauvoo, 1844, Joseph Smith, and the four gunmen at the well. This book is also for you.

In the next canvass, we shall be influenced by no party consideration . . . so the partizans in this county, who expect to divide the friends of humanity and equal rights, will find themselves mistaken—we care not a fig for Whig or Democrat; they are both alike to us, but we shall go for our friends, our tried friends, and the cause of human liberty, which is the cause of God. We are aware that "divide and conquer" is the watchword with many, but with us it cannot be done.

Joseph Smith, December 1841

I am a Whig, and I am a Clay man. I am made of Clay, and I am tending to Clay, and I am going to vote for Henry Clay; that's the way I feel . . . But I won't interfere with my people religiously, to affect their votes, though I might to elect Clay, for he ought to be president . . . I am a democrat myself. I am a Washington democrat, a Jefferson democrat, a Jackson democrat, and I voted for Harrison [in 1840], and I am going to vote for Clay [in 1844].

Joseph Smith, August 1843

Tell the people we have had Whig and Democrats [as] Presidents long enough. We want a President of the United States . . . There is oratory enough in the Church to carry me into the Presidential chair the first slide.

Joseph Smith, January 1844

[O]ur candidate for this high office, has been butchered . . . to prevent him from being elected.

John Taylor, "The Next President"
Times and Seasons, August 1844

Introduction

Assassination of a Candidate

JOSEPH SMITH DECLARED HIS CANDIDACY in the 1844 presidential race as a political reformer on an independent ticket. Joseph never gave his own movement an official name; he believed that all political parties were degraded, their leaders corrupt, and that the entire United States government was in need of reform. In print and from the pulpit he advocated a return to the "holy principles of '76," the republican ideals espoused by America's founding fathers. Smith's supporters established a political newspaper in New York City, published by the Society for the Diffusion of Truth. Its editors reported on Jeffersonian conventions promoting General Joseph Smith (he was a lieutenant general in the Illinois state militia), described as a man who would be "neither a Whig, a Democrat, or pseudo democratic President, but a President of the United States, not a Southern man with Northern principles, or a Northern man with Southern principles, but an independent man with American principles."

Joseph Smith was not simply one more third-party candidate for the presidency of the United States. He was the mayor of Nauvoo, Illinois, a flourishing Mississippi River community second only to Chicago in population. And, he was the charismatic founder of the Church of Jesus Christ of Latter-day Saints, with tens of thousands of followers who sustained him as a prophet of God.

For the thirty-eight-year-old prophet Joseph, the American presidency was only the beginning. His publicly stated motivation for seeking the presidential chair was to facilitate compensating the Saints for their losses—of life, land, and property—during years of persecution in Missouri and their subsequent expulsion from the state. His private vision (initially made known only to a select inner circle of confidants) was even more ambitious. He prophesied the demise of the United States government within his own lifetime and proclaimed that his political Kingdom of God would ultimately overthrow all earthly regimes in fulfillment of Old Testament prophecy. Smith's dual political agendas were managed by a secret Council of Fifty, organized as the nucleus of a new world government.

For Joseph and his followers, the prospect was glorious: a heavenly-inspired theocratic democracy where "God and the people [would] hold the power to conduct the affairs of men in righteousness," a literal fulfillment of the Christian prayer for God's kingdom to become established "on earth as it is in heaven." To Joseph's opponents, the prospect of merging church and state in America meant a frightening, and unacceptable, repudiation of a cornerstone of the constitution.

GENERAL SMITH'S

VIEWS

OF THE POWERS AND POLICY OF THE

GOVERNMENT

OF THE

UNITED STATES.

———•———

JOHN TAYLOR, PRINTER:

NAUVOO, ILLINOIS.

1844.

Title page of *General Smith's Views of the Powers and Policy of the Government of the United States.*

A nominating convention held in the spring of 1844 confidently expressed the belief that Joseph Smith could carry between two hundred thousand and five hundred thousand votes, or nearly 15 percent of the American electorate, in the upcoming November election. Commentators observed that even if Smith wasn't successful in his presidential campaign, he was quite possibly in a position to determine the outcome of the contest. On a tide of rising optimism, nearly four hundred political missionaries departed Nauvoo throughout the spring and early summer, preaching the gospel of Mormonism and promoting their prophet's presidential bid. Many carried *General Smith's Views of the Powers and Policy of the Government of the United States*, which they preached from the pulpit or stump as if it were an inspired religious tract. The pamphlet soon became the most widely reprinted of all Latter-day Saint publications.[1]

On the afternoon of Thursday, June 27, 1844, Joseph's campaign for the presidency and the Kingdom of God came to an abrupt and bloody end. Shortly after 5:00 P.M. a dozen armed men overpowered the guard posted at Carthage jail (in western Illinois's Hancock County) and ran up the stairs to a landing just outside the jailor's sitting room. Inside were Joseph Smith and his brother Hyrum, prophet and patriarch of the Church of Jesus Christ of Latter-day Saints. Both men were in jail on a trumped-up charge of treason against the state for having declared martial law in Nauvoo without direct orders from the governor. Earlier in the day the brothers had been joined by two trusted confidants and fellow Mormons, John Taylor and Willard Richards.

The intruders forced the door open just enough to allow the entry of gun barrels and shot wildly into the room. Hyrum pulled a single-shot pistol out of his waistband but died from a bullet to the face as he fired. Richards and Taylor pressed against the door and with broad swipes of their canes fended off the gun barrels that jabbed through the opening. Joseph responded with three shots from a six-shooter smuggled to him just hours before, striking a man each time. Three times the gun misfired. As he retreated to the window opposite the door, Joseph was shot in the thigh.

---

1.   Thanks to Gordon C. Thomasson for suggesting the title "Assassination of a Candidate." William Daniels's 1845 pamphlet, *A Correct Account of the Murder of Generals Joseph and Hyrum Smith*, written with the assistance of Lyman O. Littlefield, recognized the political motivation behind Joseph Smith's death. Although written in a primitive nineteenth-century prose style intended as Mormon propaganda, the assertions put forward in *A Correct Account* are largely corroborated by *Junius and Joseph*: "Joseph Smith was the choice of many thousands of his countrymen, to guide his country's destiny," they wrote. "He was hailed as a patriot—untrammelled by . . . party predilections . . . His principles harmonized with the primitive organization of the government, from which it has been wrested by disloyal spirits. None but bigots and hot-spurs opposed, who trembled at the loss of power and place, and immunities from the government crib. Their antipathy to him was very warm, which soon fanned a blaze of political persecution from the public journals throughout the Union. This, probably, was one engine of destruction that contributed to his death." (p. 1). Daniels's *A Correct Account* (which appeared in pamphlet form in the spring of 1845), was written, in part, as a response to the August 1844 publication of *An Authentic Account of the Massacre of Joseph Smith* by Illinois Whig editor G. T. M. Davis. The passage was first published in an unauthorized publication of the Daniels-Littlefield manuscript, "A Complete Latter-Day History of the Murder of Joseph and Hyrum Smith, At the Carthage Jail, on the 27th day of June, 1844. By Scape-Gallows Daniels," *Warsaw Signal*, 25 December 1844. See Vetterli, *Mormonism*, 280–81.

Outside, random gunshots and grey smoke filled the air. As he rested on the window ledge, Joseph could see more than a hundred outraged citizens and militiamen gathered in the yard below, many with their weapons loaded and aimed directly at him. In order to disguise their identities a number of the men wore their clothes inside out and had painted their faces with a dark mud made from wet gunpowder. The head of the militia, Colonel Levi Williams, commanded his men to shoot the Mormon leader hanging in the second-story window. No one dared.

After some hesitation, Joseph cried, "O Lord, My God," and leaped to the ground some fifteen feet below. He fell heavily. Joseph's broken, nearly lifeless body was propped up against the well-curb beside the jail. The men in the yard signaled to those inside that "Old Joe" had jumped out of the window. The assailants rushed down the stairs and faced the Mormon prophet. A four-man firing squad was called out. Within moments, Joseph Smith—lieutenant general of the Nauvoo Legion, mayor of Nauvoo, prophet of God, master mason, and candidate for the presidency of the United States of America—was dead.

John Taylor was critically wounded in the attack. Willard Richards received a minor nick in the ear. After hiding Taylor under some hay in an adjoining jail cell, Richards descended the stairs in search of a doctor.

The October grand jury was faced with nearly sixty proposed indictments for the murders. After prolonged deliberation, the jurors could agree to prosecute only nine individuals. Five of the men were prominent in Hancock County's anti-Mormon movement: Thomas C. Sharp, publisher of the *Warsaw Signal*, Illinois's leading anti-Mormon newspaper; Levi Williams, colonel of the Fifty-ninth Regiment of the Illinois Militia; Mark Aldrich, major in command of the Warsaw Independent Battalion; William N. Grover, captain of the Warsaw Cadets; and Jacob C. Davis, captain of the Warsaw Rifle Company. Four others were indicted because they were known to have been at the jail at the time of the murders or had been wounded in the exchange of gunfire. Sharp, Williams, Aldrich, Grover, and Davis were arrested and released on bail. The other men fled the county.

Following six days of trial testimony, on May 30, 1845, the jury was assigned the task of weighing the evidence in the case. It didn't take them long. The jury reached its unanimous verdict in less than three hours: "Not guilty." The indicted men were free to return to their homes and occupations. The bereaved Mormons braced themselves for more unrest.

Joseph Smith's murder has been characterized as a violent "mob" reaction to the Mormon prophet's political extremism. Robert V. Remini, the preeminent scholar of Jacksonian America (and author of the standard biographies of Andrew Jackson, Henry Clay, and Daniel Webster), for example, has recently written that "it is probable that [Smith] was executed for the simple reason that his political activities had become extremely dangerous to the citizens of surrounding towns" in western Illinois. Remini points out that Joseph Smith headed a "theocratic dictatorship in Nauvoo" and was attempting to form an independent, sovereign state in America. "Finally," Remini concludes, "Joseph had the audacity to run for the presidency of the United States . . . His candidacy was the last straw. In the minds of many he had become a menace to freemen everywhere and had to be eliminated. The courts repeatedly failed to rein him in, so a mob took it upon themselves to end his life and the danger he posed. His murder was a political act of assassination."[2]

Junius and Joseph examines Joseph Smith's nearly forgotten presidential bid, the events leading up to his assassination on June 27, 1844, and the tangled aftermath of the tragic incident. It extends Remini's political perspective regarding Joseph Smith's death in two key areas. First, this study establishes that Joseph Smith's murder, rather than being the deadly outcome of a spontaneous mob uprising, was in fact a carefully planned military-style execution. It is now possible to identify many of the key individuals engaged in planning his assassination as well as those who took part in the assault on Carthage jail. And second, this study presents incontrovertible evidence that the effort to remove the Mormon leader from power and influence extended well beyond Hancock County (and included prominent Whig politicians as well as the Democratic governor of the state), thereby transforming his death from an impulsive act by local vigilantes into a political assassination sanctioned by some of the most powerful men in Illinois. The circumstances surrounding Joseph Smith's death also serve to highlight the often unrecognized truth that a full understanding of early Mormon history can be gained only when considered in the context of events taking place in American society as a whole.

It has been long suspected that the Democratic governor of Illinois, Thomas Ford, was engaged in the plot to kill Joseph Smith. While the evidence assembled here reaffirms that assertion, the plan to murder the first Mormon prophet was not spearheaded by the Democrats. In fact, Joseph Smith's assassination is best described as the deadly result of a Whig-backed conspiracy that arose when it was determined that the Mormon prophet's candidacy might well disrupt the outcome of the 1844 presidential election. Many of the key players in this drama were supporters of Kentuckian Henry Clay, the elder statesman of the American Whig party, and his 1844 bid for the American presidency. Indeed, Clay firmly believed he was destined to become the next president of the United States. "Clear the Way for Henry Clay" resounded in party newspapers and political gatherings across the country.[3]

The lead architect in the campaign to claim Illinois as a Whig state in 1844 was John J. Hardin, a cousin of Mary Todd Lincoln and stepnephew of Henry Clay. As the only Illinois Whig serving in U.S. Congress from 1843–45, Hardin oversaw a vast network of political organizers and local operatives throughout Illinois.

---

2.   Remini, *Joseph Smith*, 177–78. Other recent examples include the website of the Church of Jesus Christ of Latter-day Saints, which stated (January 2004) that Joseph Smith was "killed by a mob" (lds.org). The influential *Church Almanac*, 487, similarly notes, "June 27 [1844] — Joseph and Hyrum Smith were killed by a mob that rushed the Carthage Jail in Carthage, Ill." Countless historical markers, exhibit labels, and survey texts use similar language to describe the circumstances surrounding Joseph Smith's death. Critical studies generally recognize that the disbanded Warsaw militia (in collaboration with the Carthage Greys) was largely responsible for the fatal assault on the jail. The first major scholarly corrective was Oaks and Hill, *Carthage Conspiracy*, published in 1975.

3.   On Whig political disloyalty regarding the Latter-day Saints, the *Quincy Herald* noted, "The Mormons would doubtless feel much mortified and chagrined that the opinions of their fast friends, Browning, Jonas, &c. should undergo such a radical change were it not for the expectation that they will change back again before the next election." (Copied by the *Illinois State Register*, 20 October 1843.)

One of these organizers was Abraham Jonas, of Columbus, Adams County, to the east of Quincy. Jonas was a long-time Freemason who masterfully transformed his prominence within the Masonic community into tangible political clout. In 1842, as Grand Master of the Illinois Lodge, Jonas made Joseph Smith a "Mason at Sight" (the first instance of the honor in Illinois Masonic history) and was single-handedly responsible for the establishment of a Mormon Nauvoo lodge that same year. At the time Jonas was running for a seat in the Illinois state legislature on the Whig ticket.

Jonas's political campaign succeeded through Mormon support at the polls. When word of his victory reached Kentucky, Henry Clay (himself a fellow Freemason and former Grand Master of the Kentucky Lodge) congratulated his old friend, adding, "I anxiously hope that your opinions may prove correct of the ultimate political character of Illinois." Recently retired from the U.S. Senate to devote himself full-time to his presidential campaign, Clay hoped the Latter-day Saints would support him in 1844.

When irregularities were discovered in the Nauvoo lodges' activities, Jonas's strident plea in their behalf before the Illinois Grand Lodge went unheeded. The Mormon Lodge lost its charter and Jonas's support for the Saints soon evaporated.

In the spring of 1844 the Mormons at Nauvoo were experiencing serious internal conflict over Joseph's bold political moves and public exposure of polygamy (plural marriage). Jonas supported the dominant opposition group headed by William Law, one of Joseph's former counselors, by supplying the Mormon dissidents with a printing press. It was this press that was used to publish the incendiary *Nauvoo Expositor* on June 7, a move calculated to test the Mormon prophet's tolerance of dissent. Joseph's response, as predicted, was to have the press destroyed, a decision that led to his death fewer than three weeks later.

Another Illinois Whig who cultivated Mormon favor only when it was politically expedient to do so was Orville H. Browning, of Quincy, a close friend and associate of Abraham Jonas. It was Browning's defense of Smith during 1841 (before Judge Stephen A. Douglas) that foiled an extradition attempt by Missouri. In the course of that trial Browning eloquently and emotionally described the suffering of the Saints as they fled the state in 1839:

> Great God! Have I not seen it? Yes my eyes have beheld the blood-stained traces
> of innocent women and children, in the drear winter, who had traveled hun-
> dreds of miles barefoot, through frost and snow, to seek a refuge from their sav-
> age pursuers . . .[4]

These oft-quoted words became part of the Mormon collective identity as victims of persecuted innocence.

Browning's apparent sympathy for the plight of the Saints (and his famed success at freeing the prophet from legal entrapments) doubtless led Joseph, around noon on June 27, 1844, to request Browning's services once again, to aid in the prophet's upcoming trial scheduled for the following Saturday. This time Browning did not reply. In the end, the solicitation was immaterial, as Joseph lived only a few

---

4.   Smith, *History of the Church* 4:370.

more hours. Browning's contempt for the Saints was magnified when, months later, he agreed to defend the men accused of killing the Mormon prophet.

Abraham Jonas and Orville H. Browning, in concert with scores of other local Whig operatives, kept the Illinois electorate informed of political developments through public meetings, rallies, and by articles in local newspapers. Flyers were posted announcing the latest political gatherings that featured the best stump speakers of the day. The Whig partisan press also helped shape popular opinion through provocative editorials and the publication of letters to the editor. Extensive campaign literature was sent through the mails.

The first half of the main title of this book is taken from the name of one of the most influential series of 1844 campaign pamphlets, known as the *Junius Tracts*. These were issued by *New York Tribune* publisher and political adviser Horace Greeley, who oversaw the national effort to promote American Whig presidential candidate Henry Clay. *Junius* was originally a pen name signed to letters written by an English Whig who attacked King George III and his royalist faction for not allowing outspoken critic John Wilkes (1727–1797), a champion of freedom of the press and individual liberty, to take his elected seat in Parliament.[5]

During the 1844 American presidential campaign, newspaper articles and letters to the editor were often signed "Junius" to maintain the author's anonymity and affirm their allegiance to the Whig cause. Weeks after the Mormon prophet announced his candidacy in the 1844 race a disgruntled Illinois Whig wrote to the editor of the anti-Mormon *Warsaw Signal*. The "deadly coils of Mormon mobocracy," the writer cautioned, threatened to undermine the very principles upon which the nation was founded. Referring to Joseph's autocratic rule, his reported misuse of the right of habeas corpus, as well as his plans to establish the political Kingdom of God on the ruins of the government of the United States, the author argued that "by a long series of high-handed outrages, in violation of all law, against the rights, the peace and the liberties of the people," the Latter-day Saints have "forfeited all claims (if any they ever had) to confidence and respect, and ought justly to receive the condemnation of every individual, not only in the community but in this nation." The writer signed his letter "Junius Secondus." As will be demonstrated in the pages that follow, the anonymous Whig author was not alone in his opposition to the Latter-day Saints and their prophet's political agenda.[6]

---

5.   The *Junius Tracts* were written by Calvin Colton and published in 1843–44. The authorship of the original Junius letters has never been determined. See, for example, Jaques, *The History of Junius*.

6.   "Junius Secondus" to editor of the *Warsaw Signal* [Thomas Sharp], n.d., Mormon Collection, Beineke Library, Yale University; microfilm, Regional Archives, Western Illinois University.

THE

JUNIUS TRACTS.
No. IX.

JUNE,]   PUBLISHED EVERY MONTH.   [1844.

ANNEXATION OF TEXAS.

BY JUNIUS.

Author of "THE CRISIS OF THE COUNTRY," and other Tracts of 1840.

Price, 3 cents single, $2 50 cts. per 100, or $20 per 1000.

TRACTS PUBLISHED

☞ NOTICE :—Committees, Clubs, and all persons desirous of obtaining these Tracts, are requested to send their orders, with remittances, to the publishers, *Greeley & McElrath, Tribune Office, New York,* who will promptly forward them to any part of the Union, as may be directed. Remittances by mail, *post paid or free,* at the risk of the proprietor. Price for any one of the series, $2 50 cts. per 100 copies, or $20 per 1000.

☞ Postmasters are authorized by law to make remittances under their frank.

NEW YORK:

PUBLISHED BY GREELEY & McELRATH,

TRIBUNE BUILDINGS, 160 NASSAU STREET.

1844.

[One Sheet Periodical, Postage under 100 miles 1½ cents; over 100 miles 2½.]

Title page of *The Junius Tracts,* no. IX. University of North Texas Libraries, Denton, Texas.

Chapter One

New World Eden: The Promise of America in Late Jacksonian Politics

THE EARLY TO MID-NINETEENTH CENTURY was a time of constant and rapid change for most Americans. The period witnessed an explosion of religious fervor throughout the northern states, with scores of new religious movements all claiming exclusive authority from God; westward territorial expansion of Anglo-Protestant civilization accompanied by the displacement of native populations; the increasingly problematic position of black slavery in American society; the proposed annexation of Texas; the proliferation of urban centers and a dramatic increase in manufacturing; and the dominance of the two-party system in American politics. Some saw in these developments the glimmerings of a perfectible society. Others believed the unfamiliar social and economic landscape was an omen of the nation's downfall.

These intertwined themes of the late Jacksonian period influenced political rhetoric and discourse during the 1844 presidential campaign in very significant ways. This chapter begins with a brief overview of America's western movement and its devastating impact on the life and culture of indigenous peoples. The second section examines Democratic and Whig political philosophies and the emergence of third parties in national politics. The chapter concludes with a consideration of partisan attitudes towards black slavery and the annexation of Texas in the 1840s. The issues touched upon here will reappear in multiple forms and take on various guises throughout the subsequent narrative.

The Promise of America

"What need wee then to feare, but to goe up at once as a peculier people marked and chosen by the finger of God to possess it?"

John Rolf, Virginia Colony, 1615[1]

The vision of North America as a Promised Land arrived with the first European colonists. For them America had been saved for the civilizing grace of Christianity

---

1. The content of this section is indebted to Haynes and Morris, *Manifest Destiny and Empire*, Stephanson, *Manifest Destiny* (Virginia quotation, xii), and Hietala, *Manifest Design*.

and represented an opportunity to establish upon its soil a new utopian society. Individual liberty, the right to do as one pleased without interference, became a national ideal. Native peoples, who had possessed the land for untold generations, presented an awkward challenge to this vision of a New World Eden. To some of the newcomers the first Americans were regarded as a degraded remnant of the Lost Tribes of Israel, a people waiting to be converted to Christ. To others they were less than civilized, destined for removal or annihilation.

The Northwest Ordinance, approved by the United States Congress in 1787, was the first act following American independence to open unorganized land north of the Ohio River and east of the Mississippi to white settlement, territory that would eventually become the states of Ohio (in 1803), Indiana (1816), Illinois (1818), Michigan (1837), and Wisconsin (1848).

The same year the Northwest Ordinance was passed, John Cleves Symmes, a New Jersey Supreme Court judge, was granted permission to sell two million acres in the Ohio country, a tract located between the Great and Little Miami Rivers, tributaries of the Ohio named after one of the Indian tribes that formerly inhabited the region.

The earliest river town to be established in the Symmes Purchase on the land between the Miamis was named Columbia, at that time a popular allegorical symbol of American exceptionalism. The naming of Columbia proudly compared the settlers' task on America's newest frontier with Columbus's discovery of the New World almost three centuries before, both accepted as predestined events acted out in accordance with God's will. The initial group of Columbia settlers, made up of just over two dozen individuals (twenty men and five women), arrived in November of 1788. Four years later the settlement had grown to more than a thousand residents.

By the mid-1790s Columbia's prospects were in decline, soon to be eclipsed by rival Cincinnati three miles down river, founded shortly after the establishment of Columbia. At first called Losantiville, in 1790 the town was renamed after the Society of Cincinnati, an association of Revolutionary War officers. In 1794 Cincinnati was still "a village of about 100 log cabins, 15 rough frame houses, and 500 people. Most of the trees in the town plat had been cut down. Stores, taverns, and dwellings lined Front Street; Broadway was a cowpath . . . Sycamore Street a steep wagon road." Even so, Cincinnatians envisioned a grand future for their frontier town.[2]

Within five decades of its founding Cincinnati had fulfilled its destiny. With forty-three thousand residents in 1840, Cincinnati was the sixth largest and most ethnically diverse city in the United States, and served as the Ohio River gateway to newer settlements in Indiana, Illinois, Missouri and elsewhere further west. There were more people living in Cincinnati in 1840 than inhabited the entire state of Ohio at the time of its formation in 1803. When Charles Dickens arrived in Cincinnati by riverboat from Pittsburgh in 1842, he discovered "a beautiful city; cheerful, thriving, and animated."[3]

For indigenous peoples the promise of America was disease, death, and dislocation. Protestant missionary efforts among the eastern Indian tribes during the late

---

2.   *Cincinnati: A Guide to the Queen City*, 13 (quote). Beaver, "The Miami Purchase."
3.   Glazer, *Cincinnati in 1840*. Dickens, *American Notes.*

eighteenth and early nineteenth century were aimed at convincing Native Americans of their "savagery" and of their need to adopt the superior ways of Christian society. Conversion was seen as "inevitable as it was desirable." As one historian has noted, "missionaries, in short, tried to make Indian men and women into farmers, artisans, and homemakers, mirror images of the supposedly more advanced whites."[4]

Many Native Americans soon discovered, however, that converting to Christianity, adopting the English language, using Anglicized names and following American social custom did not bring them equality in white society. Furthermore, Protestant assumptions about the cultural inferiority of the American Indian were shared by most government leaders. Judged by American lawmakers to be unworthy of liberty, self-government and even citizenship, the removal of Native Americans from their ancestral lands was seen as a necessary precondition for the westward advancement of white Anglo-Protestant civilization.

The language of the Indian Removal Act approved by the United States Congress in 1830 was straightforward. On its face the act provided for "an exchange of lands with the Indians residing in any of the states or territories, and for their removal" into unorganized lands "west of the river Mississippi." The reality was much more brutal. Throughout the 1830s and early 1840s Indian tribes were taken from their native lands and forced to relocate on Western reserves. Many died from disease and never reached their new homelands.[5]

The Wyandot were the one of the last of the midwestern Indian tribes to be removed from east of the Mississippi. In 1842 Wyandot leaders concluded an agreement to cede all of their lands in Ohio and Michigan (with the exception of three burial grounds) to the United States. In return, the Wyandots were to be provided with a "permanent annuity" of $17,500 "in current specie" and receive 148,000 acres of reservation land west of the Mississippi River on which to reside. By the early 1840s, most Ohio Wyandots were baptized Methodists and had adopted Western style dress. Few were full-blooded Indians.

On July 9, 1843, the last of the Huron River band of Wyandots, comprised of about 664 tribal members, four dozen wagons and nearly three hundred ponies and horses, departed Upper Sandusky, Ohio and headed south. The weeklong journey took them to the wharfs of Cincinnati on the Ohio where they boarded two steam-ships, the *Republic* and the *Nodaway*, that would take them out West. After departing the Cincinnati docks on July 21 the steamers neared the tomb of President William Henry Harrison, prominently visible on a bluff above the river at North Bend. The Indian elders requested the captain of the *Nodaway* fire a "big gun" salute to the hero of Tippecanoe. The men of the tribe assembled on the hurricane roofs of the steamships, removed their hats and silently waved them aloft in reverence to the old warrior. A chief stepped forward and spoke for his people. "Farewell Ohio and her braves!"[6]

---

4. Hietala, *Manifest Design*, 135.
5. "An Act to provide for an exchange of lands with the Indians residing in any of the states or territories, and for their removal west of the river Mississippi," 28 May 1830.
6. *The Western Star* (Lebanon, Ohio), 4 August 1843, quoted in Bowman, "The Wyandot Indians of Ohio," 95.

Republicanism and Third Parties

> *"The two great parties are so nicely balanced that a straw may decide the fight."*

D. T. Disney to James K. Polk, October 28, 1844[7]

Republicanism was a founding principle of the American political order that espoused "equality in a society of yeomen freeholders." For Thomas Jefferson the ideal society was a nation of independent farmers, a republican vision that was never fully realized in the United States due to inequalities that were already present in late colonial times with the onset of the market and manufacturing revolutions.[8] One key philosophical change was that the republican ideal of civic virtue, which originally relied upon the "selfless independent citizen as the basis of social harmony," was replaced by "personal ambition and devotion to the acquisition of wealth." By the late eighteenth century the "spirit of free enterprise" became a defining feature of the republican ethic.[9] Political discourse during the Jacksonian period never fully resolved the tension between a rhetoric of social equality and the reality of unbridgeable disparities of wealth and occupation that had already begun to polarize the American electorate.

By the late 1830s a vigorous two-party system had emerged in American politics. The Whig and Democratic parties, each with their own well-defined platforms and political alliances that transcended divisions of geography and social class, determined the agenda of American political life for more than two decades through systematic state and local party organizations. The "two great parties" contested four main issues: the power of the federal government in regional and national development; control over banking, currency and credit; land policy; and internal improvements.

Whigs	*Democrats*
Federal control and initiative	Laissez-faire, state initiative
Protective tariff	Free trade
Federally-sponsored projects	State control of projects
National bank, a well-regulated currency	Chartering of banks by individual states
Raising revenue through land sales	Reducing land prives to encourage settlement and expansion
Opposition to expansion	
Restrictions on immigration	Relaxation of strict immigration and naturalization laws

The Democratic Party claimed descent from the Democratic-Republican Party of Thomas Jefferson, author of the Declaration of Independence and third president

---

7. D. T. Disney [Cincinnati] to James K. Polk, 28 October 1844, quoted in Holt, *Party Politics in Ohio*, 208, note 210.
8. Shalhope, "Republicanism," 347–48.
9. Ibid.

of the U. S. from 1801 to 1809. Andrew Jackson assumed leadership of the Democratic-Republicans in the mid-1820s. Jackson's two-term presidency (1829–37) and that of his successor, his former vice president Martin Van Buren (1837–1841), set the tenor of life and the outlook of an entire generation of Americans. Beginning in 1840, the organization introduced the practice of announcing the official campaign platform during a national convention and became known as the Democratic Party.

The Democrats of the early 1840s were largely neo-Jeffersonians who promoted the (by then anachronistic) view that agriculture was the economic backbone of American society. Democrats actively discouraged the spread of manufacturing and wanted more land in order to sustain the unique character of American social and political life. They believed that the field, and not the factory, nurtured virtue and promoted equality. Workers were happier toiling in the fields than on the factory floor; mines, mills and factories should remain in Europe, they argued. As one historian has noted, there was "no place for a national bank, spindles or assembly lines in the Jeffersonian garden." Progress came to be defined in terms of an ever-expanding frontier, which "obviated the need for an active government and made social reform unnecessary." Indeed, Democrats looked unfavorably upon any government intrusion into the private lives of individuals and believed the federal government should "do nothing" while the states should "do for themselves."[10]

For most Democrats the expansion of the factory system and rise of urbanization as a fact of American life were viewed as a menace to social stability and harmony. The undesirable effects of mob rule and worker unrest witnessed by the major metropolitan centers of New York, Chicago, Cincinnati, Boston, and Philadelphia during the economic recession of 1837 proved that the menace of modernization was real and had to be forestalled. Democrats believed it could be thwarted, at least in part, by allowing access to new lands out West, removing barriers to foreign markets for American agricultural products, and reducing tariffs on imported goods.

Although westward territorial expansion was generally favored by the Democrats, they found it difficult to decide whether newly incorporated states should be slave or free, an issue which also divided America's industrialized north from the agricultural south. The Missouri Compromise of 1820 maintained the awkward symmetry of free and slave states in the Union. (Slave state Missouri was balanced by the admission of a free Maine.) The proposed incorporation of Texas into the Union in 1837 kept slavery and annexation at the forefront of national policy discussions, a double issue that remained unresolved until well after the 1844 presidential election. (See below.)

The American Whig party was founded in 1836 as a coalition to oppose President Andrew Jackson and the Democrats. Henry Clay of Kentucky and Daniel Webster of Massachusetts, both former National Republicans, dominated the party during the first decade of its existence. They promoted what became known as the "American System" of protective tariffs, federally sponsored internal improvement projects, a national bank in order to foster a stable currency, and the conservative

---

10. Hietala, *Manifest Design*, 108 (garden quote). See also 101, 104, 107.

use of federal land sales to benefit individual states. Whigs sought a strong federal government and were opposed to territorial expansion. Whigs wanted to consolidate and develop existing land and feared sectional crises that might result from uncontrolled land acquisitions. Mines, mills, and factories, distrusted by the Democrats due to their socially destabilizing tendencies, were an essential part of the Whig program.

For most Americans the two sides of the political debate were sharply defined. Jacksonian Democrats became self-described as "egalitarian and progressive" populists, and characterized the Whigs as "aristocratic and reactionary." Another contemporary formulation has the Democrats preferring "freedom and fertile fields" to the "monarchy, mines and manufactories" of the Whig program.[11]

The stability and effectiveness of the two-party system was strained by the unexpected death of the first Whig president, William Henry Harrison, a month following his inauguration in 1841 and the accession to the presidential chair of his vice president, John Tyler. A Whig in name only, Tyler adopted Democratic strategies in many of his policy decisions and in the end became a president without a party.

During the 1840s the Whigs and Democrats could each count on support from about half of the American electorate. In 1844 the voting population of the United States consisted of only adult white males, at that time approximately 2,700,000 strong. (Because women and slaves were dependents, they were deemed ineligible to participate in the electoral process.) In a procedure established by the Twelfth Amendment to the Constitution, adopted in 1804, the American president was not voted for directly; instead, local elections determined state electors who, in turn, voted for the nation's chief executive.

"The two great parties are so nicely balanced that a straw may decide the fight," a political observer astutely remarked in late 1844. The straw was the unpredictable entrance into the race of a third party, still a relatively new phenomenon in the 1840s, bringing with it the potential to siphon off a sufficient number of votes in order to shift the electoral balance in favor of one or another candidate. Although they tended to be single-platform movements with an underdeveloped national organization, it was soon discovered that third parties exercised political clout beyond that suggested by their relatively small size.

The 1844 presidential campaign began as a struggle for leadership by the Whigs and the Democrats and a play for political influence by the Liberty Party, the first American political party to denounce slavery. Founded in 1839, its 1844 national campaign platform, adopted at Buffalo, New York on August 30, 1843, argued for the "unqualified divorce of the general government from slavery, and also the restoration of equality of rights among men." The Buffalo resolutions emphasized that the Liberty Party "is not a new party, nor a third party, but is the party of 1776, reviving the principles of that memorable era, and striving to carry them into practical application." The party's power and attractiveness to voters, then, lay not only in proclaiming the injustice of black slavery, but also in promoting the restoration of American political ideas as expressed in the Declaration of Independence and a

---

11. Ibid., 116.

Joseph Smith as prophet, ca. 1842. Library-Archives, Community of Christ, Independence, Missouri. Reproduction by Office of Graphics Arts.

belief that the "moral laws of the Creator are paramount to all human laws . . . we ought to obey God rather than men."[12]

The potential impact of the Liberty Party came to the notice of national politicians following in the failed bid of Thomas Corwin, a Clay Whig from Lebanon, Ohio, to be re-elected as governor of his home state in 1842. The Liberty Party, which polled 5,405 votes in the Ohio gubernatorial race, divided Whig partisans on the issue of slavery and turned what would have been a Whig victory over to the Democrats. Corwin lost by fewer than four thousand votes.[13]

The Libertymen first put forward a national presidential candidate in 1840. And they would do so again in 1844. Although neither effort was successful, in both races the Liberty Party succeeded in eroding the Whig political base in a number of states, most notably New York, and contributed to Henry Clay's narrow defeat in 1844.

The Liberty Party's entry into the 1844 race was not the only destabilizing factor, however. The rise of political Mormonism was also a significant concern, especially in Illinois, where the Latter-day Saints were a commanding presence. "I am a third party, and stand independent and alone," the prophet Joseph Smith, Jr. had declared before thousands of his followers at Nauvoo in the fall of 1843. Mormons were known for voting as a bloc and had attracted the attention of both Whig and Democratic electioneers. In recent elections the Latter-day Saints had overwhelmingly supported Democratic candidates. Anticipating that the Latter-day Saints would once again support the Democrats, the Whigs redoubled their efforts to influence the Mormon vote. The Democrats were only slightly less active.

Amidst increased Whig and Democratic campaign posturing, Joseph Smith recognized the potentially strategic role he could play in the upcoming national campaign. To the surprise of nearly everyone (except perhaps himself) within six months Joseph was prepared to enter the presidential race "on his own hook," without benefit of support by either major political party.[14]

As was noted earlier, Joseph Smith was not simply another independent candidate for America's highest office. He was a prophet of God. And, more than just wanting to secure redress for the injuries suffered by the Saints during their years

---

12. *National Party Conventions*, 29. "1844 Platform Liberty Party, Buffalo, New York," 30 August 1843, Resolution 2, 5, 18. www.geocities.com/CollegePark/Quad/6460/doct/844lib.html (Accessed December 28, 2004).

13. See Chapter Five: The Third Party.

14. Smith, *American Prophet's Record*, 401 [6 August 1843] (third party quote). "Another candidate for the Presidency," *Lee County Democrat*, 2 March 1844 (hook quote).

of persecution in Ohio, Missouri, and Illinois, Joseph Smith also believed that he was chosen to establish the Kingdom of God on the earth, providing the two prime motivations—the one taught publicly, the other revealed only to a select few—for his presidential candidacy in 1844.

In order to understand the rationale behind these two interwoven agendas, it is important to review the early history of Joseph Smith's religious movement, popularly known as Mormonism. Born in Sharon, Vermont, in 1805, Joseph Smith expounded a unique and multifaceted restoration theology, departing from both mainstream Protestant and Catholic teachings. Even before the Church's formal organization in 1830, Joseph Smith preached that after the death of the apostles in the first century the world had fallen into a state of apostasy. God chose him, a young farm boy then living in upstate New York, to restore the gospel of Jesus Christ to the earth. In 1830 Joseph became the "first elder" in the newly-organized Church of Christ.

Soon after the publication of the Book of Mormon that same year, a religious history of the ancient inhabitants of the Americas that Joseph claimed to have translated from golden plates delivered to him by a heavenly messenger, the name of the book was attached to his followers and the church he founded. The story opens with the ancient Hebrew prophet Lehi and his family, including his sons Nephi, Laman, and Lemuel, escaping Jerusalem and making the difficult sea voyage to the Americas. From its earliest chapters, the Book of Mormon identifies America as the "promised land."[15]

Joseph Smith taught that Laman and his followers, cursed with a dark skin because of their unbelief, were the ancestors of the American Indian. Some of the earliest Latter-day Saint missions were dedicated to bringing the message of Christ to America's native population, with the object of removing the Lamanite curse, and teaching them of their forgotten Old World heritage. Because of this special relationship between Mormons and the American Indian, the time soon came when the Latter-day Saints were accused of "plotting with the Indians" against the United States government.[16]

In 1837 the official name of the organization became the Church of Jesus Christ of Latter-day Saints, reflecting more accurately the movement's central belief in the imminent return of Jesus Christ and the commencement of His millennial reign on the earth. Joseph served as the Lord's "Prophet, Seer and Revelator" to his followers.

The chief presiding officers of the church consisted of the First Presidency (made up of the prophet and his two counselors) and the Council (or Quorum) of the Twelve Apostles, special witnesses of Christ to the world "equal in authority and power" to the First Presidency. At the local level, congregations were organized into wards or branches, headed by a bishop or branch president. Following Old Testament tent symbolism, these units were gathered into stakes, each with its own presidency and High Council of presiding elders.[17]

---

15. Book of Mormon references to America as the "promised land" include 1 Nephi 2:20, 1 Nephi 5:5, 1 Nephi 7:13, 1 Nephi 10:13, 1 Nephi 12:1, 1 Nephi 13:14, 1 Nephi 13:20, 1 Nephi 14:2, 2 Nephi 9:2, 2 Nephi 10:11 ("land of liberty"), and Alma 46:12–22 ("title of liberty").

16. Arrington and Bitton, *The Mormon Experience*, 146.

17. Doctrine and Covenants 107:23–24 [28 March 1835]. Marquardt, *Joseph Smith Revelations*, 268.

Sidney Rigdon, Joseph's counselor, vice presidential running mate and polygamy opponent. Courtesy of the Church Archives, the Church of Jesus Christ of Latter-day Saints.

In the summer of 1831, little more than a year after the organization of the church, twenty-five-year-old Joseph Smith arrived in Hamilton, seat of southwest Ohio's Butler County, twenty-five miles north of Cincinnati on the Great Miami River. Traveling with Joseph was thirty-eight-year-old Sidney Rigdon. The two men called on Sidney's older brother, Dr. Laomi Rigdon, at his home on Main Street.

Dr. Rigdon was a leading Butler County physician. He married Rebecca Dunlevy, of Lebanon, Warren County, Ohio, in 1816 and in the 1820s established a medical practice in partnership with her younger brother John. Hamilton remained Laomi's home until his death in 1865.

Even before the arrival of Joseph and Sidney, the Dunlevys and Rigdons, both distinguished southern Ohio Baptist families, had encounters with some of America's most innovative religious movements. Rebecca's uncle, John Dunlevy, had joined the Shakers in 1805 and was the author of an influential Shaker treatise, *The manifesto: or A Declaration of the Doctrines and Practice of the Church of Christ*, first published in 1818. The Shakers differed from most other Christian sects of the period in that they believed that celibacy was the means to "live free from sin" in the coming millennium. There was a sizeable Shaker settlement at Turtle Creek, on the outskirts of Lebanon. Rebecca's father, Francis Dunlevy, often acted on behalf of the religious community during conflicts with local citizenry.

Sidney Rigdon, Joseph's traveling companion, had been a follower of restorationist Alexander Campbell for several years in the 1820s and commanded a substantial following in the northern Ohio village of Mentor. Like Joseph Smith, Campbell preached the need for a restoration of primitive Christianity. They differed in how that was to be accomplished. Campbell made no claims of a higher calling from God; for him the heavens were no longer open. Joseph Smith, on the other hand, claimed that as a young man he had been visited by God the Father and Jesus Christ, who personally announced his mission of restoration. In the course of his relatively short career Joseph Smith received numerous revelations concerning God's will for His people and for the world.

Sidney met Joseph Smith in the fall of 1830, and was soon converted (together with much of his congregation) to the gospel of Mormonism. Nearby Kirtland, Ohio, became a gathering place for the new religious movement.

It was with a great deal of interest, then, that Rigdon and Dunlevy family members assembled in the doctor's home on Main Street in Hamilton that summer of

1831. Anthony Howard Dunlevy, Rebecca's brother (and Sidney's brother-in-law), was not impressed with the new prophet. "Sidney did all the talking," he would later recall. "Jo. Smith had little to say, but deferred to his companion on all matters of explanation." In Dunlevy's view, the advent of Sidney Rigdon was essential to the survival of the Mormon movement. Sidney, he noted, "would quote by memory whole passages with great facility, giving to them meaning and views which no other person would see in them. In that particular he was exactly suited to give to the Book of Mormon a significance which no other person, not even Jo. Smith himself, could conceive, much less impart to others."[18]

Following the family visit Joseph and Sidney journeyed westward to Independence, Jackson County, Missouri. The prophet declared Jackson County to be the future site of Zion, the New Jerusalem of Biblical tradition. In August of that year the two men dedicated a portion of southwestern Missouri "to the Lord for a possession and inheritance for the Saints." Their *Evening and Morning Star* newspaper, published in Independence, promoted the gathering of the faithful to Missouri.

In the summer of 1833 conflict with the old settlers of Jackson County resulted in the destruction of the Mormon press there (which was preparing to publish the prophet's revelations) and the expulsion of the Saints by the end of the year. Church leaders petitioned the state for compensation for the lands and property that had been lost or destroyed during the forced exodus. Their request was ignored.

Kirtland, Ohio, prospered for several years. But by 1838, Kirtland, too, was effectively abandoned, leaving behind the first Latter-day Saint temple (completed in 1836), a monument to the dedication and sacrifice willingly undertaken by the early Saints, a failed banking experiment, and growing disaffection among less stalwart church members.

The headquarters of the church soon gravitated to Far West, in northern Missouri's Caldwell County, where Joseph Smith arrived in mid-March of 1838. Joseph taught his followers that this was the location of the Garden of Eden, that Adam, the first man, had lived nearby at a place known as Spring Hill (restored by Joseph to Adam-ondi-Ahman, "the land where Adam dwelt"). Joseph even identified the very pile of stones Adam had made into an altar where he "offered up sacrifice after he was cast out of the garden." Missouri, then, represented both the beginning of human time (Adam-ondi-Ahman) and, with the coming of the millennium, the place where time would end (Independence).[19]

By the fall of 1838 reports circulated that the Mormon prophet was claiming his "prophecies are superior to the laws of the land . . . he would tread down his enemies, and walk over their dead bodies; and if he was not let alone, he would be a second Mohammed to this generation." Joseph fully intended to take over the

18. Hughes and Allen, *Illusions of Innocence*, 115 (Shaker quote). Anthony Howard Dunlevy to [editor of *Baptist Witness*] n.d., *Baptist Witness*, 1 March 1875.

19. *Fulness of Times*, 107 (inheritance quote). Doctrine and Covenants 116 [19 May 1838]. A useful compilation of references to Adam-ondi-Ahman can be found in "Adam-ondi-Ahman: Where Mormons Plan to Move to Again Someday," www.lds-mormon.com/adam_ond.shtml. See also McConkie, *Mormon Doctrine*, 19–20. Whitney, *Life of Heber C. Kimball*, 209–10, quoted in Otten and Caldwell, *Sacred Truths of the Doctrine & Covenants* 2:278–79.

Nauvoo in 1848. Henry Lewis, *Das Illustirte Mississippithal* (Leipzig, 1848).

reigns of government by virtue of his divine call to establish the Kingdom of God on the earth.[20]

On October 27, 1838, Missouri Governor Lilburn W. Boggs issued an order to his state militia: "The Mormons must be treated as enemies and must be exterminated or driven from the state, if necessary for the public good." During the outbreak of hostilities Joseph established a private militia. Popularly known as the Danites, the brotherhood was named after the Book of Daniel in the Old Testament, which prophesied that in the last days the temporal Kingdom of God, described as a stone "cut out of the mountain without hands," would roll forth and destroy the nations of the world. The prophecy was emphatic: "And in the days of these kings shall the God of heaven set up a kingdom, which shall never be destroyed; and the kingdom shall not be left to other people, but it shall break in pieces and consume all these kingdoms, and it shall stand forever" (Daniel 2:44). One purpose of the Danite order was "to put right physically that which is not right, and to clense the Church of very great evils which hath hitherto existed among us inasmuch as they cannot be put

---

20. Orson Hyde and Thomas B. Marsh affidavit, 18 October 1838, in Smith, *History of the Church* 3:167, also quoted in *Fulness of Times*, 199. While the importance of establishing the Kingdom of God was noted as early as the Kirtland years, Joseph Smith's first formal revelation on the political Kingdom of God was received in Nauvoo, on 7 April 1842. The revelation is not included in the LDS (Latter-day Saints) Doctrine and Covenants. See Marquardt, *Revelations*, Doc. 164, and Joseph Smith's early comments on theocratic rule in "The Government of God," *Times and Seasons* 3 (15 July 1842): 855–56. Hill and Oaks, *Carthage Conspiracy*, 7, Hill, *Quest for Refuge*, 188, note 36, and Cartwright, *Autobiography*, 345, quoted in Godfrey, "Causes of Conflict," 63.

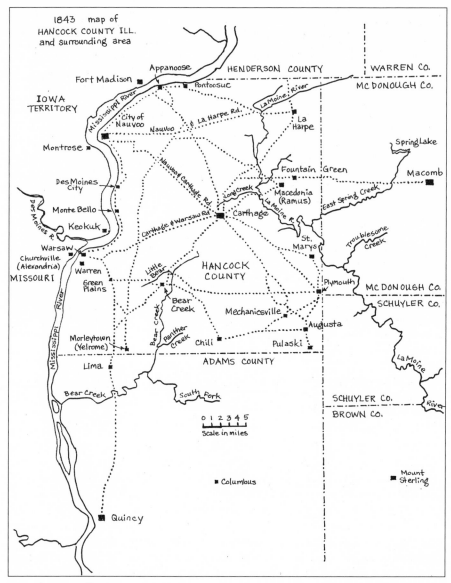

Map of western Illinois.

to right by teachings and persuasyons." Although the Danite band was in existence only for about six weeks in the fall of 1838, the symbolic impact of the organization (and the prominence of individual members) continued to be felt throughout the nineteenth century, attaining an almost mythic status for the sometimes merciless actions that the Danites carried out in the name of their prophet and their God.[21]

---

21. Smith, *History of the Church* 3:175 (extermination quote). The term "extermination" was first used in Sidney Rigdon's famous 4 July 1838 oration, published as Rigdon, *Oration Delivered...*, quoted

Joseph, Sidney, and other church leaders were arrested by Missouri officials in early November and charged with treason—in part for allegedly claiming they would eventually take political control of the state and fulfill the prophecy of Daniel. The men were imprisoned in the jail at Liberty, Missouri. Joseph remained incarcerated throughout the harsh winter of 1838–39. On account of his poor health Sidney Rigdon was released in January.

The main body of the Saints left Missouri in early 1839 and settled, temporarily, in the vicinity of Quincy, Illinois, a Mississippi river town of 1,200. As thousands of Saints arrived in western Illinois, without food, clothing, or shelter, the local population found itself unable to accommodate the massive influx of refugees. A new home for the Latter-day Saints was desperately needed.

While still confined in Liberty jail, Joseph Smith instructed church leaders to purchase land to establish once again a refuge for the beleaguered Saints. When Joseph escaped from his Missouri captors in April of 1839, he moved quickly to finalize several large land purchases. These included a tract of swampland near a bluff overlooking a bend on the Mississippi River. Known to earlier settlers as Venus, and later Commerce, Joseph renamed the town Nauvoo, "the beautiful."

The prophet received a revelation that the Saints should appeal to the federal government for assistance in receiving compensation from the state of Missouri for losses resulting from their forced expulsions. Nearly five hundred affidavits documenting the maltreatment of the Saints in Missouri were collected and sent to the United States Congress.

Joseph Smith led a delegation to Washington City, where he met with Democratic president Martin Van Buren. The chief executive was not sympathetic. The issue of states rights versus the power of the federal government and the fear of alienating his political constituencies colored Van Buren's response to the prophet's entreaty. "Gentlemen, your cause is just," Van Buren reportedly told the Mormon delegates, "but I can do nothing for you." The petition to Congress was unsuccessful. Joseph concluded, "if all hopes of obtaining satisfaction for the injuries done us be entirely blasted, that they then appeal our case to the Court of Heaven, believing that the Great Jehovah, who rules over the destiny of nations, and who notices the falling sparrows, will undoubtedly redress our wrongs, and ere long avenge us of our adversaries."[22] In addition to displaying his growing disdain for organized political parties and partisan politicians, this passage also skillfully promotes the prophet's mantra of "persecuted innocence." Joseph taught that because the Latter-day Saints were God's

in Roberts, Comprehensive History 1:441, Givens, *Viper on the Hearth*, 32, and *Fulness of Times*, 192. The speech still resonated in Nauvoo. See, for example, Davis, *Authentic Account*, 42–43. Smith, *American Prophet's Record*, 198 [27 July 1838] (Danite quote). On the Danite order and the prophecy of Daniel, see Brigham Young, 28 September 1862, *Journal of Discourses* 1:320, and Brigham Young, 29 April 1877, *Journal of Discourses* 19:63. A balanced perspective on the outbreak of anti-Mormon violence in Missouri and the origins of the Danite order is LeSueur, *The 1838 Mormon War*, especially 204–5. See also Quinn, *Origins of Power*, 479–90 ("Danites in 1838: A Partial List"). For an LDS apologetic perspective on Daniel, see Whittaker, "The Book of Daniel in Early Mormon thought."

22. *Fulness of Times*, 221–22 (government quotes). See also Johnson, *Mormon redress petitions*, Smith, *History of the Church* 4:80, 108, *Fulness of Times*, 219–22.

chosen people, the Lord was on their side. Any opposition to their cause was unjustified and unrighteous persecution, a concept that retains enormous power and influence among the Latter-day Saints even today.

With the assistance of Dr. John C. Bennett, a prominent Springfield-area physician who converted to Mormonism shortly after meeting the prophet in the summer of 1840, a city charter was granted to Nauvoo by the Illinois state legislature. In common with charters granted to Springfield and other Illinois cities, the document allowed Nauvoo to organize a municipal council, a municipal court, a local militia (to be called the Nauvoo Legion, in which Joseph Smith was commissioned a Lieutenant General by the governor of Illinois), and a university.

Significantly, political power at Nauvoo was consolidated in five individuals: "the mayor, four aldermen, and nine councilors. The mayor and aldermen also served as judges of the municipal court . . . This meant that five men controlled the legislative, executive, and judicial branches of the local government." The combination would prove to be both the fountain of the city's power and the germ of its eventual destruction.

Another provision that gave unexpected force to the authority of Nauvoo's government was a clause that directed the city's militia (composed of all able-bodied males, their arms supplied by the state of Illinois) to "be at the disposal of the mayor in executing the laws and ordinances of the city corporation, and the laws of the State."[23]

The Nauvoo swamp was drained. The town was surveyed and laid out on a neat grid. Grist mills, general stores, private dwellings of rough-hewn logs, clapboard, and brick, and a river landing were constructed. The former mosquito-infested town with a handful of residents soon numbered in the thousands, with more arrivals docking nearly every day.

Plans for a temple on the bluff above the city were also completed, the Saints donating a tenth of their income or labor to assist in the effort. The cornerstones of the Nauvoo temple were laid on April 6, 1841, the eleventh anniversary of the organization of the church. Joseph was finally realizing his dream of establishing a sanctuary for the persecuted Saints and building a House of the Lord in which to perform His sacred ordinances for the salvation of the faithful.

With ten to twelve thousand inhabitants in 1843, Nauvoo was the second largest city in Illinois, rivaled only by Chicago. The Holy City, as it was often called, dominated the economy of the region. Hancock County could claim just two additional settlements of any significance: Warsaw, "a business place a little below Nauvoo" on the eastern shore of the Mississippi, and Carthage, the county seat, "another trading village or town in the interior." Each had a population of about four hundred inhabitants.[24]

Shortly after announcing his candidacy in the spring of 1844, Joseph Smith proceeded to organize an efficient political machine to forward his dual ambitions. His political writers included accomplished editors and experienced newspapermen. A

---

23. *Fulness of Times*, 223 (mayor quote), Smith, *History of the Church* 4:244 (militia quote). Allman, "Policing in Nauvoo," 86. Flanders, *Nauvoo*, 100–101.
24. *New York Herald*, quoted in *The Prophet* 13 July 1844.

Warsaw in 1848. Henry Lewis, *Das Illustirte Mississippithal* (Leipzig, 1848).

secret committee, known as the Council of Fifty, was convened to both establish the political Kingdom of God and manage his presidential campaign.

Joseph Smith's main political newspaper in the east was published by the Society for the Diffusion of Truth in New York City. Called *The Prophet*, the paper reported on Mormon "Jeffersonian Conventions" promoting the candidacy of "General Joseph Smith." [25]

Unlike the Liberty Party, with its single-minded focus on the abolition of slavery, Joseph Smith presented a multiplank platform before the American people. His *Views on the Powers and Policy of the Government of the United States* was first issued as a small pamphlet from Nauvoo, Illinois in February of 1844 and later reprinted or excerpted by several national newspapers. One Indiana businessman noted that Joseph Smith was "the first man since the days of Washington and Jefferson, who had been frank and honest enough to give his views to the people before being elected."[26]

According to his electioneers, Joseph Smith's political views "took a line between the two [major] parties," influenced more by personal experience than affiliation with a particular political cause. Smith's support for "liberty, freedom and equal rights" together with "protection of person and property" guaranteed by a strong federal government, for example, were policy positions forged out of the persecutions and

25. The Society for the Diffusion of Truth emulates the name of the popular Society for the Diffusion of Useful Knowledge. For a slightly earlier (mocking) example, see Robertson, *The Language of Democracy*, 79 and note 24.
26. Lyman Wight and Heber C. Kimball to Joseph Smith, 19 June 1844, in Smith, *History of the Church* 7:137.

losses suffered by the Saints in Ohio, Missouri, and Illinois. Joseph's proposal to cre-
ate a national bank, although no doubt based in part upon the disastrous results of
his own banking experiment in Kirtland, Ohio, echoed the long-declared position
of Whig party leaders. Joseph Smith's promotion of free trade and the idea that the
people (and not the government) are the true "sovereigns of the soil," aligned him
more closely with Jeffersonian Democrats.[27]

Aside from the catchy slogans and campaign posturing, however, Joseph Smith,
together with the other presidential candidates, recognized that far more than political rhetoric was at stake in the upcoming election. The outstanding issue of the 1844
campaign was slavery and the annexation of Texas.

Slavery and the Question of Texas

> *"In connection with the wonderful events of this age, much isdoing towards
> abolishing slavery, and colonizing the blacks, in Africa."*

Mormon political writer W. W. Phelps, 1833[28]

When Stephen F. Austin led a colony of three hundred southerners (many of them
slave owners) into the Texas wilderness in 1821, the land was still under the control of Spain. Mexican independence was declared less than a year later. After nearly
fifteen years under Mexican rule, Texas proclaimed itself an independent republic
on March 2, 1836. The United States of America recognized Sam Houston and his
Republic of Texas the following year. The question of annexation became an issue
almost immediately and was still unresolved at the time of the American presidential
election in 1844. If Texas was admitted into the Union it was assumed by some, and
feared by others, that it would become a slave state.

The antislavery campaign in the United States was headed by men who recognized the inherent wrongness of owning another human being yet at the same time
questioned the propriety of giving black men full civil rights. Most antislavery movements supported gradual emancipation, segregation of the races, unequal rights for
blacks, and colonization, sentiments that crossed party lines. In his public remarks
on the 1857 U.S. Supreme Court decision in the Dred Scott case, which upheld the
denial of citizenship rights to blacks, for example, Republican Abraham Lincoln expressed agreement with his opponent, Democrat Stephen A. Douglas, that the races
should not mix. "Judge Douglas is especially horrified at the thought of the mixing
of blood by the white and black races: agreed for once—a thousand times agreed,"
Lincoln replied. "There are white men enough to marry all the white women, and
black men enough to marry all the black women; and so let them be married . . . A
separation of the races is the only perfect preventive of amalgamation but as all immediate separation is impossible the next best thing is to *keep* them apart *where* they

---

27. See Chapter Ten: What Will Be the End of Things?

28. *Evening and Morning Star* 2 (July 1833), 11, quoted in Bush, "Mormonism's Negro Doctrine,"12.
    The content of this section is indebted to Hietala, *Manifest Design*, especially "Texas, the Black Peril,
    and Alternatives to Abolitionism," 10–54 and Merk, *Slavery and the Annexation of Texas*.

are not already together."[29]

The 1840 census of the United States appeared to support the desirability of slavery and exposed the horrible consequences if abolitionism were adopted as a national program. The census "showed that, under the kindly paternalism of plantation masters, slaves flourished, and that by contrast, free Negroes in the North, living under an impersonal wage system, disintegrated." Doctor Edward Jarvis, a New England specialist on the insane, discovered that the census figures were in error. Dr. Jarvis noted that "the columns of the white insane were next to those of the colored insane," and, as is well known by every genealogist who has worked in the records of the period, "these columns were long and many towns on a page, and it required a very accurate eye and careful discipline to select the proper column for a fact, and to follow it down from the heading." Because the census was carried out by individuals who frequently failed to exercise proper care, "the figures representing the white lunatics of many towns were placed in the column of the colored." The results were deceiving. "Towns which had no colored population on one page, were represented on the other as having colored lunatics; and in many others the number of colored lunatics was more than that of the colored living; others were stated to have a large part of their colored people insane." It was soon published abroad that "cold is destructive to the mental health of the African . . . in the United States where only one in 2,117 is insane in Georgia the warmest state, and one in fourteen in Maine, the coldest."[30]

A Georgia representative in Congress agreed with Jarvis that the census and the environmental interpretation of black mental health was in error, "but," he added, "it is too good a thing for our [southern] politicians to give up, and many of them have prepared speeches based on this, which they cannot afford to lose." The political argument was appallingly simple: "Humanity . . . demands that Texas be added to our nation, and opened to the occupation of our surplus slaves to save them from mental death."[31]

In February 1844, a "Letter of Mr. Walker of Mississippi, Relative to the Annexation of Texas," was issued to convince northern Democrats and Whigs of the benefits that would accrue from annexation, that it was "the surest and most peaceful mode of solving the slavery and race problems." Senator Walker claimed that annexation would draw slaves and their owners from all the "worn-out lands" in the South. When Texas's soils were depleted, the planters would free their slaves, who could simply cross the Rio Grande into Mexico and the lands southward. "There they would not be a degraded caste," as in America, Walker continued, "but equals among equals,

---

29. "Abraham Lincoln on the Dred Scott Decision," 26 June 1857, transcription in afroamhistory.about. com/library/blincoln_dred_scott.htm.

30. See Hietala, *Manifest Design*, 28–29 and 39–40 and Merk, *Slavery*, 61–67 and passim. Jarvis, *Autobiography*, 62–63.

31. Jarvis, *Autobiography*, 63, quoted in Merk, *Slavery*, 119. Due to a transcription error, Davico identifies the Georgia senator as "Mr. Bencan". Merk correctly identifies him as Whig leader John M. Berrien. On Berrien, Clay, and the Latter-day Saints, see Chapter Two, note 5. The census argument was also made in the Walker Letter (see below). Appended to the letter is "Table No. 1, compiled from census of 1840, of deaf and dumb, blind, idiots, and insane." On p. 14, Walker writes, "[In Mexico] cold and want and hunger will not drive the African, as we see it does in the North, into the poorhouse and the jail, and the asylums of the idiot and insane." (Merk, *Fruits of Propaganda*, 234).

not only by law, but by feeling and association." Walker's argument became known as the "safety-valve" thesis.[32]

Possibly influenced by the Walker Letter, independent presidential candidate Joseph Smith proposed a similar solution to America's slavery problem. Joseph Smith opposed the then-current situation in the United States where "two or three millions of people are held as slaves for life, because the spirit in them is covered with a darker skin than ours." He called for liberty for all men "without reference to color or condition: ad infinitum" and advocated "national equalization" for blacks, although he, like most Americans of the time, also believed they should be segregated from whites and confined "by strict law to their own species." Liberty was not to be color-blind.[33]

In order to accomplish his goal of abolishing slavery in the United States by 1850 *and* maintaining racial segregation, Smith proposed to annex Texas. He would "liberate the slaves in two or three [southern] States," compensate their owners, "and send the [free] negroes to Texas, and from Texas to Mexico, where all colors are alike." If there was insufficient land in Mexico to handle the influx of newly freed blacks, he would "call upon Canada, and annex it."[34]

White Americans had struggled with the "problem" of free blacks for decades. The Walker Letter and Joseph Smith's Texas solution were identical in effect to the scheme proposed by the American Colonization Society, an organization dedicated to returning freed slaves to the colony of Liberia ("liberty") on Africa's western coast. "There is a moral fitness in the idea of returning to Africa her children," Henry Clay asserted during a speech before the ACS in 1827, "whose ancestors have been torn from her by the ruthless hand of fraud and violence. Transplanted in a foreign land, they will carry back to their native soil the rich fruits of religion, civilization, law and liberty." The ACS argument was remarkably similar to that made by politicians justifying the removal of the American Indian. In any case, in contrast to the Indian Removal Program, the Colonization Society was never very successful at achieving its goals and over the course of its existence returned no more than eleven thousand free blacks to the African coast.[35]

During an unofficial election tour of the South in early February of 1844, Henry Clay learned from a gentleman "just arrived . . . from Texas," that following a secret vote forty-two American senators were found "in favor of the annexation of Texas, and have advised the President," John Tyler, "that they will confirm a treaty to that effect; that a negotiation has been opened accordingly in Texas, and that a treaty will be speedily concluded." This was devastating news for the former Kentucky senator.

32. Robert J. Walker [Washington, D.C.] "Letter of Mr. Walker, of Mississippi, Relative to the Annexation of Texas" 8 January 1844, 14–15 (Washington) *Globe*, 3 February 1844, in Merk, *Fruits of Propaganda*, 234–35. See also Merk, *Fruits of Propaganda*, 95–120.

33. Smith, *Views* (darker skin quote), Smith, *Teachings*, 269 (species quote), also quoted in Bush, "Mormonism's Negro Doctrine," 18. Smith, *History of the Church* 5:217 and 6:197–98.

34. Smith, *History of the Church* 6:244. Compare Smith, *American Prophet's Record*, 457 [7 March 1844]. The supposed equality of the races in Mexico is also stressed in the Walker Letter, 15, in Merk, *Fruits of Propaganda*, 235.

35. 1827 Henry Clay speech quoted by Abraham Lincoln, "Eulogy on Henry Clay," 6 July 1852, Springfield, Illinois, in Lincoln, *Collected Works*.

An acknowledged opponent of annexation, Clay wrote to a friend, "If it be true, I shall regret extremely that I have had no hint of it."[36]

On April 12, 1844, a treaty of annexation was concluded between Texas and the U.S. Henry Clay, himself a slaveholder and antiabolitionist, felt obligated to speak out before the treaty was submitted to the Senate for ratification. In a letter written from Raleigh, North Carolina, Clay pointed out that Mexico had not abandoned its right to Texas. "Under these circumstances, if the Government of the United States were to acquire Texas, it would acquire along with it all the incumbrances which Texas is under, and among them the actual or suspended war between Mexico and Texas . . . Annexation and war with Mexico are identical." His concerns went further than war, however. The future of slavery was at stake.

"Suppose Great Britain and France, or one of them," Clay continued, "were to take part with Mexico, and by a manifesto . . . maintain the independence of Texas, disconnected with the United States, and to prevent the further propagation of slavery from the United States." Abolitionists, both in the U.S. and in England, Clay knew, wanted a Texas without slavery. In late 1843 the British had entered into secret negotiations with Sam Houston for establishing an *independent* free-soil Texas, with the goal of "abolish[ing] slavery, not only in Texas, but throughout the world." If an independent Texas republic became a reality, slaveholding Southern Democrats and Whigs feared that their "slaves in the great valley of the Mississippi . . . would all run over to Texas and under British influence [be] liberated and lost to their owners."[37]

If, on the other hand, Texas were to become part of the Union, Clay believed that Texas was "susceptible of a division into five states of Convenient size and form . . . two slave and three Free," a move that would upset the precarious balance negotiated by the Missouri Compromise of 1820.

Clay's letter was published in the *Daily National Intelligencer* on April 27, 1844, less than a week before the national Whig nominating convention in Baltimore. Although the Raleigh Letter engendered heated debate off of the convention floor, the official Whig campaign platform for 1844 made no mention of Texas, slavery, or annexation. And while Clay's public opposition to accepting Texas into the Union did not cost him the Whig presidential nomination, it significantly weakened his national appeal.[38]

Martin Van Buren, former U.S. president and frontrunner for the Democratic presidential nomination in 1844, also issued a statement opposing annexation. When it appeared in the press on the same day as Clay's letter, collusion between the two men, although unproven, was widely suspected. Earlier that month Clay had written that Van Buren, "if he does not alter his position, stands opposed. We shall

36. Henry Clay to John J. Crittenden, 15 February 1844, in Hopkins and Hargreaves, *Papers of Henry Clay* 10:6–7.

37. Henry Clay [Raleigh, North Carolina] to the editors of the Washington *Daily Intelligencer* [Joseph Gales & William W. Seaton], 17 April 1844, in Hopkins and Hargreaves, *Papers of Henry Clay* 10:43–44. Andrew Jackson to William B. Lewis, 8 April 1844, quoted in Hietala, *Manifest Design*, 24 (world and Mississippi quotes).

38. Henry Clay [Raleigh, North Carolina] to the editors of the Washington *Daily Intelligencer* [Joseph Gales & William W. Seaton], 17 April 1844, in Hopkins and Hargreaves, *Papers of Henry Clay* 10:45–46.

John McLean of Cincinnati, Ohio. Cincinnati Public Library, Ohio.

therefore occupy common ground. And his present attitude, renders it necessary that I should break silence. If he change his position, and come out for annexation, it will be so much worse for him." In fact, by publishing his antiexpansionist "attitude" Van Buren lost the Democratic nomination.[39] The Democratic national convention assembled at Baltimore in late May, three weeks after the Whigs' gathering. Following eight unsuccessful ballots, a compromise dark horse candidate from Tennessee, James K. Polk, was accepted as their presidential nominee. In an effort to compensate for Van Buren's public letter opposing annexation, the Democratic campaign platform called for "re-occupation of Oregon" and the "re-annexation of Texas," claiming that the United States had full legal right to the western territories.[40]

* * * * *

The campaign for 1844 did not begin with the formal votes for Whig and Democratic presidential candidates in Baltimore. And it didn't begin when the official campaign platform was approved and sent to press. The campaign for 1844 began years earlier when aspiring men determined that the presidential chair was their life's ambition. Kentucky senator Henry Clay was one such individual. U.S. Supreme Court judge John McLean was another. As national Whig leaders both men understood that only one could win their party's presidential nomination. One of them would lose.

Our narrative begins in June 1843, almost a full year before the Whig and Democratic nominating conventions. The scene shifts from metropolitan Baltimore to the Illinois prairie. Judge John McLean, recently arrived by riverboat from Cincinnati, has settled into his courtroom on the second floor of the capitol building in Springfield, Illinois, prepared to hear four weeks of cases brought before the Circuit Court of the United States for the Seventh District.

---

39. Henry Clay to John J. Crittenden, 21 April 1844, in Hopkins and Hargreaves, *Papers of Henry Clay* 10:48. Although he cites this letter, Remini, *Henry Clay*, 641, insists, "This coincidence—and it was coincidence—generated all kinds of rumors." *National Party Conventions*, 29.
40. *National Party Conventions*, 30. This dual argument was also made in the Walker Letter (see above). Merk, *Fruits of Propaganda*, 121–28.

Chapter Two

"Clear the Way for Henry Clay"

T HE 1844 WHIG CAMPAIGN FOR the American presidency is best understood as a refinement of strategies developed during the successful 1840 presidential bid of William Henry Harrison. Many of the same individuals figured prominently in both races.

Horace Greeley, founding editor of the *New York Tribune*, in large part responsible for Harrison's success in 1840, became one of Clay's most powerful supporters in 1844. Greeley published the widely distributed *Junius Tracts*, which included partisan critiques of political issues (such as the annexation of Texas) as well as a life of Henry Clay. He also issued the *Clay Tribune*, Clay's national campaign newspaper. Perhaps most important, Greeley maintained a network of correspondents throughout the United States which enabled him to keep a finger on the pulse of the American electorate and strengthen political allegiances through a sustained media campaign.

Not all of the American Whigs supported Henry Clay, however. One of the most notable holdouts was Cincinnati businessman Jacob Burnet, manager of William Henry Harrison's campaign four years earlier. Burnet was now promoting Henry Clay's chief Whig rival, U.S. Supreme Court judge John McLean. Soon after McLean's arrival in Springfield, Illinois, in June of 1843, Henry Clay's representative (and step-nephew) John J. Hardin visited the Supreme Court justice and proposed that the two Whig factions forge a political alliance.[1]

"A great many strangers are in town," wrote a Springfield correspondent for Horace Greeley's *New York Tribune*, "drawn here by the session of the Court." The business of the U.S. Circuit Court for the Seventh District was conducted in Springfield, Illinois, when the legislature was out of session and concluded before the oppressive heat of high summer was upon the prairie. Springfield was declared the seat of Sangamon County in 1821 by planting a wooden stake at "a certain point in the prairie, near John Kelly's field, on the waters of Spring creek." Sixteen years later the town was named Illinois's state capital. In 1843, the city of three thousand residents

---

1.   The earliest use of the slogan "Clear the Way for Henry Clay" inserted a comma between 'way' and 'for'; it was soon abandoned. See *Daily Cincinnati Enquirer*, 11 July 1842. Lambert, *Presidential Politics*, 105, noted, "The man about whom Henry Clay was most concerned was none other than Judge McLean of Ohio."

HORACE GREELEY.

Horace Greeley, New York City publisher and political manager. Miami University Libraries, Oxford, Ohio.

remained isolated; Springfield lacked a navigable waterway and railroads to the capital were still under construction.[2] Travelers with business in Springfield usually boarded shallow-draft vessels at the Mississippi river ports of Alton (on the eastern shore) or St. Louis (on the Missouri side) which inched their way up the placid Illinois River. From Meredosia, the first town of any consequence on the Illinois's eastern bank, visitors took an overland stage to the capital, still more than sixty miles due east. Jacksonville, about halfway between Meredosia and Springfield, became a required stopover before continuing on to Illinois's geographical and legislative center.

The capitol building, placed in the middle of a large public square surrounded by unpaved and often muddy streets, was begun in 1837, the year the capital was moved to Springfield from Vandalia. Constructed of Illinois dolomite that shone golden in the sunlight, the building (about the size of a typical midwestern county courthouse) was only partially finished in the summer of 1843 and still lacked its portico of stacked columns. On the interior, a temporary flight of stairs led to the Representatives' Chamber on the west wing of the second floor where fifty-eight-year-old justice John McLean presided. Sessions of the court typically lasted the entire month of June, after which the judge returned to his home in Cincinnati.[3]

Judge McLean, a large man of "imposing presence," had served as an associate justice of the United States Supreme Court since his appointment by President Andrew Jackson in 1829, "the first justice appointed from the old Northwest, and the first Ohio lawyer to be elevated to the U.S. Supreme Court." McLean's *Reports of cases argued and decided in the Circuit Court of the United States for the Seventh District*, begun in 1840, was required reading for advocates throughout the Union. McLean was also known for his opposition to political extremism. "Demagogues," he said repeatedly, "must be put down."[4]

2. Springfield, Illinois correspondent to Horace Greeley, 7 June 1843, *New York Weekly Tribune*, 22 June 1843. *Springfield, Illinois, and It's Advantages*, 11 (creek quote). "District Court United States—Judge McLean," *Illinois State Register*, 16 June 1843, mentions that Judge Nathaniel Pope was also in Springfield. See also original of John McLean to Augustus Fisher 10 August 1843, McLean Papers, Library of Congress. Population for Springfield was 1,419 in 1835 and 3,900 by 1848. "Illinois as Lincoln Knew It," 40, note 25.

3. "Illinois as Lincoln Knew It," 38. John McLean to Augustus Fischer, 10 August 1843, McLean Papers, Library of Congress.

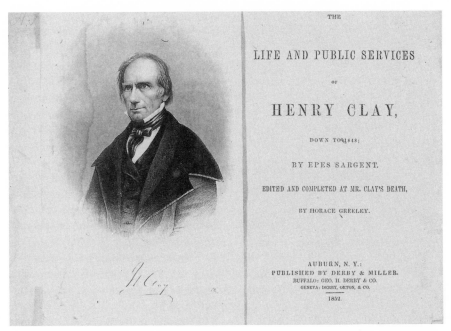

Portrait of Henry Clay and title page from *The Life and Public Services of Henry Clay, down to 1848.* Auburn, New York: Derby & Miller, 1852. Miami University Libraries, Oxford, Ohio.

For all of his success on the bench Judge McLean was above all a politician who had long sought democracy's highest prize, the presidential chair. One contemporary noted that McLean "thinks of nothing but the Presidency by day and dreams of nothing else by night." McLean's name had been first put forward as a presidential contender by Charles Hammond (editor of the *Cincinnati Gazette*) in 1832. In the 1836 presidential race McLean was supported by Hammond, as well as John Woods, publisher of the Hamilton (Ohio) *Intelligencer* who had studied law under McLean before being admitted to the bar in 1819. Neither effort was successful. In late 1842 a group of Ohio congressmen again began voicing support for McLean as a presidential favorite.[5]

At the time of McLean's 1843 Supreme Court sessions in Springfield, the movement to place his name on the 1844 Whig ticket was well underway. "We should not be greatly astonished . . . if [McLean] . . . is looking higher than the exalted seat he now occupies," the *Illinois State Register* (published in Springfield) speculated in mid-June. "If the Whigs set aside Mr. Clay, of which there are strong indications in some

4. James Wickes Taylor, Diary [3 July 1843], 27 (imposing quote). John McLean to John Teesdale, 27 March 1846 and 9 July 1846, McLean Papers, Ohio Historical Society (demagogue quote). See also Weisenburger, *John McLean*, vii (northwest quote), 81–98, 103–4.
5. John Quincy Adams, *Memoirs* 8:537 [14 March 1833] (night quote). Henry Clay to John M. Berrien, 4 September 1843, in Hopkins and Hargreaves, *Papers of Henry Clay* 9:854. As Chairman of the Senate Judiciary Committee, Berrien was also approached by the Latter-day Saints for assistance. See, for example, Orson Pratt to John M. Berrien, 11 May 1844, cited in Crowley, *Descriptive Bibliography*, 271–72.

Jacob Burnet of Cincinnati, Ohio. Henry Howe, *Historical Collections of Ohio,* The Ohio Centennial Edition (1906) 1:316.

quarters, then why is not Judge McLean's chance for a nomination as good as that of Gen. Scott or any other whig?" McLean had two chief Whig rivals, the *Register* noted, General Winfield Scott, hero of the War of 1812, and Kentucky senator Henry Clay.[6]

Shortly after the *Register* article appeared McLean received an unexpected visit from a local candidate for U.S. Congress, John J. Hardin. A native of Kentucky, Hardin had moved to Jacksonville, Illinois, in 1830 after graduating in law from Lex-ington's Transylvania University. Hardin was a staunch Clay Whig and a stepnephew of the elder statesman. Hardin's mother Elizabeth had married Henry Clay's brother, Porter Clay, in 1830 following the death of her husband, former U.S. senator Martin D. Hardin. Porter and his new wife removed to Jacksonville in 1833 so that Elizabeth could be closer to her son. The couple would remain there through the 1840s.[7]

Hardin was a member of Henry Clay's inner circle, known as his "secret commit-tee" to opponents, a network of political informants and confidants assembled over more than four decades of public service. Henry Clay had served as a U.S. congress-man from Kentucky beginning in 1806 and was elected Speaker of the House of Rep-resentatives in 1811, a position he retained for much of his earlier political career.

Clay first ran for the presidency of the U.S. in 1824. In an unusual circumstance, none of the four candidates secured a simple majority of electoral votes. The final decision as to who would become the next president of the U.S. was left up to the House of Representatives. After courting by "friends" of the three more successful candidates, Clay put his support behind John Quincy Adams. With the election of Ad-ams, Clay took the oath of office as secretary of state. Rumors of a "corrupt bargain" between the two political leaders could not be denied. The charge would plague Clay to the end of his life. Nonetheless, Clay's appointment as secretary of state survived the Adams administration. Clay returned to the U.S. Senate in 1831 and only retired from that body in 1842 in order to devote himself to the 1844 presidential race.

John J. Hardin's visit to Judge McLean was prompted by Henry Clay's fear that the "intrigue of 1839"—involving Jacob Burnet and the successful presidential cam-paign of William Henry Harrison—might be repeated in 1844. Clay refused to be "set aside" again.[8]

---

6. "District Court United States—Judge McLean," *Illinois State Register,* 16 June 1843.
7. "Judge McLean, Mr. Clay, and a Foreign Mission," *Illinois State Register,* 20 June 1843.
8. The best contemporary reference to Henry Clay's "secret committee" is Cassius M. Clay to Henry Clay, 13 April 1848, in Hopkins and Hargreaves, *Papers of Henry Clay* 10:435–39. The "corrupt bargain" charge is examined in Remini, *Henry Clay,* 251–72. Clay uses the phrase "intrigue of 1839" in at least two letters—Henry Clay to Benjamin W. Leigh, 20 June 1843, in Hopkins and Hargreaves,

In December of 1839 delegates from twenty-two of the twenty-six states in the Union were gathered at Harrisburg, Pennsylvania, to select the 1840 Whig presidential ticket. Following a heated debate (and last-minute changes in balloting procedures) the convention nominated William Henry Harrison. General Winfield Scott and Senator Henry Clay were eliminated from the race.

Harrison's campaign manager was Cincinnatian Jacob Burnet, "a man of wealth, a lawyer of the first eminence, a Supreme Court Judge, a Senator in Congress, a citizen of extensive influence." The oldest son of Dr. William Burnet, surgeon general during the Revolutionary War and member of the Continental Congress, and a 1791 graduate of Princeton University, Jacob Burnet arrived in Cincinnati from New Jersey in 1796. Burnet managed his father's investments in the Symmes Purchase, served on the legislature of the Northwest Territory (1798–1802), and was a major contributor to the Ohio Constitution, working closely with judges William Goforth and Francis Dunlavy. He was elected to the Ohio House of Representatives (1812–1813), a position he resigned in order to replace Senator William Henry Harrison, who had been appointed as U.S. minister to Colombia. Burnet was named justice of the Ohio Supreme Court in 1821 and elected U.S. senator from Ohio (1828–1831), replacing, once again, the departing William Henry Harrison. In addition to his political service, Burnet was president of the Cincinnati branch of the Bank of the United States for several years prior to its demise in 1832.[9] Jacob's younger brother, Isaac Gouverneur Burnet, was elected the first mayor of Cincinnati following the town's incorporation in 1819, a post he held for more than a decade. Another brother, David G. Burnet, was elected interim president of the Republic of Texas in 1836.[10]

At Harrisburg in December 1839 Jacob Burnet was called upon to deliver Harrison's nomination speech. His remarks were prefaced with comments about Henry Clay, the Whig statesman nearly everyone thought (before the convention, at least) was certain to win the nomination. Without directly naming the defeated senator, Burnet declared, "Long, and ardently have I desired to see him in the Presidential chair, and many a battle have I fought for the accomplishment of that desire. But few men on this floor bear more of the scars of political warfare, received in his defense than I do."

The paths of the two men had crossed frequently. Both were militant anti-Abolitionists. Burnet headed the Cincinnati chapter of the American Colonization Society (Henry Clay was the national president), which had as its object the repatriation of free blacks to the colony of Liberia in west Africa. Most recently Burnet and Clay had worked to settle a boundary dispute between Kentucky and Virginia.

Papers of Henry Clay 9:826–27, and Henry Clay to John M. Clayton, 21 June 1843, in Hopkins and Hargreaves, *Papers of Henry Clay* 9:827. To Clayton, Clay added, "They claim to be Whigs, full of ardent devotion to the cause, and expressing unbounded admiration of me. but, with grief and sadness, declaring that I cannot be elected, and that John McLean of Ohio ought to be brought out! . . . I thought it right to apprize you of this new movement." The New York Whigs behind McLean were Thurlow Weed and Moses H. Grinnell, a strong Daniel Webster supporter. See Hopkins and Hargreaves, *Papers of Henry Clay* 9:828, note 5.

9.   Gunderson, *The Log-Cabin Campaign. Narrative . . . Liberty of the Press*, 26 (influence quote).

10.   Hobby, *Life and Times of David G. Burnet. Biographical Directory of the Texan Conventions*, 60.

To soften the blow dealt by Clay's inability, once again, to receive the Whig nomination, Burnet continued, "General Harrison entertains towards him the same feelings, and has long ardently desired to see him at the head of the nation; nor would [Harrison] have been a candidate in 1836, had it not been distinctly announced that Mr. Clay had withdrawn from the canvass."

With preliminaries out of the way, Burnet addressed the president of the convention. "I hope, sir, I shall not be charged with vanity when I say that I have been [Harrison's] intimate companion and friend for more than forty years. The free and continued intercourse that has existed between us for so long a period, must necessarily enable me to speak with some confidence as to his character, acquirements, and course of life." Burnet's able recounting of General Harrison's accomplishments was widely praised, often described as his last notable public act.[11]

The convention over, the work of the canvass was yet ahead. Whig organizers were assembled throughout the Union. Burnet's speech was translated into German and Welsh in order to attract the immigrant vote. The log-cabin campaign, which appealed to the populace through catchy slogans ("Tippecanoe and Tyler too!") and hard cider, was a grand success. Harrison, "the poor man's friend," was sworn in as the nation's ninth president in February of 1841. During his lengthy inaugural address the seventy-one-year-old Harrison fell ill, and died of pneumonia less than a month later. He was replaced by his vice president, John Tyler, a former Jacksonian Democrat.

Some time after the Harrisburg convention, Burnet met with Henry Clay in Washington, D.C. In an effort to console the elder statesman, Burnet insisted: "You were the choice of 99 out of a hundred of the Whigs of the U[nited] States." Clay was incensed at what he saw as Burnet's deliberate underhandedness and later wrote, "Believing that, how could he consistently go for another? Or does he think that the wishes of the many should always yield to the desire of the few?" From the results at Harrisburg, Clay knew that Burnet, though a fellow Whig, could be a dangerous opponent.[12]

If Burnet had been triumphant in his promotion of Harrison, Clay no doubt reasoned, there was every likelihood he could repeat his success with McLean. The threat to the Clay camp was even greater now that McLean and Burnet were in-laws; in 1838 McLean's son Nathaniel had married Jacob Burnet's daughter Caroline.[13]

Hardin proposed that McLean withdraw his name from further consideration in the 1844 race. Then, Hardin assured him, when Henry Clay was president, McLean would be rewarded with a foreign ambassadorship. The intent of the offer was clear. Clay saw McLean as a dangerous political rival who had to be neutralized. At the same time, Clay wanted McLean to back him in the upcoming election in order to strengthen the Clay ticket. McLean was not yet prepared to concede the contest, for even as the two men in Springfield contemplated their political futures, Jacob Burnet and former Ohio congressman John C. Wright (editor of the Cincinnati *Daily*

11. Burnet, *Speech of Judge Burnett*, 3.
12. Henry Clay to John Sloan, 27 October 1843, in Hopkins and Hargreaves, *Papers of Henry Clay* 9:874.
13. *Cincinnati Daily Gazette*, 10 September 1838.

Gazette following the death of Hammond in 1840) were in Boston seeking support for McLean's cause. Henry Clay would wait several months for his answer.[14]

Even before he could hope to impact Henry Clay's national presidential campaign, however, John J. Hardin had to convince the Illinois electorate of his own viability as a representative from Illinois's newly formed Seventh Congressional District, politically the most important region in the state outside of Chicago.

---

14. "Judge McLean, Mr. Clay, and a Foreign Mission," *Illinois State Register,* 20 June 1843. Henry Clay to Robert P. Letcher, 26 June 1843, in Hopkins and Hargreaves, *Papers of Henry Clay* 9:830.

Chapter Three

"To Save the District for the Whigs"

IN 1843, THE ECONOMY OF Illinois had not yet recovered from the economic decline of the late 1830s. The state suffered from a crushing public debt burden brought on by a succession of Democratic administrations and the limitations of a barely functioning money economy with almost no gold or silver coin in circulation. Paper currency was accepted only at a steep discount. These conditions favored a Whig revival with a promise of "relief and reform."

When congressional redistricting was completed in early 1843, Illinois was divided into seven nearly equal precincts. John J. Hardin's drive to represent Illinois's newly formed Seventh Congressional District, which included Springfield, the state capital, was seen as an opportunity by the Whigs to deliver Illinois from "the fangs of Loco-focoism," *locofoco* being a popular term for Democrats named after a strike-anywhere friction match.[1]

To prevent party infighting, Springfield Whigs Abraham Lincoln, Edward D. Baker, and John J. Hardin had agreed to be "successively nominated and elected to Congress." Eighteen-forty-three was Hardin's year to run. The canvass was uneventful. Hardin's greatest challenge was how to overcome hoarseness from "riding in the hot weather of the day, and then speaking for five or six hours in the evening." Other Whig aspirants for Congress were not so fortunate.[2]

In western Illinois's new Sixth District the Whigs chose as their candidate Cyrus Walker, a criminal defense attorney from Macomb, McDonough County. Walker was an older Kentucky gentleman, regarded as "the peer of the leading lawyers" at Springfield and widely considered the best chance to "save the district for the whigs." A Whig "of the Henry Clay school," (the two men knew each other from the Lexington bar) Walker was not an office seeker. His three terms in the Kentucky House of Representatives had eliminated any desire for an active political career. Now, however, with larger party interests at stake, Walker could no longer refuse to run.[3]

---

1. John J. Hardin to John T. Stuart, 28 December 1842, Hardin Papers, Chicago Historical Society. J. K. Dubois to John J. Hardin, 24 August 1843, Hardin Papers, Chicago Historical Society, quoted in Cox, "Hardin," 80, note 11.

2. Abraham Lincoln to John J. Hardin, 19 January 1845, in Lincoln, *Complete Works* 1:271–274 (successively quote). Cox, "Hardin," 79 (riding quote).

3. Gregg, *History of Hancock County*, 291 (peer quote). *History of McDonough County* (1885), 388–90. "Obituary [of Cyrus Walker]," *Macomb Weekly Journal*, 2 December 1875. Collins, *History of Kentucky*, 2:770–77.

John J. Hardin of Jacksonville, Illinois. Illinois State Historical Library, Old State Capitol, Springfield, Illinois.

The Democrats expected to retain the counties they had secured in the previous election—including the Mormon-controlled county of Hancock, with its decisive bloc of more than one thousand votes in the city of Nauvoo alone—and selected a young lawyer, Joseph P. Hoge, of Galena, "talented, energetic, and a good stump speaker" to go against Walker.[4]

The Whig strategy for the Sixth District also depended upon the Mormon vote. Walker's trunk "was full of letters from all parts of the district," one acquaintance recalled, "urging him to allow the use of his name for congress." This correspondence included two letters from Joseph Smith, the Mormon prophet, who "pledged the Mormon vote to Walker, if he would allow his name to be used, but would not agree to vote for any other whig." Walker had been one of Smith's defense counsel (together with O. H. Browning, and others) in 1841 during an unsuccessful extradition attempt by Missouri authorities. Several supportive letters came from George Miller, a well-to-do farmer and fellow Freemason who had been a "brother elder" with Walker in Macomb's Presbyterian church prior to Miller's conversion to Mormonism. In the end it was "at the earnest solicitation of the leading Whigs in the Galena District" that Walker "consented to become a candidate for Congress." Cyrus Walker's success in Mormon-dominated Hancock County was at first limited. Then a circumstance arose which virtually assured his victory.[5]

On Tuesday, June 13, a grand jury indictment against Joseph Smith—on the old charge of treason against the state of Missouri and for having "fled from justice"—was signed by the governor of Missouri and forwarded to Springfield, Illinois. On that same day Joseph Smith and his wife Emma departed Nauvoo to visit her sister who lived near Dixon, Illinois, some two hundred miles to the north.[6]

Illinois's Democratic governor Thomas Ford issued a writ for Joseph's arrest on Friday, June 16. By previous arrangement the papers were delivered to the Hancock County constable, Harmon T. Wilson, and took effect the next day.

Apparently ambivalent about the forces he was unleashing, late that night Governor Ford informed Judge James Adams "he was obliged to issue a writ for Joseph

---

4. Gregg, *History of Hancock County*, 291.
5. "The Late Cyrus Walker," *Carthage Gazette*, 5 January 1876 (letters quote). "Death of Cyrus Walker. Some Reminiscences Connected with the Deceased," *Carthage Gazette*, 8 December 1875 (name quote). *History of McDonough County* (1885), 389 (whig quote). "Obituary [of Cyrus Walker]," *Macomb Weekly Journal*, 2 December 1875 (candidate quote).
6. Smith, *History of the Church* 5:432, 439, 464–65 [Missouri writ, 13 June 1843, Illinois writ, 17 June 1843]. Samuel C. Owens to Thomas Ford, 10 June 1843, in Smith, *History of the Church* 5:422.

Capitol building, Springfield, Illinois. Illinois State Historical Library, Old State Capitol, Springfield, Illinois.

and that it would start tomorrow." Adams, who had converted to Mormonism several years earlier and was their champion in the capital, dispatched an express rider to Nauvoo. He arrived on Sunday evening. William Clayton and Stephen Markham, Joseph's clerk and bodyguard, departed Nauvoo after midnight to warn the prophet of his impending arrest. After riding hard for sixty-six hours they reached Dixon the following Wednesday.[7]

The prophet would not stay safe for long. Disguised as Mormon elders "seeking the Prophet Joseph," Constable Harmon T. Wilson of Hancock County, Illinois, and Sheriff Joseph Reynolds of Jackson County, Missouri, arrested Smith on June 22 and took him to a tavern near Dixon's Ferry, where he was placed under close guard. William Clayton returned to Nauvoo with word that Joseph had been captured.[8]

Several lawyers offered legal assistance to the prophet, and at first were refused admittance by the arresting officers. Cyrus Walker, who was campaigning in the neighborhood at the time, was eventually permitted to consult with the prisoner. Walker consented to represent the Mormon leader on the condition that Smith would deliver him the Mormon vote in the upcoming congressional contest. This

7. Smith, *American Prophet's Record*, 387 [16 and 18 June 1843]. Smith, *History of the Church* 5:433–39.
8. Charlotte Haven to [her parents], 2 July 1843, in Haven, "A Girl's Letters," 634. Smith, *American Prophet's Record*, 387–88 [23 June 1843].

William Clayton, clerk of the Kingdom.
Courtesy of the Church Archives, the
Church of Jesus Christ of Latter-day Saints.

was agreed. A writ of habeas corpus in behalf of the prophet was secured, which released him from custody and permitted the prophet's case to be reviewed by a justice of the peace. Joseph intended the hearing to take place before his own Mormon-friendly municipal court of Nauvoo.

On June 29, word reached Nauvoo that the prophet would return to the Holy City "the next day and wanted the band to meet him." Joseph arrived with his attorneys (Cyrus Walker among them) sitting in a "buggy followed by stage and carriages" sporting the arresting officers, sheriff Reynolds and constable Wilson, displayed like trophies of war. Two rows of horses, about forty in all, completed the entourage. An "immence [sic] carnival of people met the cavalcade" and escorted the general to his house.[9]

After resting for a time the prophet spoke to those who had given him such a joyous welcome. "The congregation is large," the prophet began, addressing the thousands of Saints assembled in the grove near the temple site, eager to hear of his recent exploits. "I shall require attention . . . I meet you with a heart full of gratitude to Almighty God; and I presume you all feel the same . . . Thank God, I am now a prisoner in the hands of the municipal court of Nauvoo, and not in the hands of Missourians. It is not so much my object to tell of my afflictions, trials, and troubles as to speak of the writ of habeas corpus, so that the minds of all may be corrected. It has been asserted by the great and wise men, lawyers and others, that our municipal powers and legal tribunals are not to be sanctioned by the authorities of the state." (Complaints had arisen that the municipal court of Nauvoo was taking upon itself more powers than were actually granted to it by the state of Illinois.) "Relative to our city charter, courts, right of habeas corpus, etc., I wish you to know and publish that we have *all* power; and if any man from this time forth says anything to the contrary, cast it into his teeth."

"There is a secret in this," Joseph assured his audience. "If there is not power in our charter and courts, then there is not power in the state of Illinois, nor in the congress or constitution of the United States; for the United States gave unto Illinois her constitution or charter, and Illinois gave unto Nauvoo her charters, ceding unto us our vested rights, which she has no right or power to take from us." He repeated his point for emphasis. "*All* the power there was in Illinois she gave to Nauvoo; and any man that says to the contrary is a fool." No one in the vast crowd disagreed with this assessment.

---

9. Smith, *American Prophet's Record*, 388–89 [29 and 30 June 1843]. Smith, *History of the Church* 5:442–44.

"I have no doubt but I shall be discharged by the municipal court," he went on. "Were I before any good tribunal, I should be discharged, as the Missouri writs are illegal, and good for nothing—they are 'without form and void' . . . Go ye into all the world and preach the gospel. He that believeth in our chartered rights may come here and be saved; and he that does not shall remain in ignorance. If any lawyer shall say there is more power in other places and charters with respect to habeas corpus than in Nauvoo, believe it not."

He had more proof of his legal position. "I have converted this candidate for congress," Joseph declared, pointing to Cyrus Walker, seated next to him on the stand, "that the right of habeas corpus is included in our charter. If he continues converted, I will vote for him."

The prophet related the circumstances of his arrest at Dixon and the refusal of the officers, initially, to grant him the privilege of applying for a writ of habeas corpus. "I pledged my honor to my counsel that the Nauvoo city charter conferred jurisdiction to investigate the subject; so we came to Nauvoo, where I am now prisoner in the custody of a higher tribunal than the circuit court. The charter says that 'the city council shall have power and authority to make, ordain, establish, and execute such ordinances not repugnant to the constitution of the United States, or of this state, as they may deem necessary for the peace, benefit, and safety of the inhabitants of said city.' And also that 'the Municipal Court shall have power to grant writs of habeas corpus in all cases arising under the ordinances of the city council.' The city council have passed an ordinance 'that no citizen of this city shall be taken out of this city by any writ, without the privilege of a writ of habeas corpus.'"

Joseph concluded his remarks. "There is nothing but what we have power over, except where restricted by the constitution of the United States . . . The constitution of the United States declares that the privilege of the writ of habeas corpus shall not be denied. Deny me the writ of habeas corpus, and I will fight with gun, sword, cannon, whirlwind, and thunder, until they are used up like the Kilkenny cats . . . And the great Elohim has given me the privilege of having the benefits of the constitution, and the writ of habeas corpus; and I am bold to ask for this privilege this day, and I ask, in the name of Jesus Christ, and all that is sacred, that I may have *your* lives and all *your* energies to carry out the freedom which is chartered to us."

He looked over the vast audience. "Will you all help me? If so, make it manifest by raising the right hand." The response by the thousands there gathered was unanimous, "a perfect sea of hands being elevated." Joseph responded with pleasure to the spontaneous show of support. "Here is truly a committee of the whole," he said proudly. He confided to lawyer Cyrus Walker, in a voice still loud enough for those close by to hear, "These are the greatest dupes, as a body of people, that ever lived," he said, "or [else] I am not so big a rogue as I am reported to be."

Joseph again gestured towards Walker before the assembled congregation. "I understand the gospel and you do not," he said. "You understand the quackery of law, and I do not."

Walker was presented to the gathering of Saints. His comments were brief. He stressed that "from what he had seen in the Nauvoo City Charter, it gave the power to try writs of habeas corpus."

Joseph closed the meeting. "The lawyers themselves acknowledge that we have *all* power granted us in our charters that we could ask for—that we had more power than any other court in the state. For all other courts were restricted, while ours was not; and I thank God Almighty for it. I will not be rode down to hell by the Missourians any longer; and it is my privilege to speak in my own defense; and I appeal to your integrity and honor that you will stand by and help me, according to the covenant you have this day made."[10]

The Nauvoo municipal court commenced a hearing to consider Joseph Smith's writ of habeas corpus on July 1. "After a patient investigation" (and the prophet's homecoming oration firmly in mind) Smith was "discharged and the court adjourned." Having achieved his goal of freeing the Mormon prophet, Walker's election seemed certain.[11]

The Fourth of July celebrations at Nauvoo were triumphant. The prophet addressed a crowd estimated to be some fifteen thousand strong. He told of his recent arrest and he spoke of politics. "With regard to elections, some say all the Latter-day Saints vote together, and vote as I say," Joseph noted. "But I never tell any man how to vote or whom to vote for. But I will show you how we have been situated by bringing a comparison. Should there be a Methodist society here and two candidates running for office, one says, 'If you will vote for me and put me in governor, I will exterminate the Methodists, take away their charters.' The other candidate says, 'If I am governor, I will give all an equal privilege.' Which would the Methodists vote for? Of course they would vote *en masse* for the candidate that would give them their rights. Thus it has been with us."[12]

The 1842 Whig gubernatorial candidate, Joseph Duncan, the prophet noted, "said if the people would elect him he would exterminate the Mormons, and take away their charters. As to Mr. Ford," a Democrat, "he made no such threats, but manifested a spirit in his speeches to give every man his rights; hence the members of the Church universally voted for Mr. Ford and he was elected governor." (Joseph even named his favorite horse 'Joe Duncan,' so that he could literally whip the opposition.) Recent events, however, suggested that the Democratic governor Ford was not a true friend of the Latter-day Saints. "He has issued writs against me the first time the Missourians made a demand for me," continued Joseph, "and this is the second one he has issued for me, which has caused me much trouble and expense."[13]

Walker was confident the tide had turned in his favor. A Whig victory in August appeared certain.

Within days, the Democrats unleashed a devastating counterattack. On July 7, an article appeared in the *Illinois State Register* charging Joseph's arrest and Cyrus Walker's appearance at Dixon as a "Whig conspiracy." The evidence presented was convincing,

10. "An Address by President Joseph Smith, Delivered on the evening of his arrival from Dixon, June 30, 1843, in the Grove, near the Temple, Nauvoo," in Smith, *History of the Church* 5:467–68, 170, 471, 472, and 473. Compare Smith, *American Prophet's Record*, 389–91 [30 June 1843]. See also *Journal of Discourses* 2:163 and Hallwas and Launius, *Cultures in Conflict*, 92–97.

11. Smith, *American Prophet's Record*, 392 [1 July 1843].

12. Smith, *History of the Church* 5:490. Roberts, *Comprehensive History* 2:194.

13. Ibid., 5:60, 91, 292, 450. 6:398 (horse reference). Smith, *History of the Church* 5:490.

Thomas Ford (1800–1850), governor of Illinois. Illinois State Historical Library, Old State Capitol, Springfield, Illinois.

even if chiefly circumstantial. The article began by noting a letter apparently written early in the year "from the notorious John C. Bennett" (who had been expelled from the Mormon church in 1842 for alleged sexual improprieties) which urged the importance of reissuing an indictment against Joseph Smith for a nearly six-year-old charge of treason. "This charge had been made once before and afterwards abandoned by Missouri," the paper noted. "This is the same charge on which Smith was arrested and carried before Judge [Stephen A.] Douglass and discharged two years ago. After that decision the indictment against Smith was dismissed and the charge wholly abandoned." Bennett, however, after his public exposure and expulsion from Nauvoo, would not give up. It was widely considered that Bennett was "a mere tool in the hands of the Whig junto at Springfield," a group that included Abraham Lincoln, Edward D. Baker, and John J. Hardin.

Furthermore, according to the intercepted letter, Bennett insisted that his Missouri agent "go to the [Missouri] Judge and never leave him until he appoints a special term of the court; never suffer the court to adjourn until an indictment is found against Smith for treason; . . . go immediately to the Governor and never leave him until you get a demand on the Governor of Illinois for Smith's arrest, and then, despatch some active and vigilant person to Illinois for a warrant . . . and then let him never come back to Missouri without Smith." With the exception of the unforeseen complication that Joseph would be successful in having the warrant examined before a friendly court, Bennett's description of the proposed kidnap drama was remarkably accurate.

The *Register* went on to claim that Reynolds, "after he had obtained the custody of Smith at Dixon refused to employ a democratic lawyer and insisted upon having a whig lawyer of inferior abilities [Walker] simply upon the ground as he stated that the democrats were against him." And, "let it also be borne in mind," the paper continued, "that Cyrus Walker the whig candidate for congress miraculously *happened* to be within six miles of Dixon when Smith was arrested, ready and convenient to be employed by Smith, to get him delivered from custody." The paper stressed that Walker succeeded because that was part of the plan.

"It is true that the evidence is circumstantial," the *Register* concluded. "But it is strong. Positive evidence of such a dark laid conspiracy could not be expected. Nevertheless, circumstantial as it is, so strong is the force of it, that many a man has been convicted of capital offences upon evidence not more conclusive."[14]

---

14. "The Federal Whig conspiracy to obtain the Mormon votes for Browning and Walker—Unexampled villany," *Illinois State Register*, 7 July 1843, Smith, *History of the Church* 5:513–15, under date of 18 July 1843 with new title, "Was the arrest of the Prophet a political trick?"

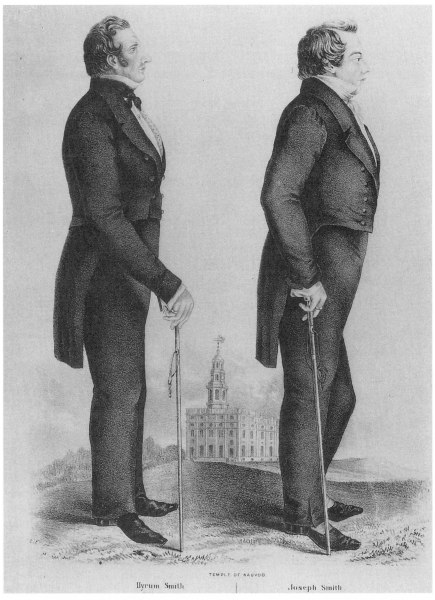

TEMPLE OF NAUVOO

Hyrum Smith | Joseph Smith

Joseph and Hyrum Smith. Nauvoo temple (incomplete at their death in 1844) in background. Courtesy of the Church Archives, the Church of Jesus Christ of Latter-day Saints.

By early August it was rumored that Hyrum Smith, Joseph's older brother, himself an able politician, had promised the Mormon vote to Democratic candidate Joseph P. Hoge in exchange for his own Democratic seat in Congress the following term. In concert with this appealing offer, a leading Democrat in Springfield quelled Mormon fears of an armed attack against the city of Nauvoo by pledging the state's "militia should not be sent against them . . . if the Mormons voted the democratic ticket."[15]

Sensing a clear Democratic victory with Mormon support, candidate Hoge (in company with Hyrum) called on Joseph Smith at his office in Nauvoo. There Hoge "acknowledged," somewhat belatedly, "the power of the Mormon Habeus Corpus."[16]

The two candidates gave stump speeches at Nauvoo in the early evening of August 1. These were little more than verbal sparring matches during which time Hoge and Walker "politically castigate[d] each other." Walker's speech was brief as usual. He was followed by Hoge, who spoke "for over two hours, having lit candles for the purpose." The two men would remain in Nauvoo until polling day, almost a week later, "making speeches, caressing and flattering" the Mormon voters, angling for approval from the people they knew would decide their political futures.[17]

On August 2, the *Nauvoo Neighbor* published two letters—one in support of Walker, the other supporting Hoge—and counseled the Saints about the upcoming election:

> We would suggest the necessity of unanimity, after weighing the matter over, and fixing on the man the best calculated to represent their interests in Congress for it can answer no good purpose that half the citizens should dis-franchise [sic] the other half, thus rendering Nauvoo powerless as far as politics are concerned. In this city we have one interest alone and should not be divided.

Under the editorship of John Taylor, one of the twelve apostles and a member of the Nauvoo city council, the *Neighbor* clearly supported Hoge, described in its pages as a man who favored "Equal Rights, and Equal Privileges . . . now and forever." The communication by "A Democrat" roundly attacked Walker's character and actions. "What reasons have you to support [Walker]?" it asked. "Is it because he defended Joseph Smith in his late arrest [at Dixon], as a Lawyer, and obtained Five Hundred Dollars for his services?"[18]

---

15. Ford, *History of Illinois*, Quaife, ed., 2:151. The phrasing has been reversed in this passage, as indicated by the ellipsis. According to Ford, he was unaware of this agreement until October 1846, after the Mormons had departed the state. (Ford, *History of Illinois*, 317–18 and Roberts, *Comprehensive History* 2:196, note 5.) The go-between was William Backenstos, "a managing democrat of Hancock county" and a former clerk for Stephen A. Douglas. Smith, *History of the Church* 5:532–36 and William Law, Interview, Cook, *William Law*, 125. See also Clayton, Nauvoo Journal 2 [18 May 1843], Clayton, *Intimate Chronicle*, 104.

16. Smith, *American Prophet's Record*, 401 [1 August 1843]. Smith, *History of the Church* 5:524.

17. Smith, *History of the Church* 5:524 (castigate and candles quotes). Charlotte Haven to [her family], 8 September 1843 (flattering quote), Haven, "A Girl's Letters," 636.

18. *Nauvoo Neighbor*, 2 August 1843. Several writers insist that Walker was paid $10,000 for his legal services. See Ford, *History of Illinois*, Quaife ed., 2:148, note 26. Quaife follows Brodie, *No Man*

John Taylor, Mormon apostle and editor of *Nauvoo Neighbor* and *Times and Seasons*. Courtesy of the Church Archives, the Church of Jesus Christ of Latter-day Saints.

On Saturday evening, two days before the elections of August 7, Hyrum Smith took the stand at the grove.[19] He addressed "a large concourse of people" who had gathered. With obvious authority as the church's patriarch and the prophet's elder brother, Hyrum told the assembled "how to vote, and whom to support if they considered their own interest and good of the place." He "advised them to go for Hoge."

William Law, Joseph's counselor in the First Presidency of the church, silent until now, strongly objected to Hyrum's action but was kept from the stand. It was nearly dark when he was finally able to address the congregation. Law "stated that to his certain knowledge the Prophet Joseph was in favor of Mr. Walker and that the prophet was more likely to know the mind of the Lord on the subject than the patriarch." When Law showed "the people how shamefully they had treated Mr. Walker . . . they began to shout" for the Whig candidate. "I am as obedient to revelation as any man," continued Law. "Bro. Hyrum does not say he had a revelation." Many in the crowd agreed.[20]

Not to be undone, Hyrum rose and took the stand a second time. He told the people he knew with a certainty how they were to vote the coming Monday, for "he had sought to know, and knew from knowledge that would not be doubted, from evidences that never fail, that Mr. Hoge was the man, and it was for the interest of this place and people to support him." He raised both arms and held up an election ticket ("printed on yellow post office wrapping paper"). "Thus saith the Lord," Hyrum proclaimed, giving his words the stamp of heavenly approval, "those that vote this ticket, this flesh colored ticket, this Democratic ticket, shall be blessed; those who do not, shall be accursed." A resounding cheer went up from those present. The Mormons were to vote for Hoge.[21]

Knows My History, 349. Brodie cites George Albert Smith, *Journal of Discourses* 13:109 and Smith, *History of the Church* 5:444. As the *History of the Church* makes clear, the $10,000 was the claim for damages, not Walker's fee.

19. There are no details of Hyrum's comments in Smith, *History of the Church* 5:525 or Smith, *American Prophet's Record*, 401 [5 August 1843].

20. William Law, Interview, Cook, *William Law*, 125 (shout quote). Ford, *History of Illinois*, Quaife ed., 2:152. "B" to *Macomb Weekly Journal*, 22 January 1877, *Macomb Weekly Journal* 25 January 1877 (revelation quote). Confirmed by "K" to *The Tribune* 7 August 1843, "The Vote of the Mormons—Hoge Elected," *New York Weekly Tribune*, 26 August 1843 (interest quote).

21. "B" to *Macomb Weekly Journal*, 22 January 1877 (*Macomb Weekly Journal* 25 January 1877) (accursed quote). "K" to *The Tribune* 7 August 1843, "The Vote of the Mormons—Hoge Elected," *New York Weekly Tribune*, 26 August 1843 (interest quote).

The prophet took the stand at the Sunday meetings. He would not preach at that time, he said, but would wait until the following Sunday. He would speak instead about the coming election. "I have not come to tell you to vote this way, that way, or the other in relation to National matters," the prophet began. "I want it to [go] abroad to the whole world that every man should stand on his own merits. The Lord has not given me Revelation concerning politics. I have not asked Him for one. I am a third party [and] stand independant and alone. I desire to see all parties protected in their rights. In relation to Mr. Walker, he is a Whig candidate, a highminded man. Mr. Walker has not hung onto my coat tail to gain his election as some have said. I am going to give a testimony, but not for electioneering purposes. Before Mr. Walker come to Nauvoo rumor come up that he might become a candidate for Congress. Says I, he is an old friend, [and] I will vote for him. When Mr. Walker come to my house, I voluntarily told him I was going to vote for him. When I dictated to him the laws of Nauvoo," in relation to writs of habeas corpus, "he received them on my testimony." Walker, continued the prophet, "withdrew all claim to your vote and influence *if* it will be detrimental to your interest as a people."[22]

Joseph let the meaning of what he had just said settle in the minds of those present and shifted to his real concern, the possibility of dissent within his own ranks. "I never authorized Brother Law to tell my private feelings," he called out, "and I utterly forbid these political demagogues from using my name henceforth and forever." Now certain he had their attention, the prophet went on. "Brother Hyrum tells me this morning that he has had a testimony to the effect it would be better for the people to vote for Hoge . . . I never knew Hyrum to say he ever had a revelation and it failed. Let God speak and all men hold their peace." Joseph turned the stand over to Hyrum who once again "explained at some length concerning the election." The crowd dispersed and "runners" from surrounding counties returned to their congregations with a clear message—vote Democratic. First abandoned, Walker's fate was now sealed.[23]

On Monday in Nauvoo, "The polls were crowded . . . from the time they opened 'till they closed, and Hoge, Hoge, Hoge, was all the rage." The prophet and Mr. Walker "rode to the polls together." As promised, Joseph voted for Mr. Walker. Of the 1,191 votes cast in the Holy City, 1,092 went for Democrat Hoge. There was now little doubt about the outcome of the contest.

At one Nauvoo polling location ("which gave Hoge 495 majority") the voting proceeded so slowly that men were returning to their farms without casting their vote. This would have been disastrous to the Hoge camp. Beginning at noon additional clerks were called in, and rather than recording the vote in the presence of the voter as was required by law, "the ticket was taken by one of the Judges who called

---

22. Smith, *American Prophet's Record*, 401 [6 August 1843]. Emphasis added. Compare Smith, *History of the Church* 5:526. Roberts, *Comprehensive History* 2:195. Smith, *History* adds "I am above the kingdoms of the world, for I have no laws." (526)

23. Smith, *History of the Church* 5:526 (demagogue, peace, forever, and election quotes). The order used here accords with Smith, *American Prophet's Record*, 402 [6 August 1843]. Cook, *William Law*, 125. Smith, *Words*, 237. See also Ford, *History of Illinois*, Quaife ed., 2:152–53. Charlotte Haven to [her parents], 8 September 1843, Haven, "A Girl's Letters," 636. "B" to *Macomb Weekly Journal*, 22 January 1847, *Macomb Weekly Journal*, 25 January 1877.

out the name of the voter, while one of the clerks wrote it upon the back of the ticket, and then deposited it, afterwards to be recorded." Some called for a declaration that the vote was invalid. None was forthcoming.[24]

When the votes were counted it became clear that Walker had maintained a solid lead over Hoge outside of Nauvoo, with an 895 vote majority in thirteen counties—Henry, Knox, Mercer, Ogle, Stark, Warren, Jo Davies, Stephenson, Winnebago, Carroll, Whiteside, Rock Island, and Henderson. Hoge led in two counties, Lee and McDonough, with a majority of only 114 votes. Hancock County figures were 2,088 in favor of Hoge, and 733 (chiefly non-Mormon votes outside of Nauvoo) in favor of Walker. The Mormon bloc vote had determined the contest.[25]

Similar evidence of Mormon electoral control was noted in Adams County to the south. The final tally of votes confirmed that most of the Saints in the Fifth District had voted for Quincy attorney O. H. Browning, a longtime friend to the Mormons, as "there was not sufficient time, or it was neglected, to send orders from Nauvoo into the Quincy district to effect a change there." Even with Mormon support, Browning was defeated by his old Democratic adversary, Judge Stephen A. Douglas, who garnered 51 percent of the vote.[26]

When the votes in the 1843 congressional race were counted, John J. Hardin became the only Illinois Whig to gain a seat in U.S. Congress. Joseph Smith's power over the ballot box in Hancock County presented an almost insurmountable challenge with the result that Hardin found himself fighting an uphill battle for Whig political control of the state in 1844.

24. "K" to *The Tribune* 7 August 1843, "The Vote of the Mormons—Hoge Elected," *New York Weekly Tribune*, 26 August 1843 (rage and recorded quotes). "Illinois—Walker's Probable Defeat—Locofoco Intrigue with the Mormons," *New York Weekly Tribune*, 26 August 1843. Roberts, *Comprehensive History* 2:196.

25. Pease, *Illinois Election Returns*, 140.

26. Ford, *History of Illinois*, Quaife ed., 2:154.

Chapter Four

"Nauvoo is no place for rational people"

There seems to be already the premonitory symptoms of a convulsion among them. Many are the spirits that hesitate not to manifest their disaffection and disloyalty to their prophet and leader.

Correspondent to the *New York Tribune*, August 27, 1843[1]

WHEN THE RESULTS OF THE Sixth District congressional elections were published, "everything connected with the Mormons became political," and marked the beginning of an uneasy alliance between Illinois Whigs and Democrats in opposition to Joseph Smith's autocratic rule. Internal dissent at Nauvoo also threatened to hasten the downfall of the Mormon prophet.[2]

William Law was not alone in his outspoken criticism of Hyrum's political revelation and the deliberateness with which Joseph Smith had manipulated the Mormon vote to favor the Democrats. "The Mormons now have all the power, elect whom they please and have taken the entire government of the county into their own hands," complained a Hancock resident. "They recently determined the election for Congressman by pretended revelations." A young woman visiting Nauvoo agreed. "Our Gentile [non-Mormon] friends say that this falling of the prophetic mantle on to Hyrum is a political ruse," she wrote to relatives in the northeast. "[W]hen Joseph was in the meshes of the law, he was assisted by some politicians of the Whig party, to whom he pledged himself in the coming elections. Now he wants the Democratic party to win, so Hyrum is of that party, and as it is revealed for him to vote, so go over all the Mormons like sheep following the bell sheep over a wall."[3]

Joseph Smith took the stand during the first Sunday meetings following the elections. He reproved the citizens of Nauvoo for their inappropriate behavior— young men "crowding onto the ladies' seats on the meeting ground," for "laughing

---

1. "The Mormons at the West," *New York Daily Tribune*, 12 September 1843. Letter dated Keokuk, Iowa, 27 August 1843. The chapter title comes from Charlotte Haven to [her parents], 15 October 1843, in Haven, "A Girl's Letters," 638. She tells "Isa" a secret: "Judge E.[mmons] has gone East. You can't think how I miss him, and it is uncertain whether he returns,—indeed Nauvoo is no place for rational people." Sylvester Emmons would become the editor of the ill-fated *Nauvoo Expositor*.
2. Ford, *History of Illinois*, Quaife ed., 2:154.
3. B. F. Morris to Milton Badger, 15 August 1843, quoted in Hampshire, *Mormonism*, 97. Charlotte Haven to [her parents], 8 September 1843, Haven, "A Girl's Letters," 635–36.

and mocking during the meeting." This conduct was intolerable, he insisted, and requested assistance from the city marshal in maintaining order. "The city is enlarging very fast," he said. "We have many professedly learned men in this city, and the height of their knowledge is not to know enough to keep in their place."

Walter Bagby, Hancock County's non-Mormon tax assessor and collector, was singled out for scorn. Bagby, claimed the prophet, "exercised more despotic power over the inhabitants of the city than any despot of the eastern country over his serfs." The two men had an altercation about two weeks before, when Bagby was in Nauvoo attending to county business. "He gave me some abusive language," said the prophet, "taking up a stone to throw at me: I seized him by the throat to choke him off."[4]

And, just a week earlier, as Joseph toured the area "on the hill" above the city on election day, he was accosted by Old Father Perry, a Gentile resident of Nauvoo. "Why, you can't vote in this precinct," the man informed him. A constable took Joseph "by the collar" and told him to go away. "I was abused and regulated at the ground," complained the prophet, "and there was not a man in the crowd to say, 'This is Bro[ther] Joseph, or this is the Mayor.'"

He blamed the politicians for the deplorable state of affairs in the city. "All our wrongs have arisen under the power and authority of democracy [the Democrats] and I have sworn that this arm shall fall from my shoulder, and this tongue cleave to the roof of my mouth before I will vote for them, unless they make me satisfaction and I feel it sensibly." He prepared to give the stand over to another speaker and then recalled he had "forgotten one thing." "We have had certain [traitors] in this city who have been writing falsehoods to Missouri," Joseph said. "There is a certain man in this city who has made a covenant to betray me and give me up and that too before Governor Carlin [of Illinois] commenced his persecutions. . . . This testimony I have from gentlemen from abroad whose names I do not wish to give."[5]

Joseph's sword fell on Sidney Rigdon. A trusted counselor and confidant since 1830, Sidney was nonetheless plagued by poor health, brought on, at least partially, by head injuries suffered while being dragged by a horse as a young boy, a traumatic mobbing he and Joseph endured in 1832, and the weeks he spent incarcerated with the prophet in the damp and cold Liberty jail. Even so, Joseph struck hard. "In the name of the Lord," he began, "I most solemnly proclaim the withdrawal of my fellowship from this man on the condition that the Judging be true and let the Saints proclaim it abroad that he will no longer be acknowledged as my counselor and all who feel to sanction my proceedings and views will manifest it by uplifted hands." The vote was unanimous. Sidney was disfellowshiped; his license as an elder in the Church of Jesus Christ of Latter-day Saints was revoked. Sidney moved quickly to clear his name and undo the damage inflicted by this arbitrary action.[6]

---

4.   Smith, *History of the Church* 5:531. Compare Smith, *American Prophet's Record*, 405 [13 August 1843]. For a fuller account, see Smith, *History of the Church* 5:524 and *Warsaw Message* 11 October 1843.

5.   Ibid., 531–32. Compare Smith, *American Prophet's Record*, 405–06 [13 August 1843].

6.   Smith, *American Prophet's Record*, 405–06 [13 August 1843]. See also Hampshire, *Mormonism*, 161 and 276, note 72. "In the name of the Lord" is recorded by William Clayton (Smith, *Words*, 243). See also Smith, *History of the Church* 5:537 and Leonard, *Nauvoo*, 299.

Thomas Gregg of Warsaw, Illinois. Western Illinois University, Regional Archives.

Two hundred of the Old Citizens assembled in Carthage on August 19, "to consult about the Mormons" and their growing influence in county politics. A "committee of six" drew up a list of concerns. The prophet had "most absolute contempt for the laws of man . . . [and] a most shameless disregard for all the forms and restraints of law," the Old Citizens argued. Joseph Smith's lawlessness, they believed, originated in a provision of the Nauvoo city charter that allowed the municipal court to issue writs of habeas corpus. Their main complaint was directed at this concern. The committee proposed a solution to halt Joseph Smith's contemptuous behavior. "If the authorities of the State of Missouri shall make another demand for the body of Joseph Smith, and our Governor shall issue another warrant," they would "stand ready at all times to serve the officer into whose hand such warrant may come . . . as a *posse*." They also attacked the political question. " As it has been too common for several years past for politicians of both political parties, not only of this county, but likewise of the state, to go to Nauvoo and truckle to the heads of the Mormon clan for their influence, we pledge ourselves that we will not support any man of either party in future who shall thus debase himself." The central corresponding committee at Carthage (which included Harmon T. Wilson and Walter Bagby), served as a "general committee of supervision" for anti-Mormon undertakings in the county. Precinct committees, of two members each, were established in Hancock's smaller settlements.[7]

Former Illinois governor Thomas Carlin responded to Sidney Rigdon's request for assistance on August 18. "It gives me pleasure to be perfectly able to disabuse you," Carlin wrote. "I have not seen you to my recollection, nor had any correspondence with you until the present, since 1839 and in all the intercourse I have had with you, I have always looked upon you as one of the most devoted followers of Joseph Smith and one of the pillars of the Church of the Latter-day Saints. I never sought through the aid of any person to entrap Joseph Smith. A faithful discharge of my official duties was all that I attempted or desired."[8]

The prophet read Governor Carlin's letter to an open meeting of the Saints on the morning of August 27. Joseph was not satisfied. "The letter is one of the most

7. Ibid., 407 [19 August 1843] (consult quote). See also Smith, *American Prophet's Record*, 403 [12 August 1843] and Smith, *History of the Church* 5:528. Gregg, *History of Hancock County*, 209. "Anti-Mormon Meeting at Carthage, Seat of Hancock County Illinois," in Smith, *History of the Church* 6:5, 7 (resolution quotes). Edson Whitney and Levi Williams served in Green Plains. Edson Whitney was chair of the meeting. Smith, *History of the Church* 6:8.

8. Smith, *American Prophet's Record*, 410–11 [27 August 1843].

evasive things and carries with it a design to hide the truth," he argued. "Has any man been concerned in a conspiracy to deliver Joseph Smith to Missouri? If so who?"

Sidney Rigdon rose to respond. "I never saw Governor Carlin but three times and never exchanged a word with any man living on this subject," insisted Rigdon. "I ask your pardon for having done anything which should give a reason to make you think so." No move was made to restore Rigdon's status in the church. A special conference to hear the case was called for early October.[9]

David N. White disembarked at the Warsaw dock in late August. The scene had changed little since he had last visited the town in 1840. White was the former editor of Warsaw's *Western World* newspaper, and met with his successor, *Warsaw Message* publisher Thomas Gregg, himself "a strong Whig," who offered to take White to the Mormon city of Nauvoo. As the Whig editor of a major eastern newspaper (the *Pittsburgh Gazette*), White hoped to speak with the Mormon prophet about politics. White knew that "the Mormon vote had been given to the Locofoco member of Congress, thereby defeating Cyrus Walker, Esq, whig, who had defended 'Joe' in several law suits with the Missourians." He wanted to find out why Joseph had not supported someone who was widely regarded as a friend to the Mormons.

The editor and the prophet met a few days later. In the course of the interview Joseph acknowledged his close friendship with Mr. Walker, "and said he had voted for him, but would not interfere with his people in the matter. He said he had never asked the Lord anything about politics; if he had done so, the Lord would have told him what to do. The Lord," Joseph Smith informed Mr. White, "has promised to give us wisdom, and when I lack wisdom I ask the Lord, and he tells me, and if he didn't tell me, I would say he was a liar; that's the way I feel. But I never asked him anything about politics. I am a Whig, and I am a Clay man. I am made of Clay, and I am tending to Clay, and I am going to vote for Henry Clay; that's the way I feel." Joseph laughed. "But I won't interfere with my people, religiously, to affect their votes, though I might to elect Clay, for he ought to be president. I have sworn by the eternal gods—it's no harm to swear by the gods, because there [are] none; if there is only one God, there can't be gods, and it's no harm to swear by nothing." He laughed again, doubtless reflecting on the impact his bold (some would say blasphemous) theological pronouncement might have on readers of the *Pittsburgh Gazette*. Joseph repeated his provocative oath, extending its significance with a reference to Old Testament practice. "I have sworn by the eternal gods that I never will vote for a democrat again," he continued, "and I intend to swear my children, putting their hands under the thigh, as Abraham swore Isaac, that they never will vote a democratic ticket in all their generations." The Democrats, who for so long had depended upon the support of the Mormon electorate, had become an enemy to the Saints.

"It is the meanest, lowest party in all creation," he said. "There is five-sixths of my people so led away by the euphonious term 'democrat,' that they will vote the Locofoco ticket. I am a democrat myself. I am a Washington democrat, a Jefferson democrat, a Jackson democrat, and I voted for Harrison [in 1840], and I am going to vote for Clay [in 1844]."

---

9. Ibid., 408–10 [27 August 1843] and Smith, *History of the Church* 5:554–56.

Joseph clarified his deliberate play on the word "democrat." "The Locofocos are no democrats," he went on, "but the meanest, lowest, most tyrannical beings in the world. They opposed me in Missouri, and were going to shoot me for treason, and I have never committed any treason whatever."

Following its initial publication in the *Pittsburgh Weekly Gazette*, the Joseph Smith interview was copied by numerous eastern newspapers. It was hoped the press exposure would keep Joseph from changing his mind about the Democrats, and about Henry Clay.[10]

Grand Master Meredith Helm presided over the convocation of the Grand Lodge of Illinois in early October. Freemasons from seventeen lodges throughout the state gathered in the third story of a brick building in Jacksonville, widely considered the finest in the city.

Freemasonry had its origins in the stone-cutting guilds of medieval Europe. To preserve the specialized knowledge of their craft and prevent infiltration by outsiders, lodges introduced passwords and secret handshakes. The first formal organization of nonworking (or "accepted") masons dates to the seventeenth century. Stone, and the tools used to work it—such as the ubiquitous compass and square, both instruments of the builder—became allegories for the life of a moral individual. Initiates passed through a series of levels or degrees, the first three of which (belonging to what was often called the Blue Lodge) were: entered apprentice, fellowcraft, and master mason. At each stage a symbolic ritual drama was enacted which revealed ancient truths designed to restore within each brother an "inner light" of wisdom. Masons pledged themselves to secrecy in not revealing lodge ritual to the uninitiated. Penalties for divulging Masonic secrets were spelled out in graphic detail.

Freemasonry provided members with an extensive social network that had at its core a belief in God and the sacredness of oath keeping. In the nineteenth century it was widely believed that the origins of Freemasonry were ancient, extending back in time to King Solomon and the building of his temple. The order was thought to possess keys to early wisdom that had been lost to the world at large. Masons covenanted to assist members of the lodge who were in need and promised never to harm a fellow brother, his wife, or his family. Lodges were often dedicated to St. John the Baptist, who, according to tradition, was an ancient Christian patron of Freemasonry. June 24 was celebrated as his anniversary, a day commemorated by public lectures, picnics, and other activities.

Each state possessed a Grand Lodge, which granted authority to groups of individual Masons wishing to organize locally. The first step in the process was to apply for permission to assemble "Under Dispensation" before a permanent charter was granted to the local unit.

---

10. David N. White [Warsaw, Illinois] to *Pittsburgh Gazette* 30 August 1843, in "The Prairies, Nauvoo, Joe Smith, the Temple, the Mormons, &c.," *Pittsburgh Weekly Gazette* 15 September 1843. Other publications of the letter include the *Western Star* (Lebanon, Ohio) 20 October 1843. An abbreviated version is included in Hallwas and Launius, *Cultures in Conflict*, 39–44. The fact that the Joseph Smith interview was published in full in Lebanon, Warren County, Ohio, is significant, as it was the home to several of the men who became key Ohio intermediaries in the Whig conspiracy against Joseph Smith—Thomas Corwin, John McLean, and Anthony Howard Dunlevy.

Orville Hickman Browning of Quincy, Illinois. Miami University Libraries.

Brother Helm notified his fellow Masons that "the whole matter" of a Mormon Lodge "is again before the Grand Lodge." He reviewed the beginnings of Mormon Freemasonry in Illinois. Helm reminded the gathering that Abraham Jonas, there present, had been elected Grand Master at the Second Grand Lodge of Illinois in April of 1840. The election had taken place in the very room they now occupied. That honor was no accident.[11]

Jonas, an English Jew, came to the U.S. sometime before 1820 and in that year participated in the first Passover in the West, held together with his brother Joseph, a Cincinnati silversmith. In 1823 Abraham was initiated into Cincinnati's Miami Lodge No. 46. He soon moved to Williamstown, Grant County, in northern Kentucky, where he became the founding master of Grant Lodge in 1827. Beginning in 1830 Jonas was successively elected Grand Junior Warden of the Kentucky Grand Lodge, Grand Senior Warden, Deputy Grand Master, and finally Grand Master from 1833–34, a feat never before accomplished nor since repeated. Jonas represented Grant County in the Kentucky legislature during this same period.

Shortly after his arrival in Illinois in 1838, Abraham moved his personal residence to the small town of Columbus, near the geographic center of Adams County. There he became the founding master of the Columbus Lodge. Since Illinois lacked a recognized Grand Lodge at that time, Jonas organized under a charter granted by the Grand Lodge of Missouri.[12]

The renewed Masonic effort in Jacksonville in 1840 was in response to the disappearance of the First Grand Lodge of Illinois (established in 1824) during the anti-Masonic movement of the 1830s. In 1840 there were fewer than 150 Freemasons in Illinois, and just over 2,000 in the entire United States. To regain its former influence, the fraternity had to rebuild upon whatever foundation was available. Jonas was absent from Jacksonville at the time of his election, and was installed by proxy by Judge James Adams, one of the few Masons present at Illinois's First Grand Lodge. Adams was elected to serve with Jonas in the office of Deputy Grand Master.[13]

One of Abraham's first moves as Grand Master was to curry Mormon favor, most likely at the urging of Judge Adams, who had been baptized a Mormon in 1836. Jonas easily positioned himself as an ally of the Latter-day Saints. He was, after all,

---

11. Carr, *Freemasonry and Nauvoo*, 24. Hogan, *Mormonism and Freemasonry: The Illinois Episode*.

12. Hogan, "Grand Master Abraham Jonas of Illinois." Sarna and Klein, *The Jews of Cincinnati*, 32.

13. Hogan, "The Initial Interfaces Between Mormonism and Freemasonry," 5. On Jonas's political agenda, see Thomas, "Freemasonry and Mormonism," 7 and Hogan, "Freemasonry and the Lynching at Carthage Jail," 22. On the relationship between Joseph Smith and Judge James Adams at this time, see Smith, *History of the Church* 5:85.

a close associate of two prominent Mormon supporters—Orville Hickman Browning and Judge James Adams. Furthermore, Jonas was the brother-in-law of Joshua Seixas, Joseph Smith's second Hebrew teacher in Kirtland, Ohio.[14]

John C. Bennett, an Ohio-born Freemason, recent convert to Mormonism and newly-elected mayor of Nauvoo, had been unsuccessful in finding a sponsor for the proposed Mormon Lodge there. Bennett had written to Quincy's Bodley Lodge for endorsement. This was a deliberate tactical move on the part of the Mormon Freemasons. Under the 1840 Grand Lodge reorganization at Jacksonville, Bodley Lodge was "Lodge No. 1" in the state, a rank that gave Quincy's lodge special prominence and voice within the fraternity. Bodley, however, declined Bennett's request on grounds that Bennett and his fellow petitioners were unknown to them as Masons.

Grand Master Jonas overcame this hurdle by single-handedly issuing a dispensation for a Mormon Lodge in Nauvoo at the Illinois Grand Lodge in early October of 1841. Objections by the Bodley Lodge caused the approval to be withdrawn. Jonas next obliged Bennett by conveying (ten days *after* the close of the Illinois Grand Lodge) a dispensation for the Nauvoo Lodge under his hand and "private seal" on October 15, 1841. Jonas's concession (accomplished through highly irregular means by having his own Columbus Lodge vouch for the Nauvoo petitioners as "worthy and fit Master Masons") allowed the Nauvoo Lodge to operate Under Dispensation, "until the next annual session . . . of the Grand Lodge [of Illinois], *and no longer.*"

At the lodge's first meeting, on December 29, 1841, John C. Bennett was installed as secretary under founding master George Miller. Instead of waiting for the October meeting of the Grand Lodge as was customary, the Nauvoo Lodge was formally installed on March 15, 1842. Jonas again broke with tradition and chose to make the installation a public ceremony, leading a "procession . . . to the grove, near the [Mormon] Temple," then under construction. Joseph Smith officiated as grand chaplain.

Masonic brethren from seven states were present—Illinois, Iowa, Ohio, Pennsylvania, New York, Maine, and Vermont. The two states that had been most active in establishing new lodges in the west, Kentucky and Missouri, were not represented at the Nauvoo installation. Their absence conveyed strong disapproval of Jonas's great Masonic experiment at Nauvoo.[15]

During the evening meeting ("at early candle lighting") Jonas gave the Nauvoo Lodge authority, "to receive the petitions of Joseph Smith, and Sidney Rigdon . . . [and] . . . confer the three several degrees of Ancient . . . Masonry on the said Joseph Smith and Sidney Rigdon — as speedily as the nature of the case will admit." (Initiates typically progressed through the three degrees over a minimum of

---

14. Smith, *American Prophet's Record*, passim, and Stern, *First American Jewish Families*, 136.
15. Smith, *Saintly Scoundrel*, 75. Bodley Lodge Minutes, 28 June 1841, quoted in Carr, *Freemasonry and Nauvoo*, 8. Carr, *Freemasonry and Nauvoo*, 9. *Proceedings/Reprint*, 51. Hogan, "Grand Master Abraham Jonas of Illinois," 18. Hogan, *The Founding Minutes of the Nauvoo Lodge*, 3 (text). *Proceedings/Reprint*, 52. Carr, *Freemasonry and Nauvoo*, 11–13. Hogan, *Official Minutes of the Nauvoo Lodge*, 17 and 19. Jonas circumvented accepted procedures by issuing a "Special Communication, by order of Grand Master Jonas." Hogan, *Founding Minutes of the Nauvoo Lodge*, 11. Smith, *History of the Church* 4:550.

two months.) Following a unanimous ballot, the men "were duly initiated Entered Apprentice Masons." Next morning, at nine A.M., Joseph and Sidney were advanced to the Fellowcraft degree. At two P.M. Joseph became a master mason. Sidney was made a master mason at seven that evening.[16]

The *Columbus Advocate* (an Adams County newspaper sponsored by Abraham Jonas) afterwards published an anonymous letter to dispel any negative perceptions of the Latter-day Saints and the recent goings on at Nauvoo:

> There was a Masonic celebration, and the Grand Master of the state was present for the purpose of publicly installing the officers of a new lodge. An immense number of persons assembled on the occasion, variously estimated from five to ten thousand persons, and never in my life did I wittness [sic] a better-dressed or a more orderly and well-behaved assemblage: not a drunken or disorderly person to be seen, and the display of taste and beauty among the females could not well be surpassed anywhere.[17]

Jonas's unorthodox procedures did not go unchallenged. The installation of the Nauvoo Lodge was witnessed by at least one brother from Quincy's Bodley Lodge No. 1. When the Nauvoo Masons invited the Bodley Lodge to "participate with them in celebrating the anniversary of St. John, the 24th of June [1842]," the latter declined on grounds of insufficient funds and poor roads, further maintaining that "the peculiar characteristic of Masonry, that she has sent forth her pure flame of living light, before the world, [must remain] *uncontaminated by political doings, and untinged by religious distinctions.*"[18]

One of the chief reasons for Bodley Lodge's unwillingness to support the Nauvoo Masons was the growing political strength of the Mormon electorate. They recognized that Jonas was attempting to gain favor with the Latter-day Saints by promoting Freemasonry among the very group that could benefit him the most at the polls. In addition to the 1,000-plus potential votes in Hancock County, there were significant numbers of Mormons who remained in Adams County even after Nauvoo became a gathering place for the Saints. Jonas also no doubt believed the Mormons could assist him in his campaign to make the town of Columbus capital of Adams County.

The "Friends of Quincy" and the "Friends of Columbus" sparred frequently in regional newspapers. Significantly, the "Friends of Quincy" committee opposed to moving the county's capital to Columbus included J. T. Holmes, John Wood, and Hiram Rogers, all founding members of the Bodley Lodge in 1834. (Hiram Rogers was present at the 1840 organization of the Second Grand Lodge of Illinois and was passed

16. Hogan, *Founding Minutes*, 12–13. Hogan, *Mormonism and Freemasonry*, 276–77. The minutes read "York," also known as the Blue Lodge degrees. Smith, *History of the Church* 4:550–52. Hogan, "Grand Master Abraham Jonas of Illinois," 18. Carr, *Freemasonry and Nauvoo*, 13.

17. "Nauvoo and the Mormons," *Columbus* [Illinois] *Advocate*, in Smith, *History of the Church* 4:565–66 under date of 22 March 1842. Signed, "An Observer, Adams County."

18. "History of Bodley Lodge No. 1, Quincy, Illinois," 1, 3, 4 (emphasis added). Hogan, *Founding Minutes*, 11, notes that "Thomas C. King, Bodley 1, Ill." was among the "visiting brethren". Warvelle, *Freemasonry in Illinois*, 129. Carr, *Freemasonry and Nauvoo*, 15.

over in favor of Jonas for the position of grand master.) These were men of wealth and influence in the Quincy community, and Jonas's effort to promote Columbus as the seat of Adams County was a direct threat to their economic well-being.

Beginning in January of 1842 a central mechanism in Jonas's movement was the publication of a weekly newspaper, the earlier mentioned *Columbus Advocate*. Although his name does not appear as editor or publisher, it was known that Jonas supplied the printing press and wrote much of the editorial matter.[19]

It also came to light at this time that Dr. John C. Bennett, so instrumental in several Nauvoo ventures, having been expelled from his home lodge in Ohio, was not a Mason in good standing. Abraham Jonas wrote to George Miller on May 4, 1842, requesting an immediate investigation, adding that Bennett, "must be a very bad man, as certain occurrences have taken place between us—which I can only explain when I see you." In a matter of weeks Bennett resigned his position as mayor of Nauvoo, was expelled from the lodge, excommunicated from the Church of Jesus Christ of Latter-day Saints, and began publication of what he claimed would be a devastating exposure of Mormonism.

Poorly written, sensationalist in tone, and overtly self-serving, Bennett's small volume, *The history of the saints: or, An exposé of Joe Smith and Mormonism*, was never as influential as he had hoped. Nonetheless, it did bring before the public two chief concerns regarding the controversial doctrines and practices of the Mormons—the rise of polygamy and the planned establishment of a Mormon theocracy with Joseph at its head. Regarding the latter, Bennett promised his readers that "the documents that will hereafter be introduced, will clearly show the existence of a vast and deeplaid scheme . . . for conquering the states of Ohio, Indiana, Illinois, Iowa, and Missouri, and of erecting upon the ruin of their present government a despotic military and religious empire, the head of which, as emperor and pope, was to be Joseph Smith, and his minister and viceroys, the apostles, high-priests, elders, and bishops, of the Mormon church." Bennett's warning was blunted by its brashness; the promised documents were never produced.[20]

Later that summer, as Bennett's inflammatory letters were appearing in the Illinois press, the Bodley Lodge passed a resolution requesting the Illinois Grand Lodge investigate "by what authority the Grand Master [Jonas] initiated, passed and raised Messers Smith and Rigdon to the degree of Entered Apprentice, Fellow Craft and Master Mason, *at one and the same time*." This rapid advancement was known as being made a "Mason at Sight." Jonas's action constituted the first documented instance of the practice in Illinois Masonic history.[21]

19. Richardson, "Many contests for the County Seat," 369–80. "County Seat Question," *Quincy Whig*, 31 July 1841. Warvelle, *Freemasonry in Illinois*, 84. Hogan, "The Initial Interfaces Between Mormonism and Freemasonry," 4. Abraham Jonas, "A Card," *Quincy Whig*, 27 November 1841. Editorial, *Quincy Whig*, 4 December 1841. Hogan, "Grand Master Abraham Jonas of Illinois," 9. The *Columbus Advocate* ceased publication in 1843.

20. Abraham Jonas to George Miller, 4 May 1842, quoted in Smith, *The Saintly Scoundrel*, 76 (explain quote). Bennett was expelled from the Nauvoo Lodge on 8 August 1842. Hogan, *Mormonism and Freemasonry*, 282. Bennett's letters were first published in the *Sangamo Journal* beginning 8 July 1842. Bennett's *The History of the Saints* (empire quote, 5–6) appeared in October of that year. See Crawley, *Descriptive Bibliography*, 202.

Furthermore, initiation of more than one person at a time into the fraternal organization was specifically forbidden. Despite this, during the five months it had been in operation (between March 15 and August 11, 1842), the Nauvoo Lodge initiated 285 individuals into the fraternity and made 243 Master Masons. By late 1842, nearly two thirds of all the Freemasons in Illinois were members of a Mormon lodge. (Non-Mormon lodges in the state averaged fewer than thirty individuals.) It also became known that Joseph Smith had acted as a grand chaplain (a privilege that included sitting on the stand to the immediate right of the Grand Master) before he had become a Mason. These were serious breaches of Masonic protocol. The Bodley Lodge insisted that the "Grand Master of this State [Jonas] . . . suspend the authority which has been granted the Nauvoo Lodge by the Grand Master of this State." Jonas would wait to act on this request until after the August elections.[22]

Even with the growing Mormon-Masonic scandal, Jonas's political gamble paid off. Elections for representatives in Illinois's Thirteenth General Assembly were held August 1, 1842. In a field of twenty-one candidates vying for five seats in the legislature, Jonas ran third, with 1,297 votes, behind fellow Whig Orville Hickman Browning (with 1,937) and Democrat Almeron Wheat (with 1,620). This was a very respectable showing for someone who had lived in Adams County for only four years. Jonas waited until the election results were in, and on August 11, 1842, suspended the Nauvoo Lodge.[23]

Upon hearing news of Jonas's successful campaign, Kentucky senator and fellow Mason Henry Clay (himself a past grand master of the Kentucky Lodge) wrote to his old friend. "I am very glad to perceive from your election to the Legislature that you enjoy the same consideration which was entertained for you in Kentucky, and I hope you will never have any cause to repent your emigration. We however miss you very much. I anxiously hope that your opinions may prove correct of the ultimate political character of Illinois." Indeed, Henry Clay anticipated that, with Jonas's endorsement, the Mormons would support him in his 1844 presidential bid.[24]

The third convocation of Illinois's Second Grand Lodge met in Jacksonville, October 3–5, 1842. Jonas was succeeded as grand master by Dr. Meredith Helm of Springfield. A special committee was appointed to investigate the Nauvoo Lodge. As no irregularities were reported by the committee, the injunction suspending its work was lifted in early November.

---

21. Bodley Lodge Resolution, 15/16 July 1842, quoted in Warvelle, *Freemasonry in Illinois*, 130 and Carr, *Freemasonry and Nauvoo*, 16–17. Italics added.

22. Warvelle, *Freemasonry in Illinois*, 130. Thomas, "Freemasonry and Mormonism," 7–8, notes there were 286 initiates and that the Lodge "passed and Raised nearly as many." Thomas gives 330 total Mormon membership in Illinois and Iowa Territory and 172 non-Mormon Lodge membership. See also Hogan, *Mormonism and Freemasonry*, 111–12, Carr, *Freemasonry and Nauvoo*, 16–17 (suspend quote), Warvelle, *Freemasonry in Illinois*, 130 and "History of Bodley Lodge, No. 1, Quincy, Illinois," 3.

23. Pease, *Illinois Election Returns*, 362, 369, 526. Carl Landrum, "Abraham Jonas—early leader here," *Quincy Herald-Whig*, 29 August 1982. Hogan, *Mormonism and Freemasonry*, 277. Hogan, "Grand Master Abraham Jonas of Illinois," 18. Warvelle, *Freemasonry in Illinois*, 30. Jonas maintained his connections with the Mormons. See Smith, *American Prophet's Record*, 336 [25 March 1843].

24. Henry Clay to Abraham Jonas, 16 September 1842, in Hopkins and Hargreaves, *Papers of Henry Clay* 9:768.

Abraham Jonas, of Columbus, Illinois, as grand master of the state of Illinois.

In the fall of 1843, "The authority therein granted," Grand Master Meredith Helm concluded, "now ceases, and the whole matter [of the Nauvoo Lodge] is again before the Grand Lodge, upon their application for a charter." Helm recommended that the Nauvoo Lodge be divided into "at least four, if not more distinct Lodges." This had been proposed by the Mormons somewhat earlier, "but as this application was made at a period very near to our annual meeting, I thought it proper to wait and refer the whole matter, as I now do, to the Grand Lodge."[25]

The Committee on Returns and Work took the matter under consideration. After examining the lodge records submitted for review, they "reported them fair, but recommended that the Grand Lodge should suspend the [Nauvoo Lodge] another year <u>for fear there might be something wrong</u>." The committee also reported that they found "the work in some measure correct, but in many instances there appear[ed to be] irregularities and matters to your committee inexplicable."

One member of the three-man committee was Brother Hiram N. Rogers, a founding member of Quincy's Bodley Lodge in 1834 and a political adversary of Abraham Jonas.

Jonas, who as grand master was responsible for establishing the Nauvoo Lodge Under Dispensation in 1842, appeared before the committee and "made a flaming speech in behalf of the Nauvoo Lodge." The records of the Nauvoo Lodge, Jonas asserted, "were the fairest books and papers that had been brought from any Lodge to the Grand Lodge . . . [and he] verily believed that if they were not Mormons, that Lodge would stand the highest of any Lodge that had come to that Grand Lodge." Past grand master Jonas stood alone. Without the advocacy of Judge James Adams, who had died in early August, the Nauvoo Lodge had lost one of its most influential supporters. Probably for the first time in his political career Jonas's convictions did not prevail. His support of the Mormons began to falter.[26]

A representative from Nauvoo asked why the Quincy Lodge had been unwilling to recommend the Nauvoo Masons. The reason given was "an unacquaintance with [them] as Masons and other things." Rogers insisted that "other things" did not mean Mormonism. The Mormon delegates then inquired what was the source of the "reliable information" supporting the injunction against the Nauvoo Lodge. It was finally acknowledged that the objection was received "from the Quincy Lodge, who got it from the Hannibal Lodge [in Missouri], who obtained it from [Dr. John C.] Bennett."[27]

---

25. Carr, *Freemasonry and Nauvoo*, 17–22, 24–25 (quotes). *Proceedings/Reprint*, 46–47, 49–50. Hogan, "Grand Master Abraham Jonas of Illinois," 28.

26. Hogan, *Mormonism and Freemasonry*, 281–82. Carr, *Freemasonry and Nauvoo*, 26. *Quincy Herald* editorial, copied by *Illinois State Register*, 20 October 1843.

27. Hogan, *Mormonism and Freemasonry*, 281–82.

The delegates also learned that on September 29, less than a week before the Grand Lodge was scheduled to convene in Jacksonville, Quincy's Bodley Lodge had passed two resolutions for its delegates to the convention. The first resolution was to examine "the propriety of granting a charter to Nauvoo Lodge," then Under Dispensation. The second resolution stated, "From what we have seen and heard from sources to be relied on, that it would be unwise to grant a charter or continue the dispensation longer among *that people*," meaning the Mormons, and instructed its delegates to vote against any such moves. With such strong political forces at work, the outcome was predetermined. The committee's recommendation that the dispensation be revoked and their charter refused was adopted. The Mormon Lodge in Nauvoo was now clandestine.[28]

At the October conference in Nauvoo, Joseph Smith found himself in a difficult position. He explained to his followers the "supposed treacherous correspondence" that Sidnet Rigdon had exchanged with Ex-Governor Carlin. But this was as far as he was willing to compromise. Joseph Smith was disposed to allow Rigdon to "retain his station" on a single condition, that he "magnify his office, and walk and conduct himself in all honesty, righteousness, and integrity." However, the prophet was not convinced this was possible "judging from their past intercourse" and maintained his lack of confidence in Rigdon's "integrity and steadfastness."[29]

In truth, Joseph was most concerned about Sidney's opposition to plural marriage, a practice the prophet had been advocating for some time. One elder had recently returned to Nauvoo "from a two years' mission in England, bringing with him a [new] wife and child, although he had left a wife and family here when he went away." The first wife's "husband and some others" eventually persuaded her that since the doctrine of the "plurality of wives is taught in the Bible, that Abraham, Jacob, Solomon, David, and indeed all the old prophets and good men, had several wives, and if right for them, it is right for the Latter Day Saints." Joseph promoted polygamy as part of "the restoration of all things," but took the practice one step further than the ancients by linking plural marriage to exaltation in the world to come. Husbands and multiple wives were "sealed" to one another for "time and eternity," their heavenly reward predicated upon their righteousness in this life.[30]

At Nauvoo the doctrine (also called celestial marriage or spiritual wifeism) was taught in secret and was not generally known to the church membership. Negative reaction within Joseph's own ranks (and the fact that polygamy was illegal under Illinois law) made open acknowledgment of the doctrine nearly impossible. Church leaders publicly condemned polygamy, claiming that any reports to the contrary were apostate or anti-Mormon attempts to discredit the Latter-day Saints. Joseph's 1843 revelation on the subject would not be made public until 1852 and only added to the LDS Doctrine and Covenants in 1876.[31]

---

28. "Minutes of Bodley Lodge No. 1," 29 September 1843, quoted in Carr, *Freemasonry and Nauvoo*, 24 [italics added]. *Proceedings/Reprint*, 58–59. Carr, *Freemasonry and Nauvoo*, 26.

29. There are several different interpretations of this event. See Smith, *History of the Church* 6:47–49 (heavily edited).

30. Charlotte Haven to [her parents], 8 September 1843, in Haven, "A Girl's Letters," 635.

31. Marquardt, *Revelations*, Doc. 169. Doctrine and Covenants, section 132. Compton, *In Sacred Loneliness*.

Sidney Rigdon had a very personal reason for opposing "celestial marriage." More than a year earlier, in April 1842, the prophet had attempted to take Sidney's daughter, nineteen-year-old Nancy, as one of his plural wives. Joseph told Nancy he had an "affection for her for several years, and wished that she should be his . . . the Lord was well pleased with this matter . . . there was no sin in it whatever . . . but, if she had any scruples of conscience about the matter, he would marry her privately." Nancy refused. Undaunted by her initial rejection, days later Joseph wrote a concilia-tory letter. "That which is wrong under one circumstance, may be, and often is, right under another," he insisted. Certainly, Joseph continued, "everything that God gives us is lawful and right; and it is proper that we should enjoy His gifts and blessings . . . Blessings offered, but rejected, are no longer blessings . . . Our Heavenly Father is more liberal in his views, and boundless in his mercies and blessings, than we are ready to believe or receive." Again, Nancy rejected the prophet's offer.

When the affair became public, Joseph at first denied he had propositioned his counselor's daughter. Confronted with the letter, the prophet eventually acknowl-edged he had "approached Nancy Rigdon and asked her to become his spiritual wife." Feeling betrayed by his longtime friend, Sidney resolved that Joseph Smith "could never be sealed to one of his daughters with his consent as he did not believe in the doctrine." The rift between the two leaders would never fully mend.[32]

Contrary to the prophet's wishes, the October 1843 conference voted to retain Rigdon as Joseph's counselor. Sidney was supported by Joseph's elder brother Hy-rum, William Law (Joseph's second counselor), William Marks (the Nauvoo stake president) and Almon W. Babbit (Joseph's attorney). Still, Joseph was unmoved. "I have thrown him off my shoulders, and you have again put him on me. You may carry him, but I will not."[33]

"I see by the newspapers that there has been a meeting of citizens at Carthage relative to the Mormons," Horace R. Hotchkiss wrote to the prophet in late Sep-tember. A New York City land speculator with significant commercial interests in Nauvoo, Hotchkiss was worried "that several severe resolutions have been passed condemning the conduct of the Mormons . . ."[34]

"In answer to your very candid inquiry and interest relative to our welfare, brev-ity will suffice," Joseph replied in mid-October. To the prophet's mind, "Unprincipled men and disappointed demagogues, with here and there an 'untamed sucker' [a Mis-sourian], composed that disgraceful and disgracing as well as mobocratic assemblage," which issued resolutions promising to fight against the Saints. "I feel proud to say that patriots and honest men generally frown upon such audacious proceedings as beneath the dignity of freemen. It is to be hoped that public opinion will continue to spurn such doings, and leave the actors to fester in their own shame." Joseph assured Hotchkiss that the Latter-day Saints were victims, once more, of persecuted innocence, and that "with the blessings of Jehovah, we shall reap the reward of virtue and goodness."[35]

---

32. George W. Robinson to James Arlington Bennet, 27 July 1842, quoted in Van Wagoner, *Sidney Rigdon*, 295. Van Wagoner, *Sidney Rigdon*, 295–97. Smith, *History of the Church* 5:134–36.
33. Smith, *History of the Church*, 6:49.
34. Horace R. Hotchkiss to Joseph Smith, 27 September 1843, in Smith, *History of the Church* 6:55.
35. Joseph Smith to Horace R. Hotchkiss, 12 October 1843, in Smith, *History of the Church* 6:55.

Hotchkiss' concerns about the viability of his investments in Nauvoo were shared by politicians who were apprehensive about the inconstancy of the Mormon electorate. Furthermore, even before the Whigs could hope to secure the Mormon vote, they had to establish unanimity within their own party ranks. There remained deep-seated animosities among the Whig frontrunners, with little certainty as to who would be nominated as the Whig candidate for president of the U.S. in 1844.

Chapter Five

The Third Party

HENRY CLAY SEALED HIS LETTER of October 5 and marked it "Confidential." It was addressed to former Ohio governor Thomas Corwin, then residing in his hometown of Lebanon, seat of Warren County, northeast of Cincinnati. "I have not been unaware of the project of bringing out J[ohn] McLean" as the Whig presidential nominee, "by my retirement either voluntary or compulsively, of Judge [Jacob] Burnett and Judge [John C.] Wright concurring in it," Clay confided to his old friend. "But I did not suppose that the latter would hold such opposite language in his paper and in his oral communications."[1]

Thomas Corwin was the member of Clay's "secret committee" with the closest ties to both the Burnet-McLean coalition and the Mormon leadership of Nauvoo. Following a failed bid for a second term as governor of Ohio, Corwin had recently resumed his Lebanon legal practice in association with Sidney Rigdon's brother-in-law, Anthony Howard Dunlevy. McLean, Dunlevy, and Corwin attended school together in Lebanon during the late 1790s. All three men maintained homes there.[2]

Corwin was a longtime Clay supporter. The two men first met shortly after Clay's appointment as secretary of state under President John Quincy Adams. In the summer of 1825, Henry Clay, together with his wife and daughter, left his Ashland estate south of Lexington and set out for Washington City. At Cincinnati twelve-year-old Eliza was struck down by a fever. Unaware of the severity of her illness, the family pressed on to Lebanon, one day-stage to the northeast. There a doctor advised Clay that Eliza required several weeks of bed rest to recover. Anxious to continue his journey to the capital, Clay wrote to President Adams on July 21. "I cannot say when her situation will admit of my continuing the journey," Clay began, "but I shall resume it, without any unnecessary delay. I regret extremely the occurrence, as it protracts an absence from my post which had been previously extended beyond my expectations."[3]

Clay used his time in Lebanon to visit the Shaker settlement at Turtle Creek, and met with local politicians to review plans for an east-west canal to intersect

---

1. Henry Clay to Thomas Corwin, 5 October 1843, Corwin Papers, Warren County (Ohio) Historical Society.
2. Strohm, *Speeches of Thomas Corwin*. Hack, *Genealogical History*.
3. Henry Clay to John Quincy Adams, 21 July 1825, in Hopkins and Hargreaves, *Papers of Henry Clay* 4:546–47.

with the Miami Canal at Middletown. Upon Clay's return to Lebanon one evening, a delegation of southern Ohio's political leaders headed by Thomas Corwin, Francis Dunlavy, Anthony Howard Dunlevy, and John Woods, met with the newly appointed secretary of state.

Francis Dunlavy, at sixty-four, a former judge and schoolmaster, was the eldest of the deputation. A Revolutionary War veteran, Dunlavy served in the 1802 convention that framed Ohio's Constitution and was a member of the first state legislature following statehood. Thirty-three-year-old Anthony Howard Dunlevy, oldest son of Francis, had spent much of his early life in Lebanon, where he and Thomas Corwin, one year his junior, were pupils in his father's school. Dunlevy and Corwin were admitted to the Ohio bar together in May of 1817. In 1825, Anthony Howard became the new editor and publisher of the *Western Star and Lebanon Gazette* (earlier established by John McLean); Henry Clay was one of his first subscribers. Thomas Corwin was prosecuting attorney for Warren County, and had just completed a term in the Ohio House of Representatives. Twenty-nine-year-old John Woods, proprietor of the *Hamilton Intelligencer*, was running for a seat in U.S. Congress. His bid would be successful.

Following his local political meetings, and assured by the doctors that Eliza would regain her health, Clay embarked once again for Washington City. When he had nearly reached the nation's capital, Clay was dismayed to read a notice of his daughter's death in the national newspaper. She had died on August 11, five days after his departure. Eliza's funeral was solemn, "attended by a respectable concourse of citizens to the Baptist Church yard [in Lebanon] and there interred." When, months later, Clay decided to make Lebanon Eliza's permanent resting place, the secretary of state asked Anthony Howard Dunlevy to supervise the carving and installation of her memorial.[4]

By the 1840s, the Woods-Dunlevy-Corwin contingent of Clay supporters extended into the next generation. Rebecca and Laomi Rigdon's only son was named after his grandfather, Francis Dunlavy, who died in 1830. Francis Dunlavy Rigdon graduated from Miami University in nearby Oxford in 1838 and became the junior legal partner of John Woods in 1841. Woods was Hamilton's foremost citizen, having served as US. representative from Ohio 1825–1829, and the leading member of the Butler County Whig Central Committee. During the 1844 presidential campaign, F. D. Rigdon contributed pro-Henry Clay editorials to Woods's newspaper and organized the Young Whigs of Butler County.[5]

Clay's concerns weren't limited to competition from Judge John McLean. Although unstated in his 1843 letter to Corwin, Clay was also worried about the

4. Thomas Corwin et al. to Henry Clay, Recommendation, 16 July 1825, in Hopkins and Hargreaves, *Papers of Henry Clay* 4:539–40. Hack, *Genealogical History*, 260, 272, 275–76. Henry Clay to Anthony Howard Dunlevy and I. (?) Morris, 25 August 1825, in Hopkins and Hargreaves, *Papers of Henry Clay* 4:592. Dunlevy (the son deliberately changed the spelling of his last name from "avy" to "evy") published a special edition of the paper called *The Spirit of Freedom*. Remini, *Henry Clay*, 282. Obituary of Eliza Clay, *Lebanon* [Ohio] *Star*, 15 August 1825, copied by the *Liberty Hall and Cincinnati Gazette*, 19 August 1825. Anthony Howard Dunlevy to Henry Clay, 7 February 1826, in Hopkins and Hargreaves, *Papers of Henry Clay* 5:89.
5. Woods Papers, Butler County (Ohio) Historical Society.

emergence of third-party politics. Corwin, Clay knew, was one of its first victims, having lost his 1842 gubernatorial re-election bid due to the unexpected strength of what Whigs described as the "Ultra-abolitionist" Liberty Party. In that campaign, Corwin received 117,902 votes to the Democratic candidate's 119,774. The Liberty Party polled 5,134 votes, many from former Whig supporters. Two percent of the electorate had decided the election and prevented Corwin from retaining the governorship. Corwin's defeat was sobering; the rise of a third party posed a constant threat to the predictable symmetry of a two-party race. Presidential candidates in the 1844 campaign feared their election might suffer a similar fate at the hands of the Liberty Party or some other political upstart. Their apprehension was well-founded.[6]

Henry Clay received his long-awaited answer from Judge John McLean within days of sending his confidential letter to Tom Corwin. It arrived in the form of a widely published letter, "not written for the press," in which McLean unofficially withdrew from the 1844 presidential race. "The friends of Mr. Clay, in consideration of his eminent qualifications and long public services, are looking with no ordinary solicitude to his nomination," wrote McLean. "I do not desire and would not receive the presidency, if within my reach, as an instrument of a party . . . To bring back the government to its old foundations, to restore its character, its former purity, energy, and elevation would be an achievement second only to that of Washington . . . And short of this object, no honest man can desire the presidency."[7]

Kentuckian Leslie Combs, longtime Clay associate and political advisor, wrote to the judge in mid-October. "Henry Clay for President & John McLean for Vice Prest," the letter began, "and then John McLean . . . would be President in 1848." Combs was suggesting that in four years McLean would be rewarded the prize he sought simply by agreeing to serve as Clay's running mate in 1844. It was a tempting offer.[8]

McLean did not take long to reply. "On my return yesterday, after an absence on my circuit of four weeks I received your letter and feel greatly obliged by the kind interests expressed in it." Even so, McLean had to decline. "So long as I remain in public life, I greatly prefer a position which requires action." He believed it would be injurious to their common cause to "select a candidate for the second office from a state adjoining that in which the candidate for the first office resides."[9]

With McLean publicly withdrawn from the 1844 presidential race, Henry Clay still faced one remaining obstacle. Clay understood that in order to have any hope of

---

6. Henry Clay to David Francis Bacon, 27 October 1843, in Hopkins and Hargreaves, *Papers of Henry Clay* 9:872: "You will find all wooing of the Ultra-abolitionists vain and useless . . . They opposed Tom Corwin." Weisenburger, *Passing of the Frontier*, 409–10, 435. Hopkins and Hargreaves, *Papers of Henry Clay* 9:872, note 2. See also Durham, *Joseph Smith, Prophet-Statesman*, 203–04. D. T. Disney to James K. Polk, 28 October 1844, quoted in Holt, *Party Politics in Ohio*, 208, note 210.

7. John McLean to A. L. G. Fischer, 10 August 1843 (*New York Daily Tribune*, 4 October 1843), original in McLean Papers, Library of Congress, with longer introductory not included in published version: "Your letter of the 24th of May arrived at this city [Cincinnati] while I was absent on my circuit [in Springfield, Illinois] and was not received by me until my return a few weeks ago." See also Weisenburger, *John McLean*, 104.

8. Leslie Combs to John McLean, 14 October 1843, in McLean Papers, Library of Congress.

9. John McLean to Leslie Combs, 26 October 1843, in McLean Papers, Library of Congress. See also John McLean to John J. Hardin, 18 April 1844, in Hardin Papers, Chicago Historical Society, where he responds, once again, to a Whig request to run as VP to Henry Clay.

a Whig triumph in 1844, the McLean and Clay camps would have to combine their political fortunes. The alliance, as a marriage of convenience, would be fragile. If it could hold together through the Whig nominating convention in May, a Clay victory in November was practically assured.

By late October, most likely at the urging of Thomas Corwin and Anthony Howard Dunlevy, McLean finally agreed to place "such influence as he had," referring to the political clout of Jacob Burnet, behind Clay's candidacy. The Kentucky senator was especially relieved that Burnet's "schemes . . . are now abandoned" and that the Cincinnati businessman would publicly (and privately, he hoped) advocate Henry Clay as the only viable Whig candidate for president of the U.S. in 1844.[10]

In mid-November Henry Clay received a letter postmarked Nauvoo, Illinois. It began simply enough. "We understand you are a candidate for the Presidency at the next election." The letter next informed Clay that "the Latter-day Saints (sometimes called Mormons, . . . now constitute a numerous class in the school politic of this vast republic)." The correspondence was signed, "Most respectfully, sir, your friend and the friend of peace, good order, and Constitutional Rights, Joseph Smith. In behalf of the Church of Jesus Christ of Latter Day Saints." These opening and closing words signaled the emergence of a new and formidable constituency in the American body politic.

Joseph Smith had written to the five major candidates for the United States presidency to "enquire what their feeling[s] were or what their course would be towards the Saints if they were elected." In addition to Clay, copies of the letter were sent to John C. Calhoun of South Carolina, Richard M. Johnson of Kentucky, Lewis Cass of Michigan, and former president Martin Van Buren. A postscript was added to Van Buren's letter: "Also whether your view or feelings have changed since the subject matter of this communication was presented you in your then official capacity at Washington, in the year 1841, and by you treated with a coldness, indifference, and neglect, bordering on contempt."[11]

Each candidate was requested to provide "an immediate, specific and candid reply" to the question of how to properly redress Mormon losses in Missouri. "What will be your rule of action, relative to us as a people, should fortune," that is, the Mormon vote, "favor your ascension to the chief magistracy?"[12]

Calhoun, Johnson, Van Buren, and Cass were Democrats. Clay was the only Whig. It was universally understood that the Whig ticket would be headed by the old

---

10. Henry Clay to John Sloan, 27 October 1843, in Hopkins and Hargreaves, *Papers of Henry Clay* 9:874. See John McLean to John Teasdale, 27 March 1846, McLean Papers, Ohio Historical Society and Weisenburger, *John McLean*, 105. A pro-Henry Clay letter written by Jacob Burnet appeared in the *Cincinnati Gazette* for 18 April 1844.

11. Joseph Smith to [presidential candidates], 4 November 1843, in Smith, *History of the Church* 6:64–65. Smith, *American Prophet's Record*, 425 [2 November 1843] (enquire quote). The letter was published numerous times, including *Times and Seasons*, 5.1 (1 January 1844), 393–94, *Nauvoo Neighbor*, 10 January 1844, *New York Herald*, 26 January 1844, *New York Evening Post*, 27 January 1844, *Niles' National Register*, 3 February 1844, *New Orleans Courrier de la Louisiane*, 3 February 1844, *American Beacon and Daily Advertiser* [Norfolk and Portsmouth, VA], 22 February 1844. See Calhoun, *Papers* 19:531.

12. Joseph Smith to [presidential candidates], 4 November 1843, in Smith, *History of the Church* 6:64–65.

George T. M. Davis of Alton, Illinois. Courtesy *Alton Telegraph,* Alton, Illinois.

Kentucky senator. The Democratic ticket was less settled, although Van Buren, as a former president, was frequently held up as the only Democratic candidate who could successfully oppose Clay.

Clay wanted the Mormon vote yet was uncertain how to respond to Joseph's inquiry. Just weeks before, the Latter-day Saint newspaper *Times and Seasons* (published in Nauvoo) had posed the question, "Who shall be our next President?" It assured its readers that the Mormons would "fix upon the man who will be the most likely to render us assistance in obtaining redress for our grievances" arising out of Mormon losses in Missouri. The editor promised the Saints would "not only give our own votes, but use our influence to obtain others; and if the voice of suffering innocence will not sufficiently arouse the rulers of our nation to investigate our case, perhaps a vote from fifty to one hundred thousand may rouse them from their lethargy. We shall fix upon the man of our choice, and notify our friends duly."[13]

Clay knew from Abraham Jonas's experience that the Mormons had successfully supported a Whig candidate in the past. Joseph's interview published in the *Pittsburgh Gazette* was dramatically pro-Clay. And yet Cyrus Walker's defeat three months earlier betrayed the inconstancy of the Mormon vote.

Clay sought a middle ground. Writing from his Ashland estate on November 15, he evaded the vital question of favors for votes posed by the Mormon prophet. "Should I be a candidate, I can enter into no engagements, make no promises, give no pledge to any particular portion of the people of the United States," Clay responded. "If I ever enter into that high office I must go into it free and unfettered." At the same time Clay wanted the Mormon prophet to understand he was not unaware of the plight of the Saints and their recent trials. "I have viewed with lively interest the progress of the Latter-day Saints," Clay assured Joseph, "I have sympathized in their sufferings under injustice . . . which have been inflicted upon them; and I think, in common with other religious communities, they ought to enjoy the security and protection of the Constitution and the laws."[14]

Joseph did not reply. Only after the Whig national convention the following May would Smith respond to Clay's inability to take a firm stand on the Mormon question.

Illinois Whig editor and publisher John Bailhache notified patrons of the *Alton Telegraph & Democratic Review* that beginning November 25, 1843, George T. M.

---

13. "Who Shall be Our Next President?" *Times and Seasons,* 1 October 1843, in Smith, *History of the Church* 6:40.

14. Henry Clay to Joseph Smith, 15 November 1843, in Smith, *History of the Church* 6:376.

Davis would be employed as a corresponding editor "until the termination of the pending contest for the next Presidency." Above the notice was a declaration, "For President, HENRY CLAY."[15]

Bailhache had moved to Alton, Illinois, from Columbus, Ohio, in 1837 to promote William Henry Harrison's presidential campaign in the West. Harrison was one of Bailhache's political heroes; the men first became acquainted when the General passed through Chillicothe (Ohio's capital at the time) during the War of 1812. Bailhache's other political idol was Henry Clay, whom he met in 1821. The two men became regular correspondents.

As a newspaper editor, Bailhache recognized the political realities of his business, yet never allowed the lack of monetary support to interfere with his personal convictions. In 1836, unlike the majority of Ohio Whigs, Bailhache was unwilling to support Judge John McLean in his bid for the presidency, favoring instead Senator Henry Clay. This reluctance probably factored into Bailhache's decision to rid himself of the *Ohio State Journal*, which he had successfully and ably edited for ten years.

After serving as mayor of the city of Columbus, Ohio, and heartbroken at the death of his last surviving daughter in early 1836, Bailhache determined to find a better position. Following a failed attempt to purchase a working interest in the *Missouri Republican* (he had relatives living in St. Louis), Bailhache was encouraged to buy the *Alton Telegraph*, represented as "being in a most prosperous state." At the time Bailhache took over the *Telegraph*, in May of 1837, not only did he discover the precarious condition of the finances associated with the press, but he was also faced with a general economic downturn in which specie payments were suspended throughout the country. The survival of the newspaper would depend upon generous support from Illinois Whigs.

Bailhache eventually succeeded in producing one of the most widely respected (and quoted) Illinois Whig newspapers. Early on in the 1840 campaign, Bailhache described himself as "warmly attached to Gen. Harrison — whom I have personally known for upwards of a quarter of a century —and I flatter myself competent to defend and support him during the ensuing campaign." His reasons were strictly ideological. "I have uniformly acted with the Whig party, in the full persuasion that it was not only composed of the best men in the Union . . . but also, that the measures for which it has contended were for the most part judicious and patriotic." A sometime politician himself, Bailhache was elected to the Illinois House of Representatives during the 1842–1843 session, where he served with Abraham Jonas, O. H. Browning, and other prominent Illinois Whigs.[16]

---

15. "Notice," *Alton Telegraph and Democratic Review,* 25 November 1843.

16. J. Hogan [?] and B. F. Edwards to John Bailache, 17 January 1837, Bailhache Papers, Illinois Historical Society, Springfield. Letter was addressed: "To Judge Balash, Late Editor of the Journal Ohio State Gazette, Columbus, Ohio." See also Fisk, "John Bailhache: A British Editor in Early Ohio," 143, Hopkins and Hargreaves, *Papers of Henry Clay* passim, Weisenburger, *John McLean,* 97, Martin, *History of Franklin County,* 444, John Bailhache, "Brief Sketch of the Life and Editorial Career of John Bailhache of Alton, Illinois," [1855], 23–24, 27, Bailhache Papers, Ohio Historical Society (patriotic quote). John Bailhache to George T. M. Davis, 20 January 1840, Bailhache Papers, Illinois Historical Society, Springfield (Harrison quote). Bailhache's legislative session lasted from 5 December 1842–6 March 1843. Clayton, *The Illinois Fact Book,* 209–11.

George T. M. Davis, Bailhache's new editorial associate, was a passionate Whig, "a man of great activity and enterprise" often criticized for the "rather unscrupulous . . . means he employed" to achieve his political objectives. Following his arrival in Illinois in 1832, Davis established a successful law practice in Alton, and would be elected mayor of the city in 1844. Davis managed some of Henry Clay's land holdings across the river in Missouri, and was a devoted admirer of the elder statesman. "Henry Clay was the Gamaliel at whose feet I had been taught the political principles that I then and now profess," Davis would later write, referring to Paul's New Testament teacher. "My heart was bound up in seeing him made the . . . President of the United States." Davis was equally strident in his opposition to Mormonism, and described his attitude toward "this evil sect" as "remorseless and implacable hatred." Indeed, Davis claimed that "From the day of their coming to that of their final exodus from the State [in 1846], I never ceased to raise my voice, or employ my pen against them."[17]

Bailhache and Davis were preparing to launch the journalistic campaign in Illinois to promote Henry Clay as the Whig candidate for president of the U.S. in 1844. Their partnership would allow Davis to travel throughout the state advocating the Whig cause.

In early December 1843, the Illinois Whig State Convention convened in Springfield's Hall of Representatives. About 140 delegates were present. G. T. M. Davis was among those in attendance. Archibald Williams of Adams County was elected president of the convention. Forty-two-year-old Williams, a native of Kentucky, moved to Quincy in 1829. He served with fellow Quincy attorney O. H. Browning during Illinois's Black Hawk War of 1832; the two men later rode the circuit together as they represented opposing sides in land title disputes. (This practice was not considered a conflict of interest for either party but a matter of convenience and companionship in the sparsely populated Military Tract.) Williams was elected to the Illinois state legislature for several sessions and became president of the Board of Trustees of Quincy upon its incorporation in 1834. In the late 1830s Archibald was active organizing the Whigs of the state (working closely with Browning, Abraham Lincoln, and Edward D. Baker) in preparation for the 1840 presidential campaign. Archibald was respected as a "sound lawyer" of "high moral character." Williams addressed the assembly of Illinois Whigs, "promising to discharge the duties that devolved upon him with the strictest fidelity and impartiality."[18]

The business of the convention included the appointment of state senatorial and district delegates to the Baltimore Convention for the nomination of president and vice president of the United States, which was to be held the following May. "The gentlemen selected as Electors are men of high character and standing, and the best

---

17. Ford, *History of Illinois*, Quaife ed., 1:274 (employed quote). George T. M. Davis to Henry Clay, 18 March 1843, quoted in Hopkins and Hargreaves, *Papers of Henry Clay* 9:806. Davis, *Autobiography*, 299 (Gamaliel quote), 73 (evil quote) and 76 (hatred quote).

18. Baxter, *Orville H. Browning*, 8 and 29. Asbury, *Reminiscences of Quincy, Illinois*, 47–49. Pease, *Illinois Elections Returns*, 590. John T. Stuart to Daniel Webster, 12 December 1841, Archives, Dartmouth College Library. "Whig State Convention!" *Alton Telegraph & Democratic Review*, 16 December 1843 (impartiality quote).

stump speakers in the State," exulted Horace Greeley's *New York Tribune,* "and are devoted heart and soul to the election of Henry Clay."[19]

The State Central Committee, chaired by Anson G. Henry, oversaw the Central Committees for each congressional district in Illinois. In the Fifth District, Archibald Williams was elected chairman, assisted by Abraham Jonas and others.

John J. Hardin had already reached Washington, D.C. by the time of the Whig State Convention, and was finalizing plans for the 1844 contest. George T. M. Davis reported on the Springfield meeting to the Congressman. "It is admitted upon all hands to have been the best [convention] ever held by the Whigs in Illinois. We have gone into a thorough systematic organization, and every Whig that had been here this winter has left determined to conquer in 1844 or perish in the effort."

Davis outlined the Whig program for Illinois. "We have instructed our congressional central committees that they must raise at least twenty five dollars in each of their districts to be transmitted to you for Junius tracts and other publications for general distribution," he said. "If a life of Mr. Clay with the leading views of his public policy gotten up in a succinct form is printed in German," Davis informed Hardin, "we will order and pay for at least a thousand copies." The convention had already agreed to sponsor the publication of a campaign paper in German to attract the immigrant vote.

Davis was concerned about the weight of responsibility upon Hardin. "I am well aware of the arduous and almost insupportable labor you are called upon to perform as the only Whig Representative from this state. And while I am too sensible of the vast efforts you will make in the Whig cause, [I] must urge upon you the absolute necessity of not undertaking too much. I tremble for your health."

"Another source of excitement," Davis told Hardin, "has grown out of the kidnapping of two Mormons by the Missourians from the neighborhood of Nauvoo . . ."[20]

---

19. "Illinois," *New-York Weekly Tribune,* 30 December 1843. *Sangamo Journal,* 4 January 1844. Thompson, "Illinois Whigs Before 1846," 125.

20. G. T. M. Davis to John J. Hardin, 29 December 1843, Hardin Papers, Chicago Historical Society.

Chapter Six

"Missourians seem determined not to let us alone"

S EVERAL DAYS BEFORE THE ILLINOIS Whig State Convention in December, Quincy attorney Orville Hickman Browning assured his longtime friend, Congressman John J. Hardin, that he needn't worry about the August 1843 defeat of Cyrus Walker (due to the last-minute awarding of the Mormon vote to the Democrats) or even his own loss (*with* Mormon support) to Democrat Stephen A. Douglas. "We are nothing daunted by the disasters of the past year," Browning wrote, "and do not despair of being able to give <u>even this State</u> to the Great Kentuckian." Browning was certain that "Van Buren can never get the strength of the Democratic party in this State and there are certain courses operating which I think will certainly give Clay *more* than the strength of the Whig party." The "*more* than the strength of the Whig party" in Browning's electoral calculus was the increasing likelihood that the Mormons would support Henry Clay in 1844. His confidence was well founded.[1]

As Browning wrote these lines, nearly two dozen men of Illinois (with the assistance of three sympathetic Missourians) were engaged in a double kidnap of a Mormon farmer and his son from the neighborhood of Nauvoo. Unless the Mormons discovered that the Illinois Whigs were behind the plot, it was anticipated that the outrage generated by the "Avery Kidnap," as it became known, would prove sufficient, once and for all, to turn Joseph Smith against the Democrats and bring him firmly into the Whig camp.

The plan was deceptively simple. The Latter-day Saints lived under constant threat of attack by the Missourians, especially following the 1842 attempt on the life of former Missouri governor Lilburn W. Boggs (the individual who issued the infamous anti-Mormon "extermination order"), an act reportedly undertaken by one of Joseph Smith's own bodyguards and carried out through his orders. It was feared that the Missourians might once again attempt to kidnap Joseph Smith and take him across the river to be tried for his alleged role in the crime.

Threat of an invasion from Missouri wasn't the only concern. Newspaper articles and popular hearsay alleged that the Holy City of Nauvoo harbored numerous criminals, and even maintained that the prophet Joseph approved of (and participated

---

1. Orville Hickman Browning to John J. Hardin, 4 December 1843, Hardin Papers, Chicago Historical Society. Emphasis added.

in) their illicit activities. If any of these stories could be proved, it would strike a convincing blow against Mormon claims of persecuted innocence. If facts were not available, they could always be manufactured.

The final shape of the Whig scheme more than likely was suggested by an editorial published in the Latter-day Saint *Nauvoo Neighbor*, responding to claims made by the *Quincy Whig* that some of Nauvoo's resident outlaws were horse thieves.

> The editor [of the *Quincy Whig*] "has had some '*private* conversation' . . . about certain charges brought against the Mormons, particularly that of screening horse thieves. . . .
>
> Come, Mr. *Whig*, out with it, and let us know who it is that is found transgressing. Who knows but that, far fallen as we are, there yet may be virtue enough left to prosecute a horse thief! We have tried this more than once, and prosecuted them as far as Carthage; but no sooner do they arrive in jail there than we lose track of them. The lock of the door is so slippery, that it lets them all out. We presume, however, that it is on account of the honesty of the people. We are pleased to find that the *Whig* is in [on] the secret![2]

In mid-November Ebenezer Richardson invited Philander Avery, a twenty-one-year-old Mormon farmer from Bear Creek, to accompany him to Warsaw, a small commercial town on the Mississippi about ten miles distant. Due to the burgeoning economic presence of Mormon Nauvoo to the north, which drew business away from the town, many of Warsaw's four hundred residents were antagonistic towards the Latter-day Saints. Avery had no reason to distrust Richardson, however, as the two men had become friends when Avery's family lived in Lee County, Iowa Territory, following the Mormon exodus from Missouri.

At Warsaw, Richardson and Avery were met by Captain Joseph McCoy of Clark County, Missouri. The young Avery was seized and bound, bundled aboard a small skiff tied up at the Warsaw dock, and conveyed across the Mississippi. When the men reached the Missouri shore, Avery was taken on horseback to Lewis County's Monticello jail.

One of Avery's captors swore that he knew Philander "had stolen . . . McCoy's horse and colt" and that his father had hidden them from the authorities. Richardson reminded his prisoner that in Missouri horse stealing was a crime punishable by "death or seven year's imprisonment." If Avery was to be set free, he had little choice but to testify against his own father. A menacing bowie knife added to the intimidation. In the space of a few hours, the men had what they were seeking: a signed affidavit by a professed eyewitness that Daniel Avery, Philander's father, had stolen a horse and colt from Joseph McCoy's Clark County farm four years earlier. Following his confession, Philander would linger in jail for several more weeks. With their bait safely in hand, the men prepared to set the trap.[3]

---

2. "Concerning Horse Thieves," *Nauvoo Neighbor*, 27 September 1843, in Smith, *History of the Church* 6:38. Smith, *History of the Church* 6:43–44.

3. The main compilation of documents related to the Avery Kidnap can be found in Smith, *History of the Church* 6:98–153. Delmore Chapman affidavit, 6 December 1843, in Smith, *History of the*

Colonel Levi Williams of Green Plains, an Illinois militiaman and one of the leaders in the Hancock County anti-Mormon movement, took on the job of organizing a posse. The forty-nine-year-old former Kentuckian was tall, just under six feet, with a dark complexion. He wore buckskin clothes and kept his black hair long, colonial style, tied in a queue behind his head. Born in Madison County, Kentucky, in 1794, Williams moved to Kentucky's northern Grant County in 1820, settling two hundred acres along Eagle Creek just outside of Williamstown. Williamstown, approximately halfway between Lexington and Covington (opposite Cincinnati on the Ohio River), was a welcome stopover for stagecoach traffic and circuit riders. It was here that Williams's political identity was formed. He named a son born in 1829 after Henry Clay, and became closely associated with Abraham Jonas, who, in addition to being a prominent Grant County politician and Freemason, ran the only store in Williamstown.[4]

In 1832, Williams took his family to Illinois, traveling by flat boat down the Ohio and up the Mississippi River to Warsaw. For some months after their arrival in Hancock County, Williams and his family lived with a cousin, Wesley Williams, brother to Quincy attorney Archibald. Williams purchased land some six miles southeast of Warsaw in 1835, built a cabin, and plowed a 113-acre farm attached to a settlement then known as Whitney's Grove. It was soon renamed Green Plains. The Williams home functioned as the local post office.[5]

Williams's target, Daniel Avery, was a forty-five-year-old Mormon farmer, "a stout, athletic" man, but "slow-spoken." Daniel worked land at Bear Creek with his wife, Margaret, and son, Philander. The elder Avery had been a witness to the anti-Mormon depredations in Missouri; his redress petition was among those submitted to Congress in 1840. Following the Missouri exodus Daniel was ordained president of the Elder's Quorum at Montrose, Lee County, Iowa Territory. Within two years, the Averys had relocated across the Mississippi River to Hancock County,

---

Church 6:100. Smith, *American Prophet's Record*, 430 [6 December 1843]. On Richardson's "repentance" for his actions, see Smith, *American Prophet's Record*, 435 [24 December 1843] and Smith, *History of the Church* 6:133. Philander Avery affidavit, 20 December 1843, in Smith, *History of the Church* 6:122 (stolen and death quotes). See also Jackson, *Adventures*, 16 on a "bogus [counterfeiting] press" in Nauvoo and John C. Elliott's role in the Avery kidnapping.

4. Pease, *Kentucky County Court Records*, 12:7, 12, (1830 Tax List). 11:77 (1827 Tax List). 11:90 (1828 Tax List). 11:104 (1829 Tax List). Sally Black, Hancock County genealogy page query (19 June 1998). Conrad, *History of Grant County, Kentucky*, 463 and Kentucky Grand Lodge *Proceedings*: (1826) 5, 12, 63, (1827) 8, 53, (1828) 18, 25–28, (1829) 12–13, 15, 18–19, 24–25, 49, (1830) 7–8, 12, 15, 16–17, (1831) 15, 21, 22–23, (1832) 16–17, (1833) 5, 8 15, (1834) 12. Abraham Jonas was a business partner with his brother Samuel, a relationship they maintained in Illinois. Abraham Jonas served on the committee that probated Levi Williams father's estate. (Grant County, Kentucky, Probate Book B, 1833–1845, 95 [July term 1835, will of John Williams]). William Conrad, a preacher who also lived in Williamstown, Kentucky, would in later years visit the Jonas brothers in Quincy, Illinois. Conrad, *Life and Travels*, 61 [23 October 1855].

5. Levi Williams enrolled in the company of Captain James White on 30 April 1832 (Whitney, *The Black Hawk War*, 467). Some sources say they arrived in 1831. *Biographical Review of Hancock County, Illinois*, 485, has the family arriving in 1832. *Biographical Review of Hancock County, Illinois*, 641–42. John Reid Williams purchased a 112.79-acre tract in 1835, Illinois State Archives, Springfield, Illinois land record 11246. Contrary to some reports (e.g. Littlefield, *The Martyrs*, 55), Levi was not the postmaster, nor was he a preacher, Baptist, Methodist, or otherwise.

Illinois. Bear Creek homesteaders with business in Warsaw had to pass through Green Plains.[6]

To ensure that the arrest of Daniel Avery went according to plan, Williams was joined in his enterprise by twenty-seven-year-old John C. Elliott, a Warsaw-area schoolteacher and a man known to be "perfectly devoid of fear."

One morning Elliott remarked to Sisson Chase, a Mormon day laborer at the Freeman farm south of Warsaw where Elliott was staying, that he was "going a shooting turkies." "What are you going to shoot them with?" inquired Chase. Elliott displayed a "brace of pistols and a large hickory cane." "He could not kill turkies with such weapons," thought Chase. "There is a certain cock I mean to take before night and they will do for that," countered Elliott.[7]

Colonel Levi Williams, as the "principal," together with his twenty-seven-year-old son John Reid Williams, John C. Elliott, William Middleton, and Captain Joseph McCoy, the last two of Clark County, Missouri, and about a dozen other Illinois men, "armed with pistols, dirks and bowie knives" converged on Vernon Doty's mill in the Bear Creek precinct on the evening of Saturday, December 2, 1843. The men "served process" upon Daniel Avery, who was conducting business at the mill. It was almost two weeks since his son had disappeared.

Avery told the men to stand off.

"We have a writ."

"I will not resist legal authority," responded Daniel. But as the intruders prepared to take him, he became defiant. "I understand you: you will take me to Warsaw, and there pass me over the river to Missouri," he said.

"Lay hold of him," one man shouted. "God damn him, lay hold of him: there's no use of parleying."

Colonel Williams, "with a large bowie-knife in his hand" along with several others, forced Avery to comply, "telling him . . . that his life would be taken if he did not submit." As he was being secured with silk handkerchiefs, Avery cried out to two men standing nearby.

"Tell my friends where I am gone."

"Hold your peace," Colonel Williams commanded. "It is of no use."[8]

About midnight Avery was propelled into a launch, securely bound, and sent across the river accompanied by five men. He would never forget their names: William Middleton, William Clark, Joseph McCoy, John C. Elliott, and Charles

---

6. Black, *Membership of the Church* 2:843. Daniel Avery affidavit, 4 March 1840, in Johnson, *Mormon Redress Petitions*, 127–28 [21? March 1840, before D. W. Kilbourn [sic], JP, Lee County, Iowa]. Kilbourne would later report on the murder of Joseph Smith. See David W. Kilbourne to Rev. T. Dent, 29 June 1844, in Hallwas and Launius, *Cultures in Conflict*, 226–28, also quoted in Launius, "Murders in Carthage," 30. Smith, *History of the Church* 4:42. Daniel Avery was denied membership in the Nauvoo Masonic Lodge on 16 June 1842. See Carr, *Freemasonry and Nauvoo*, 23. Morcombe, "Masonry and Mormonism," 451–52. This Masonic record is the source of Avery's physical description.

7. Cone, *Biographical Sketches*, 184 (fear quote). Sisson A. Chase testimony, 18 December 1843, in "Kidnapping," *Nauvoo Neighbor*, 20 December 1843. Sisson A. Chase affidavit, 11 December 1843, in *Nauvoo Neighbor*, 20 December 1843, Smith, *History of the Church* 6:109 (shooting quotes).

8. Andrew Hamilton and James Hamilton affidavit, 20 December 1843, in Smith, *History of the Church* 6:123.

Coolidge. The skiff landed on the south side of the mouth of the Des Moines. After unloading the boat of its illicit cargo, Elliott, Coolidge, and Clark returned to Illinois. Missourians Middleton and McCoy took the prisoner to the jail in Palmyra, Missouri. A blacksmith "ironed" him "to the middle of a great chain that was fast to the floor." There he would remain, without heat, with little light and poor food, for two weeks.

On Sunday evening at the Freeman farm outside of Warsaw, Sisson Chase asked Elliott "if he had caught his turkey."

"Yes," said Elliott, "a Mormon Elder."

"Who was he?"

"Daniel Avery."

"Did you have writs or authority to take Mr. Avery?"

"We all had writs," replied Elliott.

Chase wasn't sure if Elliott meant the men had legal papers authorizing Avery's arrest or if they had simply taken him by force of arms.[9]

Nauvoo citizens held a public meeting the following Thursday. Affidavits were collected on the kidnap and sent to Illinois governor Ford. Resolutions were passed responding to the recent kidnaps perpetrated (so the citizens believed) "to keep up a system of persecution against the Church of Latter-day Saints, for the purpose of justifying the said State of Missouri in her diabolical, unheard of, cruel and unconstitutional warfare against said Church." There was also a rumor that "the Governor of Mo. [had] issued another writ for President Joseph Smith & [was] about to make an appeal or demand of the Governor of Illinois." The Saints prepared for an invasion from across the Mississippi.[10]

As an added legal protection, the Nauvoo Municipal Council passed "An extra ordinance for the extra case of Joseph Smith and others."

> If any person or persons shall come with process, demand, or requisition, founded upon the aforesaid Missouri difficulties, to arrest said Joseph Smith, he or they so offending shall be subject to be arrested by any officer of the city, with or without process, and tried by the Municipal Court, upon testimony, and, if found guilty, sentenced to imprisonment in the city prison for life; which convict or convicts can only be pardoned by the Governor, with the consent of the Mayor of said city.
>
> . . . And be it further ordained that the preceding section shall apply to the case of every and all persons that may be arrested, demanded, or required upon any charge founded in the aforesaid Missouri difficulties.[11]

9. Daniel Avery affidavit, 28 December 1843, in Smith, *History of the Church* 6:147 (chain quote). Sisson A. Chase affidavit, 11 December 1843, in *Nauvoo Neighbor*, 20 December 1843, Smith, *History of the Church* 6:109. Sisson A. Chase trial testimony, 18 December 1843, in "Kidnapping," *Nauvoo Neighbor*, 20 December 1843.

10. Smith, *History of the Church* 6:101–102 (diabolical quote). Woodruff, *Journals* 2:330 [7 December 1843] (writ quote). Smith, *American Prophet's Record*, 430 [5–7 December 1843]. Sisson A. Chase affidavit, 11 December 1843, in *Nauvoo Neighbor*, 20 December 1843. Smith, *History of the Church* 6:100, 109–110, 147.

11. Smith, *History of the Church* 6:103–106. Smith, *American Prophet's Record*, 431 [8 December 1843].

The *Nauvoo Neighbor* attempted to reassure the citizens of the Holy City by claiming that the depredations by the Missourians could be controlled and that the actions of the municipal council were within the law. "What are we to say about these kidnappers who infest our borders and carry away our citizens—those infernals in human shape? . . . Great God! Has it come to this, that freeborn American citizens must be kidnapped by negro drivers [slave catchers of Missouri]?" The Whig plan was working.[12]

After reviewing the circumstances of the "Avery Kidnap" and the legal documents supplied to him by the Mormons, Governor Ford believed that the remedies available to the Saints were few. "If a citizen of the State has been kidnapped, or if property has been stolen from this State, and carried to the State of Missouri," the governor wrote to the prophet Joseph, "those who have done either are guilty of an indictable offense." But, he went on, "the constitution and the laws have provided no means whereby either the person or property taken away can be returned, except by an appeal to the laws of Missouri. The Governor has no legal right to demand the return of either."[13]

Joseph Smith found Ford's "milk-and-water" response to the Avery Kidnap unacceptable. The prophet applied to Congress for protection, recommending that the Nauvoo Legion be considered U.S. troops. This time his efforts would not fail. "I prophecy by virtue of the Holy Priesthood vested in me in the name of Jesus Christ," Joseph Smith told his followers with certain assurance, "that if Congress will not hear our petition and grant us protections they shall be broken up as a government and God shall damn them. There shall nothing be left of them, not even a grease spot."[14]

About a dozen men under Constable King Follett departed Nauvoo the evening of Sunday, December 17, and rode to Schrench Freeman's farm. Just before daybreak the men rousted John C. Elliott from his bed. Thinking the Mormon Danite band was upon him, Elliott braced for an armed confrontation. King Follett read the writ for his arrest. Elliott asked to go before the nearest magistrate at Warsaw. Follett refused.[15]

Word soon spread that Elliott had been arrested. Green Plains was a scene of preparation and anticipation. Men gathered their arms. What would happen if the governor

---

12. "Public Meeting at Nauvoo—The Aggressions of Missouri," *Nauvoo Neighbor,* 13 December 1843, in Smith, *History of the Church* 6:113.

13. Thomas Ford to Joseph Smith 12 December 1843, in Smith, *History of the Church* 6:113–15.

14. Smith, *American Prophet's Record,* 432 [16 December 1843]. Compare Smith, *History of the Church* 6:113–16, Hill, *Quest for Refuge,* 137, and Clayton, Nauvoo Journal 2 [18 May 1843] , in Clayton, *Intimate Chronicle,* 104. The Smith, *History of the Church* version inserts asterisks after "they shall be broken up as a government. * * * *" B. H. Roberts adds an explanatory note below, arguing that "this prediction doubtless has reference to the party in power; to the 'government' considered as the administration party; not to the 'government' considered as the country." George Laub includes the "grease spot" reference in his autobiography, began 1 January 1845 in Nauvoo and continued into 1846. Laub makes a direct reference to Joseph's presidential campaign. "Brother Joseph Smith declare[d] while filled with the spirit of the living God in the name of Jesus Christ that if they put him in for ruler of this nation, he should save them and set them at liberty, but if they refused they shall and will be swept off that there will not be any more than a grease spot of them left." (*New Mormon Studies* CD-ROM)

15. Smith, *American Prophet's Record,* 432 [17 December 1843]. See note 18.

did not sanction their course of action, one man asked. "Damn the Governor!" chorused the men. "If he opens his head [mouth], we will punch a hole through him! He dare not open his head! We will serve him the same sauce we will the Mormons."[16]

Follett and his men took their prisoner to Nauvoo. Not far behind, thirty armed men pursued the Mormon posse for several miles before turning back to Green Plains.

Elliott's hearing was held in Nauvoo on Monday afternoon, December 18. Justice Aaron Johnson presided at the meeting, which occupied the large second-story assembly room over Joseph Smith's red brick store. The Nauvoo clerk of court headed the entry in his docket book, "Kidnaping."[17]

Sisson Chase was called to the stand. His testimony revealed that the kidnap of the Averys was just a trial run for much bigger game. Chase recalled that John C. Elliott "said that Joseph Smith was a bad man, that he would be taken—I said that they had tried it before but had failed—he said that they would not fail this time, that a plan was in operation that would succeed—that he would be popped over [killed]."

Joseph Smith, acting as chief justice, "asked what [more] was said about him." Elliott's counsel objected. Smith felt "he had a right to hear concerning himself." The court decided "it might be heard inasmuch as other Mormons were mentioned."

Chase detailed once again what he knew about "the design of Missouri" to take the prophet Joseph and "some three or four more." Chase was dismissed.

Stephen Markham was sworn in. As one of the men in the party that arrested Elliott, Markham recalled that he "heard Mr. E. say that he assisted in taking Daniel Avery—that there was nine of them engaged in it, six belonging to Illinois and three to Missouri. He was taken in this county." As far as Markham knew, Elliott did not make any threats. "Not to me," insisted Markham, "only in taking him. He swore he would shoot us, and pointed his pistol. I told him to stand or I would shoot him if he offered resistance—that we were officers of the peace—had a writ for him—that if he gave himself up he should be civilly treated." Markham said Elliott could identify the other conspirators, and was willing to "assist in taking the leaders, McCoy, Clark, Williams and his son . . . there was nine in [the] company."

King Follett took the stand. Constable Follett confirmed Markham's testimony, stating that Elliott "confessed to me that he had been guilty of kidnapping—he said he was led into it by others—did not know what he was doing. He said there was Mr. Clark who was far more guilty than he, and wanted me to take them; I said I could not do it—I had no authority. He acknowledged the whole circumstance and said he would do so to the court."

The judge turned to Elliott and asked if he had any pleas to make. "Not at this time," he responded.

The court declared that John C. Elliott was to "be held to bail in the sum of 3000 dollars [and] to appear on the first day of the sitting of the county court at Carthage"

---

16. Amos Chase affidavit, 19 December 1843, in Smith, *History of the Church* 6:121.

17. "The Late Arrest," *Warsaw Message*, 3 January 1844. Smith, *History of the Church* 6:120. "Kidnapping," *Nauvoo Neighbor*, 20 December 1843. Dockett Book of Civil and Criminal Cases Tried in Nauvoo, Ill. 1841–45, [18 December 1843], Mormon Collection, Chicago Historical Society.

the following May.[18]

Joseph Smith, again acting as chief justice, rose to speak. "The gentleman [Elliott] was a stranger," Smith observed. "He might not be able to get bail," Joseph went on, and "suggested the propriety of the bond being reduced." Given the nature of the crime, the court thought this inadvisable. Elliott was discharged into the custody of the sheriff.[19]

Another writ was issued. Joseph Smith had sworn an affidavit before Justice of the Peace Robert D. Foster, "that one John Elliot of said county is guilty of a breach of the peace for this, that on or about the second instant, the said John Elliot did use threatening language concerning your deponent . . ."

Sisson Chase was once again sworn in. He testified that "in conversation I had with [Elliott] he carried the idea that a conspiracy was formed against Joseph Smith and others, and that some of them would be shot . . . He carried the idea that there was a conspiracy against [Joseph Smith's] life, and said we have a plan in operation that will pop him over."

Several lawyers and justices spoke "pertaining to the outrageous proceedings of Missouri. The diabolical conduct of those wretches who could be engaged in destroying and kidnapping their fellow men was portrayed in glowing colors." Joseph Smith rose to speak, making "an eloquent speech upon the subject." The prophet "manifested mercy towards his enemies," lifting up his hands " towards heaven" and declaring "that if Missouri came against us any more he would fight them & defend his rights."[20]

In the middle of the prophet's presentation an express rider arrived with distressing news: an anti-Mormon mob was collecting at Warsaw and around the home of Colonel Williams in Green Plains. (A Nauvoo warrant for Williams's arrest had been returned unendorsed.) Messengers had been sent into Missouri to "reinforce the mob."

Joseph withdrew his action. He told the court he would "forgive Elliot and the 2 men who followed him from 4 ½ miles below Warsaw and take them home give them supper and lodging and breakfast and see that they were protected." Elliott was discharged into Smith's custody.[21]

Nauvoo was put in a state of high alert. The editor of the *Nauvoo Neighbor* informed his readers that "we have received information that Mr. John Elliot is now

---

18. Sisson A. Chase testimony, 18 December 1843 ("Kidnapping," *Nauvoo Neighbor*, 20 December 1843). Elliott was not the only person willing to perform the deed. "[Mr. Thompson told a group of Mormons missionaries that he would not mind shooting] Joe Smith and said if there was any chance of him being elected that there was a man not far off [himself] that would shoot him . . . there was no chance of him [Smith] taking his seat in Washington." James Burgess, Diary, 3 March 1844, quoted in Godfrey, "Causes of Conflict," 66. Stephen Markham testimony, 18 December 1843, in "Kidnapping," *Nauvoo Neighbor*, 20 December 1843. King Follett testimony, 18 December 1843, in "Kidnapping," *Nauvoo Neighbor*, 20 December 1843. John C. Elliott testimony, 18 December 1843, in "Kidnapping," *Nauvoo Neighbor*, 20 December 1843.

19. "Kidnapping," *Nauvoo Neighbor*, 20 December 1843.

20. Joseph Smith affidavit, 18 December 1843, in "Kidnapping," *Nauvoo Neighbor*, 20 December 1843. Also Smith, *American Prophet's Record*, 433 [18 December 1843]. Woodruff, *Journals* 2:331 [18 December 1843].

21. Smith, *History of the Church* 6:119–20. Smith, *American Prophet's Record*, 433 [18 December 1843] (protected quote) and 433–34 [19 December 1843].

in the Carthage jail, where, no doubt, he will be safely kept. We have also received information that the celebrated mober, Col. Williams, with his possey, have left for Missouri."[22]

Still, fear and uncertainty prevailed in the Holy City. "I suppose you will hear that there is trouble among us before you get this," one woman wrote on December 21.

> The Missourians seem determined not to let us alone. They keep kidnaping our people. It is not safe for them to go out of Nauvoo . . . The civil authorities have taken one of the kidnapers; he is under three thousand dollars bond; we are going to send to our governor to have him send to the governor of Missouri for the release of our people. I expect he will not give them up unless our governor will give up Joseph Smith. I don't think they will ever have the pleasure of taking him. God will ere long come out in vengeance against them.[23]

With no firm evidence to keep him in prison any longer, Daniel Avery was released from his confinement on Christmas Day. He arrived in Nauvoo about sundown, "so crippled from the iron bondage and hard usage of Missouri, that he [was] hardly able to walk."[24]

George T. M. Davis wrote to Congressman John J. Hardin from his office in Springfield on December 29. "Another source of excitement has grown out of the kidnapping of two Mormons by the Missourians from the neighborhood of Nauvoo, and the refusal of Gov. Ford upon the request of the Mormons . . . to demand them of the authorities of Missouri." Two Mormon delegations "have been down here to see Ford," Davis said, "both of whom have gone home very much incensed . . . Joe has lately made a most violent public speech against [Democratic presidential hopeful] Van Buren among the Mormons, and declared he 'would swallow a bull horns and all' before he would vote for Van Buren."

Davis believed Joseph Smith's animosity towards the Missourians, Governor Ford, and Van Buren opened the door to the Whigs. He noted that the Saints had recently requested fifty subscriptions ("for one year") to the *Sangamo Journal*, a leading Illinois Whig newspaper. Davis had cautioned the editor of the journal "not to come out and *fluff* the Mormons but rather to pass them bye *sub silentio*," he informed Hardin. "This however is between ourselves," Davis cautioned. Davis's use of the term *sub silentio* referred to the legislative practice of accepting (or passing) legislation without a formal reading; in other words, without analysis. Davis believed this was the best editorial approach to dealing with the Mormons during the coming campaign. Not surprisingly, when the *Sangamo Journal* reported on the Avery

---

22. *Nauvoo Neighbor*, 20 December 1843. "The Late Arrest," *Warsaw Message*, 3 January 1844. Smith, *American Prophet's Record*, 434 [20 December 1843]. W. W. Phelps [for Joseph Smith, Jr.] to J. White, 21 December 1843, in Smith, *History of the Church* 6:132–33.

23. Martha Haven to [her family], 21 December 1843, in Partridge, "Mormon Dictator," 590–91. See also Addendum to "Kidnapping," *Nauvoo Neighbor*, 20 December 1843.

24. Clark County, Missouri, Courthouse, Book A, 426. Avery discharge order, 25 December 1843, in Smith, *History of the Church* 6:143. See also Smith, *American Prophet's Record*, 436 [25–26 December 1843]. Daniel Avery affidavit, 28 December 1843, in Smith, *History of the Church* 6:148.

affair, the headline read simply, "The Kidnapping near Nauvoo." There was no fin-ger-pointing or editorializing.[25]

For the remainder of the presidential campaign G. T. M. Davis fully intended to be the main source of reporting on Mormon affairs. "You will see an article I wrote upon the subject of [the] kidnapping in this weeks *Telegraph*," Davis continued in his letter to Hardin, "and can tell me in your next how it meets your views. I feel now more confident than ever that we can carry the Mormon vote for Mr. Clay if the Whig papers will only act circumspectly and [not] to go to praising them too quick. The Mormons themselves do not require this."[26]

G. T. M. Davis's article, "Kidnapping—Unheard-of Out-Rage" first appeared in the *Alton Telegraph*, and was soon copied or excerpted in newspapers throughout Il-linois and the Union. Not yet privy to Davis's Mormon strategy of deflecting blame for the affair away from the Whigs, Thomas Gregg, editor of the *Warsaw Message*, criticized the *Telegraph* for its blanket condemnation of the kidnap. Gregg agreed with the *Telegraph*, "that the conduct of the so-called 'kidnappers' was reprehen-sible." Even so, Gregg concluded that Davis and Bailhache went too far in their criti-cism of the affair, as "there is more excuse for them than the editors of the paper seem to appreciate."[27]

On January 10, 1844, a "large and respectable meeting of the citizens of Han-cock County" was held in the Carthage courthouse. Resolutions proposed by Walter Bagby, Colonel Levi Williams, and others were "unanimously adopted". The citizens expressed outrage that the Nauvoo authorities were "continually passing ordinances in derogation of the laws and Constitution of the State of Illinois and of the United States." These actions by the municipal authorities of Nauvoo under the command of Joseph Smith, "the most foul-mouthed blackguard that was ever commissioned by Satan to vex and torment the children of men," left the Old Citizens with but two alternatives—to submit themselves to Mormon "tyranny and oppression," or to ex-ercise "a bold and fearless resistance."

The minutes of the meeting, together with relevant documents—Nauvoo City ordinances, Mormon resolutions attesting to the "innocence of Jo Smith" in the Mis-souri troubles—were to be published in the *Warsaw Message*. Gregg was requested to furnish "1000 copies of his paper containing said documents, over and above a sufficiency to supply his subscribers; and we bind ourselves to purchase said extra copies."

The *Warsaw Message: Extra Edition* was published on January 17. Many sub-scribers would have been startled to read, in capital letters at the head of the min-utes, and at the end, surrounded by an ample border of white so that it could not be missed: "John C. Elliott, Secretary."[28]

When the grand jury met to consider the accusations against Elliott in the Avery kidnap, the case file was found empty. The court ordered "that the said defendant be

---

25. "The Kidnapping near Nauvoo," *The Sangamo Journal*, 4 January 1844.
26. G. T. M. Davis to John H. Hardin, 29 December 1843, Hardin Papers, Chicago Historical Society.
27. "Kidnapping—Unheard-of Out-Rage," *Alton Telegraph & Democratic Review*, 30 December 1843.
    "Unheard-of Outrage and the Alton Telegraph," *Warsaw Message* Extra Edition, 17 January 1844.
28. "Meeting of the citizens at Carthage," *Warsaw Message* Extra Edition, 17 January 1844.

discharged from his recognizance herein and that he go hence without delay." The lock on the door of the Carthage jail was slippery indeed.[29]

At the time the Avery kidnap was being reported in leading newspapers across the country, national presidential contenders were penning their responses to Joseph's November inquiry into their candidacies and their positions regarding Mormonism's Missouri grievances. With the increasing likelihood of additional acts of violence against the Latter-day Saints, Joseph Smith contemplated an even more ambitious political strategy.

---

29. "The People vs. John Elliott} Recognizance," 24 May 1844. Hancock County (Illinois) Court Records, 1841–1846, 134.

Chapter Seven

The Candidate

"I will show you, sir, that I will raise up a government in these United States which will overturn the present government, and I will raise up a new religion that will overturn every other form of religion in the country."

Joseph Smith to Peter Cartwright, 1839[1]

Did Joe Smith . . . say . . . he would be President of the United States, (God would give him the office if he wanted it), and then he would show them what a Bonaparte could do?

Warsaw Signal July 7, 1841[2]

JOSEPH SMITH'S NOVEMBER 1843 INQUIRY to presidential hopefuls summoned a predictable response from Democratic senator John C. Calhoun. "As you refer to the case of Missouri," responded the South Carolinian, "candor compels me to repeat what I said to you at Washington," in 1839, "that, according to my views, the case does not come within the jurisdiction of the Federal Government, which is one of limited and specific powers." Joseph requested one of his political writers, William W. Phelps, to draft a response, highlighting "the folly of keeping p[e]ople out of their right[s] and that there *was* power in government to redress wrongs."[3]

Smith's reply was biting. "Permit me, as a law-abiding man, as a well-wisher to the perpetuity of constitutional rights and liberty, and as a friend to the free worship of Almighty God by all, according to the dictates of every person's own conscience, to say that *I am surprised* that a man or men in the highest stations of public life should have made up such a fragile 'view' of a case." If one accepted Calhoun's reasoning, Joseph continued, "a 'sovereign state' is so much more powerful than the United States, the parent Government, that it can exile you at pleasure, mob you with

---

1. Conversation recorded in Cartwright, *Autobiography*, 345, also quoted in Godfrey, "Causes of Conflict," 63.
2. "Question for the 'Times and Seasons,'" *Warsaw Signal*, 7 July 1841, also quoted in Gayler, "The Mormons and Politics," 63.
3. John C. Calhoun to Joseph Smith, 2 December 1843, in Smith, *History of the Church* 6:156. Smith, *American Prophet's Record*, 436 [27 December 1843], emphasis added.

impunity, confiscate your lands and property, have the Legislature sanction it—yea, even murder you as an edicto of an emperor, *and it does no wrong;* for the noble Senator of South Carolina says the power of the federal Government is *so limited and specific, that it has no jurisdiction of the case!* What think ye of *imperium in imperio?*"[4]

Joseph's presidential correspondence became a popular topic of Nauvoo conversation. Joseph had brother Phelps read his letter to John C. Calhoun before visitors to the Nauvoo Mansion. The prophet gave evening lectures on "the Constitution and candidates for the Presidency."[5]

"John C. Calhoun cant [sic] be president of the United States!" the anti-Mormon *Warsaw Message* exclaimed in mock seriousness. "'Cause why:' Joe Smith has declared against him." The Smith-Calhoun correspondence was soon published in the national press, giving Americans their first glimpse of Joseph Smith's political agenda.[6]

Political observers in Illinois detected a decidedly anti-Democratic bias in Joseph's rhetoric. "The Mormons are in favour of Tarriff, Bank & a Distribution of the proceeds of the sales of the public Domain," a Cass County Whig reported to Congressman John J. Hardin in mid-January. "Being in favor of the[se] three propositions [the Mormons] are of course in favour of Mr. Clay [and] . . . We intend to carry Illinois for Mr. Clay."

Clay Clubs were formed throughout the state. Monthly meetings were large and spirited. "We are on the eve of a political turnover in Illinois," one Whig organizer promised. "The Dems are quarrelling among themselves daily. We are like a band of Brothers . . . You can't find a Whig that will agree not to vote for Clay."[7] Henry Clay himself was encouraged by the Whig movement. "I should be extremely happy to see Illinois added to the Whig states," Clay wrote to one organizer, "and with the Clubs which you have formed and a system of organization, extending to all the Counties, I do not see why that desirable object might not be accomplished."[8]

In Hancock County the editor of the *Warsaw Message,* Thomas Gregg, expressed concern about the lack of Whig political organization at the local level. "We have heard considerable talk, at different times, about the formation of Clay Clubs in our Village," Gregg began, "but no steps have yet been taken to carry out such an object." The *New York Tribune* had "many valuable & cheap publications, intended for distribution through the Mail." He recommended several for local use, including *The Life and Speeches of Henry Clay* and *The Junius Tracts.* "The enemy are already marshaling their forces, and strengthening their fortresses, in preparation for the conflict in

4.   Joseph Smith to John C. Calhoun, 2 January 1844, in *Times & Seasons* 5.1:394, Smith, *History of the Church* 6:156–57. Significantly, Joseph Smith used the power of states' rights to argue for his own interpretation of habeas corpus as well as to promote the Mormon political kingdom.

5.   Smith, *American Prophet's Record*, 438 [5 January 1844]. Compare to Smith, *History of the Church* 6:170. Smith, *American Prophet's Record*, 441 [19 January 1844]. Smith, *History of the Church* 6:180.

6.   "Important to the Locos," *Warsaw Message* 24 January 1844. Calhoun's letter to Joseph Smith was published in *New York Herald,* 26 January 1844 and *Niles' National Register,* 3 February 1844. See Calhoun, *Papers* 19:662–67.

7.   Mark W. Delahay to John J. Hardin, 15 January 1844, Hardin Papers, Chicago Historical Society.

8.   Henry Clay to James T. B. Stapp, 16 November 1843, in Hopkins and Hargreaves, *Papers of Henry Clay* 9:891.

November next. Nine short months have only to pass . . . Shall we not have a Clay Club?" An organizational meeting was scheduled for late February.[9]

Anson G. Henry, the State Central Committee chairman responsible for coordinating Whig organizing efforts throughout Illinois, reported to Hardin in late January. "We are not idle and intend in good earnest to make a struggle to carry Illinois . . . I am making every effort to perfect the organization of the state, and . . . we are urging the formation of 'Clay Clubs' at every county seat and in every precinct. Our project of a 'German paper' will succeed. I have already recd. 250$ and have $390 more promised, and this from 30 counties. The remaining 69 counties not yet heard [from] will certainly make up the $1000 which is all that is required."

Henry had also begun publication of a single-sheet political newspaper, *The Olive Branch*. "With a paper of this kind we can place in the hands of every voter in the state all the important facts and documents," Henry told Hardin. "We would like to grace the first No. with one of your best 'Beaucomb' speeches on the tariff and things in general, with a reasonable share of soft soap for the 'Mormons' and abolitionists if you think it will do any good. The abolitionists proper won't go for Clay anyhow unless he liberates his slaves and moves into a free state, and this we know he won't do. The Mormons are worth coaxing a little. They are violent against Van [Buren] and inclined to go for Clay. Their vote will about turn the scale in the state."[10]

The *Niles' National Register* (published in Baltimore) concurred with Henry's views:

> This singular community contrive to make themselves of importance. Numbering as they do, many thousand persons, all moving with perfect devotion at the nod of their prophet, and burning with ardor in a cause which most of them believe to be of divine authority,—holding as they do, grants made to them from time to time by the legislature of Illinois, of very large, not to say unusual corporative powers,—and wielding as they are well aware the balance of power between the two great political powers in the state, they feel their importance, and contrive to make others feel it also.

James Gordon Bennett, editor of the Democratic *New York Herald*, went even further than Niles. "It appears," he wrote, "that the Mormons are preparing to regulate matters so as to control the presidential question in the ensuing election." Realistic or not, Bennett was the not alone in his recognition that the Mormons were gravitating to the very center of national political discourse.[11]

---

9. "Clay Clubs," *Warsaw Message* 24 January 1844. See also "Warsaw Clay Club," *Warsaw Message*, 7 February 1844 and "Arouse!!! Ye Whigs!!!" *Warsaw Signal*, 17 April 1844.

10. Anson G. Henry to John J. Hardin, 24 January 1844, Hardin Papers, Chicago Historical Society. See also Henry Clay to Anson G. Henry, 17 June 1844, in Hopkins and Hargreaves, *Papers of Henry Clay* 10:70.

11. "Illinois, the Mormons," *Niles' National Register*, 3 February 1844. This article commented on the James Arlington Bennett-Joseph Smith correspondence. *Niles' National Register* also published "Correspondence of Gen. Jos. Smith and Hon. J. C. Calhoun" the same day. The *Nauvoo Neighbor*, 21 February 1844, is quoting from the *New York Herald* of uncertain date. Also published in the *Pittsburgh Christian Advocate*, 21 February 1844, quoting from the *Cincinnati Chronicle* of uncertain date. Graham, "Presidential Campaign," 53, note 21, remarks, "This is another example of how pervasive was the newspaper network of this period."

John F. Cowan (one of Joseph's non-Mormon aides-de-camp and a lieutenant general of the Nauvoo Legion) was dispatched by the prophet to confer personally with the presidential frontrunners. Cowan met Henry Clay in late January during the senator's unofficial campaign tour of the South. "I had a long conversation with Mr. Clay," Cowan reported from New Orleans. "He told me he had received a letter from you in regard to his views of the Mormons. There is one thing very certain; that he is a very good friend of yours, and speaks highly in favor of your church." Cowan advised Smith to be circumspect in his public statements about the elder statesman. "General, Mr. Clay is sure to be elected if he lives—so be cautious . . . Had you better not put up some of your boys—to start a 'Clay Club' in Nauvoo, so to make the matter shine up right." That way there could be no question about how the Mormons voted ("in case you should want any help") when Clay became president.[12]

The Council of the Twelve Apostles—together with Joseph Smith, his brother Hyrum, and Nauvoo city marshal John P. Green—met in the Nauvoo mayor's office on Monday, January 29, 1844. The men recommended "that we have independent electors and that Joseph Smith be a candidate for the next presidency [of the United States] and that we use all honorable means to secure his election." The motion passed unanimously.[13]

"To accomplish this you must send every man in the city who [can] speak through the land to electioneer," Joseph advised the assembled body, to give "stump speech[es]—[about the] Mormon religion-election Laws &c &c." Men would campaign in their home states, he said. Elder Erastus Snow would be assigned to Vermont; counselor Sidney Rigdon would return to Pennsylvania.[14]

"After the April [church] conference we will have gen[eral] conferences all over the nation and I will attend them," Smith pledged. The message would be simple. "Tell the people we have had Whig[s] and Democrats [as] Presidents long enough." The Mormons could not support Henry Clay because "The Whigs [were] striving for a king under the garb of Democracy." By advocating a nonpartisan platform Joseph was defying the current political order. "We want a president of the United States," he said. "If I ever get in the Presidential chair I will protect the people in their rights and liberties. I will not electioneer for myself," Joseph determined, following the lead of Henry Clay and other presidential hopefuls. Others must go. "There is oratory enough in the church to carry me into the Presidential chair the first slide." Victory was certain.[15]

Next day, a visitor from Quincy toasted the prophet-candidate: "May all your enemies be skined [sic], their skins made into drum heads for your friends to beat upon. Also may Nauvoo become the empire seat of government."[16]

12. John F. Cowan to Joseph Smith, Jr., 28 January 1844, LDS Archives. See also Picklesimer, "To Campaign or Not to Campaign: Henry Clay's Speaking Tour through the South," 235–42 and Remini, *Henry Clay*, 634.
13. Smith, *American Prophet's Record* 443 [29 January 1844]. See also Willard Richards to James Arlington Bennet, 4 March 1844, in Smith, *History of the Church* 6:231–33.
14. Ibid.
15. Ibid., spelling modernized.
16. Ibid., 443–44 [29 January 1844]. See also George Rockwell [to his parents], 3 August 1844, in Hallwas and Launius, *Cultures in Conflict*, 234–37.

The prophet's campaign quickly took shape. W. W. Phelps was instructed to compose "an address to the paper," clarifying Smith's "views on the powers and policy of the Government of [the] United States &c." A draft of the document was completed in early February. The troublesome municipal ordinances, "Extra case of Joseph Smith" and "unlawful search and seizure of person and property in Nauvoo," were repealed.[17]

On February 6, Joseph and his advisers drew up a document outlining a new government of the United States. A presidential cabinet was appointed, House and Senate seats were assigned, governorships were allocated. All were to be members of the Church of Jesus Christ of Latter-day Saints. Joseph's public pronouncements were careful not to reveal the full extent of his radical vision for a new political order.[18]

A campaign meeting was held in the assembly room above Joseph's store two days later. There "Bro[ther] Phelps publicly read [his] views of the Gen[eral] Government for the first time." *General Smith's Views*, as the document came to be known, advocated giving the president powers to intervene in the internal affairs of individual states, when necessary to preserve civil liberties; a more economical federal government by reducing the size of Congress and cutting congressional pay; the abolishment of slavery by 1850, with compensation to former slaveholders to be paid by the federal government from proceeds arising from the sale of public lands; the pardoning of prisoners currently being held in state penitentiaries and the creation of public works projects for convicts; the establishment of a national bank with branches in each state and territory as well as a uniform currency; receiving Texas, Oregon, and other potential territories into the Union; and electing a nonpartisan president who recognized the power of the people as sovereign.[19]

Within the church the document was praised as "big with meaning and interest, clearly pointing out the way for the temporal salvation of this Union, shewing what would be our best policy, pointing out the rocks and quicksand where the political bark is in danger of being wrecked, and the way to escape it and evincing a knowledge and foresight of our political economy."[20]

After the campaign meeting the prophet spoke publicly about some of the reasons why he allowed his name to be presented as a candidate for the presidency of the

---

17. Ibid., 444 [29 January 1844], 445 [5 and 8 February 1844], 445 [10 February 1844], 446 [12 February 1844]. This decision was due, in part, to receipt of a letter from the governor of Illinois. See Thomas Ford to citizens of Hancock County, 29 January 1844, in *Times and Seasons* 5.4:443–44.

18. Unsigned document dated 6 February 1844, LDS Archives, cited in Godfrey, "Causes of Conflict," 65, note 85. Godfrey wrote, "Not only was he [Joseph Smith] ordained a king but the leading members of the Church were assigned governmental responsibilities . . . This document is not signed but lists all of the various officers and officials in this new government." Sylvester Emmons and the Reformers knew of this movement. See "Introductory," *Nauvoo Expositor*, 10 June 1844.

19. Smith, *American Prophet's Record*, 445 [8 February 1844]. The publication history of Joseph Smith's *Views* can be found in Crawley, *A Descriptive Bibliography*, 240, 244–47, 254, 257–61, 309–11. *Views* was the most widely reprinted work associated with Mormonism before the great exodus to Utah in 1846. In addition to the original document, there are several useful summaries and partial transcriptions, including *Fulness of Times*, 270–71, G. Homer Durham, *Joseph Smith: Prophet-Statesman*, 144–67, and Smith, *History of the Church* 6:197–209.

20. *Times and Seasons* 5:441, in Smith, *History of the Church* 6:211.

United States. "I would not have suffered my name to have been used by my friends on anywise as President of the United States, or candidate for that office," he said, "if I and my friends could have had the privilege of enjoying our religious and civil rights as American citizens, even those rights which the Constitution guarantees unto all her citizens alike." Joseph's decision to run was strategic. "But this as a people we have been denied from the beginning. Persecution has rolled upon our heads from time to time, from portions of the United States, like peals of thunder, because of our religion; and no portion of the Government as yet has stepped forward for our relief." That inaction left Joseph no choice, he claimed. "In view of these things, I feel it to be my right and privilege to obtain what influence and power I can, lawfully, in the United States, for the protection of injured innocence; and if I lose my life in a good cause I am willing to be sacrificed on the altar of virtue, righteousness and truth, in maintaining the laws and Constitution of the United States, if need be, for the general good of mankind." The new third-party candidate had stepped boldly into the fray.[21]

News of Joseph's momentous political decision soon spread beyond the Mormon stronghold of Nauvoo. Thomas Gregg withdrew as editor of the *Warsaw Message*, reportedly because of an "inability to make payments on the [printing] establishment." Gregg moved to Rock Island, in the northern part of the state, to work as an assistant editor of the *Upper Mississippian*, a newspaper "firmly and decidedly Whig!" dedicated to advocating "with enthusiasm, and with all the ability with which we are capable, the election of HENRY CLAY to the Presidency of the United States." Even at a distance, Gregg remained fully informed of events in Hancock County. His brother James lived in Warsaw. In the spring Gregg's sister-in-law would marry Franklin Worrell, Carthage militiaman, local business leader, and assistant postmaster.[22]

The last issue of the *Warsaw Message* under Gregg, dated February 7, 1844, concluded with a premonition of increased conflict with the Mormons. In "A Word of Parting to Brother Joe," Gregg warned, "If the vengeance of the law shall not overtake you, and stretch you up as quick as lightning to the gallows, and thus end your career, rest assured that individual vengeance will!" A poem by a Nauvoo insider, "Buckey's Lamentation for Want of More Wives," exposed Joseph's "secret doctrine" of polygamy which "in public they deny." The paper also contained notice of an "Anti-Mormon Meeting" to take place three days later "at the Church in Warsaw." It was signed by Thomas C. Sharp, William N. Grover, and Henry Stephens.

Attorney Thomas Sharp proposed to resuscitate the *Warsaw Signal* (which he had published before Gregg took over the paper and renamed it the *Message*), "believing that the head of the Mormon church is capable of any outrage, which can secure for him supremacy over our county." Thomas Sharp was twenty-two when he established his legal practice in Warsaw in 1840. Unable to properly represent clients

---

21. Smith, *History of the Church* 6:210–11. See also Woodruff, *Journals* 2:348–49 [8 February 1844] and Woodruff, *Waiting for World's End*, 68.

22. *Warsaw Message* 7 February 1844. "Notice," and "Prospectus," *Upper Mississippian*, 23 March 1844. An earlier effort to sustain the enterprise by joining with a Whig paper in McDonough Country had failed. Gregg was assistant editor of the *Upper Mississippian* from 23 March 1844–5 October 1844. *Past and Present of Rock Island County, Illinois*, 155.

due to a hearing problem, within months of his arrival he purchased the *Western World* newspaper from David N. White and renamed it the *Warsaw Signal*. Sharp's anti-Mormon outlook was formed in early 1841 when he perceived that the Mormons had begun to move beyond "the proper sphere of a religious denomination, and become a political body." He disapproved of the special powers granted Nauvoo by the Illinois legislature and was moved to action when he witnessed the Nauvoo Legion parade in full splendor. Sharp felt "bound to oppose the concentration of political power in a religious body, or in the hands of a few individuals."[23]

To broaden his base of support, the new *Signal* was to be a "neutral sheet" of a nonpartisan aspect. Sharp had never been a fervent Whig or Democrat. Instead, his energies were focused on what he perceived to be the greater enemy, the rising tide of Mormonism. "On political topics, so far as they are of a party character, we will be silent . . . We have a common cause, and we want a common advocate." Sharp began publication of the revitalized *Signal* on February 14, 1844.[24]

The first public notice of Joseph Smith's presidential candidacy appeared a day later, in the February 15 issue of the *Times and Seasons*. An editorial, "Who Shall be Our Next president?" posed the question as a matter of vital importance to the Mormons.

> In the event of either of the prominent candidates, Van Buren or Clay, obtaining the presidential chair, we should not be placed in any better situation [than we are at present]. In speaking of Mr. Clay, his politics are diametrically opposed to ours; he inclines strongly to the old school of federalists, and as a matter of course, would not favor our cause, neither could we conscientiously vote for him. And we have yet stronger objections to Mr. Van Buren, on other grounds. He has sung the old song of Congress—Congress has no power to redress your grievances."

The editor of *Times and Seasons*, John Taylor, had been informed of rumors of an "understanding" reached between Democratic senator Thomas Hart Benton of Missouri and former president Martin Van Buren, that if Benton used his unfluence to elect Van Buren in 1844, Van Buren would wipe away the stain from Missouri, by a further persecution of the Mormons. "Under these circumstances," Taylor continued,

> the question again arises, who shall we support? GENERAL JOSEPH SMITH—A man of sterling worth and integrity and of enlarged views—a man who has raised himself from the humblest walks in life to stand at the head of a large, intelligent, respectable, and increasing society, that has spread not only in this land, but in distant nations—a man whose talents and genius are of an exalted nature, and whose experience has rendered him every way adequate to the onerous duty. Honorable, fearless, and energetic, he would administer justice with an impartial hand, and magnify, and dignify the office of Chief Magistrate of this land; and we feel assured that there is not a man in the United States more competent for the task.

---

23. "The Mormons," *Warsaw Signal*, 19 May 1841, quoted in Hamilton, "Thomas Sharp," 20.
24. "Proposals for resuscitating the Warsaw Signal," *Warsaw Message*, 31 January 1844.

... Whatever may be the opinions of men in general, in regard to Mr. Smith, we know that he need only to be known, to be admired; and that it is the principles of honor, integrity, patriotism, and philanthropy, that has elevated him in the minds of his friends, and the same principles if seen and known, would beget the esteem and confidence of all the patriotic and virtuous throughout the Union.

Whatever therefore be the opinions of other men our course is marked out, and our motto from henceforth will be—*General Joseph Smith.*[25]

General Smith's Views issued from the press on February 24. Fifteen hundred copies of the twelve-page pamphlet were printed. Next day, a Sunday, a special prayer meeting ("over the store") petitioned that "Gen[eral] Smith's views. . . . might be spread far and wide and be the means of opening the hearts of the people." Early the following week some two hundred copies of his *Views* were mailed to "the President and Cabinet, Supreme [Court] Judges," which would have included Judge John McLean, "Senators, Representatives, principal papers in the U.S. all the Governors, and many postmasters and individuals."[26]

The atmosphere in Nauvoo was optimistic. The *Nauvoo Neighbor* and *Times and Seasons* advised their readers:

The step that we have taken is a bold one, and requires our united efforts, perseverance, and diligence . . . Some have nominated Henry Clay, some Colonel Johnson, others John C. Calhoun, others Daniel Webster, and others Martin Van Buren . . . if others think they have made the wisest selection, so do we. If others think they have nominated the greatest statesman, so do we; and while those several committees think that none of the nominations made are so good as their own, we think that the man of our choice is the most able, the most competent, the best qualified, and would fill the Presidential chair with greater dignity to the nation; and that his election would be conducive of more happiness and prosperity at home and abroad, than that of any other man in these United States.

This is a thing that we, as Latter-day Saints, know, and it now devolves upon us, as an imperative duty, to make others acquainted with the same things, and to use all our influence at home, and abroad, for the accomplishment of this object.

Mr. Smith is not so generally known personally as are several of the above-named candidates, and although he has been much spoken of as man, he has been a great deal calumniated and misrepresented, and his true character is very little known.

It is for us to take away this false coloring; and by lecturing, by publishing, and circulating his works, his political views, his honor, integrity, and virtue, to stop the

---

25. "Who Shall be Our Next president?" *Times and Seasons*, 15 February 1844, in Smith, *History of the Church* 6:214–17. Although dated the 15th, the actual issue date of the sheet varied.
26. Smith, *American Prophet's Record*, 446 [18 and 19 February 1844] and 448 [24 February 1844]. Dr. Bernhisel assisted Phelps and Smith with the final editing of the pamphlet. Smith, *American Prophet's Record*, 448 [25 February 1844], 449 [27 February 1844]. See also Van Orden, "William W. Phelps . . . Political Clerk" and W. W. Phelps to Brigham Young, 6 August 1863, LDS Archives.

ERROR

VERITAS

SUPER HANC PETRAM ÆDIFICABO.

FOR PRESIDENT,
GEN. JOSEPH SMITH,
OF NAUVOO, ILLINOIS.
FOR VICE PRESIDENT,
SIDNEY RIGDON,
OF PENNSYLVANIA.

The Prophet (New York City). "For President, Gen. Joseph Smith, of Nauvoo, Illinois. For Vice President, Sidney Rigdon, of Pennsylvania." This cut appeared in *The Prophet* between June 8 and November 2, 1844. Storm clouds (ERROR) with rays of sunlight breaking through (VERITAS or "truth") and the words SUPER HANC PETRAM AEDIFICABO ("upon this rock I will build") below. The phrase is taken from the Latin translation of Matthew 16:18: *Tu es petrus, et super hanc petram aedificabo ecclesiam meam* ("Thou art Peter, and upon this rock I will build my Church"). The play on words by *The Prophet* is no doubt intentional, extending the phrase's meaning to include the ancient heritage of Freemasonry as well as Joseph Smith's efforts to establish the political Kingdom of God on the earth.

foul mouth of slander, and present him before the public in his own colors, that he may be known, respected, and supported.[27]

Springfield's Whig newspaper, the *Sangamo Journal*, was one of the first newspapers outside of Hancock County to respond to Joseph's candidacy. The editor followed G. T. M. Davis's admonition to give the Mormons as little press coverage as possible. "Gen. Joseph Smith, of the Nauvoo Legion, is announced in the Nauvoo paper, as a candidate for President of the United States," it reported without comment or flourish. "Another candidate for the presidency has entered the field," Iowa's *Lee County Democrat* reported. "We have not learnt whether he intends to submit his claims to a [Democratic or Whig] National Convention, or whether he will run upon his own hook."[28]

The *People's Organ* of St. Louis did not take the prophet's campaign seriously. "Gen. Joseph Smith, priest, prophet, military leader (we had almost said king) among the Mormons, is out as candidate for President of the United States. There is no joke in the matter—Gen. Jo received seven votes for President on board of a steamboat the other day; shouldn't wonder if he beat Tyler." *Niles' National Register* also announced, again somewhat tongue-in-cheek, "A New Candidate in the Field! Stand out of the way-all small fry." The Democratic *Illinois State Register* struck out at the Whigs where they were the weakest by declaring that General Joseph Smith "ought to be regarded as the true Whig candidate for president, until Mr. Clay can so far recover from this shuffling and dodging."[29]

In Nauvoo, Joseph contemplated the selection of a running mate. His Anointed Quorum met to consider the matter. This body, organized over the fall and winter of 1843–44, was composed of selected Nauvoo Mormons (about sixty men and women, most of them husbands and wives) who earlier had received their own endowments. The Mormon endowment was a sacred ritual composed of an anointing, promises, keys, and sealings unto eternal life tied to an individual's faithfulness in keeping the commandments of God. These endowed individuals were then further blessed with a "second anointing" (the Holy Spirit of Promise or "calling and election made sure") that guaranteed their exaltation with God the Father and Jesus Christ in the world to come. Joseph was sustained as the body's president and king.[30]

The Anointed Quorum chose James Arlington Bennet (a baptized, though unpublicized, Mormon), proprietor of Long Island's Arlington House, to run as vice

---

27. Smith, *History of the Church* 6:226–27.

28. *Sangamo Journal*, 29 February 1844. "Another candidate for the Presidency," *Lee County [Iowa] Democrat*, 2 March 1844. See also "Joe Smith's Views of the Powers and Policy of the General Government," *Warsaw Signal*, 13 March 1844.

29. "New Candidate," *People's Organ [St. Louis]*, 6 March 1844. "A new Candidate in the Field! Stand out of the way-all small fry," *Niles' National Register*, 2 March 1844. "Gen. Joseph Smith a Candidate for President," *Illinois State Register*, 15 March 1844, in Smith, *History of the Church* 6:268. Godfrey, "Causes of Conflict," 66–67, claims, "At about the same time [early March of 1844] a meeting was held in Carthage by a group of political leaders in which they plotted and planned the assassination of the Prophet should he become a real political threat in terms of the United States presidency." He lists no sources. More than likely Godfrey is referring to the Hamilton Hotel meeting of 26 June 1844. See Chapter Thirteen for details of this meeting.

30. On the Anointed Quorum, see Quinn, *Origins of Power*, 491ff, "Meetings and Initiations of the Anointed Quorum ("Holy Order"), 1842–45."

Willard Richards, recorder of the Kingdom. Courtesy of the Church Archives, the Church of Jesus Christ of Latter-day Saints.

president on Joseph's independent presidential ticket. Willard Richards wrote to inform Bennet of the decision. "During the short space since [Joseph Smith's] name has been published [as a presidential candidate], his friends have been astonished at the flood of influence that is rolling through the Western States in his favor, and in many instances where we might have least expected it." There was no doubt, Richards went on,

what the wisest of the wise admit without argument—that General Smith is the greatest statesman of the 19th century. Then why should not the nation secure to themselves his superior talents, that they may rise higher and higher in the estimation of the crowned heads of the nations, and exalt themselves through his wisdom? ...

General Smith says, if he must be President, Arlington Bennett must be Vice-President. To this his friends are agreed—agreed in everything; and in this consists our power ... we will go it with the rush of a whirlwind, so peaceful, so gentle, that it will not be felt by the nation till the battle is won. Dear General, if glory, honor, force, and power in righteous principles are desired by you, now is your time. You are safe in following the counsel of that man who holds communion with heaven; and I assure you, if you act well your part, victory's the prize.

Richards advised Arlington Bennet to embark on a political mission. "Commence at your own mansion and stay not, only for electioneering purposes, till by some popular route you reach Nauvoo; and if you preach Mormonism it will help you. At every stage, tavern, boat and company, expose the wickedness of Martinism in saying, if he is elected President, he will annihilate the Mormons, and proclaim the sycophancy of the candidates generally, and uphold Joseph against every aspersion and you shall triumph gloriously." There would be a special conference at Nauvoo on April 6. "From that period our Elders will go forth by hundreds or thousands and search the land, preaching religion and politics; and if God goes with them, who can withstand their influence?"[31]

In early March, word was received that James Arlington Bennet was apparently not a native-born American and therefore ineligible to run for the vice presidency. Even so, Bennet's name appeared as Joseph's running mate in the March 6 issue of the *Nauvoo Neighbor*. The Quorum of the Anointed was again convened and

31. Willard Richards to James Arlington Bennet, 4 March 1844, in Smith, *History of the Church* 6:231–32. See also Smith, *American Prophet's Record*, 451–52 [5 March 1844]. Quinn, *Origins of Power*, 118 and notes 69–72. Cook, "James Arlington Bennet," 247.

nominated Colonel Solomon Copeland, a non-Mormon living in Paris, Tennessee, for the vice presidential position. His solicitation, too, would be unsuccessful.[32]

At a meeting of the Nauvoo Temple Committee on Thursday, March 7, W. W. Phelps read aloud General Smith's *Views.* The body voted "unanimously, with one exception, to uphold General Smith for the Presidency of the United States." The single dissenting vote was cast by Charles A. Foster (brother of Dr. Robert Foster), accused by the prophet of writing "some of the most disgraceful things possible to name" to Horace Greeley's *New York Tribune.* The two men engaged in a verbal sparring match until Joseph threatened to fine him for disturbing the meeting and using menacing language.[33]

John Taylor spoke to the gathering that afternoon. "Of General Joseph Smith some are afraid, and think it doubtful about his election," he said, "and, like the ostrich, stick their heads under a bush, and leave their bodies out, so that we can all see them; and after this it will be a by-word—'That man is an ostrich who hides his head in this cause.' Taylor's message was clear: every Mormon must support Joseph's candidacy or be subject to public ridicule.[34]

Joseph maintained the political theme in his remarks. "As to politics, I care but little about the presidential chair," he said. "I would not give half as much for the office of President of the United States as I would for the one I now hold as Lieutenant-General of the Nauvoo Legion." Indeed, by virtue of a commission signed by the governor of Illinois, the Mormon prophet was the first man since George Washington to hold that venerated military rank. Political meetings nearly always referred to the prophet as "General Joseph Smith."[35]

Smith argued that political activism was completely in keeping with his function as a religious leader, in part because it was a means to an end, namely the preservation of the rights of the Latter-day Saints. "We have as good a right to make a political party to gain power to defend ourselves, as for demagogues to make use of our religion to get power to destroy us," he continued. "In other words, as the world has used the power of government to oppress and persecute us, it is right for us to use it for the protection of our rights. We will whip the mob by getting up a candidate for President. When I get hold of the Eastern papers, and see how popular I am, I am afraid myself that I shall be elected; but if I should be, I would not say, 'Your cause is just, but I can do nothing for you.'"[36]

Martin Van Buren's thinly disguised disdain would become the catalyst for Joseph's most radical proposal yet put before the Latter-day Saints.

---

32. Smith, *History of the Church* 6:245 and Smith, *American Prophet's Record*, 457 [8 March 1844], 460 [20 March 1844]. See also Quinn, *Origins of Power*, 118.

33. Ibid., 6:239–40. Smith, *American Prophet's Record*, 453–54 [6 March 1844]. Quinn, *Origins of Power*, 119. Wandle Mace, "Excerpts from the Life Story of Wandle Mace 1809–1890," 12.

34. Smith, *American Prophet's Record*, 456 [6 March 1844]. Smith, *History of the Church* 6:243.

35. Smith, *History of the Church* 6:243. Smith, *American Prophet's Record*, 456 [6 March 1844]. Also, Roberts, *Comprehensive History* 2:209.

36. Ibid., 6:243. Complete minutes of meeting, Smith, *History of the Church* 6:236–44. See also Smith, *American Prophet's Record*, 456 [6 March 1844]. Woodruff, *Journal* 2:358 [7 March 1844]. "Excerpts from the Life Story of Wandle Mace, 1809–1890," 12. This statement is often held to have been made tongue-in-cheek. See, for example, Roberts, *Comprehensive History* 2:209 and Smith, *History of the Church* 6:xxxiv.

Chapter Eight

Thy Kingdom Come . . . in Texas

An express has just arrived here from the city of Mexico, bringing the important intelligence that JOE SMITH, the celebrated Mormon Prophet, of the Latter-day Saints, has concluded a treaty with President Santa Anna for the purchase of Texas.

news parody in *Lee County* (Iowa) *Democrat*, January 20, 1844[1]

It would seem that the entire Indian tribes, and their vast territories, were already under his jurisdiction in a great measure, and ready to cooperate with him, and that some of our western states, together with Texas and Mexico were in a fair way to strike hands politically at least with the Prophet.

Boston Correspondent to *The Prophet* (New York City) May, 1844[2]

"WHAT I HAVE SAID IN my 'Views' in relation to the annexation of Texas is with some unpopular," Joseph continued in his remarks before the Temple Committee on the afternoon of March 7. Everyone in attendance knew the Texas question was one of the major issues in the 1844 presidential campaign. "They object to Texas on account of slavery," Joseph pointed out. The first American settlers in Texas were slave owners. If admitted to the Union, Texas would more than likely become a slave state. Northern Whigs were opposed to annexation on this ground alone. "Why, it is the very reason she ought to be received," Joseph countered, "so that we may watch over them; for, of the two evils, we should reject the greatest." (The "two evils" were slavery and the prospect of Texas becoming a British colony. Joseph thought the two problems could be resolved.)[3]

---

1. Anonymous satirical letter to the editor *Lee County Democrat* (Fort Madison, Iowa Territory), 20 January 1844.
2. Boston Correspondent to *The Prophet*, 22 May 1844, in *Nauvoo Neighbor* 19 June 1844. See also Graham, "The Presidential Candidacy," 72–73. In part, this letter was in response to Marryat's *Narrative* which appeared in 1843.
3. Woodruff, *Journals* 2:358 [7 March 1844]. Smith, *American Prophet's Record*, 456 [6 March 1844]. Smith, *History of the Church* 6:243.

"Governor Houston of Texas, says—'if you refuse to receive us into the United States, we must go to the British Government for protection,' he noted. "It will be more honorable for us," Joseph proposed, "to receive Texas and set the negroes free, and use the negroes and Indians against our foes. Don't let Texas go . . . How much better it is for the nation to bear a little expense than to have the Indians and British upon us and destroy us all. We should grasp all the territory we can . . . The South holds the balance of power," Joseph went on. "By annexing Texas, I can do away with this evil [slavery]. As soon as Texas was annexed, I would liberate the slaves in two or three [southern] States, indemnifying their owners, and send the [free] negroes to Texas, and from Texas to Mexico, where all colors are alike. And if that was not sufficient, I would call upon Canada, and annex it."[4]

Joseph's solution to the Texas problem was suggested, in part, by a letter he had received from Elders Lyman Wight and George Miller, writing from Black River Falls, Wisconsin Territory, informing the prophet of their success in cutting timber for the Nauvoo temple. "We can deliver in Nauvoo about one million feet of lumber by the last of July next," they wrote, "which will be a great deal more than what is necessary."

Conditions in the pineries were unsettled. Mormon loggers had disputes with the local Indian agent, "a gruff, austere man," who was "determined to stop all trespassing on Indian lands." Wight and Miller were confident they could induce the Indians to "sell their lands to the United States, and go to a climate southwest (all according to the policy of the U.S. Government)." They proposed to "go to the table-lands of Texas, to a point we may find to be the most eligible, [and] there locate." This Texas sanctuary, they suggested, would become "a place of gathering for all the South (they being incumbered with that unfortunate race of beings, the negroes); and for us to employ our time and talents in gathering together means to build according to the commandments of our God, and spread the Gospel to the nations according to the will of our Heavenly Father."[5]

Members of the Anointed Quorum (and others) were organized into a new administrative structure beginning on March 10. One participant described the new body as "the perfect organization of the Church of Jesus Christ of Latter-day Saints on earth . . . with full authority to build up the Kingdom of God on earth, that his will might be done on earth as in heaven—The Kingdom thus being established." The body was charged with preparing the way for the Second Coming of Jesus Christ. Distinct from the Mormon Church, this secret organization became known by its members (and those close to the inner workings of the organization) as the Kingdom of God, the Grand Council, or the Council of Fifty. "And from day to day

---

4.   Smith, *American Prophet's Record*, 456 [6 March 1844]. Smith, *History of the Church* 6:243–44. Smith, *American Prophet's Record*, 457 [6 March 1844]. See also Woodruff, *Journals* 2:358 [7 March 1844]. Hill, "The Manipulation of History," 99, concluded, "Joseph Smith was, therefore, to some degree a racist, a segregationist, a colonizer, and only incidentally a supporter of abolition. He had some elements of liberalism in his thinking, but these had definite limits. His record, like Jefferson's and Lincoln's, is marked by ambiguity."

5.   Lyman Wight and George Miller et al., "To the First Presidency and the quorum of the Twelve of the Church of Christ of Latter-day Saints," 15 February 1844, in Smith, *History of the Church* 6:255–57.

[the prophet] called some of the brethren about him, organizing them as princes in the kingdom of God, until the number of fifty-three were thus called."[6]

Joseph Smith was the standing chairman. Membership in the spring of 1844 included the First Presidency of the Church (with the notable exception of renegade counselor William Law, who earlier had opposed Joseph and Hyrum's political manipulation of the 1843 election), the Council of the Twelve Apostles, and several non-Mormons. As one member later explained, "there may be men acting as officers of the Kingdom of God who will not be members of the Church of Jesus Christ of Latter Day Saints." Although the number of non-Mormons in the Council of Fifty never amounted to more than tokenism, their presence within the Kingdom of God served two important symbolic functions. First, it supported the idea that the Council of Fifty was to be representative of all peoples, ultimately to become a worldwide political body. And, second, the organization of the Council allowed the Latter-day Saints to maintain the public fiction that they advocated the American ideal of the separation of church and state.[7]

The deliberations of the political Kingdom of God were to be confidential. One member recorded a line later struck out: "~~Joseph required perfect secrecy of them.~~" This "perfect secrecy" was an oath-bound allegiance; the penalty for revealing decisions made by the secret council to outsiders was the prospect of a horrible death. The Council of Fifty oath reinforced promises of confidentiality previously made by many of the men. A number of its members were former Danites, an organization that had administered its own oath of secrecy. Likewise the large number of Freemasons in the council would have found the oath similar to promises made during their Masonic initiations, not to mention the covenant of secrecy entered into during the Mormon endowment ceremony.[8]

Journal entries describing the proceedings of the Council of Fifty were frequently disguised by their authors, some referring to the body as the K. of G., Council of L, or the Council of YTFIF. In his record of the March 10 organizational meeting kept for Joseph Smith, Willard Richards reversed the letters in certain key words to produce phrases which, it was hoped, would be nonsensical to an uninitiated reader. As noted, the meeting was prompted by the aforementioned letter received from Lyman Wight and George Miller,

---

6. George Miller to *The Northern Islander*, 27 June 1855, in Miller, *Correspondence*, 20 (called quote). Wight, *An Address*, 3 (established quote).

7. Quinn, *Origins of Power*, 122. Apostle George Q. Cannon's full comment: "We are asked, Is the Church of God, and the Kingdom of God the same organization? And we are informed that some of the brethren hold that they are separate. This is the correct view to take. The Kingdom of God is a separate organization from the Church of God. There may be men acting as officers in the Kingdom of God who will not be members of the Church of Jesus Christ of Latter-day Saints," in Smith, *History of the Church* 7:382.

8. Smith, *American Prophet's Record*, 459 [10 March 1844], also cited in Quinn, *Origins of Power*, 128. It is possible that the strikeout was inserted when the minutes were prepared for publication as part of the Joseph Smith History. Note similarly, Davis, *Authentic Account*, 7, "[Joseph] further impressed upon the council crowning him, that God's desire was, as revealed to him, (Joe,) that, for the time being, this was to remain a *perfect secret* until God should reveal to the contrary. And accordingly Joe swore them all to present secrecy, *under penalty of death!*" Davis's source was an unidentified disaffected member of the Council. See also Hansen, *Quest for Empire*, 69–71.

about removing to the table lands of ——— /Saxet / &c. &c . . . Joseph asked, can this council keep what I say, not make it public, all held up their hands . . . Copy the constitution of the U.S. [*blank space*] [placed in the] hands of a select committee [as a guide for drafting the constitution for the council] [*one blank line*] No laws can be enacted but what every man can be protected. [*several lines left blank*] Grant their petition, go ahead concerning the Indians and the Southern states &c [several lines left blank] . . . Send 25 men by /the yrenip [Pinery]/through to Santa Fe /Atnas Eef / &c, and if ——— /Notsuoh/ will embrace the gospel [...] [several lines left blank] [We] can amend that [Texas] constitution and make it the voice of Jehovah and shame the U. S.[9]

The objectives of the theocratic body were political. George Miller, an early member of the Council of Fifty, recorded that if Joseph Smith was elected president in 1844 the Mormons "would at once establish dominion in the United States." If the political contest was not successful, the Saints would send a representative to the Republic of Texas, "to make a treaty with the Cabinet of Texas for all that country north of a west line from the falls of the Colorado River to the Nueces; thence down the same to the Gulf of Mexico, and along the same to Rio Grande, and up the same to the United States territory, and get them to acknowledge us as a nation."[10]

Lucian Woodworth was "sent out on a mission" on March 14 as a secret ambassador from the Council of Fifty to the Republic of Texas. He was to enter into negotiations with General Sam Houston for the establishment of a Mormon kingdom within the confines of the Republic. Fewer than two weeks later the Council of Fifty approved a lengthy memorial to the U.S. Congress requesting permission for Joseph Smith to raise "a company of one hundred thousand armed volunteers in the United States and [its] Territories" in order to "extend the arm of deliverance to Texas [and other frontier regions] to prevent the crowned nations [Spain and England] from encircling us as a nation on our western and southern borders." An envoy from the Council of Fifty, with a duplicate request addressed to the president of the U.S., would depart for the nation's capital in early April.[11]

Beneath the bold proclamation "FOR PRESIDENT, GEN. JOSEPH SMITH, NAUVOO, ILLINOIS," the March 15 issue of *Times and Seasons* provided the first public communications alluding to the recent deliberations within the political Kingdom of God. An editorial, written by John Taylor, a member of the Council of the Twelve and the Council of Fifty, was on the topic of "Religion and Politics."

9. Ibid., 458 [10 March 1844]. Quinn, *Origins of Power*, 120: 'K of G' (William Clayton), 'Council of L' (Joseph F. Smith), 'Council of YTFIF' (Willard Richards and John D. Lee), 'Council of 50-Kingdom' (Franklin D. Richards). *Fulness of Times*, 270, admits the purpose of the Council of Fifty was "to organize the political kingdom of God in preparation for the second coming of Christ." Smith, *History of the Church* 6: 261 is much less eschatological. Quinn, *Origins of Power*, 122, provides a more theologically oriented description of the Council.

10. George Miller to *The Northern Islander* 27 June 1855, in Miller, *Correspondence*, 20.

11. Smith, *American Prophet's Record*, 459 [14 March 1844]. Bitton, "Mormons in Texas," 9. Memorial to Congress completed 26 March 1844, in Smith, *History of the Church* 6:275–77. Credential of Orson Hyde to Congress, 30 March 1844, in Smith, *History of the Church* 6:283.

Either God has something to do in our national affairs, or he has not ... By a careful perusal of the scriptures ... we shall find that God in ancient days had as much to do with governments, kings and kingdoms, as he ever had to do with religion. The Jews, as a nation, were under the direct government of heaven, and not only had they judges and kings anointed of God, and set apart by him; but their laws were given them of God ... Certainly if any person ought to interfere in political matters it should be those whose minds and judgments are influenced by correct principles—religious as well as political.

"Our revelations tell us to *seek diligently* for good and wise men," Taylor concluded, citing a revelation received by Joseph Smith in 1833. He issued an appeal:

No one can be more fit for the task [of president of the U.S.] than Gen. Joseph Smith: he is wise, prudent, faithful, energetic and fearless; he is a virtuous man and a philanthropist; if we want to find out who he is, his past history shows his indomitable perseverance, and proves him to be a faithful friend, and a man of exalted genius, and sterling integrity; whilst his public addresses and views, as published to the world, prove him to be a patriot and a statesman.

Let every man then that hates oppression, and loves the cause of right, not only vote himself; but use his influence to obtain the votes of others, that we may by every legal means support that man whose election will secure the greatest amount of good to the nation at large.[12]

The same issue of *Times and Seasons* included correspondence addressed to the editor of the *Quincy Whig* in response to an article critical of the Mormons copied from Horace Greeley's *New York Tribune*. The letter was even more direct than Taylor's editorial by its assertion that the Kingdom of God would not simply "triumph over the state." The writer reminded his readers that "There is one God who presides over the destinies of all nations and individuals, both religiously and politically." Those who pray "Thy kingdom come, thy will be done on earth as it is in heaven,"

virtually asks God to destroy the distinction of Church and State on earth; for that distinction is not recognized in heaven. With God, politics and religion are both one ... He also prays that God may establish a government on the earth like that in heaven, and that "the kingdoms of this world become the kingdom of our God and of his Christ." The Church [of Jesus Christ of Latter-day Saints] must not triumph over the state, but actually swallow it up like Moses' rod swallowed up the rods of the Egyptians. If this be not so, the kingdom of God can never come.

The letter was signed "A Friend to the Mormons."[13]

---

12. "Religion and Politics," *Times and Seasons*, 15 March 1844, 470–71. See Hill, *Quest for Refuge*, 138 and 255, note 108.

13. "A Friend to the Mormons" to the editor *Times and Seasons*, 15 March 1844, 476–77. See Hill, *Quest for Refuge*, 138 and 255, note 108.

"We have supplied ourselves with [the] *Tribune's Mill Boy, Olive Branch, Whig Almanac* &&, and have begun to campaign vigorously," William D. Abernethy reported to John J. Hardin (then still in Washington) on March 19. Abernethy was a Clay Club organizer and anti-Mormon from Augusta, in southeastern Hancock County. They still needed copies of *The Junius Tracts*.

"Our Clay Pole is nearly ready to go up," he said. "The old Whigs of 1840 are all here & a good crop of young ones [are] all ready to do their duty next fall . . . The Whigs are active, full of zeal and united. The other party, here as elsewhere, [is] divided, cross and discouraged . . . They will not be able to rally much till after the nomination and if VB [Van Buren] is the man, many in this region will not vote. Others will support Mr. Clay." Developments in Nauvoo made it extremely unlikely that the Latter-day Saints would vote for Clay. "Our Mormon neighbors cannot be relied on," Abernethy concluded. "Joe is a candidate for President. He will not support Mr. Clay & cannot go for Van Buren. They may yet have a Revelation to go for the Locos, they are inclined that way but have a great dislike to VB." Unless a Democratic candidate were put forward who was more to the Mormon's liking than Van Buren, a Whig victory was still possible. "If the Mormons do not join the Locos in Nov[ember] I think the Whigs can carry the State."[14]

The time had come for the Whigs to once again play a more active role in influencing the Mormon vote. An opportunity presented itself with the anticipated completion of the Masonic hall in Nauvoo.

Long an opponent to Mormon Freemasonry, the worshipful master of the Bodley Lodge reported that "the Nauvoo Lodges [are] working and finishing their hall, notwithstanding their dispensations had been withdrawn by the Grand Lodge." And, contrary to Masonic law, those contraband Mormon lodges had persisted in "receiving, passing and raising Masons." There were several reasons for concern. In addition to the fact that the Mormon lodges were openly defying the authority of the Illinois Grand Lodge, itself founded on shaky ground at Jacksonville in 1840, some feared the Mormons might take the next logical step, which was to either dominate the Illinois Grand Lodge or establish their own Grand Lodge (with Hyrum Smith as Grand Master) in direct competition with the Jacksonville body. After all, by 1844 more than two-thirds of the Masons in the state were Latter-day Saints.[15]

In a "Masonic Notice" dated March 13, 1844, (signed by William Clayton as secretary of the Nauvoo Lodge, who was also Joseph's private secretary and clerk of the Council of Fifty) the Nauvoo Lodge announced "to the Masonic world that they have fixed on Friday the 5th day of April, for the dedication of their Masonic Hall, to take place at 1 o'clock P.M. All worthy brethren of the fraternity who feel interested in the cause, are requested to participate with us in the ceremonies of dedication," one day before the annual general conference of the church.[16]

---

14. William D. Abernethy to John J. Hardin, 19 March 1844, Hardin Papers, Chicago Historical Society.
15. Minutes of the Bodley Lodge, 1 April 1844, quoted in Carr, *Freemasonry and Nauvoo*, 27. The minutes added that "brethren of the Warsaw Lodge had notified the Grand Officers on the subject." See also Hogan, "Erection and Dedication," 14.
16. "Masonic Notice," *Nauvoo Neighbor* between 13 March and 5 April 1844, quoted in Carr, *Freemasonry and Nauvoo*, 27.

Dr. William Gano Goforth, of Belleville, Illinois, was one of the first Masonic guests to arrive. He, together with his wife, disembarked "at the wharf of the city of Nauvoo" the morning of April 5 and "after visiting the house of a connection, called on Gen. Joseph Smith." Goforth's wife would be baptized into the Mormon church during their visit; Goforth himself was known to have "a strong inclination to the Mormon faith." He was an even stronger supporter of Henry Clay.

Dr. Goforth, "a living skeleton of a man," and "the most perfect personification of Don Quixote that was ever seen," was the grandson of William Goforth, an original member of New York's Sons of Liberty and one of the first settlers of Columbia on the "land between the two Miamis" in southern Ohio in 1788. His father was Dr. William Goforth, an early Cincinnati physician and Freemason. Born in 1795, William Gano Goforth was named after the Reverend John Gano, founder of the First Baptist Church of New York City and father of John Stites Gano; both men were early Columbia settlers. In 1787 Goforth's aunt, Mary Goforth, married John S. Gano, under whom future Supreme Court Judge John McLean was apprenticed between 1804 and 1806. Following the death of his father in 1816, William Gano Goforth went west, and settled in Belleville, St. Clair County, Illinois. His mother and three younger siblings remained in Ohio and moved, for a time, to Lebanon, to be near her old friends from Columbia, the Anthony Howard Dunlevy family.

Dr. Goforth practiced medicine in Belleville for many years, and was known for his "exceedingly eccentric character, [which] at times [was] intemperate." Nonetheless, Dr. Goforth became the chief physician to John Reynolds, an Illinois politician who found Goforth to be "bold and fearless in his practice." Reynolds had been a member of the Illinois state House of Representatives, Democratic governor of Illinois, and a U.S. representative from the state for nine years, between 1834 and 1843. Reynolds's brother, Thomas, was governor of Missouri from 1840 until his death in early 1844.

Like his father, Dr. William Gano Goforth was an active Freemason. His first recorded Masonic activity in Illinois took place in December 1842, when he was elected marshal of the newly constituted St. Clair Lodge No. 60, operating under authority from the Grand Lodge of Missouri.[17]

On the afternoon of April 5, following a morning session of Masonic "work," the dedication of Nauvoo's new Masonic Hall was performed by Worshipful Master Hyrum Smith. This important task was usually reserved for the grand master of the state. Indeed, the cornerstones of the building were inscribed, "M. HELM. G.M.A.L.5843"—Meredith Helm, Grand Master After Light 1843. With the Nauvoo Lodge under suspension, grand master Helm could not be expected to conduct the

17. William G. Goforth to *Belleville Advocate*, 13 April 1844, in *Belleville Advocate*, 18 April 1844. Charles Francis Adams, *Diary*, May 14, 1844. Josiah Quincy to [family] 16 May 1844, in Woodworth, "Josiah Quincy's 1844 Visit with Joseph Smith," 84. John Reynolds, *My Own Times*, 205. Thomas Jefferson Goforth (1800–1879) also moved west, to Jackson County, Missouri. It is not known if he was involved in the Mormon troubles. "A History of the Descendants," 508–509. William Gano Goforth was a close associate of John C. Bennett. See, for example, *Times and Seasons*, 2.14 (May 15, 1841), for a letter from Goforth, where he wrote, "I am and have been long acquainted with Dr. Bennett, both as a physician, and minister of the Gospel." Hogan, "The Strange Question," 3. *History of Masonry in Illinois*, 190–91.

ceremony. Even past grand master Abraham Jonas (once a valiant Mormon supporter) failed to attend the clandestine dedication.[18]

Master Mason (and Council of Fifty member) Erastus Snow "delivered a pleasing and instructive address on the beauties and benefits of the Institution." He was
followed by Hyrum Smith, Dr. William G. Goforth, and Joseph Smith, whose speeches were "all characterized by feelings of the purest friendship." When the Grand
Lodge was mentioned in one of the speeches, "a feeling of holy indignation seemed
to prevail, yet an universal expression of forgiveness was evidently in the breast of
all present and especially should our oppressors take off the iron yoke and treat us
as members of the family of mankind,—as members of the most noble of moral
institutions and as brethren of the same noble Fraternity." Following the addresses,
the visiting Freemasons were given dinner at the Masonic Hall "at the expense of the
Nauvoo Lodge."[19]

The church scheduled its regular annual conference to begin the following day,
Saturday, April 6, the fourteenth anniversary of its founding in 1830. More than ten
thousand Saints were in attendance. Joseph convened the meeting.

The prophet was confident. Despite reports there was a new conspiracy against
his life, he determined not to allow "petty difficulties" (such as William Law's opposition to polygamy) to interfere with the "instruction on the principles of eternal
truth" which had been prepared. "I feel in closer communion and better standing
with God than ever I felt before in my life," he said, "and I am glad of this opportunity to appear in your midst. I thank God for the glorious day that He has given us."
He decided not to speak at that time, on account of "the weakness of my lungs," but
would defer to others. "The Elders will give you instruction," he said. "And then, if
necessary, I will offer such corrections as may be proper to fill up the interstices."[20]

Elder Sidney Rigdon, recently rehabilitated and initiated into the Council of
Fifty, was the first speaker. Because of ill health and other concerns, it had been five
years since he last addressed the Saints during a general conference. Rigdon chose as
his topic, "The Church of Jesus Christ in the Last Days." He did not require a passage
from the Bible for inspiration.

"I can make a text for myself," he began. Involved as he was with the affairs of
the church from the first year of its existence, the history of the institution would be
his guide. "I recollect in the year 1830 I met the whole Church of Christ in a little old
log-house about 20 feet square, near Waterloo, N.Y., and we began to talk about the
kingdom of God as if we had the world at our command." He admitted that church
leaders had held "secret associations" since its organization in 1830.

"The time has now come to tell why we held secret meetings," he continued.
"We were maturing plans fourteen years ago which we can now tell. Were we maturing plans to corrupt the world, to destroy the peace of society? No. Let fourteen
years' experience of the Church tell the story. The Church never would have been
here if we had not done as we did in secret." Rigdon recited an inventory of the suc-
cesses and persecutions of the Latter-day Saints during their fourteen-year history,

---

18. Smith, *History of the Church* 6:287. Hogan, "Dedication of the Nauvoo Masonic Temple" and "Erec-
    tion and Dedication."
19. Hogan, "Erection and Dedication," 13. Smith, *History of the Church* 6:287.
20. Smith, *History of the Church* 6:287–88.

from Kirtland to Missouri and, most recently, in Illinois. "Do not be astonished, then, if we even yet have secret meetings, asking God for things for your benefit. Do not be afraid . . . There was no evil concocted when we first held secret meetings, and it is the same now . . . The things that were done in secret in the beginning are now seen openly and there is nothing secret now but what all will know in time to come."

He paused at this allusion to the recent work of the political Kingdom of God. "I am disposed to give some reasons why salvation only belongs to the kingdom of God, and to that alone. . . . I discover one thing: Mankind have labored under one universal mistake about this—viz., salvation was distinct from government; i. e., that I can build a Church without government, and that thing have power to save me!" To the contrary, Rigdon argued, "When God sets up a system of salvation, He sets up a system of government. When I speak of a government, I mean what I say. I mean a government that shall rule over temporal and spiritual affairs . . . The kingdom of God does not interfere with the laws of the land, but keeps itself by its own laws." In other words, now that Joseph Smith had organized the Kingdom of God, he was obligated to observe a higher law than that of the United States of America. He was to follow only the will of God, not man. Rigdon paused, his health still not fully recovered, and sat down to refresh himself.

Elder John Taylor was called upon to speak. His observations, like his editorials, were circumspect. "Many things have been spoken by Elder Rigdon concerning the early history of this Church," he began. "There is no person who has searched the oracles of eternal truth, but his mind will be touched with the remarks made by our venerable friend, which unfold the dispensation of Jehovah, and have a tendency to produce the most thrilling feelings in the bosoms of many who are this day present, and to promote our general edification . . . We are laying the foundation of a kingdom that shall last forever—that shall bloom in time and blossom in eternity. We are engaged in a greater work than ever occupied the attention of mortals. We live in a day that prophets and kings desired to see, but died without the sight . . . Tell your rulers that all their deeds of fame are tarnished, and their glory is departed."

The conference continued on Sunday morning. The sun was "pleasant," the air "calm and serene." Nearly twenty thousand were assembled to hear Elder Sidney Rigdon conclude his remarks on the history of the church and the Kingdom of God. "I shall preach from the same text we preached from yesterday, The Church of Jesus Christ, the Kingdom of God, the leven, the little stone spoken of by Daniel &c.," Sidney said. He answered a question raised by the recent letter published in *Times and Seasons.* "Let no man be alarmed because the Lord said that the kingdom of God should swallow up all other kingdoms. What harm would it do? For all the world would have the same spirit. The Lord said He intended to do by the whole world the same as he has done by us, & this is the thing the world is afraid of. Reflect then. This is as far as I intended to go upon this subject."[21]

---

21. Ibid., 6:288–96. See also Smith, *American Prophet's Record,* 463 [6 April 1844]. Note *History of the Church* title, "Behold the Church of God of the last days." Woodruff, *Journals* 2:376, 378, 380 [6 April 1844]. An editorial "From the Holy City," *Warsaw Signal* 10 April 1844, described Rigdon as "an old horse [that] was turned out on the commons to die," performing in "pliant submission to the dictation of his master."

The Sunday afternoon session commenced at two P.M. While waiting for the prophet to arrive, Patriarch Hyrum Smith spoke about progress on building the Nauvoo temple and admonished all missionaries departing Nauvoo to "preach the pure truth."[22]

Joseph approached the stand at three fifteen and rose to present a message before the congregation. Inspired by the untimely death of King Follet, who was killed in a well accident the previous month, Joseph announced that he would "address [them] on the subject of the dead." He began by examining the character of God. "What kind of a being is God?" he asked. The answer was startling. "God himself was once as we are now, and is an exalted man, and sits enthroned in yonder heavens! That is the great secret . . . We have imagined and supposed that God was God from all eternity. I will refute that idea, and take away the veil so that you may see. These are incomprehensible ideas to some, but they are simple." Joseph concluded his dissertation—touching on the plurality of gods, eternal progression and the nature of intelligence—more than two hours later, at five thirty that afternoon.[23]

The effect on the Saints was electric. "I have evidence enough that Joseph is not fallen," one elder joyfully recorded. "Any one that could not see in him the Spirit of Inspiration of God must be dark, they might have known that he was not a fallen Prophet even if they thought he was fallen." William Law, Joseph's estranged counselor in the First Presidency of the church, was less impressed. "Conference is over, and some of the most blasphemous doctrines have been taught by J. Smith & others," Law wrote in his diary. "Such as a plurality of Gods, other gods as far above our God as he is above us. That he wrought out his salvation in the flesh with fear and trembling, the same as we do; . . . that secret meetings are all legal and right and that the Kingdom [of God] must be set up after the manner of a Kingdom (and of course have a King)."[24]

Dr. Goforth met privately with Joseph in the evening. They spoke of politics. The prophet expressed his "disapprobation of Martin Van Buren-ism—and [his] unwillingness to vote for, or influence a vote for HENRY CLAY . . . Americans cannot sustain a man that will not inviolably protect national rights!" Afterwards Goforth wrote to the editor of the *Belleville Advocate*:

> The name of Joseph Smith, of Nauvoo, is now before the people as a candidate for President of the United States. With this name is proclaimed *Jeffersonianism* . . . Jeffersonian Democracy, and free trade and sailors' rights, and protection of person and property. The interview on this occasion was satisfactory, & I know not of hearing a sounder policy designed for public inspection and American prosperity. [25]

Brigham Young, as president of the Quorum of the Twelve, presided over the final session of Conference—an electioneering meeting—on Tuesday, April 9. Some

22. Smith, *History of the Church* 6:301.
23. Ibid., 6:302, 305.
24. Fielding, Journal, 148 (fallen quote), in Cook, *Words,* 361–62. Law, Diary, 15 April 1844, in Cook, *William Law,* 49.
25. William Gano Goforth to editor of the *Belleville Advocate,* 13 April 1844, in *Belleville Advocate,* 18 April 1844.

eleven hundred elders were present. Brigham admonished the men to preach only the "first principles"—faith, repentance, baptism for the remission of sins, and the Gift of the Holy Ghost—when they went out. They "need not go into mysteries," he cautioned. Mention of the ideal of plural marriage (one of "the mysteries") was to be avoided. Any elder found teaching the newly revealed doctrines would have his name published in *Times and Seasons* and his license to preach revoked. Brigham was insistent. "We want the Elders to electioneer for President Smith and we want to build the temple this season and by the help of God we will do it. We are acquainted with the views of Gen. Smith, the Democrats and Whigs and all factions," Brigham Young went on. "It is now time to have a President of the United States. Elders will be sent to preach the Gospel and electioneer." Remember, he told them, "The government belongs to God. No man can draw the dividing line between the government of God and the government of the children of men. You can't touch the Gospel without infringing upon the common avocations of men. They may have helps and governments in the Church, but it is all one at last."[26]

Hyrum next admonished the men. "We engage in the election the same as in any other principle," he said. "You are to vote for good men, and if you do not do this it is a sin: to vote for wicked men, it would be sin. Choose the good and refuse the evil. Men of false principles have preyed upon us like wolves upon helpless lambs. Damn the rod of tyranny; curse it. Let every man use his liberties according to the Constitution. Don't fear man or devil; electioneer with all people, male and female, and exhort them to do the thing that is right. We want a President of the U. S., not a party President, but a President of the whole people; for a party President disfranchises the opposite party. Have a President who will maintain every man in his rights."

"I wish all of you to do all the good you can," Hyrum continued. "We will try and convert the nations into one solid union. I despise the principle that divides the nation into party and faction . . . Whatever are the rights of men guaranteed by the Constitution of these United States, let them have them. Then, if we were all in union, no one dare attempt to put a warlike foot on our soil. I don't like to see the rights of Americans trampled down." He moved on to the Texas question. "I am opposed to the policy of all such persons as would allow Great Britain or any other power to take from us Oregon or any portion of our national territory; and damn all who attempt it. Lift up your voices like thunder: there is power and influence enough among us to put in a President."[27]

Brigham Young again took the stand. He "requested all who were in favor of electing Joseph to the Presidency to raise both hands." The voting was nearly unanimous, with eleven hundred elders "clapping their hand[s]" and giving "many loud cheers." Only one unidentified dissenting vote was manifested.[28]

26. Woodruff, *Journals* 2:390 [9 April 1844]. Smith, *American Prophet's Record*, 469 [9 April 1844]. Smith, *History of the Church* 6:322.

27. Smith, *History of the Church* 6:323–24. The next line notes, "I don't wonder at the old Carthagenian lawyer being afraid of Joseph Smith being elected." It is uncertain who is being referred to here.

28. Smith, *American Prophet's Record*, 469 [9 April 1844]. Smith, *History of the Church* 6:324, says, "A unanimous vote was passed."

Brigham Young as president of the LDS
Church, following exodus to Utah, notably
wearing his Masonic pin of compass, square,
and 'G.' Courtesy of the Church Archives, the
Church of Jesus Christ of Latter-day Saints.

Apostle and Council of Fifty member Heber C. Kimball spoke next. "We are going to arrange a plan for Conferences," Kimball explained, "and we design to send Elders to all the different States to get up meetings and protracted meetings, and electioneer for Joseph to be the next President." Kimball recognized the task would not be easy. "A great many of the Elders will necessarily have to leave their families," he noted, "and the mothers will have to assume the responsibility of governing and taking care of the children to a much greater extent than when their husbands were at home."[29]

At the conclusion of Elder Kimball's remarks a "call was made for the volunteers to go preaching to pass out to the green." A "great company" of men, nearly 250 in all, formed two ranks on the right of the stand. Those able to serve for six months were seated first, followed by those who could serve for three months or less. Following an adjournment, the names of the volunteers were called and their assignments made. In a few weeks the volunteers would number nearly four hundred.[30]

That afternoon, following the conclusion of the political meeting, Joseph, his wife Emma, and Dr. William Gano Goforth rode out to "the mound" together where they admired the peach groves. Dr. Goforth prepared to return to his home in Belleville. "On morning of the 10th, a strong look out for the Osprey was commenced, and late in the afternoon she approached—when my wife and I embarked, expressing for the people of Nauvoo our prayers, and receiving their expressions of reciprocity."[31]

James Arlington Bennet formally responded to Willard Richards's vice presidential proposal on April 14. He could not run for public office, he wrote, and he doubted that Joseph could be elected. "If you can by any supernatural means elect Brother Joseph President of these U. States, I have not a doubt but that he would govern the people and administer the laws in good faith, and with righteous intentions, but I can see no natural means by which he has the slightest chance of receiving the votes even of one state." He reminded Dr. Richards that "every man's hand is against the Mormons, and the Mormons against every man in a religious sense." Arlington Bennet proposed that "the Mormons should settle out of the States and have an

---

29. Smith, *History of the Church* 6:325.

30. Ibid.. Smith, *American Prophet's Record*, 469 [9 April 1844]. Robertson, "The Campaign and the Kingdom."

31. William Gano Goforth to editor of the *Belleville Advocate*, 13 April 1844, in *Belleville Advocate*, 18 April 1844.

empire of their own. Not only thousands but millions would flock to an independent people. In this case a Patriarchal government with Joseph at the head would be just the thing. In unity there is power. Nothing could resist such a people."[32]

The letter would have arrived in Nauvoo at an auspicious moment. On April 11 Joseph was anointed "Prophet, Priest and King" in the Kingdom of God, an act greeted with "loud shouts of Hosanna" by the Council of Fifty. On April 18 the prophet "declared the council full" composed of fifty-two men (including the clerk and recorder) "called upon to form the grand K. of G. by revelation." The clerk of the council, William Clayton, was nearly overwhelmed by the day's events. "It seems like heaven began on earth," he wrote, "and the power of God is with us."[33]

Democrat Francis Preston Blair, publisher of the Washington, D.C., *Daily Globe* and the *Congressional Globe*, was the first national political figure to respond to Joseph Smith's *Views*. His article, "A new Advocate for a National Bank," was published in the *Daily Globe*, and copied by newspapers throughout the U.S. It was a barbed assessment of Smith's fiscal platform. "We have cast our eyes hastily over General Smith's (Mormon Joe) 'Views of the Powers and Policy of the Government of the United States," Blair began. Instead of discovering anything original, Blair found his *Views* to be in accord with proposals by "Messrs. Clay, Webster, Sargeant, and the whig party in general, for a national bank."

Blair balked at the prophet's recommendation that state legislatures should be petitioned to "pardon every convict in the several penitentiaries; blessing them as they go, and saying to them, in the name of the Lord 'Go thy way and sin no more.'" If that were done, Blair feared "the 'specie basis' would soon disappear from Joe's mother bank and branches, including that of Nauvoo," although perhaps no more ill effect could be expected from the "small thieves" than the depression caused by the "great thieves who robbed millions from the late whig bank and its satellites" and who were never prosecuted for their crimes.

"Upon the whole, however," Blair continued, "we will do General Smith the justice to state, that we think his financial doctrines more sound, his views more honest, and his scheme more feasible, than those of the hypocrites and quacks who, supported by a great party, have fleeced the country to the very quick, and are now eager to repeat the application of the shears."

With Joseph Smith's platform supposedly so closely resembling that of the Whigs, Blair wrote, "let General Smith be the Whig candidate for the vice presidency . . . Cannot Mr. Clay persuade the General to accompany him on his electioneering tour?" Blair's suggestion was all in jest. "With . . . Joe Smith, and a few other quadrupeds to complete his menagerie," Blair jibed, Clay "could not fail to convince the moral and enlightened people of the United States of the necessity of a national bank, and of their duty to make him President."

---

32. James Arlington Bennet to Willard Richards, 14 April 1844, quoted in Godfrey, "Causes of Conflict," 68 and Hill, *Quest for Refuge*, 140 and 255, note 123.

33. Clayton, Council of Fifty minutes, 11 April 1844, in Ehat, "Heaven Began," 267. This soon became common (if not exactly public) knowledge. See, for example, "W." [Nauvoo, Illinois] to editors of the *Missouri Republican*, 25 April 1844 (reprinted in the *Clay Tribune*, 8 June 1844): "Joe, is not only Prophet, but he is Mormon King, and in his triune function of Prophet, Priest and King." See also Josiah Quincy [to family], 16 May 1844, in Woodworth, "Josiah Quincy's 1844 Visit," 85 and note 15.

Blair concluded his "analysis" of Joseph Smith's *Views* with a mock proposal. "We propose, then, that Joe Smith . . . be made president . . . of the new whig national bank that is not to be; that the mother bank be established at Nauvoo, with branches over all creation." With selected bank officials carefully chosen from the Whig party, "we should have the perfection of a whig system of finance."[34]

Joseph replied to Blair on April 15. The prophet emphasized that he rarely responded to many of the wild speculations about the Mormons that appeared in the nation's press. Written by a respected editor of two of the leading national newspapers, Blair's commentary was viewed differently.

It was "extraneous, irrelevant and kick shawing to connect me or any part of my 'Views on the Powers and Policy of the Government,' with Mr. Clay, Mr. Webster, Mr. Adams, Mr. Benton, Mr. Calhoun, Mr. Van Buren, or any of their galvanic cronies," Joseph protested. They have done "*nothing* but draw money from the treasury. It is entirely too late in the age of this Republic, to clarify a Harry of the West; deify a Daniel of the East; quidify a Quincy of the Whigs, or bigify a Benton of the Democrats; leaving Mr. Calhoun and Mr. Van Buren such fair samples of bogus-democracy, that he that runs [for public office] may read."

Even so, Joseph continued, one suggestion "worthy of commendation relative to a National Bank, in Mr. Blair's remarks, is, that the mother bank should be located at *Nauvoo*." Nauvoo was not a city adulterated by "dishonor, crime, corruption or bribery," he pointed out.

Joseph concluded his response to Blair with a summary of his political creed:

> "*As the world is governed too much*" and as there is not a nation or dynasty, now occupying the earth, which acknowledges Almighty God as their lawgiver . . . And as 'crowns won by blood, by blood must be maintained,' I go emphatically, virtuously, and humanely, for a THEODEMOCRACY, where God and the people hold the power to conduct the affairs of men in righteousness.

(Joseph's concept of precisely what constituted a *theo*democracy is never fully spelled out, although Council of Fifty member George A. Smith later preached that, "What we do [politically] we should do as one man. Our system should be Theo-Democracy,—the voice of the people consenting to the voice of God.")

Continuing his rejoinder to editor Blair, Joseph Smith maintained that government could be effective only "where liberty, free trade, and sailor's rights, and the protection of life and property shall be maintained inviolate, for the benefit of ALL." (The inclusion of "sailor's rights" in his 1844 campaign platform was part of a larger movement to ban the practice of impressing captured sailors, regardless of nationality, into service under a victor's flag.) This lead neatly to his next point, that "to exalt mankind is nobly acting the part of a God; to degrade them, is meanly doing the drudgery of the devil." He concluded his political credo with the phrase: "Unitas,

---

34. "A New Advocate for a National Bank," *Globe* (Washington, D.C.), 14 March 1844. See also *Times and Seasons*, 15 April 1844, 510–11, *Sangamo Journal*, 4 April 1844, and the *Warsaw Signal*, 24 April 1844. Also published in *The Prophet*, 18 May 1844.

libertas, caritas—esto perpetua!" [Unity, liberty, charity—forever!][35]

A list of nearly 340 political missionaries and 47 proposed general conferences appeared in *Times and Seasons* for April 15. The first conference outside of Illinois was scheduled to take place in Cincinnati, Ohio, on May 18. The final general conference (lasting nine days!), to be held in Washington, D.C., was slated for early to mid-September.

"Those Elders who are numbered in the fore going list," Brigham Young advised the prospective missionaries, will "preside over the different states, will appoint conferences in all places in their several states where opportunities present, and will attend all the conferences, or send experienced and able elders, who will preach the truth in righteousness, and present before the people 'General Smith's views of the power and policy of the General Government' and seek diligently to get up electors who will go for him for the presidency." The Council of the Twelve would serve as traveling general authorities and attend as many conferences as was possible.[36]

Simeon Francis, Whig editor of Springfield's *Sangamo Journal,* was becoming exasperated with the Mormons. "I can't understand Joe Smith," he wrote in a letter to John J. Hardin on April 2. "Some of our friends believe that he will ultimately tell his Mormons to vote for Clay." The prospect of the Mormons voting for Henry Clay was becoming even less likely, however. On that same day Joseph was visited in Nauvoo by an unnamed Vermonter (a self-proclaimed "prophet of God") who "prophesied that this government was about to be overthrown and the Kingdom of Daniel spoke of was about to be established some where in the west and he thought in Illinois."[37]

On the morning of Tuesday, April 23, a general meeting of the Nauvoo Saints was held in the Masonic Hall. Its purpose was to select delegates to attend the Whig national convention in Baltimore the first Monday in May. David S. Hollister, a member of the Council of Fifty, was among those chosen to meet with Whig representatives in Baltimore. That afternoon the body again assembled to hear electioneering speeches "about Presidents &c."[38]

In the meeting it was concluded that Joseph could count on between two hundred thousand and five hundred thousand votes "independent of any other party," some 10 to 15 percent of the electorate. Available sources indicate neither how those figures were arrived at, nor how it was thought the votes would be distributed. If the 1844 race was as close as most observers predicted it would be, the Mormon prophet was quite possibly in a position to force a repeat of Henry Clay's 1824 election compromise. Accurate or not, it was soon rumored that Joseph Smith might "withdraw from the canvass for President, if he could get to be Secretary of State or Minister to Russia,"

---

35. Joseph Smith, "The Globe," 15 April 1844 (*Times and Seasons* 15 April 1844, 508–10, *Nauvoo Neighbor,* 17 April 1844). See Smith, *American Prophet's Record,* 471 [17 April 1844], George A. Smith, Journal History 12 July 1865, quoted in Hansen, "Metamorphosis," 72, Quinn, *New Mormon History,* 229, *Times and Seasons,* 5.8 (April 15 1844), 510. Last portion is quoted in Graham, "Presidential Campaign," 66.

36. Smith, *History of the Church* 6:340.

37. Simeon Francis to John J. Hardin, 22 April 1844, Hardin Papers, Chicago Historical Society. Smith, *American Prophet's Record,* 472 [22 April 1844]. Quinn, *Origins of Power,* 136.

38. Smith, *American Prophet's Record,* 472 [23 April 1844].

Map of publication and distribution of *General Smith's Views* showing major locations mentioned in the text. Numbers in paranthesis (201) indicate entry in Crawley, *Descriptive Bibliography*. Pamphlets (P) and newspaper printings (N) together with quantity published are given when known.

an echo of John Hardin's offer to Judge John McLean the previous summer.[39]

The *Nauvoo Neighbor*'s report on of the gathering was understated and probably would have been missed by many readers. Even so, a Whig correspondent in attendance at the meeting expressed alarm at the political developments taking place

39. "Public Meeting," *Nauvoo Neighbor*, 24 April 1844. Also reported in *Niles' National Register*, 16 May 1844, *Upper Mississippian*, 11 May 1844, "Mormon Movements," *New York Herald*, 23 May 1844, and in "Mormon Politicians," *Clay Tribune*, 25 May, 1844.

in Nauvoo. Referring to Joseph's recent ordination within the Council of Fifty, the reporter wrote, "Joe, is not only Prophet, but he is [the] Mormon King, . . . in his triune function of Prophet, Priest and King." Furthermore, he warned his readers,

It is the design of these people to have candidates for electors in every state of the Union; a convention is to be held in Baltimore, probably next month. The leaders are busy organizing their plans—over a hundred persons leave in a few days for different states to carry them out as far as possible . . . He indignantly spurns the proposition to run for the second office on the same ticket with Mr. Van Buren: he thinks his chance would be much better alone . . . let no man sneer at these people or deem them of little consequence, either for good or evil. They are becoming of potent influence to the people of the State of Illinois. It is a serious question: What will be the end of things?

The letter was initially published in the *Missouri Republican* and gained wide exposure when copied by Greeley's *New York Tribune*. The story was also picked up by the *Clay Tribune* and *Niles' National Register*.[40]

Council of Fifty member Orson Hyde arrived in Washington the same day as the Nauvoo meeting. He called on Illinois representatives in the capital, Illinois Whig John J. Hardin, and Democrats Joseph P. Hoge, Stephen A. Douglas, and John Wentworth, the following day. Elder Hyde presented the men with Joseph's proposal to raise one hundred thousand army troops to protect the American frontier. The legislators saw little likelihood of passage.

Hyde felt that Joseph's plan to colonize Texas was more feasible. "Congress will pass no act in relation to Texas or Oregon at present," he wrote to the prophet on April 25. "She is afraid of England, afraid of Mexico, afraid the Presidential election will be twisted by it. The members all appear like unskillful players at checkers." Hyde pointed out that "most of the settlers in Oregon and Texas are our old enemies," however if "the settlement of Oregon and Texas be determined upon, the sooner the move is made the better; and I would not advise any delay [waiting] for the action of our government, for there is such jealously of our rising power already, that government will do nothing to favor us. *If the saints possess the kingdom* I think they will have to take it; and the sooner it is done the more easily it is accomplished. Your superior wisdom must determine whether to go to Oregon, to Texas, or to remain within these United States." Don't delay, he urged. "The present perhaps is the most proper time that ever will be."

The next day, Hyde had a long conversation with Judge Stephen A. Douglas. Hyde reported that the senator "would resign his seat in Congress if he could command the force that Mr. Smith could, and would be on the march to the [western] country in a month . . . the eyes of many aspiring politicians in this place are upon that country."

---

40. "Public Meeting," *Nauvoo Neighbor* 24 April 1844. Graham, "Presidential Campaign," 71–72, 79. "W." [Nauvoo, Illinois] to the editors of the *Missouri Republican*, 25 April 1844. Reprinted in the *Clay Tribune*, 8 June 1844, and published or noted in the *New York Tribune*, 18 May 1844 and "Political-Presidential," *Niles' National Register*, 16 May 1844.

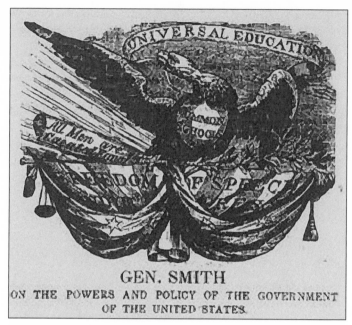

Woodcut engraving from *The Prophet,* June 8, 1844, above the New York publication of *General Smith's Views.*

Hyde's assessment of the political climate in Washington centered on the issue of slavery. "The Northern Whig members are almost to a man against Texas and Oregon; but should the present administration succeed in annexing Texas, then all the Whigs would turn around in favor of Oregon; for if Texas be admitted slavery is extended to the South; then free states must be added to the West to keep up a balance of power between the slave and the free states." Hyde also warned the prophet. "Should Texas be admitted, war with Mexico is looked upon as inevitable." Hyde reflected on the difficulties of getting any of the Saints' proposals approved. "There are many powerful checks upon our government," he noted, "preventing her from moving in any of these important matters; and for aught I know these checks are permitted to prevent our government from extending her jurisdiction over the territory which God designs to give to His Saints." Hyde reported that Judge Douglas told him "he would equally as soon go to that country without an act of Congress as with . . . and that in five years a noble state might be formed and then if they would not receive us into the Union, we would have a government of our own."[41]

At the very time the Mormon delegates were meeting with Illinois representatives in Washington, D.C., national political conventions were being planned for Baltimore and Nauvoo. Forces in opposition to General Joseph Smith's presidential campaign were also gaining momentum.

---

41. Orson Hyde to Joseph Smith, 25 April 1844, in Smith, *History of the Church* 6:369–73, Orson Hyde to Joseph Smith, 26 April 1844, in Smith, *History of the Church* 6:373–76. Quinn, *Origins of Power,* 133.

Chapter Nine

Two Conventions

For President, Senator Henry Clay. For Vice-President, Theodore Freling-huysen.

Clay Tribune, New York City, May 4, 1844[1]

For President, Gen. Joseph Smith, of Nauvoo, Illinois. "A Western man, with American principles."

The Prophet, New York City, May 25, 1844[2]

THE WHIG NATIONAL CONVENTION CONVENED in Baltimore at the Universalist Church on May 1, 1844. A roll call just before noon confirmed that all twenty-five states in the Union were represented. Ambrose Spencer, of New York, was selected as president of the convention. Vice presidents represented each state. Jacob Burnet led the Ohio delegation. The Illinois representation included George T. M. Davis. John J. Hardin was also present, although not as an official delegate. Horace Greeley conferred with his fellow Whigs and reported on the convention proceedings.

A representative from Virginia addressed the convention. In his view, "The voice of the whig party of the country was so decidedly in favor of a certain individual for the presidency that it would be unnecessary to go through the usual form of a nomination." He proposed a resolution declaring "HENRY CLAY, of KENTUCKY to be unanimously chosen as the whig candidate for the presidency of the United States, and that he be recommended to the people as such." The resolution passed by acclamation, "the cheering and bravos . . . continued for a great length of time." A committee, composed of five men, including longtime Clay supporter John McPherson Berrien of Georgia, and Clay's sometime adversary Jacob Burnet, was formed to inform Henry Clay of his nomination.

The challenge of selecting a vice presidential running mate lay ahead. The Honorable George Evans of Maine and John M. Clayton of Delaware withdrew their names from consideration. Many expected Judge John McLean of Ohio to run.

---

1. *Clay Tribune,* 4 May 1844.
2. *The Prophet,* 25 May 1844

McLean's letter declining the vice presidential nomination was read before the convention and greeted with acclaim from the floor.

With McLean no longer in the running, a New York representative suggested that each state delegation "appoint one of their number to form a Committee" which would "collect the votes of the several delegates" to determine who would run in the vice presidency slot. Jacob Burnet asked if that would mean the nomination would go "to the gentleman receiving the highest number of votes." The New York representative answered in the affirmative. The candidate "reported by the Committee" would then be accepted or rejected by the convention as a whole. Burnet objected. If a state was not fully represented at the convention, its vote would be effectively discounted. Burnet proposed that "the Delegation from each State should cast the full Electoral Vote for that State." Each delegation would choose its own candidate, he argued, thereby avoiding the potential of a split vote within a state. Burnet's block voting strategy was unsuccessful.

With two hundred and seventy-five delegates present, a simple majority of 138 votes would be required for a nomination to succeed. Four men were nominated for the vice presidency: Millard Filmore of New York, John Davis of Massachusetts, Theodore Frelinghuysen of New Jersey, and John Sergeant of Pennsylvania.

The first vote resulted in: John Sergeant, 38; Millard Filmore, 53; John Davis, 83; Theodore Frelinghuysen, 101. The two largest delegations, Ohio and New York, prevented the choice from settling on Frelinghuysen the first round—20 of Ohio's 23 votes went for Davis; 35 of New York's 36 votes went for Fillmore.

The second vote: John Sergeant, 32; Millard Fillmore, 57; John Davis, 74; Theodore Frelinghuysen, 118. Ohio's delegates remained with Davis (19), with 4 going to Fillmore. New York stayed behind Fillmore (35); only one voted for Frelinghuysen. Sergeant's candidacy, as the lowest vote getter, was withdrawn.

The third vote: John Davis, 76; Millard Fillmore, 40; Theodore Frelinghuysen, 155. As expected, Massachusetts voted with Davis (12), Ohio stayed with Davis (19), while New York supported Filmore (29). Theodore Frelinghuysen was announced as "the candidate of the convention for the office of vice president of the United States."

Burnet offered a resolution that the nomination be made unanimous. Representatives from Massachusetts and New York concurred in their support. Alfred Kelley, of Ohio, noted that because the state had brought Davis into the field, they "could not honorably desert so honorable a man." Since the convention had fairly chosen Frelinghuysen, however, "no state would support [him] with more unanimity than the state of Ohio."

The question was taken. "The resolution was unanimously adopted amidst loud and repeated cheers." Whig principles espoused by Clay and Frelinghuysen were summed up for the assembly:

> A well regulated national currency; a tariff or revenue to defray the necessary expenses of the government, and discriminating with special reference to the protection of the domestic labor of the country; the distribution of the proceeds of the sales of public lands; a single term for the presidency; a reform of executive usurpations:—and, generally—such an administration of the affairs of the country as

shall impart to every branch of the public service the greatest practicable efficiency, controlled by a well regulated and wise economy.[3]

Someone in the crowd "called out for a rhyme." Illinois State Representative in Congress, John J. Hardin, penned some lines and sent them down to the convention floor.

Our Country's flag aloft we raise—
Our hopes now high, and upward rising;
In burning words it there displays
The names of Clay and Frelinghuysen![4]

On the second of May, a Young Men's National Ratification Convention met in the same hall. The assembly was even grander than the day before. Thought to be "the largest and most imposing political assemblage ever assembled," numbering in the tens of thousands, every state in the Union was represented, "several of them by thousands of delegates."

Representatives crowded into the streets and took their assigned places in formation, to be part of a parade later in the day. Countless floats and displays struggled to outdo each other. A triumphal arch, forty-five feet high, spanned Baltimore Street at the intersection of Calvert. The base of each capital was inscribed with Whig Principles, columns were inscribed with the words: Union, Peace, Encouragement to Industry, Sound Currency, Honest Administration, Uphold the Constitution, Distribution of the Public lands, No Spoils Principles, Executive restraint—One Term.

Another arch, thirty-seven feet in height, spanning Baltimore at Hanover Street, contained likenesses of William Henry Harrison and Henry Clay. A prominent inscription read, "UNION, PEACE, AND PATIENCE," a phrase taken from Clay's Raleigh letter (published three days before the opening of the nominating convention) declaring his opposition to the annexation of Texas. A series of blocks inscribed with Whig principles added "States Rights" to the earlier list.

The Young Men's Convention ratified the choices of Clay and Frelinghuysen as the Whig presidential and vice presidential candidates in 1844. "The response [was as] loud as tens of thousands of voices could make it."

Judge John McPherson Berrien read the correspondence from the nominating committee to Henry Clay. Clay's letter of acceptance, dated May 2, was likewise read before the assembly.[5]

---

3. The convention is reported in *Niles' National Register* for 4 May 1844. The listing of delegates can be found on 147, where Cyrus Edwards of Illinois is mistakenly listed as "Silas." The *Clay Tribune* of May 4 is correct.

4. Thomas Gregg reported, "The four lines of verse in our Editorial head, are ascribed to Gen. Hardin, member of congress from this State. On the nomination of Frelinghuysen, some one in the crowd called out for a rhyme, in connection with the [names]. Mr. Hardin immediately wrote and sent up those line[s], which were received with great applause. We adopt them as our motto." *Upper Mississippian*, 18 May 1844.

5. Henry Clay to John M. Berrien, Jacob Burnet, et al., 2 May 1844, in Hopkins and Hargreaves, *Papers of Henry Clay* 10:52. See also John M. Berrien, Jacob Burnet, Erastus Root, Abbott Lawrence, and William S. Archer to Henry Clay, 1 May 1844, in *Niles' National Register* 18 May 1844.

In Nauvoo, *Times and Seasons* had just published the general conference minutes (including Sidney Rigdon's remarks on the Kingdom of God) and promised, "owing to the extensive call" for the document, to include "Gen. Smith's Views of the Powers and Policy of the Government of the United States" in the next issue. Lucien Woodworth, secret ambassador from Nauvoo to the Republic of Texas, reported on his mission before the Council of Fifty on May 3. "The prospect of our obtaining room to form a colony there [in Texas] is fair," Woodworth assured them. Joseph Smith addressed the council. "Let George Miller and Lyman Wight take the Black River company and their friends, and go to Texas," he said, "to the confines [border] of Mexico in the Cordilleras mountains; and at the same time let brother Woodworth, who has just returned from Texas, go back to the seat of government in Texas, to intercede for a tract of country which we, the Church, might have control over, that we might find a resting place for a little season." Support from the Council of Fifty was unanimous.[6]

"I have petitioned the president and Congress assembled," Joseph reminded them, "to give me the command of [one hundred thousand] men, in some part or portion of the confines [border] of Mexico, for our safety, and for the protection of the government of the United States." Not having yet received an answer from the capital, Joseph assigned George Miller to his home state of Kentucky, to "visit Henry Clay, and others of high standing in the United States government."[7]

Lyman Wight was to "go to the City of Washington, and to all the Eastern Cities of note, and hold [Joseph] up as a candidate for President of the United States at the ensuing election." At the conclusion of their political missions, Miller and Wight were to "go forth with the Black river company to perform the Mission which has been voted this day." Lucien Woodworth, George Miller, and Uriah Brown, "the oldest and most prominent non-Mormon in the Council of Fifty" were assigned as "commissioners appointed to meet the Texan Congress" in the fall of 1844, "to sanction or ratify the said treaty, partly entered into by our minister [Woodworth] and the Texan cabinet." Council support was again unanimous.[8]

"All things are going on gloriously at Nauvoo," Brigham Young and Willard Richards wrote to the head of the church's mission in England later that day. "We shall make a great wake in the nation. Joseph for President . . . We have already received several hundred volunteers to go out electioneering and preaching and more offering. We go for storming the nation . . . We shall have a State Convention at Nauvoo on the 17th inst.,—an election. A great many are believing the doctrine. If any of the brethren wish to go to Texas, we have no particular objection," Young and Richards assured the mission president. "You may send a hundred thousand there if you can." "The kingdom is organized," they went on, alluding to the recent decisions by the Council of Fifty, "and, although as yet no bigger than a grain of mustard seed,

6. Fielding, Nauvoo Journal, 148, (fair quote). Wight, *An Address*, 3 (season quote).
7. Wight, *An Address*, 3. Wight's account incorrectly reads, "200,000". George Miller to *The Northern Islander*, 28 June 1855, in Miller, *Correspondence*, 21.
8. Ibid., 3–4. Smith, *American Prophet's Record*, 476 [3 May 1844], 477 [6 May 1844]. Quinn, *Origins of Power*, 122, 128. Jackson, *Adventures*, 32. Hansen, *Quest for Empire*, 86. George Miller to *The Northern Islander*, 28 June 1855, in Miller, *Correspondence*, 21.

the little plant is in a flourishing condition, and our prospects brighter than ever. Cousin Lemuel," referring to the American Indian, "is very friendly, and cultivating the spirit of peace and union in his family very extensively."[9]

On May 6, Sidney Rigdon was selected by the Council of Fifty to serve as Joseph's vice presidential running mate. Not having forgotten their differences, Joseph gave Sidney a blessing. "Let him be a candidate for Vice President, and place upon him every mark of honour and respect, that he may have every possible inducement to abide in the truth, being borne up by the good feelings of his brethren." Rigdon prepared to leave Nauvoo and take up residence in Pittsburgh.[10]

Steamboat elections, "the common mode of testing the success of candidates for the Presidency," were held for the amusement of passengers journeying the Mississippi River to gauge the strength of the various contenders. One tally was:

General Joseph Smith	20 gentlemen	&	5 ladies
Henry Clay	16		4
Martin Van Buren	7		0

On another occasion, it was "nip and tuck" between Van Buren and Joseph Smith. Each candidate received two votes.[11]

Up on the Nauvoo hill, recently excommunicated William Law (Joseph's former counselor) met with a number of his followers. In late March Joseph Smith had been informed that Law and Foster, together with Chauncey L. Higbee and non-Mormon Joseph H. Jackson, were engaged in a conspiracy to "destroy all the Smith family in a few weeks." On April 18, a meeting of the Nauvoo High Council and the Quorum of the Twelve was held to consider the matter. William Law, his wife Jane Law, Wilson Law, and Robert D. Foster "were cut off from the church by unanimous vote." The charge was "unchristianlike conduct." Law held the first conference of the Reformed Mormon Church on Sunday April 21. Membership in the fledgling organization soon numbered in the hundreds.[12]

Francis M. Higbee, one of the leaders of the reform movement, addressed a letter to Thomas Gregg, former editor of the *Warsaw Message*, presently working in Rock Island as assistant editor of the pro-Henry Clay *Upper Mississippian*. Higbee told Gregg that he had "purchased a 5 d press" with a 25" x 38" platen, "& fixtures," scheduled to arrive in a day or two on a riverboat from Quincy. The printing

9. Brigham Young and Willard Richards to Reuben Hedlock, 3 May 1844, in Smith, *History of the Church* 6: 351, 354.

10. Smith, *American Prophet's Record*, 477 [6 May 1844]. *Hyde, Speech*, 1845, 10 (candidate quote). This is not the best source, but is apparently the only published reference (Cook, *Revelations*, 364). The authors prefer to refer to the pronouncement as a blessing regarding Rigdon's vice presidency rather than a revelation. On Rigdon's departure from Nauvoo, see *Nauvoo Neighbor*, 8 May 1844. A short notice following Joseph Smith's *Views* notes, "President S. Rigdon is about to remove to Pittsburgh, the place of his former residence."

11. "Hurrah for the General!!," *Nauvoo Neighbor*, 8 May 1844. *Sangamo Journal*, 9 May 1844.

12. *Times and Seasons*, 5.8:511. See the response in the Preamble of the *Nauvoo Expositor*, 7 June 1844, beginning, "On Thursday evening, the 18th of April, there was a council called, unknown to the Church, which tried, condemned, and cut off brothers Wm. Law . . . which we contend is contrary to the book of Doctrine and Covenants."

supplies, purchased in St. Louis, would reach Nauvoo towards the middle of the month aboard the *Die Vernon*. Higbee exercised appropriate caution in not informing Gregg that the press had been purchased from fellow Whig Abraham Jonas. If the transaction became public knowledge, attention would be drawn immediately to the fact that the Illinois Whigs were behind the Mormon prophet's impending downfall.[13]

Despite a warning by Joseph Smith that a dissident press "shall not be set up in Nauvoo," Higbee assured Gregg that they would have the first issue off the press by the last week in May. "The paper I think we will call the <u>Nauvoo Expositor</u>," Higbee said.[14]

The Reformers, as they were known, continued to believe in the Book of Mormon and the Doctrine and Covenants (containing the earlier revelations of Joseph Smith). Joseph Smith *was* a prophet, they believed, but he had fallen from grace. The Reformers aimed to reveal Joseph Smith's "peculiar and particular mode of Legislation" (especially what they saw as his abuse of the right of habeas corpus) and supply a "dissertation upon his <u>delectable</u> plan of Government."

Informing the world about the secretive Council of Fifty and its political activities was not the only objective of the *Expositor*. Mormon polygamy was a more immediate target. "Above all," Higbee promised, "it shall be the organ through which we will herald his <u>mormon</u> ribaldry. It shall also contain a full and complete expose of his <u>mormon seraglio</u>, or <u>Nauvoo Harem</u>—; and his unparalleled and unheard of attempts at seduction." In a postscript Higbee suggested that Gregg "publish that portion of this [letter] you please or all if you see fit," and concluded with the words, "Yours in great haste."[15]

The "Prospectus of the *Nauvoo Expositor*" was published on May 10. It stressed that the oversize Imperial sheet would remain politically neutral ("without taking a decided stand in favor of either of the great Political Parties of the country") while advocating, in part, "the Unconditional Repeal of the Nauvoo City Charter . . . to restrain and correct the abuses of the UNIT POWER—to ward off the Iron Rod which is held over the devoted heads of the citizens of Nauvoo and the surrounding country—to advocate unmitigated DISOBEDIENCE to POLITICAL REVELATIONS . . . [by a] . . . SELF-CONSTITUTED MONARCH . . . to oppose, with uncompromising hostility any UNION OF CHURCH AND STATE or any preliminary step tending to the same."

The first issue was scheduled to appear on Friday, June 7, 1844. Sylvester Emmons, a non-Mormon member of the Nauvoo City Council, would serve as editor. "From an acquaintance with the dignity of character, and literary qualifications of

---

13. Francis Higbee to Thomas Gregg [May 1844], Mormon Collection, Chicago Historical Society. Leonard, *Nauvoo*, 362. Hogan, "Abraham Jonas," 19, and Waller, "Some Half-Forgotten Towns," 67. Smith, *American Prophet's Record*, 477 [7 May 1844], noted, "An opposition printing press arrived at Dr. Foster's from Columbus, Ohio [sic!] as reports says." Almon C. Babbitt's 1845 statement before the Illinois legislature, "The [*Expositor*] press in Nauvoo was established for political purposes by the Whigs" (Roberts, *Comprehensive History* 2:484), suggests that among the Mormons at least Babbitt knew the actual source of the opposition press.

14. *Warsaw Signal*, 22 May 1844.

15. Francis M. Higbee to Thomas Gregg [May 1844], Mormon Collection, Chicago Historical Society.

this gentleman," the Reformers believed, "assured that the 'Nauvoo Expositor,' must and will sustain a high and honorable reputation." The prospectus was signed by William Law, Wilson Law, Charles Ivins, Francis M. Higbee, Robert D. Foster, and Charles A. Foster.[16]

The Nauvoo home of William Law became the gathering place for disaffected Mormons and others sympathetic to the cause of the Reformers. "The new church appears to be going ahead," the *Warsaw Signal* reported. "On last Sunday," May 12, "there were about three hundred assembled at Mr. Law's house in Nauvoo, and listened with much seeming pleasure to a sermon from Elder Blakely, who denounced Smith as a fallen prophet. He treated the Spiritual wife doctrine without gloves, and repudiated Smith's plan on uniting Church and State." William Law, "in strong language," gave his reasons for withdrawing from the "false prophet." Francis M. Higbee read a series of resolutions which clarified the areas of disagreement and why they found it necessary to separate themselves from the main Mormon church, calling for "the repeal of the Nauvoo City Charter," the discontinuance of all "political revelations, and unconstitutional ordinances."[17]

Robert D. Foster, a justice of the peace recently cut off from the church, began collecting affidavits documenting polygamy at Nauvoo. William Law testified before Foster that Hyrum Smith showed him a "revelation from God . . . [which] authorized certain men to have more wives than one at a time, in this world and in the world to come. It said this was the law, and commanded Joseph to enter into the law . . . and also that he should administer [it] to others." Jane Law, William's wife, affirmed that she had also read the revelation, which "set forth that those women who would not allow their husbands to have more wives than one should be under condemnation before God."[18]

The initial Mormon response to the "Prospectus" was a letter dated May 12, published in the *Nauvoo Neighbor*. Written from the Nauvoo Mansion and signed "An American," the author asserted that the Mormons "have been most woefully misrepresented and abused . . . by persons who know nothing of their principles and doctrines . . . There is not a city within my knowledge that can boast of a more enterprising and industrious people than Nauvoo," the writer proclaimed. And, "General Smith is a man who understands the political history of his country as well as the religious history of the world, as perfectly as any politician or religionist I have ever met with. He advances ideas which if carried into effect would greatly benefit the nation in point of commerce and finance . . . Mr. Smith's 'Views of the Powers and Policy of the Government' manifest a Republican spirit, and if carried out, would soon place the nation in a prosperous condition." Claiming to be a non-Mormon, the writer had "heretofore been a warm advocate of the measures of the Whig party but, considering General Smith's views and sentiments to be worthy the applause of every citizen of the United States, and especially the yeomanry of the country, I

---

16. Prospectus of the *Nauvoo Expositor,* 10 May 1844, photostatic copy, Martin Collection, Regional Archives, Western Illinois University.

17. "The New Church appears to be going ahead," *Warsaw Signal,* 15 May 1844.

18. William Law affidavit, 4 May 1844, Jane Law affidavit, 4 May 1844, in *Nauvoo Expositor,* 7 June 1844.

shall in every instance advocate his principles and use my utmost influence in his favor."[19]

What "An American" failed to note was that on the day he wrote his supportive letter, Joseph Smith made an even stronger declaration of his views and destiny during the Sunday meetings. "God will always protect me until my mission is fulfilled," the prophet informed the Saints there assembled. "I calculate to be one of the instruments of setting up the Kingdom of Daniel by the word of the Lord," he said, "and I intend to lay a foundation that will revolutionize the whole world." He clarified his position. "It will not be by sword or gun that his kingdom will roll on: the power of truth is such that all nations will be under the necessity of obeying the Gospel." And yet personal sacrifice would also be required. "It may be that the Saints will have to beat their plows into swords, for it will not do for men to sit down patiently and see their children destroyed." That moment was rapidly approaching.[20]

Word soon reached Nauvoo that Henry Clay had been nominated by the Whig national meetings in Baltimore. "I arrived in the city two days after the great Whig convention," Council of Fifty member David S. Hollister wrote to the prophet. "All is joy and enthusiasm among the Whigs, while doubt and consternation are manifested among the Democrats. The convention has been got up at immense expense; hundreds of thousands of dollars have been expended." The Democratic national convention was scheduled for Baltimore on May 27, Hollister noted. "In the meantime," he would "do what [was] in [his] power for the promotion of the good cause."[21]

Dr. Goforth returned to Nauvoo in anticipation of the Mormon political convention to be held there on May 17. He had been invited by the "Friends of General Joseph Smith" to serve as a representative to the Illinois State Convention at Nauvoo and advance the interests of the Saints at an independent national convention (hosted by the Mormons) to be held in Baltimore in July.

The invitation was not by chance. Dr. Goforth was the only non-Mormon to make an address at the dedication of the Masonic hall earlier in the spring. His political reputation was considerable. Dr. Goforth had been a leading force behind the 1823 Illinois convention that nominated General Andrew Jackson for president. At that time Goforth was appointed chairman of the Committee of Resolutions. "The resolutions, then drafted were stigmatized by the whigs as the 'Goforth Resolutions,'—they went *forth* and general Jackson was elected." The Mormons were hopeful that Goforth might be equally successful in promoting Joseph Smith in 1844. "All the difference we look for now," one observer commented, "is that they will *goforth* a little quicker, and that Gen. Smith, will be elected the first trial."[22]

Goforth was accompanied by two gentlemen from the East, Josiah Quincy Jr. and Charles Francis Adams, a son of John Quincy Adams, whom he met on the steamship *Amaranth* following its departure from Quincy. Previous to their arrival in the Holy City, Goforth confided to the two men that he was "going to Nauvoo, to promote the election of the just nominated Henry Clay." Shortly after his arrival,

19. "An American" to the *Nauvoo Neighbor,* 12 May 1844, in Smith, *History of the Church* 6:367–68.

20. Smith, *History of the Church* 6:365.

21. David Hollister [Baltimore] to Joseph Smith, 9 May 1844, LDS Archives.

22. Editorial, *Nauvoo Neighbor,* 22 May 1844.

Goforth met with members of William Law's Reform movement. They encouraged Goforth to support them by publicly opposing Joseph Smith. Knowing that supporting the Reformers would undermine his own mission, Goforth was not yet prepared to join them.[23]

Adams and Quincy visited with the prophet, who expounded on his political views. Joseph Smith "denounced the Missouri Compromise as an unjustifiable concession for the benefit of slavery," Quincy recorded. The chief topic of conversation was "Henry Clay's bid for the presidency." The Boston visitor felt that "Dr. Goforth might have spared himself the trouble of coming to Nauvoo to electioneer for a duelist who would fire at John Randolph," in a contest arising out of charges that Clay had engaged in bribery and forgery, "but was not brave enough to protect the Saints in their rights as American citizens."

Joseph Smith concluded his political discourse by informing his distinguished visitors "what he would do, were he President of the United States," and expressed the hope that "he might one day so hold the balance between parties as to render his election to that office by no means unlikely." Adams and Quincy would depart Nauvoo on May 16.[24]

The time had now come for Joseph to reply to Henry Clay's letter of November 15, 1843. On the evening of May 15 Joseph had William W. Phelps "read [his] rejoinder to Clay's letter for the first time." It was a scathing retort, running to several closely spaced sheets. On the issues highlighted in *General Smith's Views*, Joseph was especially strident. "Your *shrinkage* is truly wonderful!" the prophet admonished the Kentucky senator.

> Not only your banking system, and high tariff project, have vanished from your mind 'like the baseless fabric of a vision,' but the 'annexation of Texas' has touched your pathetic sensibilities of national pride so acutely, that the poor Texians, your own *brethren*, may fall back into the ferocity of Mexico, or be sold at auction to British stock jobbers, and all is well, for 'I,' the old senator from Kentucky, am fearful it would militate against my interest in the north, to enlarge the borders of the union in the south—Truly 'a poor wise child is better than an old foolish king, who will be no longer admonished.' Who ever heard of a nation that had too much territory? Was it ever bad policy to make friends? Has any people ever become too good to do good? No, never; but the ambition and vanity of some men have flown away with their wisdom and judgment, and left a creaking *skeleton* to occupy the place of a noble *soul*.[25]

---

23. Josiah Quincy, Autobiography, in Mulder and Mortensen, *Among the Mormons*, 132. See Smith, *American Prophet's Record*, 470 [13 April 1844] about Dr. Goforth and Dr. Foster, "taken in secret council." Dr. Goforth had been "invited into the Laws' clique," according to Smith, *Words*, 376 [26 May 1844]. Also Smith, *History of the Church* 6:411, 438.

24. Josiah Quincy, Autobiography, in Mulder and Mortensen, *Among the Mormons*, 142, Quinn, *Origins of Power*, 135.

25. Smith, *American Prophet's Record*, 479 [15 May 1844]. Joseph Smith to Henry Clay, 13 May 1844, in *Times and Seasons*, 1 June 1844, 544–48, Hopkins and Hargreaves, *Papers of Henry Clay* 10:61. This last contains miscellaneous quotes only. Later publications of the letter include Roberts, *Rise and Fall of Nauvoo*, 380–98, and Hogan, "Henry Clay."

The State Convention at Nauvoo convened "according to appointment" on May 17, 1844, in the assembly room above Joseph Smith's store. General Uriah Brown, a non-Mormon businessman, inventor and member of the Council of Fifty, was appointed chairman. Dr. Goforth and other delegates presented their letters of introduction, which were read to the gathering:

> Joseph Smith of Nauvoo is recognized respectfully as a candidate, declarative in the principles of Jeffersonianism, or Jefferson democracy, free trade, and sailor's rights, and the protection of person and property.
>
> A convention being about to be held in the City of Nauvoo on the 17th of this month (May), your name has been on every occasion given as a delegate to said convention, and through me the message to be imparted you, asking you to represent our expressions in the case.
>
> Please say for us, as Americans, that we will support General Joseph Smith in preference to any other man that has given, or suffered his name to come before us as a candidate. And at the great Baltimore Convention, to be held on the 13th of July, our delegation to said convention be authorized to proclaim for us submission to the nominee as may be by them brought before the people, in case of a failure to nominate Joseph Smith (our choice), and unite approbatively for his support.[26]

Scribe William W. Phelps read Henry Clay's letter to Joseph Smith (dated November 15, 1843) and "General Joseph Smith's rejoinder," of May 13, "which was applauded by three cheers." Dr. Goforth reprised his 1823 role as head of the Committee for Resolutions, working together with Elder John Taylor, scribe William W. Phelps, Joseph's brother William Smith, and Elder Lucian R. Foster.[27]

Correspondence from New York's Central Committee of the National Reform Association, which had requested a statement on government policy from Joseph Smith, "as a candidate for public office," was also read. Joseph's response was confident.[28]

Following a recess, the convention appointed a "committee to appoint electors" for the state of Illinois (again headed by Dr. Goforth) and a "central committee of correspondence" (headed by Dr. Willard Richards). Delegates from the "different states of the Union were then received by vote." Attendance was somewhat low on account of "very heavy rains the preceding five days." Illinois, with 15 delegates, including gunsmith John Browning, had the largest contingent; New York had 10 delegates; Pennsylvania (4); Ohio (7); Virginia (1); Massachusetts (2); New Jersey (4); Louisiana (2); Mississippi (3); Delaware (2); Vermont (2); Missouri (1); Maine (1); Tennessee (1); Kentucky (2, including General George Miller, who, although a resident of Nauvoo, represented Madison County); Indiana (1); Connecticut (1);

---

26. Friends of Joseph Smith to Dr. G. W. [sic] Goforth, 4 May 1844, in Smith, *History of the Church* 6:386–87.

27. Smith, *History of the Church* 6:387.

28. John Windt, Egbert S. Manning, James Maxwell, Lewis Masquerier, Daniel Witter, George H. Evans, Ellis Smalley to Joseph Smith, 20 April 1844, in Smith, *History of the Church* 6:388. Joseph Smith to Central Committee of the National Reform Association, 17 May 1844, in Smith, *History of the Church* 6:388.

Maryland (1); Rhode Island (2); New Hampshire (1); Michigan (1); Georgia (1); Alabama (1); South Carolina (1); North Carolina (1); Iowa (1); Arkansas (1).[29]

"It was moved, seconded, and carried by acclamation, that General Joseph Smith, of Illinois, be the choice of this convention for President of the United States."

"It was moved, seconded, and carried by acclamation, that Sidney Rigdon, Esq., of Pennsylvania, be the choice of the Convention for Vice-President of the United States."

More than a dozen resolutions were adopted by the convention:

1. *Resolved,* that from all the facts and appearances that are now visible in the United States, we believe that much imbecility and fraud is practiced by the officers of Government; and that to remedy these evils it is highly necessary that a virtuous people should arise in the panoply of their might, and with one heart and one mind correct these abuses by electing wise and honorable men to fill the various offices of Government.

2. *Resolved,* that as union is power, the permanency and continuance of our political institutions depend upon the correction of the abuses.

3. *Resolved,* that as all political parties of the present day have degraded themselves by adhering more or less to corrupt principles and practices, by fomenting discord and division among the people, being swallowed in the vortex of party spirit and sectional prejudices, until they have become insensible to the welfare of the people and the general good of the country; and knowing that there are good men among all parties in whose bosoms burn the fire of pure patriotism, we invite them, by the love of liberty, by the sacred honor of freemen, by the patriotism of the illustrious fathers of our freedom, by the glorious love of country, and by the holy principles of '76, to come over and help us to reform the Government.

4. *Resolved,* that to redress all wrongs, the government of the United States, with the President at its head, is as powerful in its sphere as Jehovah is in His.

   (This reflected a major shift in the interpretation of the role of the president of the United States. The resolution argued that the president should become a protector of the oppressed, to "redress all wrongs," referring, of course, in part to the injuries suffered by the Saints during their tribulations in Ohio and Missouri.)

5. *Resolved,* that the better to carry out the principles of liberty and equal rights, Jeffersonian democracy, free trade, and sailor's rights, and the protection of person and property, we will support General Joseph Smith, of Illinois, for the President of the United States at the ensuing election.

6. *Resolved,* that we will support Sidney Rigdon, Esq., of Pennsylvania, for the Vice-Presidency.

7. *Resolved,* that we will hold a National Convention at Baltimore on Saturday, the 13th day of July.[30]

Orson Hyde, Heber C. Kimball, David S. Hollister, Orson Pratt, and Lyman Wight, all members of the Council of Fifty, were elected to serve as Baltimore convention representatives. Sidney Rigdon addressed the meeting. He exposed "the|

---

29. "State Convention," *Nauvoo Neighbor,* 22 May 1844.
30. Smith, *History of the Church* 6:390–92.

Jeffersonian Democracy.

Protection of Person and Property,

For President,
JOSEPH SMITH.
For Vice President,
SIDNEY RIGDON,

Electors for the State of Michigan,
Mephibosbeth Sirrine,
William Van Every,
Samuel Graham,
Alvan Hood,
Seth Taft.

Electoral ticket for the state of Michigan, Jeffersonian Democracy, 1844.
"George A. Smith Collection," *Salt Lake Herald,* 27 October 1892.

political dishonesty of both Henry Clay and Martin Van Buren . . . and the present [degraded] condition of the country." Rigdon was followed by General Joseph Smith and Dr. William Gano Goforth, Lyman Wight, William W. Phelps, John Taylor, Hyrum Smith, and John S. Reid, Esquire.[31]

Dr. Goforth expounded upon "the past glories of the republic, and the wrongs suffered by the Latter-day Saints in Missouri." Doubtless unnoticed by most, Dr. Goforth also maintained his commitment to the Whig cause. At the conclusion of his political speech the esteemed doctor promised to support "JOSEPH SMITH the proclaimer of Jefferson Democracy, of Free trade and Sailors rights and protection of Person and Property" at the July Baltimore convention. Unless, of course, there was a demonstrated "want of success in the nomination." In such a case (not forgetting his commission in the letter of invitation), Goforth would "instruct our delegates to say Henry Clay."[32]

A caucus was held that evening. Unable to attend due to the illness of his wife, Emma, Joseph later joined a spontaneous street meeting. The mood was exultant. A barrel of tar burned brightly. Toasts were made. The prophet's supporters raised him up on their shoulders, carried him "twice around the fire" and escorted him to the Nauvoo Mansion by a marching band. Joseph Smith's presidential campaign was officially under way.[33]

---

31. Ibid., 6:392.
32. Ibid. *Nauvoo Neighbor,* 22 May 1844.
33. Smith, *History of the Church* 6:397.

Chapter Ten

What Will Be the End of Things?

We have now fairly entered upon our electioneering campaign: from this time forth, forward is our motto, and in order to ensure success it will be necessary for us to use every exertion . . . Let every man who is a friend to Gen. Joseph Smith . . . use every endeavor to secure the election . . . It is not an idle farce that we are engaged in; but a solid reality . . . Several presses are already beginning to advocate his cause and others are expected soon, one has started in New York and one in this state. A gentleman has just informed us that he is going to Cincinnati for the purpose of commencing a paper advocating our cause, and the prospect brightens on every hand.

"A Word to Our Friends Abroad," *Nauvoo Neighbor*, May 22, 1844[1]

"Hang out the banner for Gen. Joseph Smith, and let the world know that we are not afraid to advocate his claims to the Presidential Chair."

William Smith, June 3, 1844[2]

"We noticed not a long time since, that his friends were stirring."

Niles' National Register, June 8, 1844[3]

THROUGHOUT THE MONTH OF MAY political missionaries departed Nauvoo. The movement was unprecedented. "At no period since the organization of the church," George Miller would write, "had there been half so many elders in the vineyard, in proportion to the number of members of the church. I preached and electioneered alternately."[4]

"Our mission is to visit the Eastern States and hold large meetings in every place we can. Preach the Gospel and electioneer for General Smith," twenty-seven-year-old

---

1. "A Word to our Friends Abroad," *Nauvoo Neighbor*, 22 May 1844. See also "Funny," *Warsaw Signal*, 8 May 1844.
2. William Smith to [George T. Leach], 3 June 1844, in *The Prophet*, 22 June 1844.
3. *Niles' National Register*, 8 June 1844.
4. George Miller to *The Northern Islander*, 28 June 1855, in Miller, *Correspondence*, 21.

George Albert Smith wrote in his journal on May 9, the day he left Nauvoo. Smith was not alone. He was joined by Jedediah M. Grant, just a year older than himself, and Wilford Woodruff, then 37. Smith and Woodruff were both apostles; all three men were members of the Council of Fifty. The elders rode in a lumber wagon as they embarked on their "political mission to the east."[5]

After riding four days "through constant rains, and over roads almost impossible for man or beast," the elders took dinner and rested at Ottawa, Illinois, nearly two hundred miles to the east of Nauvoo. An "advertisement" promoted a political meeting at the courthouse promising a "lecture upon the Subject of Gen Smith views of the government & c" by one of the apostles. Three hundred of the local citizens were gathered when they reached the meeting place. Elder George Albert Smith spoke to the assembly. "General Smith [is] the smartest man in the United States, and best calculated to fill the presidential chair," he told them. His remarks were greeted with applause.[6]

✳ ✳ ✳ ✳ ✳

Saturday, May 18, 1844.

Reformers James Blakesley, Francis M. Higbee, Charles Ivins, and Austin Cowles were excommunicated by the High Council of Nauvoo. The charge was "apostasy."[7]

The *Upper Mississippian* announced that Democrat Stephen A. Douglas had been nominated for a second term in Congress from Illinois's Fifth District. The Whigs expected to run O. H. Browning in opposition.[8]

Having concluded his unofficial campaign tour of the South, Senator Henry Clay returned to his Ashland estate near Lexington, Kentucky.[9]

Volume 1, Number 1 of the Mormon political newspaper *The Prophet* was published in New York City, issued by The Society for the Diffusion of Truth. "New York has hoisted her Ensign and cast her banner on the breeze, as an Advocate for equal rights and a supporter of our new candidate for the Presidency, the renowned and mysterious Prophet of the West, General Joseph Smith."[10]

✳ ✳ ✳ ✳ ✳

At Newark, Illinois, some thirty miles northeast of Ottawa, Elder Wilford Woodruff presided over a political meeting held in the local schoolhouse. General Joseph Smith's *Views of the powers and policy of the government of the United States* was read, followed by an address demonstrating "that Gen Smith took a line between the two parties on the banking system & ever[y] thing els[e] almost." Elder Woodruff spoke of the persecutions endured by the Saints, and "the danger the whole people of the United States

---

5. George A. Smith, Journal, 9 May 1844, quoted in Godfrey, "Causes of Conflict," 67.

6. Woodruff, *Journals* 2:397 [17 May 1844]. George A. Smith, Journal, 17 May 1844, quoted in Godfrey, "Causes of Conflict," 68.

7. Smith, *History of the Church* 6:398. See Brigham Young and Willard Richards to Reuben Hedlock, 3 May 1844, on list of major Reformers, in Smith, *History of the Church* 6:354.

8. *Upper Mississippian*, 18 May 1844.

9. *New-York Weekly Tribune*, 1 June 1844.

10. Boston Correspondent to the editor of *The Prophet*, 22 May 1844, in *The Prophet*, 25 May 1844.

were in of being destroyed by misrule & mob law if they permitted that principle to triumph." He suggested that "our claims & rights to cast our votes for a president" was the only proper recourse. Elder George Albert Smith concluded with "a spirited address upon politiks . . . [and] of the [poor] treatment we had received from the hands of Vanburen & Clay, & Calhoun &c." The meeting was a success. Woodruff wrote in his journal that day, "All who had spoken had the assistance of the Lord."[11]

At Joliet, Illinois, another thirty miles due east from Newark, within a day's journey of Chicago, the elders "delivered a lecture upon politiks." Elder Woodruff "felt inspired by the spirit of God" and "declaired in their midst our rights." He spoke of "our persecutions, General Smith's views, our treatment by the government" in Missouri and Washington. "We had the best attention of the people & a good impression was made."[12]

Lyman Wight and Heber C. Kimball departed Nauvoo May 21 aboard the steamboat *Osprey*. "Joseph Smith, the next President of the United States!" resounded on the waters of the Mississippi as the steamboat left the Nauvoo shore.[13]

Many of the 165 passengers on board listened with approval (and gave appropriate applause) to "a political address" that demonstrated "what right Joseph had to the presidential chair" and "that the other candidates had disqualified themselves to all the right and title, by acts of meanness." Steamboat balloting gave Joseph Smith "a large majority over all the other candidates." At St. Louis the elders called the members of the church together, almost seven hundred strong, "and instructed them spiritually and politically."[14]

Elder James C. Snow was assigned a "special mission" to Rush County, Indiana. When he reached the mission field, he "commenced to lay before the people the views and policy of President Joseph Smith relative to the government and laws of the United States, presenting him as a candidate for the ensuing presidential election." There was opposition at first. When "the people became better acquainted with his principles; prejudice then gave way, and hundreds in Rush and other counties were turned in favor of President Smith and the saints. Twenty were baptized into the church."[15]

George Miller "started to Kentucky" in the latter part of the month. When he arrived the entire region "was in a high state of political excitement, as it was just before their general election, which was to come off on the first Monday in August." Candidates sponsored barbeques and addressed the local citizens. At Clay rallies there were "log cabin exhibitions, and live raccoons at the top of long poles."

Miller found himself "at one of those meetings" and commenced reading "to a few of my old acquaintances Joseph Smith's views of the powers and policy of

---

11. Woodruff, *Journals* 2:399 [20 May 1844]. See also Godfrey, "Causes of Conflict," 68.

12. Woodruff, *Journals* 2:400 [21 May 1844].

13. Lyman Wight and Heber C. Kimball to Joseph Smith, 19 June 1844, in Smith, *History of the Church* 7:136.

14. Smith, *History of the Church* 7:136.

15. James C. Snow, affidavit, 17 November 1845, in Smith, *History of the Church* 7:527. David Pettigrew had a similar experience. When reading General Smith's *Views* to a non-Mormon populace, he found that "it was so far beyond anything they had heard before that it took with the people surprisingly," quoted in Robertson, "Campaign and the Kingdom," note 30.

government." A gentleman in the crowd interrupted him. "I have a matter to tell you as a friend," he said. "If you do not leave this country and put a stop to preaching your religious views and political Mormonism, the negroes are employed to hang you to an apple tree." He disregarded the "friendly" warning.

By this time Miller was gathering more of a crowd than the candidate who was then on the stand. Miller "got on a large stump, and commenced reading aloud Joseph's views on the powers and policy of government," followed by a short speech. Afterwards, Miller was "loudly and repeatedly cheered," and taken to a tavern two miles distant, "where they had a late dinner prepared for [his] benefit."[16]

Some political missionaries had less success. One elder preached to a gathering about "justice, government and corrupt rulers," which so enraged the people that they nearly mobbed the speaker. "The truth is I spoke the facts," he recorded in his journal, "and truth make[s] . . . people mad!"[17]

Elder Lorenzo Snow was appointed to supervise "the political interests of General Joseph Smith, as candidate for the presidential chair, in Ohio," his native state. Smith left Nauvoo and proceeded "by steamboat and stage" to Kirtland, in the northern part of Ohio. Once there, he had printed "several thousand pamphlets" of General Smith's *Views*. Securing a horse and buggy, Elder Snow traveled through the country, "lecturing, canvassing, and distributing pamphlets."

"Many people both Saints and Gentiles, thought this a bold stroke of policy," he recalled. "Our own people . . . were quite willing to use their influence and devote their time and energies to the promotion of the object in view." To those with little firsthand knowledge of Mormonism or Joseph Smith, "the [political] movement seemed a species of insanity." Others "with no less astonishment, hailed it as a beacon of prosperity to our national destiny."[18]

Word of the Nauvoo Convention soon reached New York City. On May 23, James Gordon Bennett of the *New York Herald* reported that Mormon "delegates [had been] appointed to the Baltimore Convention, who were instructed to make the best bargain they could with the candidates. They claim possession of from two hundred thousand to five hundred thousand votes in Nauvoo and throughout the Union, and with that they calculate that they can hold the balance of power and make whoever they please president." Bennett doubted "whether Clay or Van Buren will trade with them," but that "Captain John Tyler would outbid the others." He interpreted the movement to mean "that Joe Smith does not expect to be elected president, but he still wants to have a finger in the pie, and see whether something can't be made out of it."[19]

Two days later the New York editor of *The Prophet* proclaimed: "We this week have hoisted the banner and placed before the world as a candidate for the Chief Magistracy of this Republic, the Prophet of the last days, General Joseph Smith of Nauvoo, Ill." He pledged himself to "use our utmost endeavors to ensure his election,

16. George Miller to *The Northern Islander*, 28 June 1855, in Miller, *Correspondence*, 21.

17. James Flanagan, Diary, 8 May 1844, quoted in Godfrey, "Causes of Conflict," 69.

18. Lorenzo Snow, quoted in Smith, *Biography and Family Record*, 79. Snow referred to this as "my first and last electioneering tour." See also Robertson, "Campaign and the Kingdom," 149.

19. "Mormon Movements," *New York Herald*, 23 May 1844.

being satisfyed that he will administer the laws of his country without reference to party, sect or local prejudice. We have communications from various parts of the country, hailing his nomination with joy, and we feel confident that if the intelligence of the American people prevail over their prejudices, he will be elected by a large majority."[20]

The first Mormon "Jeffersonian Convention" was convened at Boston's Franklin Hall on Friday and Saturday, May 24 and 25. Apostle Parley P. Pratt (also of the Quorum of the Anointed and the Council of Fifty) was voted as chair. The convention passed resolutions promoting equal rights for all—abolitionists, Catholics, Latter-day Saints, and "black men [who otherwise would be] burned at the stake or tree"—members of groups who were often subject to lynch law. Speakers argued that "the people of these United (*distracted*) States are entirely destitute of an effective and energetic government," no longer "possessing the disposition or ability to administer the law in equity, and execute justice to its own citizens." In order to "reform the abuses of trust and power in every department of government" the Jeffersonians recommended the people "uphold by their influence and votes, an independent candidate for the Presidency," General Joseph Smith, "who will neither be a Whig, a Democrat, or pseudo democratic President, but a President of the United States; not a Southern man with Northern principles, or a Northern man with Southern principles; but an independant [sic] man with American principles." Delegates in favor of Joseph Smith as an independent candidate would hold a Massachusetts state convention on the first of July.[21]

In Dresden, Weakly County, Tennessee, a conference of elders proposed General Joseph Smith as a "suitable candidate for the presidency of the United States." General Smith's *Views*, together "with his claims on this government," were presented for the consideration of those present. This resulted in a large mob-like gathering that broke up the meeting. On the next day an elder "delivered a lecture on party politics, as taught by aspiring demagogues of the present day; those of the dominant parties now before the people of the United States." These were contrasted with the General Joseph Smith's *Views*, concluding "with an animated eulogium on Gen. Jackson's administration and held him to view as the standard of democracy." This time the meeting proceeded without incident. The body successfully appointed an elector for the district, and three thousand copies of General Smith's *Views* were ordered printed "for immediate distribution."[22]

✶ ✶ ✶ ✶ ✶

Sunday, May 26, 1844. Nauvoo, Illinois.

"My object is to let you know that I am right here on the spot where I intend to stay," the prophet announced from the stand at the Sunday morning meetings. "I, like Paul have been in perils, and oftener than anyone in this generation . . . I glory

---

20. Editorial, *The Prophet*, 25 May 1844.
21. "Jeffersonian Convention," *The Prophet*, 8 June 1844.
22. "Minutes of the general conference of the elders of the church . . . Dresden, Weakly County, Tennessee," *Times and Seasons*, 5.12:573–74.

in persecution." He had no doubt that "when facts are proved, truth and innocence will prevail at last.

"Come on! Ye prosecutors! Ye false swearers! All hell, boil over! Ye burning mountains, roll down your lava! For I will come out on the top at last." Joseph had, for the past three years, he said, maintained a "record of all my acts and proceedings" kept by "several good and faithful, and efficient clerks in constant employ" who accompanied him everywhere he went and recorded all of his activities. "My enemies cannot prove anything against me." He reviewed the circumstances of various affidavits, indictments, and charges made against him.

He turned to the matter of William Law and the Reformers. "It appears a holy prophet has risen up, and he has testified against me." Polygamy was the chief issue. Even at the start of his ministry, Joseph acknowledged, "I had not been married scarcely five minutes, and made one proclamation of the Gospel, before it was reported that I had seven wives." William Law had testified that Joseph Smith was "guilty of adultery."

"This spiritual wifeism!" Joseph countered. "A man asked me whether the commandment was given that a man may have seven wives; and now the new prophet has charged me with adultery . . . I am innocent of all these charges [of adultery], and you can bear witness of my innocence, for you know me yourselves."[23]

* * * * *

Writing from Nauvoo on business for the Council of Fifty, Willard Richards advised Orson Hyde, then in Washington, D.C. "Our great success at present depends upon our faith in the doctrine of election," he said. "Our faith must be made manifest by our works and every honorable exertion made to elect Gen. Smith . . . The election on the principle of Jeffersonian democracy, free trade, and protection of person and property, is gaining ground in every quarter."[24]

While on board the riverboat *Louis Philippe*, Lyman Wight met with David Guard of Lawrenceburg, Indiana, a thriving town on the Ohio River southwest of Cincinnati. A wealthy businessman, Guard had "emigrated to Cincinnati when there were but three log cabins in that place." Guard was in complete accord with Joseph's political platform, he said, and pledged to have General Smith's *Views* "published in both the Lawrenceburg papers." Guard was impressed by the General's openness, calling Joseph Smith, "the first man since the days of Washington and Jefferson, who had been frank and honest enough to give his views to the people before being elected." Guard was confident in the prophet's success, telling Wight if Joseph was "not elected this time, [he] would be the next."

Lyman Wight presided over a church conference in Cincinnati on May 27, and gave an address "on the subject of politics, and perseverance in duty, and the great necessity of reform in government." Heber C. Kimball and Brigham Young spoke on the same subjects. Two thousand copies of *General Smiths Views* were ordered to

---

23. Smith, *History of the Church* 6: 408–12. Hallwas and Launius, *Cultures in Conflict*, 138–41. Smith, *Words*, 373–77.

24. Willard Richards to Orson Hyde, 26 May 1844, in Smith, *History of the Church* 6:406.

be printed, and for the elders to "scatter them with the velocity of lightning and the voice of thunder."[25]

A meeting of the "friends of General Joseph Smith" convened in New York City on May 28, and proposed to hold "a State Convention of the friends of Gen Joseph Smith" at Utica, Oneida County, on August 23. "Electors favorable to the election of Gen. Smith to the presidency, [should] be selected by his friends in each Electoral district of the State" and attend the Utica Convention.[26]

The *New York Tribune* published a letter of warning the same day. Originally written at the conclusion of the April 23 political gathering in Nauvoo, the *Tribune* withheld the correspondence from publication until it was certain the Mormons would go forward with their plans for a national campaign. The author cautioned his readers that the threat of political Mormonism was real. It ended with a question the author wanted all Americans to consider: "What will be the end of things?"[27]

Between St. Louis and Pittsburgh, the traveling elders "conversed most of the time when awake upon religion and politics." At Pittsburgh Brigham Young parted company with William Smith, Heber C. Kimball, and Lyman Wight. Young would remain in Pittsburgh while the others continued "by steamer, stage and railway," until they reached Washington City, "preaching to, and thorning everybody with politics that came our way."[28]

"Your views upon the Texas-Oregon question, are quite popular in this country," aide-de-camp John F. Cowan reported to the prophet from New York City. "They begin to say now, Joe Smith is no fool after all. I say, I could have told them that long ago, if they had asked the question." Joseph Smith's petition to Congress to raise one hundred thousand troops was another matter and had created "quite an excitement throughout the country." Cowan advised caution. "Old fellow take care of your local matters in politics. Keep them light for the present. As there are many new things springing up. I have something to communicate to you, which is of great importance to your local matters, in a political way." It is not known what Cowan was referring to specifically in this cryptic passage, nor if he communicated his concerns to the prophet.[29]

Writing from Centerville, Kentucky, (just north of Henry Clay's Ashland estate) on June 1, Dr. Wall Southwick inscribed a letter, "Hon. Joseph Smith, Nauvoo, Ill." Describing himself as an "ambitious person" whose "schemes have met with disappointments," Dr. Southwick offered his services to the prophet, "determined to make [his desires] subservient to the more fortunate man." He was young, just 29, had

---

25. Lyman Wight and Heber C. Kimball to Joseph Smith, 19 June 1844, in Smith, *History of the Church* 7:136–37.

26. "Public Meeting," *The Prophet*, 1 June 1844.

27. "W." [Nauvoo, Illinois] to the editors of the *Missouri Republican*, 25 April 1844, *New York Tribune*, 28 May 1844. Graham, "Presidential Campaign," 79. The letter would appear in the *Clay Tribune* on June 8.

28. Summary of letter from Heber C. Kimball to his family in Nauvoo. "He wrote from Pittsburgh , saying they arrived May 30." (Kimball, "Journal and Letters," 90, transcription from New Mormon Studies CD-ROM). Lyman Wight and Heber C. Kimball to Joseph Smith, 19 June 1844, in Smith, *History of the Church* 7:137.

29. John F. Cowan to Joseph Smith, 31 May 1844, LDS Archives.

a classical education, and much recent experience, both "Financial and Political," in Texas, where he had become familiar "with men, & measures in that country. A knowledge of which I am certain will be of service to you, and which I am anxious to confer with you personally." One small obstacle remained. "I was on my way to your city, when an accident deprived me of the means of doing so, the accident to which I refer, was the sinking of the [riverboat] Buckeye and loss of all my money, except a small sum which I had in my pocket at the time . . . if you will send me money enough to carry me to your place, I hope I shall be able to convince you that the small sum was not badly expended."[30]

A land developer in Galveston City, the Republic of Texas, offered the prophet a substantial parcel of Texas acreage on which to remove the Saints. "I need not point out to a mind as ambitious and discerning as yours the advantages which would certainly result to you from the settlement of such a tract in this country. Should you remove here with all of your adherents you would at once acquire the controlling vote of Texas, and might yourself aspire to and obtain any Office in the Republic." As an additional assurance of Mormon success, he added, "Mexico is doomed."[31]

✯ ✯ ✯ ✯ ✯

June 3, 1844

In the U.S. House of Representatives, Illinois Whig John J. Hardin spoke out against expansionist James K. Polk, the newly nominated Democratic candidate for president of the United States, denouncing his proposed plans for the "re-annexation" of Texas.[32]

Orville Hickman Browning wrote to Abraham Jonas, declining the Whig nomination for Congress from Illinois's Fifth District. Browning had been "almost entirely confined with severe indisposition" since mid-April, he informed Jonas, and requested that his name be removed from consideration at the Whig nominating convention scheduled for June 5. Browning would be replaced by David A. Woodson, who would face incumbent Democrat Stephen A. Douglas. In Illinois's Seventh Congressional District, Whig Edward D. Baker was selected to run for the seat vacated by John J. Hardin.[33]

Judge John McLean arrived in Springfield, Illinois, in preparation for the June session of the United States Circuit Court.[34]

William Smith, Mormon apostle and brother of the prophet Joseph, reached Philadelphia. "The news from the West is all very good," he wrote to the publisher of *The Prophet*. "I mentioned to [the Council of Fifty] concerning your publishing

30. Wall Southwick to Joseph Smith, 1 June 1844, in *Warsaw Signal*, 31 July 1844.
31. John H. Walton [Galveston City, Republic of Texas] to Joseph Smith, 3 June 1844, LDS Archives. The first portion of this letter is also quoted in Van Wagenen, *Mormon Kingdom*, 48. Van Wagenen, 47, notes that the proposed land was in "northern Texas between the Red and Trinity Rivers."
32. *Speech of Mr. J. J. Hardin of Illinois*. Cox, "Hardin," 154–55.
33. Orville Hickman Browning to Abraham Jonas, 3 June 1844, in *Quincy Whig*, 26 June 1844.
34. Complete Record Law 1-A 1843– [#1687] Circuit Court U.S.A. S.D. Illinois, 250. [#1603] 4:231 (NARA, Chicago). McLean had returned to Cincinnati by 1 July 1844. Order Book U.S. Circuit Court S.D. Ohio, 215 (NARA, Chicago).

a paper in New York, and the Prophet bid it God speed: the council also sanctioned it by a loud and general vote, to 'go ahead' and do the best you can." William Smith had also spoken at length with Elders Lyman Wight and Heber C. Kimball, then "on their way to Washington, to talk with the (would be) big men of the earth, on the state of a rotten and crumbling Government." "It is evident that there is a 'shaking among the dry bones,'" portent of a revolution in the established political order, Smith continued. He believed

> the late nomination for President and Vice President at the Baltimore Convention [James K. Polk and George M. Dallas] proves that fact: Matty's [Van Buren's] subject, "can't do nothing for you," (meaning the Mormons) has occasioned a great flare up in their ranks, and brought two entire new candidates in the field, although they say it is the great and important question of annexation that has done it:—No sir, these men, perhaps, have not committed themselves on the Missouri and Mormon question, hence must be entitled to Mormon votes.

Given the new look of presidential politics in the capital, William Smith was confident that the petitions from the Council of Fifty would receive a sympathetic hearing. "Brs. L. Wight and H. C. Kembal [sic] are in Washington, and they are regular go-ahead men, and they will unveil the mask, and give them Davy Crockett and Mormon politics, Gentile Mobocratic principles 'right side up with care.'"[35]

✳   ✳   ✳   ✳   ✳

William Smith's prediction notwithstanding, the two Council of Fifty Washington emissaries were not as successful as they had hoped. Elders Kimball and Wight did succeed in getting a petition signed, "with our names attached, in behalf of the church, asking for a remuneration for our losses [in Missouri]," however there was no mention of Mormon "rights, or redress, for they would not receive such a petition from us." Illinois Representative Semple promised "he would do the best he could" and gave the petition to the chairman of the Committee on Public lands. Perhaps sensing that their request had a poor chance of passage, Elder Kimball wrote to his wife in Nauvoo. "I want to see our Prophet here in the Chare [Chair] of Stat[e]s," he said. Then "we will go where we can find a home and worship God in his own way, and injoy our rits [rights] as free citizens."[36] But before Joseph could become president, and before the Kingdom of God could become a viable reality, dissenters at Nauvoo would strike at the very foundation of the Mormon movement.

35. William Smith [Philadelphia] to [George T. Leach, New York City], 3 June 1844, in *The Prophet*, 22 June 1844. On Leach, see Crawley, *Descriptive Bibliography*, 255.

36. Lyman Wight and Heber C. Kimball to Joseph Smith, 19 June 1844, in Smith, *History of the Church* 7:138. Heber C. Kimball to Helen Mar Kimball, 9 June 1844, quoted in Quinn, *Origins of Power*, 135.

Chapter Eleven

Retributive Justice

"THIS DAY THE *Nauvoo Expositor* goes forth to the world," Mormon dissident and reformer William Law wrote in his journal on Friday, June 7, "rich with facts, such expositions as make the guilty tremble and rage. 1000 sheets were struck and five hundred mailed forthwith. If the paper is suffered to continue it will set forth deeds of the most dark, cruel and damning ever perpetrated by any people under the name of religion since the world began."[1]

The Reform movement was initiated by church members hoping to promote change within the Church of Jesus Christ of Latter-day Saints "without a public exposition." When private negotiations proved ineffective, and William Law and others were excommunicated without a proper hearing, the dissenters determined to accomplish their objectives through the deliberate exercise of their basic rights: freedom of speech, freedom of the press, and freedom to worship God as they saw fit. "We are aware," the Reformers acknowledged in the *Expositor's* premier issue, "we are hazarding every earthly blessing, particularly property, and probably life itself, in striking this blow at tyranny and oppression."[2]

From the beginning of their opposition to Joseph Smith, the Reformed Mormon Church advocated repeal of the Nauvoo Charter. When the "opposition press" was set up in Nauvoo, and not in the safe havens of Carthage or Warsaw, some concluded that the Reformers intended more than a change in city government. As one observer noted, the *Nauvoo Expositor* was purposefully "designed as an engine to bring destruction upon the city of Nauvoo" and, ultimately, death to the prophet Joseph Smith and his brother Hyrum.[3]

Even so, the preamble of the *Expositor* made it clear the schismatics were not opposed to many of Joseph Smith's early teachings. " We all verily believe, and many of us know of a surety," the preamble stressed, "that the religion of the Latter Day Saints, as originally taught by Joseph Smith, which is contained in the Old and New Testaments, Book of Covenants, and the Book of Mormon, is verily true; and that the

---

1. William Law, Diary, 7 June 1844, in Cook, *William Law*, 55. See also Smith, *American Prophet's Record*, 488 [7 June 1844]. Robert D. Foster to Joseph Smith, 7 June 1844, in *Warsaw Signal* 12 June 1844, Hallwas and Launius, *Cultures in Conflict*, 151. Smith, *History of the Church* 6:430.
2. "Preamble," *Nauvoo Expositor*, 7 June 1844.
3. See "P. S." of [unknown author] to Thomas Sharp, 8 June 1844, in *Warsaw Signal*, 12 June 1844. Clayton, Temple History, in Clayton, *Intimate Chronicle*, 541.

NAUVOO EXPOSITOR.

—THE TRUTH, THE WHOLE TRUTH, AND NOTHING BUT THE TRUTH.—

VOL. I.]   NAUVOO, ILLINOIS, FRIDAY, JUNE 7, 1844.   [NO. 1.

But here his musings were interrupted by the clatter of horses' hoofs, approaching at a swift pace behind him, and the next moment a horseman, muffled in a large cloak, reined up his steed, with a powerful jerk, at his side. They rode on for some distance in silence, until Henry, for that was our hero's name, addressed him with—

"A fine evening, sir!"

"It is," answered the stranger—whose features and accent denoted him to be a foreigner—"It is very fine." Then, after a pause he continued: "Being a stranger in this country, I should feel obliged, sir, if you would direct me to the village of E——."

"Willingly," replied Henry; "it is to E—— that I am going, and, if I shall not intrude, shall be happy to accompany you."

The stranger expressed his thanks, and, after a short time resumed:

"I suppose you reside in E——, sir?"

"Why, not exactly a resident, but rather a frequent visitor, as you may suppose," answered the light-hearted Henry, "when I tell you that the magnet which attracts me is a lady."

"And by such a magnet," replied the stranger, with a sigh, "I have been drawn from the sunny shores of Italy; attend awhile, and, in return for your confidence, you shall hear my story, and during its relation, our horses will cool:

"About a year ago, there came to Naples an old gentleman with his wife, who was an invalid, and a lovely daughter. They engaged a villa near the one in which I resided; I, thereby, became acquainted with the gentleman, who invited me to his house; but as his daughter was constantly in attendance on her mother, I never could meet her. I called again and again for the same purpose, but was as often disappointed, until shortly after, the old lady dying, I with some other neighbors, was invited to the funeral. I saw her then in all the loveliness

ing into the bower, clasped her to his breast. The blush which overspread her face at being thus caught, was dispelled by the joy of beholding him in whom her earthly happiness was centred.

"Now, I declare," said Adeline, playfully tapping his shoulder, "that you have become quite a truant! I have not seen you for more than a *whole day*."·

"Sweetest," replied Henry, embracing her, "you must forgive me; I staid but to settle some affairs *now*, that I might not again be torn from you—though I must confess that I should have been here earlier but for nay, have not so hardly, Adeline, it was a *man*, and if you heard his story, you would, I have no doubt, forgive him the delay he caused *me*—but you shall hear it some other time."

Adeline, however, would rather hear it *then*. Henry, therefore, relating the story of the stranger, and looking at Adeline, as he concluded, was surprised to find her in tears.

"Dearest Adeline," exclaimed he, taking her hand, "let it not affect you thus; he will, I dare say, be made happy as you will make *me* to-morrow."

"Henry," replied Adeline, with a deep sigh, "I am more concerned in this unhappy tale than you imagine; I have reason for supposing that I am the female of whom he is in search."

"You! Adeline?"

"I have not mentioned this before, lest you should think me vain, but I will tell you now. You already know, my dear Henry, that my mother, being in a bad state of health, by the physician's advice, we went to reside at Naples. When we had been there but a short time, my father formed an acquaintance with an Italian nobleman, who, on the death of my mother, made me an offer in marriage; but, notwithstanding his wealth and station, the person, I felt that I could not love him, even if *you* had not already possessed my affections. On my rejec-

ses to her; so I up un told um that as how I b'lieved so, and that there was a weddin up there this morning. Lord love you, sir, he look'd the colour o' old white Peggy there, till I thought the mon war gone crazy; but he starts off all at once towards yer honer's house: so I thought, maybe, he was an old friend, and war in order 'cause ye—— didn't ax him to the wedding."

"Well, my good fellow, did he not say anything at starting, this morning?"

"Oh, he war as grumpy as may be, an' only ax'd the nearest way to the sea, so I told un the *nearest*, which, yer honer knows, lays *clean over the cliff*."

De Moncey could not help smiling at the oddity of the direction; and, rewarding the man for his information, they returned home.

"I have no longer any doubt, Henry, was my Italian friend, who, on finding the hopelessness of the case, and moreover that you, to whom he seems to have taken a liking, were his rival, has departed in despair."

They had now reached the house, when Henry, espying his beloved in the garden, ran to acquaint her with the result of their walk. She was greatly relieved by the news; and, with light hearts, they entered the breakfast-room. The breakfast was soon dispatched, and the joyous party set out on their journey to the church, which was situate at one end of the park, through which, as the cavalcade passed, it was saluted by the glad shouts of the assembled tenantry, whose merry faces bore witness of the general joy, and added additional pleasure to the good De Moncey.

They had now arrived at the church; and the happy bridegroom handing out his blushing bride, they proceeded gaily up the little path which led to the door. Approaching through the porch, Adeline slightly trembled. Henry stopped to kiss her hand; and, in an

—we forget! and when at last we arise with exhausted strength from the sick-bed, and creep to the window, the first gush, during the illness of the body, conspire to soften the feelings; the still room; the mild twilight through the window curtains; the low voices; and then, more than all, the kind words of those who surround us; their attention, their solicitude, perhaps a tear in their eyes; all this does us good; and when the wise Solomon enumerated all the good things which have their time upon the earth, he forgot to celebrate sickness among the rest.

"Better laugh than cry."—So say we. It's no use rubbing one's eyes, and blubbering over all 'the ills that flesh is heir to.' Red eyes caused by any thing but grief or its kindred are scandalous looking affairs. The best way is to "stand up to the rack," and take the good things and the evil as they come along, without repining; and always cheering yourself with that philosophical ejaculation, "better luck next time."

Is dame fortune as shy as a weasel? Tell her to go to thunder, and laugh her in the face. The happiest fellow we ever saw, slept upon a plank—and hadn't a shilling in his pocket, nor a coat to his back.

Do you find "disappointment lurking in many a prize?" Then throw it away, and laugh at your own folly for pursuing it.

Does fame elude your grasp? Then laugh at the fools that are so often her favorites. She's of no consequence any how, and never buttered a piece of bread or furnished a man a clean dickey.

Is your heart broken by
"Some maiden fair,
Of bright blue eyes and auburn hair?"
Then thank your stars that you have escaped with your neck, and make the welkin ring with a hearty laugh.
It lightens the weight of one's heart

Nauvoo Expositor masthead, vol. 1, no. 1.

pure principles set forth in those books, are the immutable and eternal principles of heaven." Mormonism as initially formulated and practiced was an uplifting religious creed, the Reformers asserted: "Its precepts are invigorating, and in every sense of the word, tend to dignify and ennoble man's conceptions of God and his atributes [sic]." Lately, however, concerns had arisen about Joseph's control of land sales in Nauvoo and several doctrinal "innovations" introduced by the prophet. Most prominent among these was the troubling doctrine of the "plurality of wives."[4]

By the spring of 1844, Joseph Smith, his brother Hyrum, Brigham Young, Willard Richards, Heber C. Kimball, and several other church leaders were actively engaged in the practice of plural marriage. The justification for polygamy, or "the principle," as it became known, was scriptural. Indeed, Joseph firmly believed the work he was engaged in involved the "restoration of all things," including the ancient Hebrew custom of having "many wives and concubines." Joseph, as the prophet, was the most

---

4. "Preamble," *Nauvoo Expositor*, 7 June 1844.

active polygamist. By spring of 1844, Joseph Smith had instituted plural marriages with more than thirty women. Eighteen of his wives were single when they entered into the "new and everlasting covenant" with the prophet; four were widows. Eleven of the women were married to other men at the time they became Joseph's plural wives; the women continued to live with their first husbands in order to conceal their relationship (consummated or not) with the prophet.[5]

Not all of the women Joseph solicited submitted to his entreaties. The most publicly embarrassing refusal was Joseph's attempt, in 1842, to marry Nancy Rigdon, daughter of counselor Sidney Rigdon, himself a vocal opponent of polygamy. At the time she was being courted by twenty-three-year-old Francis M. Higbee. By early 1844, Higbee had become an influential dissident. Jane Law, wife of former counselor William Law, was unsuccessfully propositioned by Joseph in the spring of 1844. The Reformers opposed these "abominations and whoredoms" because they were not "consonant with the principles of Jesus Christ and the Apostles."[6]

Polygamy wasn't the only issue. "Among the many items of false doctrine that are taught in the Church," the *Expositor* maintained, "is the doctrine of many Gods . . . We do not know what to call it other than blasphemy, for it is most unquestionably, speaking of God in an impious and irreverent manner." The Reform movement also opposed the practice of a "second anointing" (one of the "mysteries") bestowed upon a select few at Nauvoo (especially members of the Anointed Quorum)—an "unconditional sealing up [to eternal life] against all crimes, save that of shedding innocent blood." The Reformers requested "all those holding license to preach the gospel, who know they are guilty of teaching the doctrine of other Gods above the God of this creation . . . and all other doctrines, (so called) which are contrary to the laws of God, or to the laws of our country, to cease preaching, and to come and make satisfaction, and have their licenses renewed."

The dissenters also bridled at Joseph's bold "attempt at Political power and influence, which we verily believe to be preposterous and absurd. We believe it is inconsistent, and not in accordance with the christian religion. We do not believe that God ever raised up a Prophet to christianize a world by political schemes and intrigue." The Reformers allowed that Joseph could certainly "plead he has been injured, abused, and his petitions treated with contempt by the general government, and that he only desires an influence of a political character that will warrant him redress of grievances." Despite their own claims of unjust persecution, they protested, "we care not—the faithful followers of Jesus must bear [abuse and injury] in this age as well as Christ and the Apostles did anciently."[7]

Sylvester Emmons, the non-Mormon editor of the *Expositor*, wrote an introductory statement of principles. "We believe religious despotism to be incompatible with our free institutions," he said. "In relation to [partisan] politics, whatever our own views may be upon the federal measures that now, or may, hereafter agitate the country,

---

5.   Compton, *In Sacred Loneliness.* LDS scriptural passages on "many wives and concubines" include Doctrine and Covenants 132:37, 38, and 39. On the "new and everlasting covenant" see Doctrine and Covenants 22, 45:9, 131:2, 4, 6, and 19.

6.   "Preamble," *Nauvoo Expositor,* 7 June 1844.

7.   "Preamble" and "Resolution 14," *Nauvoo Expositor,* 7 June 1844.

the *Expositor* will not be the exponent thereof; and all the strife and party zeal of the two great antagonistical parties for the success of their respective candidates for the Presidency, we shall remain neutral, and in an editorial capacity, inactive."

Of greater concern was the rise of Joseph Smith's independent political movement that "has sprung up in our midst, the leader of which, it would seem, expects, by a flourish of Quixotic chivalry, to take, by storm, the Presidential chair." Once in the executive chair, Emmons noted correctly, Joseph planned to "distribute among his *faithful* supporters, the office of governor in all the different States, for the purpose, we presume, of more effectually consolidating the government." Emmons himself was "disposed to treat" the movement "with a little levity, but nothing more."

There remained one other crucial matter—the prophet's controversial use of the right of habeas corpus—which Emmons believed was far more serious in its potential consequences than even Joseph's political aspirations. A case in point was the matter of one Jeremiah Smith, who had been indicted for embezzlement. Arrested by a U.S. marshal who had tracked the fugitive to Nauvoo, Smith was released by Joseph's municipal court on a writ of habeas corpus. That an accused federal fugitive could be protected and aided by Nauvoo civil authorities was an outrage. "It is too gross a burlesque," submitted Emmons, "a subterfuge too low to indicate any thing but a corrupt motive." Jeremiah Smith, as it so happened, was a blood relation of the Mormon prophet.[8]

An article in the main body of the *Expositor* examined Joseph Smith's bid for the presidency in more detail. "It appears to be a new rule of tactics for two rival candidates to enter into a discussion of their respective claims to that high office, just preceding an election," the author noted. On May 29 the *Nauvoo Neighbor* had published the incendiary correspondence between Joseph Smith and Henry Clay. "If . . . any individual voter, who has a perfect right to know a candidates [sic] principles, should not be satisfied," by a glance at his *Views* and this new correspondence, "he may further aid his inquiries, by a reference to the record of the grand inquest of Hancock County [where] Joseph Smith, the candidate of another 'powerful' party has two indictments against him, one for fornication and adultery, another for perjury. Our readers can make their own comments."[9]

The approaching August elections were of more immediate concern. "Hiram Smith is already in the field as a [Democratic] candidate for the legislature," Francis M. Higbee noted in an article addressed to the non-Mormon citizens of Hancock County. He prompted his readers to recall the events of the previous summer. "Will you support him, that same Hyrum Smith the devoted follower and brother of Joe, who feigned a revelation from God, directing the citizens of Hancock County to vote for J. P. Hoge, in preference to Cyrus Walker, and by so doing blaspheming the name of God? Will you . . . support a man like that . . . one who will trifle with the things of God, and feign converse with the Divinity, for the sake of carrying an election?"

Higbee's second charge went beyond local politics. "In supporting Hyrum Smith, you, citizens of Hancock County, are supporting Joseph Smith, for whom he (Hyrum) goes tooth and toe nails, for President of the United States. The question

---

8.   "Introductory," *Nauvoo Expositor*, 7 June 1844.
9.   "Joe. Smith-The Presidency," *Nauvoo Expositor*, 7 June 1844.

may arise here, in voting for Joseph Smith, for whom am I voting? You are voting for a man who contends all governments are to be put down and the one established upon its ruins. You are voting for an enemy to your government . . . You are voting for a sycophant, whose attempts for power find no parallel in history. You are voting for a man who refuses to suffer criminals to be brought to justice . . . a man who stands indicted, and who is now held to bail, for the crimes of adultery and perjury; two of the greatest crimes known to our laws. Query not then for whom you are voting; it is for one of the blackest and basest scoundrels that has appeared upon the stage of human existence since the days of Nero, and Caligula."[10]

Joseph Smith lost no time in responding to the charges levied by the *Expositor* and called for an extraordinary meeting of the city council on Saturday June 8. Joseph "made a long speech in favor of having an ordinance to suppress Libels &c. in Nauvoo." A committee was formed to draft a document which would "prevent misrepresentations and libelous publications, and conspiracies against the peace of the city." The prophet also spoke to the desirability of "first purging the City Council." Sylvester Emmons, a current city councilman, was suspended from council and "cited to appear at the next regular term of the Council on impeachment."[11]

The "character of the paper and proprietors" were next attacked. Council of Fifty member Theodore Turley, a gunsmith who was later valued for his skill at producing dies for minting counterfeit coin, testified that William and Wilson Law "had brought Bogus Dies for him to fix."[12]

"What good has Foster, and his brother, and the Higbee's, and Laws ever done?" Hyrum inquired of the council. "Who was Judge Emmons? When he came here he had scarce two shirts to his back, but he had been dandled by the authorities of the city." Emmon's "right-hand man" was Francis M. Higbee, "who had confessed to [Hyrum] that he has the P** [pox, syphillis]."

Joseph Smith, as mayor, went before the city council, arguing that the *Expositor* printing establishment should be declared a nuisance. He read aloud Sylvester Emmon's editorial in the *Expositor*. "Who ever said a word against Judge Emmons until he attacked this council?" Joseph asked. "Or even against Joseph H. Jackson [a non-Mormon with close ties to the dissenters who claimed Joseph Smith was actively engaged in counterfeiting U.S. coin] or the Laws, until they came out against the city? Here is a paper that is exciting our enemies abroad . . . They make it a criminality, for a man to have a wife on the earth, while he has one in heaven, according to the keys of the Holy Priesthood."[13]

---

10. Francis M. Higbee, "Citizens of Hancock County," *Nauvoo Expositor*, 7 June 1844.
11. "City Council, Regular Session minutes," *Nauvoo Neighbor*, 19 June 1844. On the proceedings, see Smith, *American Prophet's Record*, 488–90 [8–11 June 1844]. The most accessible version of the minutes, and that used here, can be found in Hallwas and Launius, *Cultures in Conflict*, 150–56. Smith, *American Prophet's Record*, 489 [8 June 1844]. Clayton, Nauvoo Journal 2 [10 June 1844], in Clayton, *Intimate Chronicle*, 132. G. T. M. Davis, *Authentic Account*, 13. Smith, *American Prophet's Record*, 489 [10 June 1844], reads, "I immediately ordered . . ." Compare Smith, *History of the Church* 6:448.
12. On Turley and counterfeiting see Clayton, Nauvoo Journal 3, in Clayton, *Intimate Chronicle*, 230 and Quinn, *Origins of Power*, 529, 650, 654.
13. See Jackson, *Adventures*, 11–12 and 15–16 on Joseph Smith's counterfeiting activity. Brooke, *Refiner's Fire*, 268–71, also discusses Mormons and counterfeiting at Nauvoo.

William Law's affidavit describing Joseph's 1843 revelation on plural marriage was read, followed by several additional statements regarding the practice of polygamy at Nauvoo. Joseph protested "that he preache[d] on the stand from the Bible, shewing the order in ancient days, having nothing to do with the present times."

"I would rather die to-morrow and have the thing smashed," Joseph said, "than live and have it go on, for it [is] exciting the spirit of mobocracy among the people and bringing death and destruction upon us."

Hyrum concurred with his brother, and reaffirmed that the revelation on plural marriage referred to "was in reference to former days, and not the present time." Joseph "said he had never preached the revelation in private . . . [and] . . . had not taught [it] to the anointed in the church in private." The "truth" of his statements denying the practice of plural marriage were confirmed by many council members then present. Ironically, several of the men were themselves active polygamists.

Mayor Joseph Smith read Francis M. Higbee's article from the *Expositor* and took offense at its strident language. "Is it not treasonable against all chartered rights and privileges, and against the peace and happiness of the city?" Joseph asked.

Hyrum expressed his support "in favor of declaring the *Expositor* a nuisance."

"No city on earth would bear such slander," John Taylor added. He was "decidedly in favor of active measures." Referring to previous minutes of the municipal body, Taylor pointed out, "Wilson Law was president of this [Municipal] Council during the passage of many ordinances . . . William Law and Emmons were members of [the City] Council, and Emmons has never objected to any ordinance while in the Council," he said. Judge Emmons, Taylor felt, was "more like a cypher, and is now become Editor of a libelous paper, and is trying to destroy our charter and ordinances." Taylor read from the United States Constitution concerning freedom of the press. "We are willing they should publish the truth," Taylor said. "But it is unlawful to publish libels; the *Expositor* is a nuisance, and stinks in the nose of every honest man."

Mayor Joseph Smith read from the Illinois Constitution, Article 8, Section 12, "touching the responsibility of the press for its constitutional liberty."

Citing the legal authority of Blackstone on private wrongs, another councilman pointed out that "a nuisance was any thing that dtsturbs [sic] the peace of a community," and thus can be suppressed.

Hyrum "believed the best way [to be rid of the nuisance] was to small the preess [sic] and 'pi' the type."

After considerable discussion, Councilman Warrington, who "did not belong to any church or any party," spoke up. He "thought it might be considered rather harsh for the council to declare the paper a nuisance, and proposed giving a few days limitation and assessing a fine of $3,000 for every libel and if they would not cease publishing libels to declare it a nuisance and said the statues made provisions for a fine of $500."

Orson Spencer, a Mormon alderman, disagreed. He considered the *Expositor* a nuisance, and did not think it "wise to give them time to trumpet a thousand lies, their property could not pay for it; if we pass only a fine or imprisonment, have we any confidence that they will desist? None at all! We have found these men covenant breakers with God! With their wives!!"

William W. Phelps reported on his investigation of the "constitution, charter, and laws." The Municipal Council of Nauvoo, he said, had "the power to declare that office a nuisance" and that "a resolution declaring it a nuisance is all that is required."

One man provided testimony that "Francis M. Higbee, and Wm. Law, declared they had commenced their operations, and would carry them out, law or no law." Stephen Markham reported that "Francis M. Higbee said the interest of this city is done, the moment a hand is laid on their press."

On Monday afternoon, an "ordinance concerning Libels" was approved by Nauvoo's City Council, followed by a resolution (which passed "unanimously, with the exception of Councillor Warrington") declaring the *Nauvoo Expositor* a public nuisance. "The Mayor is instructed to cause said printing establishment and papers to be removed without delay, in such manner as he shall direct. Passed June 10th, 1844." The time was 5:30 P.M.

Joseph "immediately ordered the marshal to destroy it without delay." Joseph also instructed Jonathan Dunham, Major General of the Nauvoo Legion, "to assist the Marshal with the Legion if called upon to do so."[14]

At the time the resolution was approved, William Law and several other dissidents were at the county seat. That morning, Law, Dr. Foster, and Charles Ivins "went to Carthage. It was the day of the sale of lands for taxes." The dissidents had been invited "by twenty five of the most respectable citizens in Carthage vicinity" to "deliver a lecture or more" at the court house, "on the subject of Nauvoo legislation, usurpation &c. &c." Law advised restraint, "allowing the law to have its course." He "was told that [his] press would be destroyed, but [said he] did not believe it. [He] could not even suspect men of being such fools," Law claimed. The citizens "urged [him] to come to Carthage with the press immediately."[15]

Francis M. Higbee, who had remained in Nauvoo, received word that the press might be in danger. "If they lay their hand upon it or break it," Higbee promised the informant, "they may date their downfall from that very hour."[16]

About sundown, some two hundred Nauvoo police and citizens gathered at the temple site, where the men organized and then proceeded to the *Expositor* office a few blocks distant. Two hours later, Marshal J. P. Green filled out the return. "The within-named press and type is destroyed and pied according to order, on this 10th day of June, 1844, at about 8 o'clock P.M." The marshal and his men continued to the Nauvoo Mansion where Joseph Smith greeted them. After Green "reported that he had removed the press, type, and printed papers and fixtures into the street and fired them," the prophet addressed the men. He "told them

---

14. For citations to the Council Minutes, see note 11.

15. William Law, Nauvoo diary, 10 June 1844, in Cook, *William Law,* 55–56. William Law, Interview, in Cook, *William Law,* 126. Lyndon Cook, referring to Law's diary entry for 11 June 1844, notes, "Some strike-outs and interlineations in the diary suggest that portions of the document may have been written with substantial hindsight." (56, note 47). While it is apparently true that neither the Laws nor Fosters were in Carthage on the day of the murder of Joseph Smith, William Law also effectively covers the trail of his involvement in the conspiracy, claiming to the end of his life that he knew of no movement to assassinate the prophet.

16. Smith, *American Prophet's Record,* 490 [11 June 1844] and 489 [10 June 1844].

they had done right." They had executed his orders as required of him by the city council. Joseph was adamant. He would never submit, he said, "to have another libelous publication . . . established in this city . . . I [care] not how many papers there [are] in the city if they would print the truth but [I] would submit to no libe[l]s or slander from them." The men cheered the prophet and returned to their homes.[17]

Upon his arrival in Nauvoo that evening, William Law discovered that the "unthinkable" had occurred. "[W]e rode over our type, that they scattered in the street, and over our broken office furniture," he later recorded. Upon further inquiry, Law was told by Charles A. Foster and Francis M. Higbee, who had attempted to prevent the men from entering the *Expositor* press building, that "The Marshal had the office door broken upon by sledges, the press & type carried out into the street and broken up, then piled the tables, desks, paper &c on top of the press and burned them with fire." The destroyed property included "fifteen hundred pounds of printing type, four hundred reams of paper, twenty five kegs of ink." If any resistance was offered, the marshal had been instructed to "burn the houses of the proprietors." The two-story brick building "had been perfectly gutted, not a bit had been left of anything." The destruction was more horrible than Law had imagined it would be, a clear sign that his life was in danger.[18]

William Law took his family to his brother's home for the night and prepared to depart the Holy City. "While we had people packing our things at my house, we rode, my brother and I, through the city in an open carriage, to show that we were not afraid." They were leaving behind considerable property. William Law had a "steam flouring mill at Nauvoo—& several dwelling houses—the one in which he . . . resided being a fine two story brick home."[19]

On June 11, the William and Wilson Law families left Nauvoo on a steamboat "laden with men, women & children. With horses, waggons, furnitures, etc." and proceeded to Burlington, Iowa. There Law "intended to secure quarters for the women & children & return to Nauvoo to fight if necessary." In Nauvoo that night "two attempts were made to fire his mill & house."[20]

Francis M. Higbee remained in Nauvoo. "He was very sorry," he said, for they had "set up the press for the destruction of the city," and now that the press was destroyed, "he meant to kill Joseph Smith and Hyrum Smith."[21]

Charles A. Foster departed Nauvoo for Warsaw where he wrote an account of the destruction of the *Expositor* press for *Warsaw Signal* editor Thomas Sharp.

---

17. Davis, *Authentic Account*, 13, reads, "six o'clock P.M." Smith, *American Prophet's Record*, 489 [10 June 1844].

18. William Law, Interview, in Cook, *William Law*, 126. William Law, Diary, 10 June 1844, in Cook, *William Law*, 56.

19. Ibid., in Cook, *William Law*, 126. David Wells Kilbourne to T. Dent, 15 June 1844, in Hallwas and Launius, *Cultures in Conflict*, 161.

20. David Wells Kilbourne to T. Dent, 15 June 1844, in Hallwas and Launius, *Cultures in Conflict*, 162. Kilbourne notes, "Mr. Law told me . . . " Smith, *American Prophet's Record*, 491 [14 June 1844]. L[yman Littlefield] to *The Prophet*, 13 June 1844.

21. Joseph Jackson affidavit, 21 June 1844, in Smith, *History of the Church* 6:524. This is not the same individual as the infamous Joseph H. Jackson.

I hasten to inform you of the UNPARALLELED OUTRAGE, perpetrated upon our rights, and interests by the ruthless, lawless, ruffian band of MORMON MOB-OCRATS, at the dictation of that UNPRINCIPLED wretch, Joe Smith. We were privately informed that the CITY COUNCIL, which had been in extra session, for two days past, had enacted an ordinance in relation to libels, providing that any thing that had been published, or any thing that might, be published tending to disparage the character of the officers of the city should be regarded as LAWLESS. They also declared the "Nauvoo Expositor" a "*nuisance*," and directed the police of [the] city to proceed immediately to the office of the Expositor, and DESTROY the PRESS and also the MATERIALS by THROWING them into the STREET!!. If any resistance were made, the officers were directed to demolish the building, and property, of all who were concerned in publishing said paper; and also take all into custody, who might refuse to obey the authorities of the City. Accordingly, a company consisting of some 200 men, armed and equipped, with MUSKETS, SWORDS, PISTOLS, BOWIE KNIVES SLEDGE-HAMMERS, &c, assisted by a crowd of several hundred minions, who volunteered their services on the occasion, marched to the building, and breaking open the doors with a sledge hammer, commenced the work of destruction and desperation. They tumbled the press and materials into the street, and set fire to them, and demolished the machinery with a sledge hammer, and injured the building very materially. We made no resistance; but looked on and felt revenge, but leave it for the public, to avenge this climax of insult and injury.[22]

Later that day Foster took the steamer *Osprey* to St. Louis where he prepared a longer account of the affair for the *St. Louis Evening Gazette*.[23]

⋆ ⋆ ⋆ ⋆ ⋆

That same evening, a thousand miles to the east, Jeffersonian gatherings were held in New York City and Petersborough, New Hampshire. Fifty men, twenty women, and "a few boys" attended the New York City meeting, held at the Bowery's Military Hall. Parley P. Pratt was the featured speaker. He struck out against men like Martin Van Buren and Henry Clay for not supporting legislation compensating the Saints for their losses in the Missouri persecutions. "Are not the members of Congress murderers and robbers, as accessories after the fact, when, after coming to the knowledge of these things, they still fellowship Missouri and refuse redress?"

Pratt concluded his remarks with another question. "Who then shall we vote for as our next President? I answer, General Joseph Smith of Nauvoo, Ill. He is not a Southern man with Northern principles, nor a Northern man with Southern principles, he is an Independent man with American principles, and he has both knowledge and disposition, to govern for the benefit and protection of ALL. And what is more, HE DARE TO IT, EVEN IN THIS AGE, and this can scarcely be said of many others.

---

22. Charles A. Foster to Thomas Sharp, 11 June 1844, in *Warsaw Signal*, 12 June 1844.
23. Charles A. Foster to editor, 11 June 1844, in *St. Louis Evening Gazette*, 12 June 1844, in Hallwas and Launius, *Cultures in Conflict*, 157–59.

Come then, O Americans!
Rally to the Standard of Liberty.
And in your generous indignation trample down
The Tyrant's rod, and the Oppressor's crown,
That you proud eagle to its height may soar,
And peace triumphant reign for-ever more."[24]

The following day Horace Greeley's *New York Tribune* sharply criticized the organizers (who had promoted the political meeting as a nonsectarian gathering) because "reference was made to [Mormonism's] peculiar opinions upon religious tenets." This the editor of *The Prophet* denied. He also disagreed with the *Tribune* that Elder Pratt "denounced Henry Clay or any other men as murderers because they would not pledge themselves to support 'OUR PRETENSIONS.'" On the contrary, Pratt "denounced only as murderers" those men (including "the President and members of Congress") who had "aided or abetted murder in Missouri" by "refusing just and lawful redress and protection, when, as officers of this Republic, it was in their power to have done otherwise." By doing nothing to help the Latter-day Saints in their tribulations, national political leaders had become their active persecutors.[25]

The Petersborough, New Hampshire, political meeting resolved that only "the watchful energies of a virtuous people . . . are capable of maintaining, or worthy of enjoying the blessings of free institutions." The political system was near its breaking point, the conveners concluded. "[W]e will by all lawful ways and means endeavor to reform the abuses of trust and power in every department of the government, and rear the fallen standard of equal rights and universal liberty to every soul of man."

"[I]n all his publications and public acts," one resolution asserted, General Joseph Smith, "has exhibited a largeness of soul, an indifference of thought, a decision of character, a bold genius, a philanthropic and patriotic spirit, a statesman's views, and all the qualities that might render him worth the suffrages of a free and enlightened people."[26]

✶ ✶ ✶ ✶ ✶

The *Nauvoo Neighbor* published an *Extra* on June 12, heading its description of the *Expositor* affair "Retributive Justice," an undisguised reference to the Biblical principle that all "sin must be balanced . . . with equivalent punishment and suffering." The men behind the opposition press were characterized as a "knot of base men . . . blacklegs and bogus-makers [counterfeiters]." Despite the fact that the *Expositor* presented no fact that was untrue and no assertion that was unsubstantiated, the destruction of the newspaper was justified on the grounds it was "filled with libels and slanderous articles upon the citizens and City Council from one end to the other." The church had suffered enough, the article went on, claiming that the paper had vilified and slandered "the innocent inhabitants of this city," with the intent of raising another mob "to drive and plunder us again as they did in Missouri." Under

---

24. "Jeffersonians Attend!" *The Prophet*, 8 June 1844. "Jeffersonian Meeting," *The Prophet*, 15 June 1844.
25. *New York Tribune* quoted in *The Prophet*, 15 June 1844.
26. "Jeffersonian Meeting, at Petersborough, N.H.," *The Prophet*, 29 June 1844.

these circumstances, and given the "pressing cries and supplications of afflicted innocence" by local citizens, the city council had no choice. The *Neighbor* asked, "Why start presses to destroy rights and privileges, and bring upon us mobs to plunder and murder? We ask no more than what belongs to us, the rights of Americans."[27]

Foster's letter describing the *Expositor* incident was published in the *Warsaw Signal* on June 12. Thomas Sharp finally had the opening he had been waiting for. "We have only to state, that this is sufficient!" Sharp editorialized. "War and extermination is inevitable! Citizens ARISE, ONE and ALL!!!—Can you stand by, and suffer such INFERNAL DEVILS! To rob men of their property and rights, without avenging them. We have no time for comment, every man will make his own. LET IT BE MADE WITH POWDER AND BALL!!!"[28]

Constable David Bettisworth and Dr. Thomas Barnes, both of Carthage, arrived in Nauvoo to serve process that afternoon. The writs had been sworn out by Francis M. Higbee. Joseph Smith, Hyrum Smith, William W. Phelps, John Taylor, and "a number of others" were indicted "for riot, in breaking the press of the Nauvoo Expositor." Joseph Smith pointed out that the writ stated that the case could be heard before the issuing magistrate "or some other justice of the Peace of said County." He would not leave the Holy City. The Mormons were prepared, Joseph said, "to go to trial before Esqr Johnson" of Nauvoo, "for that was their privilege allowed by the Statute."

Bettisworth objected. He intended to take the Mormons before Justice Morrison in Carthage, "the man who issued the writ," an indication of just how far the Reformers and their confederates were willing to distort the law in order to fulfill their own objectives of thwarting the Mormon prophet. Joseph Smith was expert at playing that game, too. "Do you intend to break the law?" he asked. Joseph and Hyrum called "upon all present to witness" that they offered to go "before the nearest justice of the peace" and to "witness where the officer broke the law" if he attempted to prevent them from exercising their rights.[29]

The Nauvoo Municipal Court assembled in the Seventies Hall later that afternoon. "Much testimony was brought to the point & the Court discharged J[oseph Smith] . . . and assessed the costs to F. M. Higbee the complainant." The writ was endorsed, "honorably discharged." The men accused of the destruction of the *Expositor* press were free. Higbee was charged with malicious prosecution and ordered to pay court costs.[30]

27. "Retributive Justice," *Nauvoo Neighbor* Extra 12 June 1844, first published as an Extra on 10 June. Hallwas and Launius, *Cultures in Conflict*, 159–60, note, "He employed the Mormon myth of persecuted innocence to arouse the fears of his readers and justify the destruction of the press."

28. *Warsaw Signal*, 12 June 1844. Also, "Further particulars from Nauvoo," in the same issue: "we have conversed with a gentleman of undoubted veracity, who was in Nauvoo, and present in the council room." Sharp claims his life was threatened by Hyrum Smith. See also Martha McConnell Walker [Fountain Green] to Martha Walker [Fannettsburg, PA], 18 June 1844. "The press spoke freely and last week it was burned to the ground, and a reward offered to any man or set of men that would burn the Warsaw press." Walker Papers, Regional Archives, Western Illinois University. Similarly, Davis, *Authentic Account*, 40–41. Smith, *History of the Church* 6:463–64, 500.

29. William Clayton, Nauvoo Journal 2 [12 June 1844], in Clayton, *Intimate Chronicle*, 132.

30. Davis, *Authentic Account*, 13. Smith, *History of the Church* 6:465, reads, "honorably released."

Hancock County citizens held a public meeting in Carthage the next day. Thomas Sharp claimed he was alerted by an informant present at the Nauvoo City Council hearings that "Hyrum Smith did, in the presence of the City Council and the citizens of Nauvoo, offer a reward for the destruction of the printing press and materials of the *Warsaw Signal*, a newspaper also opposed to his interests." Sharp was incensed. This "public threat made in the Council of the City" of Nauvoo, he said, "is sufficient, in connection with the recent outrage, to command the efforts and the services of every good citizen to put an immediate stop to the career of the mad prophet and his demoniac coadjutors."

With this latest provocation, manufactured or not, the citizens of Hancock County, Illinois, declared they were prepared to "co-operate with [their] fellow-citizens in this state, Missouri and Iowa, to exterminate, utterly exterminate the wicked and abominable Mormon leaders, the authors of our troubles." A Committee of Resolutions was formed, made up of some of the more prominent men in Hancock County. They included the anti-Mormons Colonel Levi Williams, Samuel Williams, Elisha Worrell (uncle of Franklin Worrell), John M. Ferris, and George Rockwell. The Nauvoo dissidents were represented by Chauncey L. Higbee and George Robinson (Sidney Rigdon's son-in-law).

Walter Bagby addressed the meeting. He "spoke long and eloquently upon the course of our grievances." The "time was at hand," he said, "when we [are] individually and collectively called upon to repel the innovations upon our liberties." Places of encampment should be designated, "at which to rendezvous our forces, that we may be ready when called upon for efficient action." Armed conflict was inevitable.

Dr. Barnes expressed his frustration "that the persons charged with the writs were duly arrested, but taken from the officers and on a writ of habeas corpus from the Municipal Court, and discharged, and the following potent words entered upon the records—honorably released." Carthage attorney Onias C. Skinner proposed that a vote of thanks be "tendered to Dr. Barnes for volunteering his services in executing said writs." This was passed. Francis M. Higbee, one of the Nauvoo Reformers and a proprietor of the now-defunct *Expositor*, was "loudly called for" and gave a history of the Mormon "problem."

The Committee of Resolutions made their report. Places of military encampment were established at Warsaw, Carthage, Green Plains, Spilman's Landing, Chili, and La Harpe. Further, it was agreed to send a "deputation of two discreet men . . . to Springfield" to persuade the governor to intercede in order to bring to justice the destroyers of the *Expositor* press. Skinner and Bagby were chosen "to bear the resolutions adopted by this meeting to his Excellency the Governor, requiring his executive interposition."[31]

"Our City and adjacent country contains some excitable elements at present," Lyman O. Littlefield wrote from Nauvoo on June 13. His letter was addressed to the New York editor of *The Prophet* and echoed the language of the *Nauvoo Neighbor*. The *Nauvoo Expositor*, Littlefield asserted, was declared a nuisance, "very properly and legally . . . the mayor was forthwith ordered to have it removed." Himself a witness to the destruction, Littlefield noted "the building was literally gutted of its contents

---

31. Davis, *Authentic Account*, 40–41. Smith, *History of the Church* 6:463–66.

which was thrown into the street and burned. While the blaze sent up its lurid light into the darkening atmosphere, making visible the calm, reconciled countenances of four or five hundred people, many of whom had been left homeless by Missouri incendiaries; we involuntarily exclaimed, 'This is but retributive justice!'"[32]

32. L[yman Littlefield] to editor of *The Prophet*, 13 June 1844, in *The Prophet*, 13 July 1844. For another, somewhat critical Nauvoo perspective on the incident, see Sarah Scott to [in-laws], 15 June 1844, in Partridge, "Mormon Dictator," 593–96.

Chapter Twelve

Gentlemen of Undoubted Veracity

JOSEPH SMITH WROTE TO GOVERNOR Thomas Ford on June 14. His letter was accompanied by several statements from witnesses to the razing of the *Expositor* reaffirming that "The whole affair was conducted by the City Marshal and his posse in the most quiet and orderly manner, without the least noise, riot or tumult."[1]

Joseph's counselor Sidney Rigdon prepared his own confidential letter to the governor. There were "difficulties in [Nauvoo] which I have had no concern," Rigdon began. The inevitable destruction of the *Expositor* press "was done without tumult or disorder," he said. "When the press was destroyed, all returned home, and everything has been perfectly quiet ever since," Rigdon concluded. "I can see no need for executive interference in this case," he said, but requested that the governor "disperse all uncalled for assemblies, and let the laws have their regular course, which they can have if these assemblies will disperse. If not, I fear the consequences."

Rigdon failed to mention that much of his information about the proceedings of the anti-Mormons would have come from his son-in-law, former Nauvoo dissident George Robinson, currently chairman of the La Harpe District anti-Mormon committee. And, at about this same time, Sidney's brother-in-law Anthony Howard Dunlevy was preparing to leave Ohio for the seat of conflict. Dunlevy's legal partner and fellow Whig, Supreme Court Justice John McLean, was already in Springfield presiding over the proceedings of the U.S. Circuit Court. McLean was one of the few people besides the governor who had the power to put a stop to the conflict that was unfolding in Hancock County.

Little wonder, then, that Rigdon desired anonymity. "I send this to your Excellency as confidential, as I do not wish to take any part in the affair, or be known in it." He would depart Nauvoo for the safety of Pittsburgh in less than a week. And although Rigdon was Joseph Smith's vice presidential running mate, as far as is presently known, he never made a political speech in support of the prophet's candidacy.[2]

The captain of an independent Hancock County militia unit entered a home in Rocky Run and requested the use of a military drum for the duration of the

---

1.   John M. Bernhisel to Thomas Ford, 14 June 1844, in Smith, *History of the Church* 6:467–68. See also Minutes of the Trial of Joseph Smith et al. before Esquire Wells—'Expositor Affair,' 17 June 1844, in Smith, *History of the Church* 6:488–91.

2.   Sidney Rigdon to Thomas Ford, 14 June 1844, in Smith, *History of the Church* 6:469–471.

Mormon conflict. The militia expected assistance from Missouri, he said, which "had offered to send over two thousand men, to come over to assist" in the capture of Joseph Smith. To make their appearance legal in form of law, summonses would be issued for "every man who was in or would come into the county." Skinner and Bagby were in Springfield, the captain added, to convince Governor Ford "to order the militia out" to aid them in taking Joseph Smith and other Mormon lawbreakers. "If the Governor ordered the [state] militia against [Hancock county's independent militia] instead of in favor of them, [the captain] would turn mob, and the [local] militia would join him." There could be no neutral stance. The local citizens "must fight either for one side or the other, or they must share the same fate as the Mormons."[3]

Joseph Smith addressed the Saints gathered in the grove that afternoon. "You know that of late some malicious and corrupt men have sprung up and apostatized from the Church of latter-day Saints," he said, referring to the Laws, Higbees, and Fosters, among others, "and they declare that the Prophet believes in a plurality of gods, and, lo and behold! We have discovered a very great secret, they cry—'The Prophet says there are many Gods, and this proves that he has fallen.' It has been my intention for a long time to take up this subject and lay it clearly before the people, and show what my faith is in relation to this interesting matter . . . I'll preach on the plurality of Gods . . . It has been preached by the Elders for fifteen years."[4]

After the meeting, cut short on account of rain, Circuit Judge Jesse B. Thomas advised the prophet to "go before some justice of the peace of the county and have an examination . . . and if acquitted or bound over, would allay all excitement answer the law and cut off all legal pretext for a mob and he would be bound to order them to keep the peace." The prophet agreed and made arrangements to have his case heard before a friendly Nauvoo magistrate.[5]

It was already too late. A messenger arrived in Nauvoo with urgent news. Fifteen hundred men were preparing to assemble at Warsaw on June 17. The Quincy Greys had supplied arms to the Hancock militia units. Warsaw had acquired five cannon. Once the men were assembled, the Missourians, "and others who would join them," would be met at Carthage by units of the Quincy Greys "and other companies from Adams county." Delegates would be dispatched to branches of the Mormon church with an ultimatum that "they must deny Joseph's being a prophet . . . [or] leave immediately." A demand would be made for Joseph, Hyrum, and members of the Nauvoo Municipal Council engaged in the *Expositor* affair. If they were not given up, the anti-Mormons would "blow up the city, and kill and exterminate all the inhabitants."[6]

Joseph again took the temple stand. Prepare arms for the defense of the city, he told the gathered brethren. Messengers were to be sent "to all the surrounding towns and villages, to explain the cause of the disturbance, and show them that all was

---

3. James Guyman affidavit, 20 June 1844, in Smith, *History of the Church* 6:511-12. See also Smith, *History of the Church* 6:481.

4. Smith, *History of the Church* 6:473–74.

5. Smith, *American Prophet's Record*, 492 [16 June 1844]. Smith, *History of the Church* 6:479.

6. Thomas G. Wilson affidavit, 16 June 1844, in Smith, *History of the Church* 6:480–81.

peace at Nauvoo, and that there was no cause for any mobs." The Nauvoo Legion was to be "in readiness to suppress all illegal violence in the City."[7]

Joseph wrote to Governor Ford later that day. "Judge Thomas has been here and given his advice in the case, which I shall strictly follow until I hear from your Excellency, and in all cases shall adhere to the Constitution and laws. The Nauvoo Legion is at your service to quell all insurrection and support the dignity of the common weal." In his capacity as mayor, Joseph issued a proclamation: "Our city is infested with a set of blacklegs, counterfeiters and debauchers, and that the proprietors of this press were of that class the minutes of the Municipal Court fully testify . . . Of the correctness of our conduct in this affair, we appeal to every high court in the state."[8]

The June 17 deadline for all Mormons in the outlying districts to return to Nauvoo was rapidly approaching. "We feel to hope for the best, and determined to prepare for the worst," Joseph wrote to his uncle, a resident of Ramus, a Mormon settlement in northeastern Hancock County. "[W]e want this to be your motto in common with us, 'That we will never ground our arms until we give them up by death.' Free trade and sailor's rights, protection of persons and property, wives and families. If a mob annoy you, defend yourselves to the very last; and if they fall upon you with a superior force, and you think you are not able to compete with them, retreat to Nauvoo." He signed the letter, "Joseph Smith, Mayor of the City of Nauvoo, and Lieut.-General of the Nauvoo Legion."[9]

Hyrum prepared a letter to Brigham Young and other members of the Quorum of the Twelve and Council of Fifty, calling them home to Nauvoo. "Mass meetings are held upon mass meetings drawing up resolutions to utterly exterminate the Saints," Hyrum reported.

> The excitement has been gotten up by the Laws, Fosters and the Higbees, and they themselves have left the city and are engaged in the mob. They have sent their runners into the State of Missouri to excite them to murder and bloodshed, and the report is that a great many hundreds of them will come over to take an active part in murdering the Saints . . . It is thought best by myself and others for you to return without delay . . . Let wisdom be exercised; and whatever they do, do it without a noise . . . Communicate to the others of the Twelve with as much speed as possible, with perfect stillness and calmness. A word to the wise is sufficient; and a little powder, lead and a good rifle can be packed in your luggage very eas[il]y without creating any suspicion.

Joseph added a hurried postscript. "Large bodies of armed men, cannon and munition of war are coming on from Missouri in steamboats. These facts are communicated to the Governor and President of the United States, and you will readily

---

7.   Clayton, Nauvoo Journal 3 [16 June 1844], in Smith, *Words*, 383.

8.   Joseph Smith to Thomas Ford, 16 June 1844, in Smith, *History of the Church* 6: 480, Hallwas and Launius, *Cultures in Conflict*, 187. "Proclamation," 16 June 1844, in Smith, *History of the Church* 6:484–85.

9.   Joseph Smith to John Smith, 17 June 1844, in Smith, *History of the Church* 6:485–86.

see that we have to prepare for the onset. JOSEPH SMITH." The desperate letters were never sent.[10]

On June 17 a *Nauvoo Neighbor Extra* declared, "Our lives, our city, our charter and our characters are just as sacred, just as dear, and just as good as other people's." Hyrum issued a statement insisting that he "did not make any threats, nor offer any reward against the [Warsaw] *Signal* or its editor [Thomas Sharp] in the [Nauvoo] City Council."[11]

✳ ✳ ✳ ✳ ✳

Elder William Smith (brother of Joseph and Hyrum, Mormon apostle and Council of Fifty member) addressed "a large and enthusiastic meeting of the friends of equal rights" in New York City that same day. His remarks were "a strain of flowing eloquence," which criticized the courses that had been pursued by "the two great political parties." The speech was met with "deafening applause." Elder (and Council of Fifty member) Orson Hyde then "alluded to the present state of anarchy" of the current government and "the impolitic movements of these who had usurped [power in] the name of Democracy." He enjoined all those who wanted to enjoy "Liberty of Speech and conscience" to support "the Peoples Candidate," General Joseph Smith. The resolutions of the May 17 Nauvoo political convention were read to "much applause."

The New York City conference concluded with its own set of resolutions. "The free American citizens opposed to tyranny over mind or body, have nominated as a candidate for the Presidency, Gen. Joseph Smith of Nauvoo Ill., the friend of the oppressed, an independent man with American principles; and for the Vice Presidency, Sidney Rigdon Esq. of Pennsylvania." All who were in favor of "Free Trade and Equal Rights" were requested to support "Gen Joseph Smith, the Philanthropist." The meeting adjourned "with nine cheers" for General Joseph Smith and Sidney Rigdon.[12]

✳ ✳ ✳ ✳ ✳

By nine A.M. on June 18' the Nauvoo Legion was assembled and organized. Several boxes of arms, forty stands in all, were distributed to the men. That afternoon, the Nauvoo Legion of three to four thousand men assembled near the Mansion, then still under construction. Lieutenant General Joseph Smith, in full dress uniform, stood on the scaffolding and placed the city under martial law.

Acting Major General Dunham, with General Joseph Smith "and staff riding in front" marched up Main Street. "The number was large and inspiring," one observer commented, "considering the number who were gone preaching."[13]

Scribe William W. Phelps read the latest *Warsaw Signal Extra* before the military assembly. The paper called upon all of the citizens of Hancock and surrounding

10. Hyrum Smith to Brigham Young with postscript by Joseph Smith, 17 June 1844, Smith, *History of the Church* 6:486–87. Smith, *History of the Church* 6:494.

11. "To the Public," *Nauvoo Neighbor*, 19 June 1844, in Smith, *History of the Church* 6:495–96.

12. "Great Jeffersonian Meeting," *The Prophet*, 22 June 1844.

13. Smith, *American Prophet's Record*, 493–94 [18 June 1844]. Smith, *History of the Church* 6:496–97.

counties to "assist the mob," he said. The anti-Mormon mobocrats, Joseph Smith replied, were waging "a war of extermination upon us because of our religion." He "called upon all the volunteers who felt to support the constitution from the Rocky Mountains to the Atlantic ocean to come with their arms, ammunition & provisions to defend us from the mob & defend the constitution."

"We have taken the counsel of Judge Thomas," he said, "and have been tried before a civil magistrate on the charge of riot—not that the law required it, but because the Judge advised it as a precautionary measure, to allay all possible pretext for excitement. We were legally acquitted . . . for we have broken no law." When Constable Bettisworth refused them the privilege of going before the local magistrate, Joseph noted, it was he who "broke the law . . . declaring that we should go before Morrison in Carthage, and no one else, when he knew that a numerous mob was collected there who are publicly pledged to destroy our lives.

"It was under these circumstances that we availed ourselves of the writ of habeas corpus, and were brought before the Municipal Court of this city and discharged from the illegal detention under which we were held by Constable Bettisworth," Joseph said. Even in the face of their proper actions before the law, he said, "all mobmen, priests, thieves, and bogus makers, apostates and adulterers" were claiming that Mormons refused to conform to legal authority and due process.[14]

Joseph drew his sword and aimed it heavenward. "I call God and angels to witness that I have unsheathed my sword with a firm and unalterable determination that this people shall have their legal rights, and be protected from mob violence, or my blood shall be spilt upon the ground like water, and my body consigned to the silent tomb . . . I call upon all friends of truth and liberty to come to our assistance."[15]

Messengers arrived in Nauvoo later that evening. Governor Ford would not support the anti-Mormon militia of Hancock County, they reported. No order would be made until Ford had been able to judge the conditions in Hancock County for himself. When the news reached the anti-Mormons, they "damned the Gov as being as bad as Joe Smith."[16]

The night of the June 18 was stormy. Sidney Rigdon and more than 150 other Mormons departed Nauvoo on board the steamship *Osprey* so that they would be out of the way when the inevitable occurred.[17]

Warsaw was in "a constant state of excitement." Commercial business of the Mississippi port town was suspended. All able bodied men were placed under arms "and almost constantly in drill." A six pounder was expected from Quincy. Additional cannon and ammunition had been secured in St. Louis.[18]

Nauvoo remained on high alert. The legion was reinforced by Mormon troops from Green Plains and Iowa who were reviewed and paraded on the bank of the Mississippi. A picket-guard under the command of Colonel Stephen Markham posted lookouts "on all the roads leading out of the city; and . . . in all the streets and alleys

---

14. Smith, *History of the Church*, 6:497–99. Smith, *American Prophet's Record*, 494 [18 June 1844].
15. Smith, *History of the Church* 6:499.
16. Smith, *American Prophet's Record*, 494 [18 June 1844]. Smith, *History of the Church* 6:502.
17. "Leaving the City," *Warsaw Signal*, 19 June 1844.
18. "The Preparation," *Warsaw Signal*, 19 June 1844. Hallwas and Launius, *Cultures in Conflict*, 199.

in the city, and also on the river bank." All the "powder and lead in the city" was to be secured, and "to see that all the arms were in use, and that all unclaimed arms be put in the hands of those who could use them." Theodore Turley was ordered to "commence Making cannon." No one could enter or leave the city without permission. Work on the temple was suspended. Joseph encouraged Hyrum to take his family and go to Cincinnati. Sidney Rigdon, Joseph's vice presidential running mate, who had recently departed Nauvoo, would be safe in Pittsburgh, Joseph said. Sidney would reach his Pennsylvania home on June 27.[19]

Wilford Woodruff replied to James Arlington Bennet's earlier correspondence regarding the upcoming election. "Your views about the nomination of General Smith for the presidency are correct," he said. "We will gain popularity and external influence. But this is not all: we mean to elect him, and nothing shall be wanting on our part to accomplish it; and why? Because we are satisfied, fully satisfied, that this is the best or only method of saving our free institutions from a total overthrow."[20]

Dr. Wall Southwick ("a man from Texas trying to get Joseph to go to Texas with the church") arrived in Nauvoo mid-morning on June 20. He reported that a cannon from Quincy had reached Warsaw. On account the local U.S. mail was no longer reliable, Joseph Smith sent letters "by express . . . to the Illinois river" to members of the Quorum of the Twelve then on political missions, requesting that they return to Nauvoo immediately. Brigham Young was in Boston; Heber C. Kimball and Orson Pratt were in Washington, D.C.; Orson Hyde and William Smith were in Philadelphia; Parley P. Pratt was in New York City; Wilford Woodruff was in Portage, New York; George A. Smith was in Peterboro, Vermont; John E. Page was in Pittsburgh; and Lyman Wight was in Baltimore. Amasa Lyman in Cincinnati, and George Miller, then in Madison County, Kentucky, were also called home to Nauvoo.[21]

Governor Ford reached Carthage on June 21 and set up his headquarters in the Hamilton Hotel. He was greeted with the energized anticipation of a military encampment. General Minor Deming had called out the militia in Hancock, McDonough, and Schuyler counties. More than a thousand men were in arms, many encamped around (and in) the courthouse. Constables of the county had summoned men to "serve as a posse comitatus" to assist in the arrest of Joseph Smith.

Governor Ford addressed the militiamen and citizens from the steps of the Carthage courthouse. He had come, he said, "to see that the law was fully carried out." Mr. William H. Roosevelt, a Whig anti-Mormon from Warsaw, disagreed. "[T]he law was not sufficient to carry out [our] measures," he argued. "We have the willing minds and God Almighty has given us strength, and we will wield the sabre

19. Smith, *American Prophet's Record*, 495. Smith, *History of the Church* 6:505–7, 519–20. "The Mormon Disturbances," *Clay Tribune* 6 July 1844, copying from the St. Louis *New Era* of 20 June 1844.

20. Willard Richards to James Arlington Bennet, 20 June 1844, in Smith, *History of the Church* 6:516–18. Hallwas and Launius, *Cultures in Conflict*, 165–68.

21. Stephen Markham to Wilford Woodruff, 20 June 1856 (Southwick reference), LDS Archives. Smith, *History of the Church* 6:507, 519. Smith, *American Prophet's Record*, 495 [20 June 1844].

Hamilton House (Hamilton Hotel), Carthage, Hancock County, Illinois.

and make our own laws!!" Roosevelt believed "the Governor . . . was too easy in his remarks . . . in saying that he wished a compliance with the laws."

Onias C. Skinner, Carthage attorney and candidate for the state legislature on an independent ticket, reminded the audience that he had been "one of the delegates appointed by the people of Carthage to go to Springfield and lay before the Governor their grievances." He believed the governor "would do what was right."

Ford gave orders to Captain Dunn: "All the people who [were] assembled in Carthage [and elsewhere in the county], should be consolidated in the militia, under [the governor's] command, to co-operate in maintaining the supremacy of the law." At the conclusion of Ford's address, "officers and men unanimously voted, with acclamation, to sustain [him] in a strictly legal course," and that the Mormon leaders (once they were brought into custody) "should be protected from violence." An additional one thousand men from the Fourth Brigade of the Fifth Division of the Illinois Militia were called out, bringing the total muster to over two thousand men, still only about half the size of the Nauvoo Legion. General Minor Deming commanded the Fifty-ninth Regiment (of five hundred men) to "rendezvous forthwith at Warsaw with 8 days provision."[22]

Governor Ford addressed a letter to "The Honorable the Mayor and Common Council of the City of Nauvoo." "As chief magistrate," he began, "it is my duty to

22. Thomas Ford, *Message from the Governor* [1844], 3 (posse and carry out quotes). Daniels, *Correct Account,* 4 (Roosevelt and Skinner quotes). Smith, *History of the Church* 6:563.

see that impartial justice shall be done, uninfluenced either by excitement here or in your city . . . I think before any decisive measure shall be adopted, that I ought to hear the allegations and defenses of all parties." Ford requested that a committee from Nauvoo be sent to Carthage to ascertain the facts in the case. Joseph prepared to forward "affidavits and handbills" to the governor in Carthage.[23]

Warsaw's parade ground was alive. Nearly three hundred men were mustered under the direction of Colonel Levi Williams, Mark Aldrich, William N. Grover, and Jacob C. Davis. Colonel Levi Williams commanded the Fifty-ninth Regiment of the Illinois Militia. Mark Aldrich was major in command of the Warsaw Independent Battalion. William N. Grover was captain of the Warsaw Cadets. Jacob C. Davis, captain of the Warsaw Rifle Company, was assisted by honorary captain John C. Elliott, of Avery Kidnap fame. Speeches by William H. Roosevelt, Thomas Sharp, and Colonel Williams kept the excitement at high pitch.[24]

George Rockwell, a Warsaw druggist, was dispatched to Alton, about 160 miles to the south, to secure arms for the militia. "I have been called on by the citizens of Warsaw to take an active and responsible part in [these] proceedings [against the Mormons]," he wrote to his father, "and I can assure you that I take much pleasure in lending my humble aid to expel a band of citizens from the State, the leaders of whom are deserving a thousand deaths. I have been constantly engaged for the last two weeks trying to accomplish it, and now take pleasure in saying that I have no doubt as to our ultimate success. Since I enlisted my self in this cause, I have . . . traveled on horseback more than 300 miles in various directions to raise men and means to accomplish our ends, knowing that our cause was just." He had little confidence in the Democratic governor, "with whose party the Mormons have voted for three years past."

Rockwell reached Alton sometime after midnight on the June 22. He had an order "from the Governor on the Quarter master General for all the Arms Cannon etc. in the arsenal [at Alton] belonging to the State," which would be taken to Warsaw on the *Die Vernon*'s return voyage up river.

Rockwell was not well rewarded for his efforts. The Alton armory produced only about "one hundred yaugers, twenty muskets, and three six pounders." Yaugers were .52 caliber model 1841 U.S. breech-loading cap-lock rifles used by sharpshooters. Parts were interchangeable, which made them a favored weapon. The remaining arms were "so out of order as to be useless." The cannon was mainly for show, to provide a deterrent, but little more.[25]

Before returning to Warsaw, Rockwell met with Whig editor George T. M. Davis. Davis would accompany Rockwell on his return to Warsaw in order to report firsthand on the Mormon conflict. Without revealing Davis's ties to the anti-Mormons in Hancock County, the *Alton Telegraph* announced that Davis "had made such arrangements as will enable him to procure the earliest and most authentic information" in order to keep his readers "constantly advised of the progress of affairs at

---

23. Thomas Ford to 'The Honorable Mayor and Common Council of the City of Nauvoo,' 21 June 1844, in Smith, *History of the Church* 6: 521–22.

24. Daniels, *Correct Account*, 5. Daniels mentions, "Captains Aldrich, Grover, [John C.] Elliott, and Col. Williams of Green Plains."

25. George Rockwell [Alton] to Thomas H. Rockwell, 22 June 1844, Kansas State Historical Society. "Authentic Information," *Alton Telegraph*, 29 June 1844 (useless quote).

Nauvoo and its vicinity."[26]

Council of Fifty member Lucien Woodworth (together with several other Nauvoo leaders) and James W. Woods, Joseph's non-Mormon attorney, departed Nauvoo just after noon to negotiate with Governor Ford in Carthage. Woodworth carried a letter from Joseph Smith to the governor. "I would respectfully recommend the bearer, Col. [Lucien] Woodworth, as one of my aides, and a man whose testimony can be relied upon," Joseph wrote. "Our troubles are invariably brought upon us by falsehoods and misrepresentations by designing men. We have ever held ourselves amenable to the law; and, for myself, sir, I am ever ready to conform to and support the laws and Constitution, even at the expense of my life. I have never in the least offered any resistance to law or lawful process, which is a well-known fact to the general public; all of which circumstances make us the more anxious to have you come to Nauvoo and investigate the whole matter."

"In regard to the destruction of the press," Joseph offered, "the truth only needs to be presented before your Excellency to satisfy you of the justice of the proceedings. The press was established by a set of men who had already set themselves at defiance of the law and authorities of the city, and had threatened the lives of some of its principal officers, and who also made it no private matter that the press was established for the express purpose of destroying the city."[27]

Following a lengthy interrogation, Joseph's delegation returned to Nauvoo at 10 P.M. that evening. They bore a letter from the governor. Illinois's chief magistrate was forthright. "After examining carefully all the allegations on the part of the citizens of the country in Hancock county, and the defensive matters submitted to me by the committee of your citizens concerning the existing disturbances," Ford informed the Mormon prophet,

> I find that there appears to be but little contradiction as to important facts, so that it may be safely assumed that the immediate cause of the existing excitement is the destruction of the press and *Nauvoo Expositor*, and the subsequent refusal of the individuals accused to be accountable therefor according to the general laws of this state, and the insisting on your parts to be accountable only before your own municipal court, and according to the ordinances of your city ... Many other facts have been asserted on both sides as tending to increase the excitement; but as they mostly relate to private persons, and committed by individuals, ... I will not further notice them in this communication.

"I now express to you my opinion that your conduct in the destruction of the press was a very gross outrage upon the laws and the liberties of the people," the governor continued. "It may have been full of libels, but this did not authorize you to destroy it ... You have violated the Constitution in at least four particulars."

First, the governor explained, the owners of the press were given no proper notice of the proceedings of the city council and were not permitted to defend themselves. "No jury was called or sworn, and most of the witnesses were permitted

---

26. "Authentic Information," *Alton Telegraph*, 29 June 1844.
27. Joseph Smith to Thomas Ford, 22 June 1844, in Smith, *History of the Church* 6:525–27. See also Hallwas and Launius, *Cultures in Conflict*, 187–89.

to give their evidence, without being under oath." Equally important, the governor stated, "there existed no general ordinance of the city, defining such a press to be a nuisance." And, Ford stressed, "the Common Council possessed legislative authority, only; and could, under no pretense, set in judgement as a court."

The governor's second criticism centered on Mormon abuse of habeas corpus. Ford acknowledged that the municipal court had power to issue writs of habeas corpus "in all cases of imprisonment arising under the ordinances of the city." However, the city council passed an ordinance giving the municipal court "jurisdiction to issue the writ in all cases of arrest and imprisonment in the city, by whatsoever authority the same might be made," be it state or federal authority. This action made it "impossible to execute the laws there, unless permitted by the municipal court."

Ford was blunt in his assessment of the affair. "The whole proceedings of the Mayor, the Common Council, and the Municipal Court, were irregular and illegal, and not to be endured in a free country." He was aware that the Mormons had been "repeatedly assured by some of the best lawyers in the State, who had been candidates for office, before that people, that it had full and competent power to issue writs of habeas corpus in all cases whatever." Nevertheless, "The Common Council violated the law in assuming the exercise of judicial power ... The Mayor violated the law in ordering this erroneous and absurd judgment of the Common Council to be executed. And the municipal court erred in discharging them from arrest."

Ford's third criticism "touched the liberty of the press, which is justly dear to any republican people, it was well calculated to raise a great flame of excitement. And it may well be questioned, whether years of misrepresentation by the most profligate newspaper could have engendered such a feeling as was produced by the destruction of this one press."[28]

Joseph's reply was cordial. "Yours of this date [June 22] is received ... A part of the same delegation, Mr. Woodworth, who was detained yesterday, started for Carthage at 12 noon, this date, who, we perceive, had not arrived at your last date. Some documents conveyed by him would tend to counteract some of the views expressed in your Excellency's communication, and we feel confident, if all the facts could be before your Excellency, you would have come to different conclusions." He disputed the governor's interpretation of habeas corpus, what constituted a nuisance, and the necessity of declaring martial law in Nauvoo. "Disperse the mob," Joseph requested, "and secure to us our constitutional privileges, that our lives may not be endangered when on trial."[29]

Joseph considered "laying the case before President Tyler," but decided against it after a short consultation. He resolved to go West, "and all would be well." That night Joseph and Hyrum fled Nauvoo and crossed the Mississippi on a small skiff. The governor's posse reached Nauvoo the next morning, June 22, intent on arresting Joseph and his brother. They returned to Carthage empty handed. Convinced that Nauvoo would be destroyed if they did not give themselves up to the authorities in Carthage, the Smith brothers returned to the Illinois shore.[30]

---

28. Thomas Ford to Joseph Smith, 22 June 1844, in Smith, *History of the Church* 6:533–34. Thomas Ford, *Message from the Governor* [1844], 4–5.

29. Joseph Smith to Thomas Ford Smith 22 June 1844, in *History of the Church* 6:538–40.

30. Smith, *History of the Church* 6:545, 547–50. Joseph Smith to President John Tyler, 20 June 1844, in Smith, *History of the Church* 6:508. Smith, *American Prophet's Record*, 495 [20 June 1844].

✶ ✶ ✶ ✶ ✶

We conversed with a gentleman of undoubted veracity just from Nauvoo, who says that the church was never more united than at present—the confidence in the authorities of the church is unabated—the disaffected, who are in favor of a reorganization of the church, number twelve individuals, four of whom are doubtful—there are many tales afloat about the Mormons, in the east, which have not the slightest foundation in truth. We would advise the saints not to give ear to such reports.

"Matters at Headquarters," *The Prophet*, New York, June 22, 1844

We have just issued from the press, a stereotyped edition of Gen. Smith's Political Writings, together with a copy of a Memorial to the Legislature of Missouri: the whole forming a neat octavo pamphlet of forty one pages . . . price six dollars per hundred, or one dollar per dozen copies . . . "Mormon Book Depository," [offers for sale copies of] Gen. Jos. Smith's views on the policy of Government; Appeal to the Green Mountain Boys; Correspondence between Gen. Smith, Col. Wentworth and J. C. Calhoun, and a Memorial to the Legislature of Missouri.

Advertisement, *The Prophet*, New York, June 22, 1844

✶ ✶ ✶ ✶ ✶

On Sunday afternoon, June 23, Joseph and Hyrum wrote to Governor Ford. They agreed to proceed to Carthage the next day, with a suitable escort, accompanied by witnesses. "We will meet your posse, if this letter is satisfactory, (if not, inform me) at or near the [Carthage] Mound, at or about two o'clock tomorrow afternoon." Theodore Turley expressed the letter to Carthage. Joseph began his search for a defense attorney.[31]

A large party of nearly thirty men on horseback—those indicted on charges of riot for the destruction of property belonging to the owners of the *Expositor*, Joseph's attorney, James Woods, and several others—departed Nauvoo in the early morning of June 24. About four miles from Carthage they were met by Captain Dunn, who had orders from the governor to collect all of the weapons of the Nauvoo Legion. Joseph countersigned the order and returned to Nauvoo, where he disbanded the legion and assisted in collecting the weapons; in all four cannons and some one thousand stand of arms. Woods went on to Carthage to seek a pledge of safety for the arriving prisoners.

Hyrum sent a trusted observer to Carthage to "see what [was] going on." The intelligence, gathered from Carthage residents friendly to the Mormons, was not encouraging. One person said, "that as sure as Joseph and Hyrum came to Carthage, they would be killed." Artois Hamilton, proprietor of the Hamilton Hotel, warned

---

31. Joseph Smith [Bank of the River Mississippi] to Thomas Ford, 23 June 1844, in Smith, *History of the Church* 6:550, Hallwas and Launius, *Cultures in Conflict*, 189. Smith, *History of the Church* 6:551–53.

the informant. "Those are the boys," he said, pointing to the Carthage Greys, "that will settle you Mormons." Hyrum was advised against going to Carthage. "Do not go another foot, for they say they will kill you, if you go to Carthage."[32]

Choosing to disregard the impassioned warning, and recognizing he had no other alternative, Joseph and his company headed for Carthage a second time that evening. Four miles west of the county seat, at the Carthage Mound, they were again met by Captain Dunn "and his company of dragoons."[33]

Joseph told his brethren not under indictment to return to Nauvoo. "Be faithful, honor the law, and keep the commandments of God," he said. Joseph was resigned to his fate. "Nothing but the interposition of Almighty God can save us now," he said. "We will give ourselves to the slaughter . . . I feel perfectly calm, never better—calm as a morning in spring. I shall die innocent."[34]

That evening a thunderstorm arose in the west.

---

32. H. T. Reid and James W. Wood to Joseph Smith, 24 June 1844, in Smith, *History of the Church* 6:558–59. Statement by Abram C. Hodge, in Smith, *History of the Church* 6:557–58.

33. Willard Richards, Journal [24 June 1844], quoted in *Old Mormon Nauvoo*, 188.

34. H. Herringshaw [Nauvoo] to William Smith [New York] 28 August 1844, in *The Prophet* 21 September 1844. The commonly accepted statement by Joseph that he was going "like a lamb to the slaughter" (e.g. Smith, *History of the Church* 6:555) is first found as a postscript in a letter from Willard Richards and John Taylor to Reuben Hedlock, 9 July 1844, in Smith, *History of the Church* 7:175. Another relatively early documented example of its usage outside of the *History of the Church* narrative is Doctrine and Covenants 135:4. More significant (on two fronts as noted below) is the following comment in Sarah Scott to [her in-laws], 22 July 1844 and a 9 August addendum by Isaac Scott: "You will likely hear a great deal about Joseph's innocence such as 'I go as a lamb to the slaughter, and if I die, I die an innocent man.' All these statements, I believe, are false and got up for the purpose of reconciling the minds of the Church. I believe they had not the least idea that they were going to be murdered. Hyrum said the last time I heard him preach, which was only a few days before he and Joseph were taken to Carthage, that their enemies could not kill brother Joseph, for he had a great work to accomplish yet. There was also considerable said in Carthage which proves beyond dispute that they did not expect death. They blame the apostates, as they term them, with being accessory to the murder of the Smiths. This is not the case: the Laws and Fosters were not in the state at the time the murder was committed, and if they had been there, they would have been the last to stain their hands with human blood." (Partridge, "Mormon Dictator," 600) The letter strongly suggests that the "lamb to the slaughter" phrase was intended to preserve the image of Joseph Smith as a prophet to the very end of his life. Another important fact, again contrary to many published assertions, is that this letter confirms that the Laws and Fosters had already left Illinois at the time of the murders and were not present at Carthage jail.

Chapter Thirteen

Carthage

THE NAUVOO COMPANY ARRIVED AT Hamilton's Hotel just before midnight. A "great crowd" of nearly five hundred soldiers greeted them, eager to catch a glimpse of the infamous Joe Smith. The governor told the men to leave, that they would be permitted to see the Mormon prophet in the morning.

After rising early, Joseph and Hyrum surrendered themselves to the constable. At half-past eight Governor Ford assembled the troops from Hancock and surrounding counties on the square near the courthouse. Many local citizens also gathered around the square, anxious to see the prisoners. George T. M. Davis, Illinois Whig leader and political editor of the *Alton Telegraph*, was among them. Brigadier General Minor R. Deming passed the Smith brothers along the lines of troops under a guard composed of the Carthage Greys. The men made three stops before each unit "so that all could see."[1]

"*General* Joseph Smith on my right, and *General* Hyrum Smith on my left," he announced at each juncture. Infuriated that the Carthage Greys had become an "*escort*, not a guard, to the two prisoners," Captain Robert F. Smith signaled for his men to break rank. General Deming ordered their arrest for mutiny.

"Boys, will you stand this?" asked Captain Smith.

"No!" chorused the Greys.

"Then load with ball cartridges!"[2]

Governor Ford stepped forward to intervene. "It was without [my] orders," he explained, "that any introduction had taken place of the Smiths to the soldiers, and that they were regarded as a guard, not as an escort." Ford countermanded the arrest. The Greys hissed as General Deming completed the "inspection."[3]

Following the display, Joseph, Hyrum, and the other Mormon prisoners were loosely guarded and allowed to move freely about Hamilton's tavern. Informants came and went throughout the day. William Prentiss, the United States marshal for Illinois,

1. "Joe Smith," *Western Star*, from the *St. Louis Republican*. Smith, *History of the Church* 6:559. Davis, *Authentic Account*, 34.

2. Davis, *Authentic Account*, 34–35. Compare Smith, *History of the Church* 6:563.

3. Davis, *Authentic Account*, 35. See also Samuel Otho Williams to John Prickett, 10 July 1844, in Hampshire, *Mormonism in Conflict*, 206–207, Lundwall, *Fate of the Persecutors*, 215–19. Williams claimed Joseph Smith fainted. A rebuttal is found in Smith, *History of the Church* 6:604. Similarly, "The Mormon Difficulties," *Lee County Democrat*, 29 June 1844. Compare Smith, *History of the Church* 6:563–64.

"called to see Joseph" later that morning. Mark Aldrich, major in command of the War-saw Independent Battalion, longtime Freemason and noted anti-Mormon, met with the prophet as well as the governor in the early afternoon. There was to be no mistake about the identity of the men in custody and the plans that were to be carried out.[4]

Governor Ford ordered Captain Singleton to march his McDonough County troops to Nauvoo, "take command of the police and forces" and maintain order there. Nearly thirteen hundred armed men were assembled at Carthage. Another five hundred militiamen were gathered in Warsaw, anxious to march into Nauvoo. Golden Point, not far from the Mississippi River, "about equidistant from Nauvoo and Warsaw," was selected as the place of rendezvous for the two bodies of troops. They were to join forces on the morning of June 27.

Colonel Levi Williams of Warsaw, commandant of the Fifty-ninth Regiment of the Illinois militia, was ordered by General Deming to take the men under his com-mand and join with the Carthage encampment "preparatory to marching into the City of Nauvoo in the order of military attack. You are further ordered to provide your Regiment with 4 days provision for this Campaign." The orders were signed by Deming's aide-de-camp, Carthage attorney Onias B. Skinner. The Warsaw troops approached Carthage before noon.[5]

Carthage Grey Captain Robert F. Smith, a justice of the peace, unexpectedly called for the examination of the case of "Joseph and Hiram Smith for 'riot.'" At the hearing, prosecutor Chauncey L. Higbee moved to adjourn. Lawyers for Joseph and Hyrum objected. While the procedure would free the defendants from jail, it would mean entering recognizances that "virtually admitted their guilt of the charge pre-ferred against them." With no other recourse, Joseph and Hyrum "waived the exami-nation of witnesses against them and entered into recognizances in the sum of five hundred dollars each" in order to guarantee their appearance at the next term of the Circuit Court for Hancock County.[6]

Shortly after Joseph and Hyrum had completed their recognizance bonds and were waiting to conduct an interview with the governor, they were approached by the constable, who served the men with new writs, this time charging them with treason for calling out the Nauvoo Legion earlier in the month. The papers had been sworn out before Justice Robert F. Smith the previous day in order to prevent the Smith brothers from ever leaving Carthage.[7]

Justice Smith remanded Joseph and Hyrum to jail to await examination on the new charge, scheduled to take place the next day. The accused were taken to the Carthage jail.[8]

4. Smith, *History of the Church* 6:564–65.
5. Special Brigade Order No. 15, to Captain Singleton, 25 June 1844, in Davis, *Authentic Account*, 15. Smith, *History of the Church* 7:14. General M. R. Deming order to Colonel Levi Williams, 25 June 1844. Minor Deming was commissioned Brigadier General, Fourth Brigade, Fifth Division, of Il-linois State Militia on 10 May 1844. Exec. Rec. 1843–1847 4.184. Illinois State Archives, Springfield.
6. Davis, *Authentic Account*, 15. Smith, *History of the Church* 6:567–68.
7. Ibid.
8. The treason charge against Joseph Smith was brought by Augustine Spencer. Hyrum was charged by Hyrum O. Norton. Both writs, dated June 24, 1844, in Smith, *History of the Church* 6:561–62. See also Willard Richards, Journal [25 June 1844, 9:15 A.M.], quoted in Holzapfel and Cottle, *Old*

* * * * *

Elder William Smith, "who was heartily cheered on coming forth," addressed a Jeffersonian Meeting at the Marion Temperance Hall on Canal Street in New York City on June 25. The gathering sang "Mobbers of Missouri," because, he said, there was no song more appropriate. Smith spoke about the "stand we have taken in unfurling our banner to the world, with the name of the friend of the oppressed, Gen. Jos. Smith, inscribed on it as a candidate for the Presidency." He pictured "in a vivid manner" the character of his brother, "the people's candidate . . . Three cheers for the General and Sidney Rigdon!"

Fellow Council of Fifty member Orson Hyde took the stand. He was grateful for the honor conferred upon him, he said, and although "the former speaker said that he did not come here to preach the scripture, but to preach politically . . . it is hard to separate them entirely, for he had noticed he had slipped them in occasionally." Elder Hyde referred to Joseph Smith's prophecies regarding the downfall of the United States as a nation, and as evidence pointed to the recent incident in which "the big gun that exploded in Washington" on board the warship Princeton had killed the U.S. secretary of state and delayed the submission of the treaty of annexation with Texas. Joseph Smith also wanted to see slavery "done away with," Hyde noted, however "he did not want to see them taken away without compensation . . . which could be made satisfactory." His remarks were greeted with "three cheers for General Smith."[9]

David S. Hollister wrote to the prophet and the Council of Fifty from Baltimore on June 26. "Newspaper publications have frighent some people crazy," he said. The ominous news from the west had frustrated his negotiations during the Democratic National Convention held in Baltimore in late May. "I was not a little chagrined at the little success we met with." He would continue to work to "prepare a place" for the Mormon independent political convention scheduled for August, call a meeting of delegates through the Baltimore city papers, and do whatever the Council of Fifty requested.[10]

* * * * *

The Carthage jail, a large recently-built two-story stone structure, was on the north side of Walnut Street on the outskirts of town, one block north and one and three-quarter blocks west of the public square, about a quarter mile from the courthouse.

Mormon Nauvoo, 188–89. Dan Jones recalled that the anti-Mormons (Joseph H. Jackson) claimed they "had eighteen accusations against Joseph, and as one failed, they would try another to detain him there, and they had had so much trouble and hazard, and worked so hard in getting him to Carthage, that they would not let him get out of it alive." (Smith, *History of the Church* 6:568–69). See also Woods, Memoirs, in Stiles, *Recollections and Sketches*. Stephen Markham to Wilford Woodruff, 20 June 1856, LDS Archives. Joseph Smith to Judge Thomas, 26 June 1844, in Smith, *History of the Church* 6:590–91. See also Smith, *History of the Church* 6:569–71, 574.

9. "Political Jeffersonian Meeting," *The Prophet* 29 June 1844. The same issue notes, "Elder Wm. Smith, of the 'Quorum of the Twelve' having accepted of the Editorship of the Prophet all letters or communications appertaining to the business must be addressed to him (post paid)."

10. David S. Hollister [Baltimore] to Joseph Smith [and Council of Fifty], 26 June 1844, LDS Archives.

View of Carthage Jail. Piercy, *Route from Liverpool to Great Salt Lake Valley.*

The building was thirty-four feet by twenty-eight feet in outer dimensions, its southern exposure standing eighteen feet back from the street. The jail yard was enclosed by a low wooden fence. A well, protected by a waist-high curbing, was on the east side of the yard. An open space to the north of the jail led to a skirt of timber and the Warsaw road.

The jailer and his family occupied the ground floor and a large upstairs parlor ("the front room"). The main floor consisted of a kitchen, an eating area (with fireplace) and the debtor's prison. The main entrance to the jail was on the south side of the building. Just inside the entryway, stairs led to an upper landing. At the top of the landing to the right was the jailer's family room, furnished with a thin panel door locked by a simple latch. The pleasant room had a fireplace and double-hung glass-paned windows, two on the south side and one on the east. They were unbarred. Immediately beyond the second-story landing was the actual jail, a windowless room with several wrought iron cages bolted to the walls, the floor covered with loose straw for mattresses and hygiene.[11]

For a time, Joseph and Hyrum were kept in the upstairs criminal cells. Later that evening Sheriff Stigall moved the men to the barred lower north room of the jail, on the ground floor, usually reserved for debtors. There the two prisoners were joined by eight other men, most of them fellow Saints, including Williard Richards,

---

11. Richards, Journal, 25 June 1844, quoted in *Old Mormon Nauvoo*, 188–189. Stephen Markham to Wilford Woodruff, 20 June 1856, LDS Archives. Good descriptions of the Carthage jail include: Jensen and Stevenson, "Infancy," 8 October 1888, 59. Thomas L. Barnes to Miranda Barnes Haskett, 6 November 1897, in Mulder and Mortensen, *Among the Mormons*, 146–51. Huntress, *Murder*, 146–53. Lundwall, *Fate of the Persecutors*, 220–23. Davis, *Authentic Account*, 21–22.

Reconstruction of the Carthage jail.

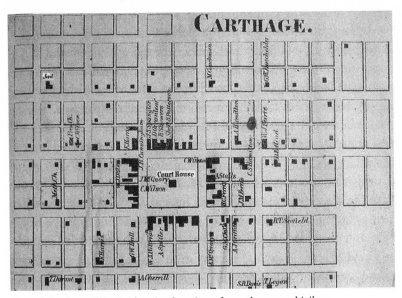

Plan of Carthage, Illinois, showing location of courthouse and jail.

John Taylor, Stephen Markham, and Dan Jones. Dr. Wall Southwick was the only non-Mormon. The room was bare. "There was no bed, cot, or char what I can recall to mind, and here, if I recollect aright," one of the men later wrote, "we spent the night amusing ourselves as best we could." Stephen Markham, who served as Joseph's bodyguard, saw "several men with their fire arms peeking through the windows." Markham secured Joseph and Hyrum "in one corner of the room where they could not be seen & guarded them all night." After a restless sleep huddled on the floor of the debtor's room, the men ate a "well prepared" breakfast with jailer Stigall and his family. The two prisoners were then escorted to the upstairs sitting room.

Stephen Markham and Dr. Wall Southwick went into town. The news was not good. There was a "good deal of exitement especialy with the Carthage Grays," because the men had rebelled and said they would "kill Joseph & H[yrum]." Dr. Southwick went to consult with the governor.[12]

Jailor Stigall and Joseph Smith spoke for a time. Stigall sympathized with the plight of the prophet. Mormon leader William Clayton's youngest sister, Lucy, who lived with the jailor and his family, was employed as their housekeeper. To console his prisoner, Stigall pointed out that the supposed "invasion" of nine thousand men from Missouri was actually closer to two hundred. Joseph asked Stigall to deliver a letter to the governor at the Hamilton Hotel. In it Smith requested another interview, "having been much disappointed the past evening." Ford was to "send an answer per bearer." Stigall returned less than an hour later, the letter endorsed. "The interview will take place at my earliest leisure to-day. [signed] Governor Ford."[13]

The governor, together with Colonel Thomas Geddes of the Illinois militia, met with the prophet in the upstairs bedroom. The discussion centered on the legality of the actions taken by Joseph Smith to protect his city and his people from "a large, organized military and mobocratic foe." Joseph maintained that his actions were fully justified. "I shall look to you for our protection," he told the governor. "I believe you are talking of going to Nauvoo; if you go, sir, I wish to go along. I refuse not to answer any law, but I do not consider myself safe here."

"I am in hopes that you will be acquitted," the governor assured him. "But if I go, I will certainly take you along. I do not, however, apprehend danger . . . you shall have protection, General Smith. I did not make this promise without consulting my officers, who all pledged their honor to its fulfillment."[14]

Governor Ford and Colonel Geddes left the jail. Reminded perhaps of the extermination order issued by the governor of Missouri six years earlier, after the two

---

12. John S. Fullmer to Wilford Woodruff, 18 October 1881, LDS Archives. Jason H. Sherman, "Reminiscences of the Mormons in Illinois," *Ithaca Journal* 26 April 1886. Smith *History of the Church* 6:575.

13. Joseph Smith to Thomas Ford and Thomas Ford to Joseph Smith 26 June 1844, in Smith, *History of the Church* 6:575–76.

14. Smith, *History of the Church* 6:576, 577–79 [Manuscript History version]. 6:579–85 [John Taylor version]. Smith, *History of the Church* 7:95 [John Taylor]. Roberts, *Rise and Fall*, 437. Note, Thomas L. Barnes, a captain in the Carthage militia, testified that he "never heard that [the] Smiths were to be killed that evening, nor did I know that Warsaw companies were coming. I had no *intimation* that the Smiths were to be killed." (Sharp, *Trial*, 15). Significantly, the Wilford C. Wood Collection transcript of Barnes's testimony adds: "I may have supposed something but my suppositions ought not to hang any one . . . the companies here themselves and not their officers had pledged themselves to the Governor to protect the Smiths." (57)

men were no longer within earshot of the jail Ford exclaimed to Geddes, "O, it's all nonsense; you will have to drive these Mormons out yet!"

"If we undertake that, Governor," Geddes queried, "when the proper time comes, will you interfere?"

"No, I will not," he said, "until you are through!" The two conspirators walked toward their military headquarters at Hamilton Hotel. Ford's promise to protect Joseph Smith was now revealed as nothing more than a ruse.[15]

Still, Ford was uncomfortable in his role as Judas. An informant approached the governor as he reached the fence just outside the two-story building. "The soldiers are determined to see Joe Smith dead before they leave here," the informant told him. Ford retorted, "If you know of any such thing keep it to yourself."[16]

Colonel Enoch C. March and George T. M. Davis, both residents of Alton, rode into Nauvoo that afternoon. March asked a Mormon acquaintance if he thought the prophet had any hope of returning to Nauvoo alive. The man "had no doubt but that he would be honorably discharged upon his trial by the court, and would be preserved in safety from the power of his enemies; that he was in the hands of his God, whom he loved and faithfully served; and He, who held the destinies of nations in His own hands, would deliver him from his enemies, as He had done hundreds of times before."

"You are mistaken, " Colonel March replied, "and I know it; you do not know what I know; I tell you they will kill Joe Smith before he leaves Carthage, and I know it, and you never will see him alive again."

"Enoch," the man said, "I do not believe it, he is in the hands of God, and God will deliver him."

Undeterred, March replied, "I know better; when you hear of him again, you will hear he is dead."[17]

The Carthage constable handed jailer Stigall a request from Justice Robert F. Smith: "You are hereby commanded to bring the bodies of Joseph Smith and Hyrum Smith from the jail of said county, forthwith before me at my office, for an examination on the charge of treason, they having been committed for safe keeping until trial could be had on such examination, and the state now being ready for such examination." Stigall refused the application because he had insufficient authority and "could find no law authorizing a justice of the peace to demand prisoners committed to his charge." Major Frank Worrell, of the Carthage Greys, compelled Stigall, by force of arms, to give up the prisoners. Joseph and Hyrum walked to the courthouse, accompanied by several of their trusted friends, under guard by the Carthage Greys, "who formed a hollow square," fixed bayonets at the ready, "with Joe and Hyrum in the middle."[18]

15. Thomas Geddes interview, in Gregg, *History of Hancock County*, 372, also quoted in Smith, *History of the Church* 6:585–86, note.

16. Alfred Randall affidavit, 12 February 1855, in Smith, *History of the Church* 6:586–87.

17. Jonathan C. Wright affidavit, 13 January 1855, in Smith, *History of the Church* 6:587–88.

18. Robert F. Smith, order to bring Joseph and Hyrum Smith to court, 26 June 1844, in Smith, *History of the Church* 6:596. The earlier false mittimus issued by Robert F. Smith, dated 25 June 1844, in Smith, *History of the Church* 6:569. See also Smith, *History of the Church* 6:570–71, on the illegality of the writ. John Taylor's lengthy account of the proceedings is in Smith, *History of the Church* 6:571–74. Counselor H. T. Reid's remarks are on 575. Order, 26 June 1844, in Smith, *History of the Church* 6:596 and 594. John S. Fullmer to Wilford Woodruff 18 October 1881, LDS Archives. Davis, *Authentic Account*, 15–16.

George T. M. Davis looked on. "The court house was crowded to suffocation, and but a small portion of those collected, could gain admittance," he recorded. "A few moments after the prisoners were brought in, and order could be restored, the justices inquired of the prosecution if they were ready to proceed with the investigation, who replied in the affirmative." Onias C. Skinner, Judge Sylvester Emmons (former editor of the *Nauvoo Expositor*), and Thomas Sharp (current editor of the *Warsaw Signal*) prosecuted the case.[19]

Joseph and Hyrum's defense attorneys remarked that they "were not prepared," and applied for a continuance. The hearing was deferred until the next day at noon. The two prisoners were returned to jail "under the same armed force, and in the same manner as they had been brought into court." Upon reaching the safety of the jailor's bedroom, Mormon elder John S. Fullmer gave Joseph "a single barrel pocket pistol, about six inches, in length, silver mounted" which he had carried "unobserved" in his boot top.[20]

Ford sent jailer Stigall a note. "I would advise the jailor to keep the Messrs. Smith in the [upstairs] room in which I found them this morning, unless a closer confinement should be clearly necessary to prevent an escape. [signed] Thomas Ford, Governor and Commander-in-Chief. June 26, 1844"[21]

That evening several dozen men met in an upstairs room of the Hamilton Hotel in Carthage. The atmosphere was somber. This was the latest meeting of the Carthage Central Committee (also known as the Vigilance Committee of Safety), initially composed of anti-Mormon "old citizens" of Hancock and surrounding counties in Illinois. Tonight, in addition to local militia leaders, the group was joined by Illinois Whig Central Committee member George T. M. Davis, Illinois Governor Thomas Ford, as well as some two dozen representatives from nearly every state in the Union and the Republic of Texas. The men had responded to a "secret national call" to join forces against the Mormons, transforming the local anti-Mormon committee into a star chamber political trial. A secretary took minutes of the proceedings. A sentinel kept guard.[22]

The men reviewed the situation confronting them. Joseph Smith and his brother Hyrum, prophet and patriarch of the Church of Jesus Christ of Latter-day Saints, were confined to the Carthage jail, on charges of treason for having illegally called

---

19. Davis, *Authentic Account*, 16.

20. John S. Fullmer to Wilford Woodruff, 18 October 1881, LDS Archives.

21. Ibid. Smith, *History of the Church* 6:596. Thomas Ford to G. W. Stigall, 26 June 1844, in Smith, *History of the Church* 6:598. See also Willard Richards, Journal [26 June 1844, 4:25 P.M.], quoted in Holzapfel and Cottle, *Old Mormon Nauvoo*, 189, and Thomas Ford, *History of Illinois*, in Smith, *History of the Church* 7:13. That an escape was planned is asserted by G. T. M. Davis, *Authentic Account*, 16 and 21.

22. Davis, *Autobiography*, 80–81, uses "Vigilance Committee of Safety" and "Committee of Vigilance". On the "secret national call," see Cone, *Biographical and Historical Sketches*, 184. Stephen Markham to Wilford Woodruff, 20 June 1856, LDS Archives. Davis, *Autobiography*, called the body a "secret tribunal." Davis's detailed remarks on the proceedings in his *Autobiography* make it apparent he was present at the Hamilton Hotel during the meeting. Sworn to secrecy, he never admitted to being in attendance. Note especially his comments in Davis, *Authentic Account*, 27 and 80. Beginning with the Joseph Smith History as published in the *Deseret News* and *Millennial Star* (see Journal History, 27 June 1844), the meeting has been erroneously placed on the morning of June 27.

out the Nauvoo Legion. Those present swore that Joseph Smith would not be released from jail alive. Delegates from the eastern states pointed out that Joseph's "Views on Government" taught by nearly four hundred Mormon political missionaries were "widely circulated & took like wild fire." It was further believed that if Smith "did not get into the Presidential chair this election, he would be sure to next," as his support included many prominent Masons and Masonic bodies throughout the United States. The fear was best expressed by Warsaw businessman and militia leader George Rockwell, who, like many of the delegates in Carthage, believed that Joseph and Hyrum Smith's "political influence was seen and felt by the whole State" of Illinois, and "had been so guided by revelation that it bid fair in a few years if they continued to prosper and increase, to sap the very foundations of our [national] government."[23]

The Committee of Safety considered two possible courses of action in order to prevent Joseph from achieving his political goals. One recommendation was that following the departure of Governor Ford for Nauvoo on the June 27, the two Smiths would be shot by a rifle detail made up of selectmen from militia units in western Illinois. A more drastic solution was to burn Mormon Nauvoo to the ground, "its men, women, and children left to the disposal of the soldiers."[24]

In the interest of "justice and mercy," the committee determined that the lives of Joseph and Hyrum would be sufficient compensation for the wrongdoings of the Saints in Illinois. Property of the Mormons would be kept intact, with the understanding that the Saints would shortly thereafter leave the state.[25]

Volunteers were called for. In all, a dozen men were selected for their bravery and marksmanship. Each man pledged "that they would neither eat nor sleep until Smith was dead" and agreed never to reveal the identities of those involved in the extralegal executions.[26]

Colonel Stephen Markham, widely recognized as Joseph's bodyguard and one of the men who had broken up the *Expositor* press, approached the room where the secret meeting was being held. When his presence became known, an alarm was sounded. The assembly quickly dispersed. In the confusion, Dr. Wall

---

23. Stephen Markham to Wilford Woodruff, 20 June 1856, LDS Archives (wild fire and chair quotes). Cartwright, *Autobiography*, 228. Cartwright noted, "When Joe Smith was announced a candidate for President of these United States, almost every infidel association [meaning Freemasons] in the Union declared in his favor. I traveled extensively through the Eastern states and cities, as well as in the West, that year; and I must say this was literally true, as far as I conversed with, or obtained reliable information of those infidel association or individuals." George Rockwell to Thomas H. Rockwell, 3 August 1844, in Hallwas and Launius, *Cultures in Conflict*, 234 (government quote). It is not known if Rockwell was present at the Carthage meeting on 26 June 1844.

24. Davis, *Autobiography*, 80–81.

25. Ibid.

26. "Man who helped kill Mormon head in 1844 Confessed in Mount Airy," *Mount Airy News*, 24 February 1927. Davis, *Autobiography*, 80, wrote, "Their fate had been sealed and their doom determined upon the night previous [to their murders]." See also Davis, *Authentic Account*, 27–28. This agreement echoes an incident recorded in Acts 23:12–14: "When it was day, the Jews made a plot and bound themselves by an oath neither to eat nor drink till they had killed Paul. There were more than forty who made this conspiracy. And they went to the chief priests and elders, and said, 'We have strictly bound ourselves by an oath to taste no food till we have killed Paul.'"

Southwick (the Texas representative) slipped the minutes book into his coat pocket and withdrew.

When Southwick and Markham reached a safe location, Southwick disclosed the minutes book and its contents that confirmed the rumors that had been circulating for the past several days. Southwick promised Markham the volume after he had made a copy for his own use. Markham returned to the Carthage jail and reported to Joseph Smith that the men at Hamilton's Hotel meant to kill him the next day. "Be not afraid," was Joseph's only response.[27]

George T. M. Davis repaired to his room in the hotel to initiate his latest propaganda campaign and began the first in a series of letters for publication in the *Alton Telegraph*. He headed the letter, "Carthage, June 26, 1844, 8 P.M."

> All is excitement and confusion on the part of the citizens, with no concert of action, and united but in one sentiment; and that is, a fixed determination to rid themselves, in some way or other, of the obnoxious leaders of the Mormons . . .
>
> Their trial was fixed for this afternoon; but, upon the application of the accused, it has been postponed until Saturday of this week, the 29th inst . . .
>
> Mr. Wood, a lawyer from Burlington, has labored hard to give a political cast to the affair, and to impress Gov. Ford with the idea of doing the same. In it, however, he has signally failed, for there is but one mind among all the citizens in regard to this matter, without distinction of party or sect . . .
>
> Notwithstanding the accumulated wrongs and injuries inflicted upon the citizens, by the Mormons, there is a commendable spirit on the part of the former, only to hold the leaders responsible; and the convictions of my mind are, that before they disband, a desperate effort will be made to visit summary punishment upon the two Smiths, and possibly one or two others at Nauvoo. The citizens state openly, that it is now reduced to the alternative, that either they in a body must abandon the county of Hancock and their property, or the leaders of the Mormons must quit the country . . .
>
> You need not be at all surprised, to hear, at any time, of the destruction of the two Smiths by the populace. The Governor has placed a guard of fifty men to protect the jail in which they are confined from attack, and destruction; but judging from what I hear and see I entertain but little hope of success of this effort. I now think of going to Nauvoo to-morrow with the army; and if so, will write you from that place.
>
> Yours truly, G. T. M. D.[28]

Another meeting was held in Warsaw later that same evening. Jacob C. Davis, captain of the Warsaw Rifle Company, William N. Grover, captain of the Warsaw Cadets, and Major Mark Aldrich, commander of the Warsaw Independent Battalion, met together to select twenty men from their forces "to go and kill Joseph and Hiram Smith in the jail at Carthage."[29]

27. Stephen Markham to Wilford Woodruff, 20 June 1856, LDS Archives.
28. G. T. M. Davis [Carthage, 8 P.M.] to John Bailhache 26 June 1844, in *Alton Telegraph* 6 July, 1844.
29. William Daniels, grand jury testimony, October 1844. P13, f41, Community of Christ Archives.

Brigadier General Deming, writing from "Head Quarters, Carthage," informed his family in Lichtfield, Connecticut, that his brother Edwin, then living in Quincy, had been killed by lightning several days earlier. Deming planned to accompany the Governor to Nauvoo on the June 27 and proceed from there to Quincy to make arrangements for Edwin's funeral.[30]

When Joseph's lawyers informed him of the new date for the trial, Elder Taylor prayed for deliverance. The longer the men were kept in jail, the less likely it was they would come out alive. John S. Fullmer, John Taylor, Stephen Markham, Dan Jones, and Williard Richards remained with Joseph and Hyrum in the front room of the jail. The men retired for the night.

After breakfast the next morning, Dan Jones, a Welsh convert and ship captain, left the jail to find out what he could about a gunshot the prisoners had heard during the night. Just outside he encountered Franklin Worrell, a local dry goods merchant and officer in the Carthage Greys. "We have had too much trouble to bring Old Joe here to let him ever escape alive," Worrell said to Jones, "and unless you want to die with him you had better leave before sundown; and you are not a damned bit better than him for taking his part, and you'll see that I can prophesy better than Old Joe, for neither he nor his brother, nor anyone who will remain with them will see the sun set today."[31]

Jones passed the military encampment on his way to inform Governor Ford about the conspiracy against the prophet's life. "Our troops will be discharged this morning in obedience to orders," Jones heard one soldier say, "and for a sham we will leave the town; but when the Governor and the McDonough troops have left for Nauvoo this afternoon, we will return and kill those men, if we have to tear the jail down." Three cheers rose up. Upon being informed of this latest intelligence, Ford told Jones: "You are unnecessarily alarmed for the safety of your friends, sir, the people are not that cruel." Ford, who had been at the Hamilton Hotel meeting the night before, knew full well what was about to transpire.

Not entirely convinced that Mr. Ford had understood what he was trying to say, Jones continued. "The Messers. Smith are American citizens," Jones pointed out, "and have surrendered themselves to your Excellency upon your pledging your honor for their safety; they are also Master Masons, and as such I demand of you protection of their lives." Ford said nothing.[32]

Jones returned to the jail, where Joseph addressed a letter to his wife. He assured her of his safety and added a note at the end, "P. S.—Dear Emma, I am very much resigned to my lot, knowing I am justified, and have done the best that could be done. Give my love to the children and all my friends . . . and all who inquire after me; and as for treason, I know that I have not committed any, and they cannot prove anything of the kind, so you need not have any fears that anything can happen to us on that account. May God bless you all. Amen."[33]

---

30. Minor R. Deming to Stephen Deming, 26 June 1844, Deming Papers, Illinois Historical Survey, Urbana.
31. Smith, *History of the Church* 6:602.
32. Ibid., 6:602–3.
33. Joseph Smith to Emma Smith, 27 June 1844 [8:20 a.m.], in Smith, *History of the Church* 6:605. Roberts, *Comprehensive History* 2:268.

The governor's meeting with the "council of officers" of the companies en-camped at Carthage that morning bordered on mutinous. The officers of Hancock (excepting the leaders of the Warsaw militia, who were not present) favored march-ing into Nauvoo. Nearly all of the officers from Schuyler and McDonough counties voted against it. A small majority wanted to march to the Mormon Holy City, pos-sibly provoking an outbreak of uncontrollable violence.

The officers insisted they had two justifiable reasons for marching to Nauvoo in full force. First, they hoped "to search for apparatus to make counterfeit money," the manufacture and possession of which was a federal offense. They also intended to "terrify the Mormons from attempting any open or secret measures of vengeance against the citizens of the county, who had taken a part against them or their leaders." Brigadier General Deming argued that disbanding the troops was the only viable option, since "it would be unsafe to control or manage them" in their present state of agitation.

Ford proposed instead to proceed to Nauvoo with a token company of troops, "search [for counterfeit], and deliver an address to the Mormons" warning them against any outbreak of violence against the Gentile citizens of the county. He coun-termanded his previous order to march on Nauvoo with an expeditionary force. Jo-seph's attorney objected. "As long as the Governor remained in Carthage, the Smiths would be safe," he believed. "As soon as he left there would be no safety." He asked for a guard.[34]

Ford ordered the Carthage Greys to disband, "with the exception of three compa-nies, two of which were retained as a guard to the jail." The third company, consisting of sixty mounted soldiers under Captain Dunn, was to accompany the commander in chief to Nauvoo. Ford had originally thought to use McDonough troops to guard the jail. The men were "in a perfect fever" to return to their families, however. There were few provisions with which to "supply them for more than a few days" and "their crops were suffering at home" from damage caused by the unusually heavy spring rains. Carthage men, on the other hand, could "board at their own houses." And, it was likely the Smith trial might not be held until autumn. Ford believed that keep-ing a force "from a foreign county for so long a time" away from their families was an unreasonable demand. Brigadier General Deming, known for his opposition to "mobocracy and violence towards the prisoners," recommended that a local force be used to guard the prisoners during their incarceration.

Two companies of Carthage Greys, under the command of Captain Robert F. Smith, were ordered to guard the jail. Ford justified his choice of guards for the Smiths by explaining that the Greys were "an old independent company, well armed, uniformed and drilled, and the members of it were the elite of the militia of the county." Captain Smith "was universally spoken of as a most respectable citizen and honorable man," the governor insisted, knowing full well that "they and their officers were the deadly enemies of the prisoners." He had little choice, he said. "It would have been difficult to find friends of the prisoners under my command, unless I had called in the Mormons as a guard, and this I was satisfied would have led to the

---

34. Ford, *History of Illinois,* in Smith, *History of the Church* 7:16–17. G. T. M. Davis to John Bailhache, 26 June 1844, in *Alton Telegraph* 6 July 1844. Woods, Memoirs, in Stiles, *Recollections and Sketches.*

immediate war and the sure death of the prisoners." Still, he had "confidence in their loyalty and integrity ... [and] relied upon this company especially because it was an independent company, for a long time instructed and practiced in military discipline and subordination. [He] also had their word and honor, officers and men, to do their duty according to law."[35]

Joseph's attorney had to give in. "All I could do was to go with them," Woods later recalled. The two companies of Carthage Greys moved their tents to the south-west corner of the public square and "took up their quarters in the court house." The guard detail assigned to the jail, five hundred yards to the west, consisted of "six men from the company, with an officer in command." The men rotated guard duty on three-hour shifts.[36]

"I am about to leave for Nauvoo," Mormon Cyrus Wheelock informed the governor, "and I fear for those men; they are safe as regards the law, but they are not safe from the hands of traitors, and midnight assassins who thirst for their blood and have determined to spill it; and under these circumstances I leave with a heavy heart."

"Your friends shall be protected," Ford replied, "and have a fair trial by the law; in this pledge I am not alone; I have obtained the pledge of the whole of the army to sustain me." He failed to mention the pledge of protection did not extend to the War-saw troops, to himself, nor to anyone else who was in the secret meetings in Carthage and Warsaw the night before.[37]

Wheelock slipped into the jail unsearched and gave Joseph an Allen's Patent Pepperbox charged with six cartridges. Joseph handed Hyrum the single barrel pistol that had been smuggled into the prison the night before. "You may have use for this," Joseph said. "I hate to use such things or to see them used," Hyrum replied. "So do I," said Joseph, "but we may have to, to defend ourselves." Hyrum took the pistol.[38]

Wheelock departed for Nauvoo with verbal instructions from the prophet to inform the commanders of the Nauvoo Legion they were to "avoid all military dis-play, or any other movement calculated to produce excitement during the Gover-nor's visit." Joseph concluded another letter to his wife Emma. "P.S.—20 minutes to 10.—I just learn that the Governor is about to disband his troops, and put a guard to protect us and the peace, and come himself to Nauvoo and deliver a speech to the people. This is right as I suppose."[39]

---

35. Ford, *History of Illinois*, in Smith, *History of the Church* 7:17–20.

36. Woods, Memoirs, in Stiles, *Recollections and Sketches*. Marsh, "Mormons in Hancock County," 48. William R. Hamilton to Foster Walker, 24 December 1902, Martin Collection, Regional Archives, Western Illinois University. See also Samuel Otho Williams to John Prickett, 10 July 1844: "A guard of six men was placed at the jail with a sergeant to command it which was relieved about every three hours." (Hampshire, *Mormonism in Conflict*, 206–7, Lundwall, *Fate of the Persecutors*, 215–19, Hallwas and Launius, *Cultures*, 222–26). Davis, *Authentic Account*, 22, says "eight men were alternately detached and stationed as immediate guards at the jail." Similarly, William Law, Nauvoo Diary, 27 June 1844, "guard the jail (8 men at a time)." (Cook, *William Law*, 60). G. W. Stigall to the *Warsaw Signal*, 3 July 1844, noted "there was a guard of seven men kept at the door of the jail." (*Warsaw Signal*, 24 July 1844).

37. Smith, *History of the Church* 6:607. See note 66.

38. Smith, *History of the Church* 6:607.

39. Ibid. Joseph Smith to Emma Smith, 27 June 1844, in Smith, *History of the Church* 6:611.

Brigadier General Minor Deming was left in command at Carthage. The governor started for Nauvoo, eighteen miles to the northwest. He was accompanied by Colonel Buckmaster of Alton, newspaperman George T. M. Davis, and Captain Dunn's company, the mounted Union Dragoons. The disbanded troops "broke camp and left for home," most departing Carthage before noon. Written orders were sent to Colonel Williams at Golden's Point, southeast of Warsaw, to disband his troops as well.[40]

The prophet instructed his lawyer. "I want you to go and prepare my people," he told Woods, "for I will never live to see another sun. They have determined to murder me, and I never expect to see you again. I have no doubt you have done the best you could for me." Woods departed for Nauvoo, where he would arrive mid-afternoon.[41]

Captain Robert F. Smith ordered two of the youngest of the Greys to "go on top of the court house and keep a sharp lookout and see if a body of men were approaching the town from any direction; and, if any were seen, to immediately report to the captain . . . at his quarters." They were supplied with "a large field glass and could clearly see in every direction save due north for several miles." Anticipating an attack by the Mormons, they "were especially ordered to keep a strict outlook over the prairies towards Nauvoo."[42]

About two hours after their departure from the county seat, the governor and his troops neared the Carthage Mound. Colonel Buckmaster took the governor aside. There was "a suspicion that an attack would be made upon the jail," Buckmaster said. He had seen "two persons converse together at Carthage with some air of mystery." Ford dismissed it. Ignoring his role in the conspiracy, Ford wrote much later that he thought that an attack on the jail was unlikely, at least not until Friday. He "could not believe that any person would attack the jail whilst we were in Nauvoo, and thereby expose my life and the life of my companions to the sudden vengeance of the Mormons upon hearing of the death of their leaders." Nevertheless, Ford sent a "special order" to Captain Robert F. Smith, "to guard the jail strictly, and at the peril of his life, until my return." At this point Ford decided that he would "omit making the search for counterfeit money at Nauvoo," and return to Carthage that evening following his afternoon address to the Mormons. The baggage wagons containing firearms were ordered "to remain where they were until towards evening, and then return to Carthage." The governor and his reduced company continued toward Nauvoo.[43]

The Warsaw companies encamped on the Chittenden farm paraded single file. Captain Jacob Davis of the Warsaw Rifle Company and Captain William N. Grover of the Warsaw Cadets "selected ten men each from their respective companies." The twenty selectmen "were marched a short distance to one side." Colonel

40. William R. Hamilton to Foster Walker, 24 December 1902, Martin Collection, Regional Archives, Western Illinois University. Davis, *Authentic Account*, 18.

41. Woods, Memoirs, in Stiles, *Recollections and Sketches*.

42. William R. Hamilton to Foster Walker, 24 December 1902, Martin Collection, Regional Archives, Western Illinois University. Apparently, at least one of the lookouts was a Mormon boy, Henry Martin Harmon, a twelve-year-old resident of Carthage. "Witness to Martyrdom," *Church News*, 12 December 1981, 16.

43. Ford, *History of Illinois*, in Smith, *History of the Church* 7:22–23.

Williams, Major Mark Aldrich, commander of the Warsaw Independent Battalion, and Captains Davis and Grover instructed the men. When asked the reason these men were sent "in advance of the troops," the men were told "they had been detailed for a picket guard." The truth was that these twenty men had been chosen the night before, with the aim of proceeding to Carthage and assassinating the Smiths, "while the residue of the army, under Governor Ford, were at Nauvoo."[44]

Several baggage wagons also left Warsaw for Golden Point that morning and were assembling at the Railroad Shanty when Governor Ford's messenger reached the men sometime before noon. Colonel Levi Williams read the disbanding order. "Head Quarters, Carthage June 27, 1844. Brigade orders. The troops at Warsaw and in its vicinity and all volunteers who may have come there from other counties are hereby ordered to be forthwith discharged. Thomas Ford Governor & Commander in chief." The men were now free to act as private citizens. Under Illinois law, they were also protected from arrest as they returned to their homes.[45]

Williams asked the men to "remain for a few moments." Thomas Sharp, "a citizen (not connected with the troops), who believed he would be murdered, if the Smiths were allowed to escape," addressed the men. "All things are understood," Sharp announced. "We must hasten to Carthage and murder the Smiths while the Governor is absent at Nauvoo . . . The news will reach Nauvoo before the Governor leaves. This will so enrage the Mormons, that they will fall upon and murder Tom Ford, and we shall then be rid of the d——d little Governor and the Mormons too." The star chamber had become a coup to unseat the governor.[46]

Some of the soldiers still wished to return to Warsaw. Others "insisted upon prompt action." The governor won't help us, exclaimed one, "[we] must either take the matter into [our] own hands, and avenge [our] wrongs, or [our] most implacable enemies [the Smiths] would escape." The majority favored immediate action.[47]

Captains Davis, Grover, and John C. Elliott gathered their men. Grover consulted with the owner of the baggage wagon containing the militia's arms. Grover would pay $4 "to take the baggage to Carthage," he said, adding that "he wanted to go to Carthage to see the Governor, to ascertain why the governor disbanded the troops with the [state] arms in their possession." Unaware of the subterfuge, the wagon man agreed. Grover requested volunteers beyond the twenty who had been chosen the night before. Finally, a company of more than eighty was assembled. The remaining men were told to go home.[48]

Willard Richards handed Dan Jones a letter from the prophet. "Take it to Quincy and return as soon as you can!" It was addressed to Orville Hickman Browning, a Quincy attorney. The letter was short. "Myself and brother Hyrum are in jail on

44. Daniels, *Correct Account*, 6–7. William M. Daniels, grand jury testimony, October 1844, P13, f41, Community of Christ Archives. Davis, *Authentic Account*, 28.

45. William M. Daniels affidavit, 4 July 1844, in Smith, *History of the Church* 7:162. Thomas Ford to Levi Williams, disbanding order, 27 June 1844, in Davis, *Authentic Account*, 20.

46. Davis, *Authentic Account*, 28. William M. Daniels affidavit, 4 July 1844, in Smith, *History of the Church* 7:163. Daniels, *Correct Account*, 8.

47. Ibid., 28.

48. Daniels, *Correct Account*, 7. Benjamin Brackenberry, October 1844 grand jury testimony, P13, F41, Community of Christ Archives.

charge of treason, to come up for examination on Saturday morning, 29th inst.," the letter read, "and we request your professional services at that time, on our defense, without fail." Concerned the request might appear too strident, Joseph added a postscript: "There is no cause of action, for we have not been guilty of any crime, neither is there any just cause of suspicion against us; but certain circumstances make your attendance very necessary."

The letter safely in his pocket, Jones was hounded as he walked through the dangerous streets of Carthage. "News of the letter went throughout the mob like the wings of the breeze," he later recalled, "and some claimed it was orders for the Nauvoo Legion to come there to save the prisoners." Jones at first took the wrong road out of Carthage but eventually headed in the direction of Warsaw and the Mississippi River.[49]

Stephen Markham sat on the bed with Joseph in the jailor's upstairs parlor room. "I wish you would tell me how this fuss is going to come out as you have at other times before hand," Markham pleaded. "Brother Markham," the prophet replied, "the Lord placed me to govern this kingdom on the earth but the people has taken away from me the [reigns] of government." He had returned from across the Iowa River, he explained, when the spirit had told him to leave. He gave in to those who criticized him for abandoning the Saints. "I gave way to them & the wisperings of the spirit left me & I am now no more [than] a common man."[50]

After a period of silence, the prophet again addressed Markham. "Brother Markham, as you have a pass to go out & in you will need to go out & get the Doctor [Willard Richards] a Pipe & tobacco to settle his stomach." Markham borrowed a pipe from Sheriff Backenstos and bought some tobacco in a nearby store. While there a man approached him "& threw out considerable threats against the Mormons" and in particular against Markham himself.

Upon hearing the commotion, Artois Hamilton, owner of the Hamilton Hotel, crossed the street to the store. "You had better go home," Hamilton insisted. "You will only get killed if you remain." Hamilton no doubt knew that Markham had been caught attempting to smuggle clothes into the prison in order to help Joseph and Hyrum break jail and escape the county in disguise. "You can do the prisnors no good . . . I will bring you your horse," Hamilton offered. "I am not going home," Markham said. "Don't bring him." A group of Carthage Greys gathered around and forced Markham onto his horse, piercing his boots "with the points of their baynets ontill the blood filled [his] shoes. They then formed a hollow square round [him] & marched [him] to the timber." Markham reluctantly returned to Nauvoo.[51]

The Warsaw troops slowed to a partial halt when they were within six miles of Carthage. There was little natural cover to shield an advancing military force. The

---

49. Jones, "Martyrdom," 91. Joseph Smith to O. H. Browning, 27 June 1844, in Smith, *History of the Church* 6:613, original document in Community of Christ Archives. Willard Richards, Journal, [27 June 1844, 12:30 P.M.], quoted in Holzapfel and Cottle, *Old Mormon Nauvoo*, 189.

50. Stephen Markham to Wilford Woodruff, 20 June 1856, LDS Archives.

51. Ibid. Davis, *Authentic Account*, 42. George Rockwell [to parents] 3 August 1844, Kansas State Historical Society. Willard Richards, Journal [27 June 1844, 4:15 P.M.], quoted in Holzapfel and Cottle, *Old Mormon Nauvoo*, 189–90.

prairie was flat with occasional streams and random vegetation growing between the rows of cultivated crops. Often the ground was muddy. Ticks were a nuisance. Colonel Williams rode into town to consult with the Greys, making several roundtrips as the men approached their objective.[52]

When the troops were within four miles of the town, a Carthage Grey came out to meet them. "If you are going to do anything, now is the time," the Grey said.

Major Aldrich opened the letter and read it to the men. It explained that Governor Ford had left for Nauvoo. The guard at the jail "understood the matter perfectly: that their guns would be loaded with blank cartridges, and would be fired over the leads of the assailants of the jail . . . [and] a portion of the guard at the jail, should be seized and held by some of the assailants." When the men had reached their agreed upon position, they were "to fire a signal of three guns . . . the Carthage Grays would form, and come down to the jail." Whichever group reached the jail first was to murder the Smith brothers.[53]

The messenger "turned off from the road to the left and went along a hollow." The selectmen followed. The remaining men and wagons stayed on the main road. "The wagons need not hurry about getting in to Carthage," Captain Grover said. In order to keep from attracting attention, the wagons were to keep one-half mile apart. "What did the Carthage Grey mean?" a wagonman asked a guard. "They were a going to take Jo Smith to [Missouri] and hang him," he was told. The man stopped his wagon, loosened the reigns and let his horses feed on the grass.[54]

Runners were dispatched to warn Carthage residents that "a mob had collected on the prairie and were on the road to Carthage." Word spread that "they were Mormans comeing to liberate the Smiths from jail and would destroy the town and everything in it." By mid-afternoon parts of Carthage were nearly deserted.[55]

Dr. Thomas Barnes was asked by "a prominent man and a man of influence" in Carthage to "go out on the road toward Nauvoo and see what was going on out that way." Barnes was captain of the Rangers, an irregular company of twenty or thirty men whose job it was to act as "spies" as well as to "go over the prairies and carry expresses from one point to another." When they had gone about three miles outside of Carthage, they had a "fine view of the country all around . . . [and] could see very plain where the Carthage and Warsaw road was." As they waited, the men discerned "quite a company going hurredly in the direction of Carthage." Barnes headed back to Carthage to report what he had observed.[56]

---

52. Daniels, *Correct Account*, 8, says, "three or four times".

53. William N. Daniels, grand jury testimony, October 1844, P13, f41, Community of Christ Archives. Benjamin Brackenbury, grand jury testimony, October 1844, P13, f41, Community of Christ Archives. Davis, *Authentic Account*, 28. Daniels, *Correct Account*, 9.

54. Ibid. Benjamin Brackenbury, grand jury testimony, October 1844, P13, f41, Community of Christ Archives.

55. Mrs. R. F. Smith, "A short sketch of the trials of Mrs. R. F. Smith at the killing of the Smiths: the Mormans Profphet." Illinois Historical Society, Springfield. She was notified to evacuate the town at 2:30 P.M. Eliza Clayton recalled they were told about the impending assault "in the forenoon of the day". (Madsen, *In Their Own Words*, 224).

56. Thomas L. Barnes to Miranda Haskett, 6 November 1897, in Mulder and Mortensen, *Among the Mormons*, 146–51. Huntress, *Murder*, 152–53. Lundwall, *Fate of the Persecutors*, 220–23.

Joseph and Hyrum, John Taylor, and Willard Richards sat on chairs in the parlor, conversing on various topics. Hyrum read from *Josephus*. During a pause in the conversation, John Taylor sang a popular hymn, "The Poor Wayfaring Man of Grief," thought by one of the jailers to be "the sweetest voice he ever heard." Joseph had him sing it again.[57]

The lookouts on top of the courthouse "saw a body of armed men in wagons and on horse approaching the low timber, a little north of west from the jail, and about two miles distant." They reported at once to Captain Smith. The boys were ordered "to keep a strict watch" and to notify him if any men "came through the timber."[58]

The four o'clock detail of Carthage Greys prepared to replace the men on guard at the jail. They were told to "withdraw the loads from the[ir] guns and substitute blank cartridges." When they refused to become part of the conspiracy, the men were relieved from duty. Another squad of seven men was sent to the jail. Lieutenant Frank Worrell was placed in command over them.[59]

Jailer Stigall entered the second-floor sitting room. The four Mormons were seated before the curtained windows, which had been opened to allow what little breeze there was to circulate in the room. The jailor looked worried. There was a rumor, Stigall informed them, "that a large body of men were approaching the town." Markham had been "surrounded by a mob," he said, and chased out of Carthage. Stigall insisted that they be locked in the nearby cells for their own safety. "After supper we will go in," the prophet assured him. Stigall left the prisoners.[60]

Joseph turned to Dr. Willard Richards, his scribe and clerk. "If we go in the jail will you go in with us?" Joseph asked.

"Bro. Joseph, you did not ask me to cross the river with you, you did not ask me to come to Carthage, you did not ask me to come to jail with you, and do you think I would forsake you now? But I will tell you what I will do, if you are condemned to be hung for treason I will be hung in your stead and you shall go free."

"You cannot."

"I will."[61]

In Nauvoo, five thousand Mormons gathered to hear the governor of the state of Illinois address the Saints. They had congregated in less than half an hour after the city marshal gave notice, eagerly expecting hopeful news of their prophet and leader.

Ford spoke from a platform "made of a few rough boards" erected atop an unfinished one-story frame building on the corner opposite the Nauvoo Mansion. The Mormons were the aggressors, Ford began. Their leaders had violated the law. The

---

57. "Some interesting facts told about old jail tragedy," *Carthage Republican*, 19 November 1942, from *Carthage Republican* of 13 July 1892.

58. William R. Hamilton to Foster Walker, 24 December 1902, Martin Collection, Regional Archives, Western Illinois University.

59. Samuel Dickinson. "Some interesting facts told about old jail tragedy," *Carthage Republican*, 19 November 1942, from *Carthage Republican* of 13 July 1892.

60. Willard Richards, Journal [27 June 1844, 4:15 P.M.], quoted in Holzapfel and Cottle, *Old Mormon Nauvoo*, 189–90. See also Smith, *History of the Church* 6:616. Marsh, "Mormons in Hancock County," 50, records that Joseph's response was, "I think they must be friends. It will be all right, Jailor. Don't worry." Her words imply Joseph was planning a jailbreak.

61. Willard Richards, Journal [27 June 1844, 4:15 p.m], quoted in Holzapfel and Cottle, *Old Mormon Nauvoo*, 189–90.

destruction of the *Nauvoo Expositor*, many of the ordinances passed by city council, "the abuse of the exercise of the Habeas Corpus Act, and their resisting the service of process, for violations of law, were all illegal, arbitrary, and unjustifiable acts. Their leaders had deceived them in all these things."

There were "many scandalous reports in circulation against them," the governor continued, and "these reports, whether true or false, were generally believed by the people." He alluded to the much-feared Danite band. "If any vengeance should be attempted openly or secretly against the persons or property of the citizens who had taken part against their leaders," Ford warned them, "the public hatred and excitement was such, that thousands would assemble for the total destruction of their city and the extermination of their people, and that no power in the state would be able to prevent it."

Many in the assembly were indignant. The Mormons were a law-abiding people, they insisted. And just as they "looked to the law alone for their protection," the Mormons said, "so were they careful themselves to observe its provisions."

As a form of insurance, the governor asked the people to manifest publicly "whether they would strictly observe the laws even in opposition to their Prophet and leaders." All present agreed. "The vote was unanimous in favor of this proposition."[62]

Stephen Markham, who had arrived in the middle of this "speech," approached the governor as he came down off the scaffolding, and met him at the door of the Nauvoo Mansion. Markham described his illtreatment in Carthage. "That is nothing to what you have done here," said Ford. Markham shot back, "You are a damned liar." The governor took up his return march to Carthage.[63]

"There's about 400 Mormons coming down the fence to the jail!" cried the lookouts at the courthouse. An officer of the Carthage Greys ran into his house. "A party of men are coming to take Joe Smith from jail," he yelled, "and hang him on the public square." He took his sword down from the mantle, buckled it, and ran to his encampment a few yards away. Already men were gathering, "some with scared looking faces."[64]

"It is a party of Mormons," said one soldier, "coming to rescue the Smiths and take them to Nauvoo and we fear the guard will all be killed—they are so few."

"The Mormons are coming; the guard will be killed," cried another.

"The Danites are coming to take him home!"[65]

"Come on you cowards damn you, come on, those boys [the guards] will all be killed," swore a Carthage officer. He broke away from his men "trying to hold him" and ran towards the jail, just four blocks away. No one followed.[66]

62. Davis, *Authentic Account*, 20. Ford, *History of Illinois*, in Smith, *History of the Church* 7:23–24. Sarah Scott to "father and Mother [in-laws]," 22 July 1844, in Partridge, "Mormon Dictator," 593–96.
63. Stephen Markham to Wilford Woodruff, 20 June 1856, LDS Archives.
64. Samuel Otho Williams to John Prickett, 10 July 1844, in Lundwall, *Fate of the Persecutors*, 218, Hallwas and Launius, *Cultures*, 222–26. Marsh, "Mormons in Hancock County," 50.
65. Marsh, "Mormons in Hancock County," 50-51.
66. Marsh, "Mormons in Hancock County," 51. See also William R. Hamilton to Foster Walker, 24 December 1902, "I have always thought the officers and some privates were working for delay." Martin Collection, Regional Archives, Western Illinois University. Similarly, Gregg, *History of*

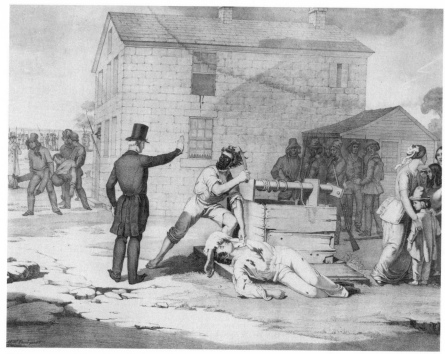

"Martyrdom of Joseph and Hiram [sic] Smith in Carthage jail, June 27th 1844," by G. N. Fasel, after C. G. Crehen. Color lithograph. New York, 1851. Library of Congress, 229906.

Captain Robert F. Smith commanded his men to form rank in front of their tents on the square. Some of the Greys had fallen asleep and were "in a half dazed state looking for uniforms, arms &c." His order, too, had little effect.[67]

The Warsaw men, many disguised with a black mud made from gunpowder smeared over their faces, others with their uniforms turned inside out, ran along a low fence next to a skirt of timber northwest of the town. Signal shots were fired as they emerged from the woods and ran towards the jail, still a half mile distant. John C. Elliott and his men jumped the low fence that surrounded the jail. The regular militiamen crowded into the open area by the well. Colonel Williams approached on horseback and commanded Elliott to proceed.[68]

Hancock County, 325, acknowledges there was a plot. "It is certain that a portion of the Greys knew that something was to be done; but others, the great body of them, knew nothing about it." Marsh concurred with the opinion of Thomas L. Barnes (note 14) that the officers were privy to the conspiracy: "I now believe that those persons, who were honorable men and good citizens—brought the news of what was intended by the mob to the officers of the Greys—(my brother-in-law being one of them) but only to the officers, not a man in the ranks knew any more than other citizens." (Marsh, "Mormons in Hancock County," 50)

67. Ibid.

68. Woods, Memoirs, in Stiles, *Recollections and Sketches*. William N. Daniels, grand jury testimony, October 1844. P13, f41, Community of Christ Archives. Daniels, *Correct Account*, 10. Cone, *Biographical Sketches*, 184–85.

The outside door to the jail was open. The Warsaw selectmen called out to the guard, some of whom were inside resting on the stairs.

"Surrender!" cried the intruders. Lieutenant Worrell ordered his men to fire. The blank cartridges had no effect. The men struggled. Worrell lost his sword. The intruders dropped a rifle and a musket.[69]

Hearing shots from outside, Dr. Richards parted the curtain. More than two hundred men, some in militia uniforms, others wearing fringed blue flannel hunting shirts, most of them armed, were crowding around the jail. The men by the well shot aimlessly into the air. The noise was like thunder. Grey acrid smoke rose to where the prisoners watched in disbelief. Anticipating an altercation, the Mormons removed their coats.[70]

Elliott and his selectmen ran up the stairs and stopped at the landing just outside the sitting room, their guns at the ready. Hyrum, Joseph, Taylor, and Richards pressed against the thin paneled door from the inside. It wouldn't keep the assailants out for very long.

The men in the hallway began their assault, firing up the stairs towards the sitting room. They regrouped on the landing.

Hyrum checked his weapon, aimed, and fired. A shot from the hallway struck him in the face. "I am a dead man!" he cried. Hyrum's pistol fell from his hand. Joseph leaned over his dying brother, called out his name, and returned to the task of securing the door. The assailants pressed against the door until the latch gave way. As the intruders poked their gun barrels into the room, Richards and Taylor beat them down with broad swipes of their canes. Joseph's shoulder pressed against the weakening door. He jammed his Allen Pepperbox through the opening and shot blindly into the landing. Three times the ball struck a man. Three times the gun misfired.[71]

The assailants forced their way into the room. Dr. Richards retreated into the corner of the room, his large form hidden from the assailants by the fully open door. John Taylor went to the window. A shot from the courtyard hit him in the chest, forcing him back inside. Taylor rolled under the bed to shield himself from further injury.

The prophet retreated to the open window opposite the door. Gunfire from the hallway filled the room with smoke. Hit in the thigh from the latest volley, Joseph sat awkwardly on the broad window ledge.[72]

69. Willard Richards, Journal [27 June 1844], quoted in *Old Mormon Nauvoo*, 189–90. Clayton, Temple History, in Clayton, *Intimate Chronicle*, 542. William M. Daniels affidavit, 4 July 1844, in Smith, *History of the Church* 7:163. Thomas L. Barnes to Miranda Haskell, 6 November 1897, in Mulder and Mortensen, *Among the Mormons*, 146–51. Huntress, *Murder*, 152–53. Lundwall, *Fate of the Persecutors*, 220–23. Woods, Memoirs, in Stiles, *Recollections and Sketches*. William Daniels, grand jury testimony, October 1844, P13, F41, Community of Christ Archives. Samuel Otho Williams to John Prickett, 10 July 1844, in Hampshire, *Mormonism in Conflict*, 206–7, Lundwall, *Fate of the Persecutors*, 215–19, Hallwas and Launius, *Cultures*, 222–26.

70. Ibid. On the appearance of the men outside, see Daniels, *Correct Account*, 9. Jeremiah Willey, 13 August 1844, LDS Archives. Samuel Otho Williams to John Prickett, 10 July 1844, in Lundwall, *Fate of the Persecutors*, 218, Hallwas and Launius, *Cultures*, 222–26.

71. Ibid. Thomas L. Barnes to Miranda Haskell, 6 November 1897, in Huntress, *Murder*, 146–53. Smith, *History of the Church* 6:620.

72. Thomas L. Barnes to Miranda Barnes Haskell, 6 November 1897, in Huntress, *Murder*, 146–53. William R. Hamilton to Foster Walker, 24 December 1902, Martin Collection, Regional Archives, Western Illinois University. Willard Richards, Journal [27 June 1844], quoted in *Old Mormon*

"Shoot him, damn you! Shoot him!" Colonel Williams cried out to the Warsaw militiamen gathered in the courtyard below. The backup company of Carthage Greys marching in formation to the prison was less than 150 feet away. Any closer and they would be forced to fire into the "mob" surrounding the jail. Even with the approaching Greys, no one dared shoot a fellow militia officer and a master mason.[73]

Joseph held out his arms in the hailing sign of a Freemason in distress. "O Lord my God . . ." he cried, uttering the first four words of the Masonic plea for help. He fell from the window and landed, nearly fifteen feet below, on his side, badly hurt and unable to move.[74]

"Old Joe jumped the window!" Williams called to the men inside the jail. The selectmen gathered in the courtyard and faced the Mormon prophet. One grabbed the dying man, and cursed as he propped him up against the well curb. "Shoot the God damned scoundrel," ordered Williams.[75]

Four men, led by John C. Elliott, took up their arms, and moved to the front rank of troops. They took position, aimed, and fired on command. Each ball found its mark. As they discharged their weapons, the threatening storm clouds parted and the rays of the setting sun illuminated the horrid scene. Several of the men struck Joseph's lifeless body with their bayonets to make certain the job was done.[76]

Nauvoo, 189–90. Jeremiah Willey, statement, 13 August 1844, LDS Archives. Samuel Otho Williams to John Prickett, 10 July 1844, in Lundwall, *Fate of the Persecutors*, 218. Tracy, *In Search of Joseph*, 57.

73. Daniels, *Correct Account*, 9–10. Samuel Otho Williams to John Prickett, 10 July 1844, in Lundwall, *Fate of the Persecutors*, 220–23, Hallwas and Launius, *Cultures*, 222–26. William Daniels, 1845 trial testimony, in Sharp, *Trial*, 7. Woods, Memoirs, in Stiles, *Recollections and Sketches*, relates that the shooting was random, into the air, to act as a diversion.

74. Smith, *History of the Church* 6:629. Roberts, *Comprehensive History* 2:286. On Joseph Smith's Masonic distress cry, see Thomas L. Barnes to Miranda Barnes Haskett, 6 November 1897, in Lundwall, *Fate of the Persecutors*, 220–23, Huntress, *Murder*, 146–53. John D. Lee, *Mormonism Unveiled*, 153, completed the phrase: "Joseph left the door, sprang through the window, and cried out. 'Oh, Lord, my God, is there no help for the widow's son!' as he sprang from the window, pierced by several balls." With the subsequent disgrace of Freemasonry within Mormonism, efforts were made to sanitize Joseph's Masonic distress cry. See, for example, B. H. Roberts, *Comprehensive History* 2:287, "Did Joseph Smith make Masonic appeal for help[?]" Not surprisingly, Roberts thought not. Significantly, Leonard, *Nauvoo*, 397, acknowledges Joseph's "Masonic signal of distress." See Chapter Twenty.

75. William M. Daniels affidavit, 4 July 1844, in Smith, *History of the Church* 7:163. William Daniels, October 1844 grand jury testimony, P13, f41, Community of Christ Archives.

76. The flash could have been lightning, although it was more likely the setting sun glaring in the gunmen's eyes. Leonard, *Nauvoo*, 725, note 49 has recently written, "There is no credence to Littlefield's distortion of William Daniels's report that all of the shots were fired execution-style on orders of Colonel Williams after Joseph was propped against the well." The actual distortion was not the firing squad itself, but the supposed interposition of a brilliant light from heaven (sometimes described as lightning) which reputedly froze the assailants in place.

It was Michael Quinn's understanding of events surrounding Joseph Smith's assassination as developed in *Origins of Power* that provided the framework for our own analysis. Quinn, *Origins of Power*, 646, reconstructs the scene as follows: "[27 June, 5 P.M.] Joseph defends himself with a pistol, jumps out the window, and begins to shout the Masonic cry of distress: 'Oh, Lord, my God, is there no help for the widow's son?' Masons in the crowd show no mercy and prop the semi-conscious Smith against a nearby well and shoot him several times at point-blank range." During the nineteenth century, Mayhew, *History of the Mormons* [1851 edition], 162–3, [1854 edition], 175, provides one of the best descriptions of the execution. "When Smith fell from the window he was not dead, but merely stunned by the fall . . . one of the gang raised him up and placed him against the well, and

"Well against which Joseph Smith was placed and shot at after his assassination," in Piercy's 1855 *Route from Liverpool to Great Salt Lake Valley*. This illustration (with the addition of a dog) and a nearly identical caption ("shot at by the mob") later appeared in *Frank Leslie's Illustrated Newspaper* for August 23, 1856. The wording of the caption reflects the impact of John Taylor's August 1844 conflated account of the martyrdom as recorded in the Doctrine and Covenants: "Joseph leaped from the window, and was shot dead in the attempt, exclaiming: *O Lord my God!* [Hyrum and Joseph] were both shot after they were dead, in a brutal manner, and both received four balls." (135:1)

---

that, while in this position, four others among the mob advanced to the front rank with loaded muskets, and fired at the 'Prophet.' From the circumstance that four bullets were afterwards found in his body, there would appear to be some grounds for believing this to be the correct account of Smith's death, and each of these four men stood at a short distance from him as to make it quite certain that every shot fired took effect." Clayton, Temple History, written in May 1845, concurs: "They raised him up and set him against the well-curb; but as yet it appears he had not been hit with a ball. However, four of the mob immediately drew their guns and shot him dead." (Smith, *Intimate Chronicle*, 542). Clayton's 28 June 1844 journal account of the martyrdom is not available to researchers.

Significantly, Thomas Ford, one of the best informed individuals concerning the murder, *History of Illinois*, 355, similarly wrote, "The fall so stunned him that he was unable to rise; and being placed in a sitting posture by the conspirators below, they dispatched him with four balls through his body."

Other early accounts (written before the spring of 1845) supporting the view that Joseph Smith was alive when he fell to the ground and was subsequently "dispatched" include, in approximate chronological order:

(1) Thomas Sharp, "Events of the Week," *Warsaw Signal Extra*, 29 June 1844. Like Governor Ford, Thomas Sharp used the term "dispatched" to refer to Joseph's last moments. (See below, p. 201.)

(2) Nathan Calhoun Cheney to Charles Beebe, 28 June 1844, LDS Archives. According to Cheney, the "mob fired hin through" while Smith was hanging in the window as well as after he had jumped to the ground.

(3) Willard Richards to Reuben Hedlock, 9 July 1844: "Joseph in attempting to leap from the same

window, was shot & fell on the outside about twenty feet descent. The mob gathered instantly round him & again shot him. Joseph & Hyrum received each four balls and were killed instantly." LDS Archives, Turley, *Selected Collections*, 1.31.

(4) Jeremiah Willey, statement, 13 August 1844, LDS Archives, relating a conversation he had with Henry Mathias of Warsaw about events of the 27 June 1844 soon after the date in question: "Charles Gullier said he then shot him at the window from the door, and Vorus shot him from the outside of the prison. and he fell out upon the ground . . . [after Vorus] turned him on his back . . . Vorus then left him, when there were more guns fired at him."

(5) William Daniels affidavit, 4 July 1844, in Smith, *History of the Church* 7:163. See p. 220, note 12.

(6) Samuel Otho Williams to John A. Pricket, 10 July 1844. "He was shot several times and a bayonet run through him after he fell." Leonard, *Nauvoo*, 394, Hallwas and Launius, *Cultures*, 222–26.

(7) William Daniels, October 1844 grand jury testimony, P13, f41, Community of Christ Archives. See p. 220, note 15.

(8) Statements by John C. Elliott in the fall of 1844, as testified by John C. Burns, "I told him [Elliott] that in all probability he [Smith] was dead when he fell from the window, or was killed by the fall. I told him that but two balls entered his body. But Mr. Elliott immediately interrupted me by saying: I *know* you are mistaken, placing great emphasis on the word *know*. I *know* (said he) he was not dead when he fell from the window, and I *know* he was shot with four or five balls. He also said something about his attempting to clamber up against the well-curb, but what he said about it I do not distinctly remember." (*Nauvoo Neighbor*, 19 February 1845) See also Jesse, "Return to Carthage," 16, note 26 and Quinn, *Origins of Power*, 374–76 for more sources.

Writers who later claimed Joseph was not shot after he fell from the window were either covering for the men who committed the crime or accommodating Willard Richards's published version of events at the jail. (See following chapters of this study.)

A bowie knife (or pewter fife) entered the story early on. Daniels, *Correct Account*, 15, wrote that a ruffian wielded a "bowie knife for the purpose of severing his head from his body." Daniels corrected this statement in his trial testimony: "The Pewter flute man went to him, or tried to—the light I suppose stopped him. I saw no bowie knife." (Sharp, *Trial*, 12). For a recent analysis of the bowie knife myth, see Turley, *Victims*, 11–13. For another example of the transmutation of the "bowie knife" into a "pewter fife" see Andrew Jensen, "L.D.S. Church Historian records light from heaven." (Historical Record 7–471, in Lundwall, *Fate of the Persecutors*, 360, Tracy, *In Search of Joseph*, 30–31). See also Leonard, *Nauvoo*, 395. It is possible that a transcription error transformed "bowie knife" into "pewter fife."

Chapter Fourteen

Distance Lent Enchantment to the View

"**F**OR GOD'S SAKE COME BACK and take away your men!" Colonel Williams cried out. His disguised militia unit was running for the safety of the trees, anxious to escape the Carthage Greys who were almost upon the jail. The wounded were just emerging into the sunlight. William Vorhees was hit in the left shoulder. Charles Gallaher was "grazed on the side of the face." John Willis was wounded in the right wrist. "I shot Hyrum!" Willis exclaimed proudly, "and Joe shot me!" The invalids were loaded into the baggage wagons and headed west.[1]

"Alight quick!" Artois Hamilton called out and grabbed the reigns of Samuel Smith's horse. Exhausted, Samuel fell from his mount into the sanctuary of the hotel. He had tried to reach Carthage by way of Bear Creek earlier in the day, he told Hamilton, but had been "sent back by the mob guard." Samuel changed to a swifter horse. When he was finally within sight of Carthage "he heard the firing of guns." He was too late. His beloved brothers were dead.[2]

A young Mormon housekeeper stood in the doorway of Captain Robert F. Smith's Carthage home, wringing her hands. "Oh, my God! Mrs. Smith!" she cried. "They are shooting them men down at the Jail and throwing them out of the window." Mrs. Smith hurried to the Greys' courthouse headquarters, hoping to locate

---

1. Davis, *Authentic Account*, 25. William N. Daniels, grand jury testimony, October 1844, in P13, f31, Community of Christ Archives. Daniels, *Correct Account*, 15. Jeremiah Willey, 13 August 1844, LDS Archives. William R. Hamilton to Foster Walker, 24 December 1902, Martin Collection, Regional Archives, Western Illinois University. William N. Daniels, 1845 trial testimony, in Sharp, *Trial*, 12. Benjamin Brackenbury, 1845 trial testimony, in Sharp, *Trial*, 24. The earliest account of Willis's altercation with Joseph Smith is in G. T. M. Davis [Warsaw, 2 P.M.] to John Bailhache, 28 June 1844, in *Alton Telegraph*, 6 July 1844. Davis mentions "Wills, Gallaher and Voorhees." A variant of the statement is recorded in William Daniels, October 1844 grand jury testimony. P13, f41, Community of Christ Archives. According to Joseph Fielding, Wills was an Irish Latter-day Saint, "who came with me from England with his wife and two children. He was an elder in the Church." This is confirmed by Davis, *Authentic Account*, 24. Fielding insists he died from his wounds. (Fielding, Nauvoo Journal, 151–52). Thomas L. Barnes, on the other hand, recalled that Wills survived. Thomas L. Barnes to Miranda Barnes Haskett, 6 November 1897, in Mulder and Mortensen, *Among the Mormons*, 146–51, Huntress, *Murder*, 146–53, Lundwall, *Fate of the Persecutors*, 220-23.
2. H. Herringshaw [Nauvoo] to William Smith [New York], 28 August 1844, in *The Prophet*, 21 September 1844.

her husband. "He's at the jail . . . Gov. Ford told him to guard the town," she was informed. The officer in charge advised her to leave Carthage immediately.[3]

Richards eased himself out of his hiding place behind the door. The shooting could start up again at any moment. He stepped over Hyrum's bloodied remains and approached the window. Looking down into the courtyard, he saw the lifeless body of his beloved prophet and dear friend. Richards turned to leave the room. "Take me," a faint voice cried out. It was John Taylor, gravely wounded but still alive. Richards pulled his dying friend from under the bed and dragged him across the floor into the cellblock next door. He covered the Mormon elder with straw from one of the mattresses to keep him hidden. Richards cautiously descended the stairs and called for the jailer.

Stigall found Doctor Barnes and brought him to the prison. As the two men walked through the bottom doorway into the dungeon-like darkness, they stepped over Joseph's body at the foot of the stairs, apparently dragged there by the mob shortly after the killing. Blood stained the floor around the prophet.

Hyrum's body lay in the upstairs parlor where he had fallen less than an hour before. The doctor approached the cellblock expecting to find another body. Even though he was severely weakened from a loss of blood, Elder Taylor refused to come out. Stigall assured Taylor it was safe, that the Gentile doctor would not harm him and only wanted to treat his wounds. A pitiful figure eventually emerged from the windowless cell. Coagulated blood and straw stuck to his clothing. He had been shot four times.

> One ball had hit him in his forearm and passed down and lodged in the hand be-
> tween the phalanges of his third and fourth fingers. Another hit him on the left side
> of the pelvis cutting through the skin and tissue leaving a superficial wound that
> you could lay your hand in. A third ball passed through his thigh . . . A fourth ball
> hit his watch, which he had in the fob in his pantaloons.

The watch would forever record the exact time of the killings: 5:16 and 26 seconds. The men prepared to transport Taylor to Hamilton's Hotel.[4]

The Carthage Greys dispatched a messenger to the governor, informing him of the death of the Smiths. Their work done, the militia disbanded. Innkeeper Artois Hamilton and Mormon Samuel H. Smith removed the bodies from the jail and took them to the hotel. Boxes were made out of pine boards to transport the remains to Nauvoo the next day. Barnes treated Taylor as best he could. Sheriff Stigall performed an inquest.[5]

3. Mrs. R. H. Smith, "Short Sketch of the Trials . . ." Illinois Historical Society, Springfield.
4. Smith, *History of the Church* 6:620. Thomas L. Barnes to Miranda Barnes Haskett, 6 November 1897, in Mulder and Mortensen, *Among the Mormons,* 146–51. Huntress, *Murder,* 146–53. Lundwall, *Fate of the Persecutors,* 220–23.
5. Davis, *Autobiography,* 81. Verdict of jury on inquest upon the bodies of Joseph and Hyrum Smith, 27 June 1844. Filed 25 October 1844, in "Original Verdict of the Coroner's Jury in the Smith Massacre," *Hancock County Journal,* 9 December 1915, "Coroner's Jury Verdict in Murder of Joseph Smith," unidentified newspaper, 2–6–58, Lundwall, *Fate of the Persecutors,* 276–77. On the inquest, see also Bernauer, "Still Side by Side," 2, note 4. William R. Hamilton to S. H. B. Smith, 18 March

Barnes turned to Willard Richards, the only other Mormon survivor of the assault.

"Richards, what does all this mean?" Doctor Barnes asked. "Who done it?"

"Doctor, I do not know, but I believe it was some Missourians that come over and have killed Joseph and Hyrum and wounded brother Taylor."

"Do you believe that?"

"I do."

"Will you write that down and send it to Nauvoo?" Richards would write the note, he said, if someone could be found who would take it safely to Nauvoo. Barnes assured him he could.[6]

> CARTHAGE JAIL, 8:05 o'clock, P.M., June 27th, 1844.
>
> Joseph and Hyrum are dead. Taylor wounded, not very badly. I am well. Our guard was forced, as we believe, by a band of Missourians from 100 to 200. The job was done in an instant, and the party fled towards Nauvoo instantly. This is as I believe it. The citizens here are afraid of the Mormons attacking them. I promise them no!
>
> W. RICHARDS.
JOHN TAYLOR.
>
> N. B.—The citizens promise us protection. Alarm guns have been fired.[7]

"The Mormons will be down upon us so soon as they hear of this," warned Samuel Otho Williams, an officer with the Carthage Greys. "We think the best plan will be for you all to leave town immediately, " he told his family. The few remaining Greys would be no match for the Nauvoo Legion, expected to descend upon Carthage before morning. "We must remain and do the best we can for the defense of the town."[8]

The women and children would go to Augusta, in southeast Hancock County. The women prepared for escape. "Placing a mattress and pillows with some blankets in the bottom of the wagon for the benefit of the little ones—taking the slender stock of silver and other valuables—and a goodly supply of the cooked food which had been so lavishly prepared for the troops, we got into the wagon." It was nearly dark. They drove past the Hamilton Hotel "where the dead and wounded had been taken, we saw lights being carried from room to room, and groups of men around who were talking in low tones, and I thought with shuddering horror of what must be lying in those rooms."[9]

1898, Martin Collection, Regional Archives, Western Illinois University. William R. Hamilton to Foster Walker, 24 December 1902, Martin Collection, Regional Archives, Western Illinois University. Hamilton recalled that the pine boards were made into "thousands of walking canes."

6. Thomas L. Barnes to Miranda Barnes Haskett, 6 November 1897, in Mulder and Mortensen, *Among the Mormons*, 146–51. Huntress, *Murder*, 146–53. Lundwall, *Fate of the Persecutors*, 220–23. Davis, *Autobiography*, 81.

7. Willard Richards and John Taylor [Carthage, 8:05 P.M.] to Nauvoo, 27 June 1844, in Smith, *History of the Church* 6:621–22. Roberts, *Comprehensive History* 2, 290, note 7.

8. Marsh, "Mormons in Hancock County," 53.

9. Ibid., 53–54.

By evening Carthage was nearly deserted. "Men, women, and children fled in wagons, on horseback and afoot, while *Delenda est Carthago* seemed sounding in their ears." Carthage is fled.[10]

Two miles outside of Nauvoo, the governor's forces returning to Carthage met two messengers. They had devastating news. "The Smiths had been assassinated in jail, about five or six o'clock of that day," they told the governor. The two men were ordered into custody. With an anticipated outbreak of violence if the Mormons were informed of the massacre, it was crucial to keep the news from them as long as possible.[11]

Thomas Sharp, riding on horseback, was the first of the killing party to reach Warsaw. "The Smiths are dead," he announced. "The men that killed them are on their way to Warsaw. Some of them are wounded. Someone must be sent to meet them with a wagon."[12]

Mr. Pinchback volunteered his team. Five or six miles east of Warsaw the wagon met up with "a straggling company of men . . . He could see by the twilight they were somewhat disguised their coats turned wrong side out—their faces blacked or covered with handkerchiefs through which holes had been made for the eyes &c." Three were wounded: Charles Gallaher, William Vorhees, and John Willis. The men were taken to a nearby farm where they ate and had their wounds dressed by a doctor from Missouri. While recuperating the three men told their stories. The farmer promised them his protection. "He would spill the last drop of his blood," he pledged, "before any of these men should be taken."[13]

Ford wrote to the citizens of Warsaw, to inform them of the horrible incident. By the time his messenger arrived there the people were already preparing to leave for safe havens in Alexandria, immediately across the river, or Quincy, further south.[14]

Captain Malin waited aboard his steamer at the Warsaw dock. He agreed to hold his ship "at the wharf until the women and children were aboard" and had been transported safely to Alexandria, on the Missouri side of the river, where they would be taken to the upper room of a large warehouse, which earlier had been "made comfortable to receive many of them."[15]

---

10. Ibid., 53, quoting J. H. S. from the *Ithaca Journal* (1886). See ch. 13, note 12.
11. Ford, *History of Illinois*, in Smith, *History of the Church* 7:24. David Wells Kilbourne to T. Dent, 29 June 1844, in Hallwas and Launius, *Cultures in Conflict*, 226–28. Kilbourne, who was with the governor that day, mentions "a messenger" only. Stephen Markham to Wilford Woodruff, 20 June 1856, LDS Archives. According to Markham, G. D. Grant was an LDS messenger sent from Carthage to Nauvoo. G. T. M. Davis identified the "two expresses . . . last night to Governor Ford" as "Snow and Bedell". G. T. M. Davis [Warsaw, 2m.] to John Bailhache 28 June 1844, in *Alton Telegraph* 6 July 1844.
12. Jeremiah Willey, statement, 13 August 1844, LDS Archives. According to Benjamin Brackenbury, 1845 trial testimony, in Sharp, *Trial*, 23, "Gregg who did live in Warsaw . . . was the first who brought the news to me that the Smith's were killed." Eliza Jane Graham also testified that Sharp arrived "with James Gregg" when Sharp first returned to Warsaw from Carthage. (Sharp, *Trial*, 19). Abraham I. Chittenden (Sharp, *Trial*, 3) and E. W. Gould (Sharp, *Trial*, 31) agreed that James Gregg brought the news. James was the brother of Thomas Gregg, the Whig editor of the *Upper Mississippian* at the time of the murders.
13. Marsh, "Mormons in Hancock County," 57. Jeremiah Willey, statement, 13 August 1844, LDS Archives. The physician was identified as, "Doc. Adams from Missouri."
14. Thomas Ford to [the people of Warsaw] 3 July 1844, in Smith, *History of the Church* 7:160–62.
15. Marsh, "Mormons in Hancock County," 56.

Dan Jones, still carrying Joseph's letter addressed to Quincy attorney O. H. Browning, approached the Warsaw dock. The people were rejoicing. "Joe and Hyrum were both shot while trying to escape from prison!" Messengers were being sent to "Quincy and the lower Counties," he was told, to raise troops to defend Warsaw against an attack by the Mormons. A *Warsaw Signal Extra*, "a slit of a paper a little larger than my hand just issued," was distributed to the crowd. "Joe and Hiram Smith are dead," Jones read, "shot this afternoon. An attack from the Mormons is expected every hour. Will not the surrounding counties rush instantly to our rescue? Warsaw, June 27th, 1844."[16]

George T. M. Davis and Colonel March left the governor at Nauvoo and headed for Keokuk, Iowa, where they hoped to catch the packet *Boreas* to Quincy. When they had been in Keokuk but a little while they "heard the report of a cannon in the direction of Warsaw" and knew "at once . . . it was intended as a signal of triumph, and that the event had occurred." Davis hired a skiff "and a couple of men" to row him to Warsaw, which he reached, after repeated forced landings by sentinels on the shore, sometime around midnight.[17]

Warsaw was in a state of high alert. "The streets were patrolled by a vigilant guard," Davis recorded. "Sentinels were placed at every point of ingress, on the outskirts of town: the few pieces of cannon, they had, were stationed at those points, where, it was believed, they would do the most signal service in case of an attack. Several of the merchants had their goods in wagons, ready for a retreat, in the event of the Mormons attacking them with an overpowering force."[18]

Davis located the company responsible for the assault on Carthage jail. "The troops who had marched from Golden's Point, to Carthage, and back again, that day," he noted, "had but a short time previous, returned, and were very much fatigued, and were partaking of some refreshments which had been prepared for them by a portion of the citizens." He gathered from the men details of the incident at Carthage and penned a quick message to Bailhache in Alton.

> Warsaw, June 27, 1844, 12 P.M.
>
> I have simply time to announce to you that Joseph Smith, the Prophet, and Hyrum Smith, his brother, as well as W. Richards, the Recorder of Nauvoo, have all fallen victim to the . . . indignation of the citizens of Hancock . . . When I left [Nauvoo] they of course had not heard of the death of the Smiths and Richards; but I do not entertain the belief they will rise against the citizens . . .
>
> Doctor Singleton, with a company of sixty men, was left in Nauvoo this evening, and some apprehend the Mormons will make an attack upon them, as well as Governor Ford and his escort of about the same number of horse, who expected, when I left, to camp within a few miles of Nauvoo on his return to Carthage. I anticipate nothing of the kind myself . . .

---

16. Dan Jones to Thomas Bullock, 20 January 1855, LDS Archives. "Death of the Prophet!! Joe Smith and Hiram Smith are Dead!" *Cincinnati Daily Enquirer & Message*, 4 July 1844 (taken from *the Quincy Herald*): "The following slip from the office of the Warsaw Signal, explains the dreadful tragedy." Dan Jones's version of the text of the *Signal Extra* is apparently based upon his memory and not a re-examination of the actual flyer.

17. Davis, *Authentic Account*, 25-26.

18. Ibid., 26.

I only allude to it, to guard against a thousand rumors, that may reach you, which will be without foundation. I have written this in great haste and in the midst of excitement, which must furnish an apology for its imperfections. I ought to have mentioned that Col. Buckmaster, of our City, constitutes one of the Governor's escort.

Yours truly, G. T. M. D.[19]

The *Boreas* lay on the opposite shore, filled with Warsaw families destined for Quincy "as a place of refuge." Davis crossed the Mississippi on a ferry "crowded with women and children, with what scattering articles of wearing apparel they could collect together in the hurry and excitement of the moment." At the suggestion of George Rockwell, Davis spoke to the departing citizens. The governor's address to the citizens of Nauvoo, he told them, had achieved its aim. The Mormons, he had no doubt, "from their dejected appearance," wished to avoid bloodshed. Davis boarded the *Boreas* and headed for Quincy with the Warsaw exiles.[20]

When Governor Ford arrived in Carthage he discovered that "one company of the guard stationed by [him] to guard the jail had disbanded and gone home before the jail was attacked, and many of the Carthage Greys departed soon afterwards." Ford advised the remaining inhabitants to desert the town. The people departed unarmed. "The cannon, arms, and ammunition of the citizens, were all left at Carthage." The public records of the county were removed to a safe location east of town. A token guard under General Deming was left to watch over the empty buildings.[21]

Residents of Carthage thought the governor was "badly scared" because he had "stopped for only a few minutes," apparently believing the town "would be in ashes before morning." The road out of Carthage was "mud and water knee deep in some places." His first stopover en route to Quincy was Augusta, eighteen miles to the southeast. Ford arrived there before daybreak and left for Quincy "directly after breakfast."[22]

It was still dark when the *Boreas* pulled up at the Quincy wharf. Dozens of women and children from Warsaw, Whig newspaper editor George T. M. Davis, Mormon Dan Jones, and two men representing the Warsaw Committee disembarked the steam packet. Alarm bells were rung. Within a half hour an immense concourse of citizens assembled at the courthouse. It was not yet 5 A.M.

William H. Roosevelt, one of the Warsaw representatives, rose to address the crowd. "About 6 o'clock, last evening," announced Roosevelt excitedly, "an attempt was made by the Mormons on the outside to rescue the Mormon prisoners from the custody of the guard." He continued his narrative of the assault:

---

19. Ibid., 26. G. T. M. Davis [Warsaw, 12 P.M.] to John Bailhache 27 June 1844, in *Alton Telegraph*, 6 July 1844.

20. Ibid., 26.

21. Thomas Ford, *Message of the Governor* [1844], 18, also in Smith, *History of the Church* 7:27. William R. Hamilton to S. H. B. Smith [son of Samuel H. Smith], 18 March 1898, Martin Collection, Regional Archives, Western Illinois University.

22. Samuel Otho Williams to John Prickett, 10 July 1844, in Hampshire, *Mormonism in Conflict*, 206–7, Lundwall, *Fate of the Persecutors*, 215–19.

A youth, about 19 years of age, (a Mormon,) began the fray, by shooting the sentinel at the door, wounding him severely in the shoulder.

Simultaneously with this attempt, the Mormons on the inside of the jail, including the Smiths, presented pistols through the windows and doors of the jail, and fired upon the guard without wounding, it is supposed, mortally, four of the old citizens of Hancock!

It is unnecessary to say that this bloodthirsty attempt, on the part of the Mormons, was the signal for certain and sure vengeance.

The lives of the two Smiths, and Richards, were quickly taken, and we believe no others!

Carthage was filled with Mormons—previous to the affray, the Mormons appeared to be collecting around the jail, it is now supposed, for the purpose of attempting the rescue of their leader.[23]

A resolution was adopted "to render the citizens of Warsaw and Carthage all the assistance in their power, against any attack that might be made upon them by the Mormons." Roosevelt's comments were rushed to the office of the *Quincy Whig* and issued as an *Extra*. Messengers left for Hannibal "and the towns below" to alert the Missourians to the cause.[24]

In less than an hour nearly three hundred volunteers ("as good men as ever pulled a trigger")—the Quincy Rifle company, the Quincy Guards, the Irish Volunteers, "and a large volunteer company"—prepared to leave for Warsaw on the *Boreas*'s return voyage upriver.[25]

Hundreds of the citizens of Quincy lined the shore as the men embarked and cheered the troops on, "their shouts like claps of thunder." George T. M. Davis wrote to John Bailhache before joining the men on the deck of the *Boreas*.

> Quincy, June 28, 1844, 6 A.M.
>
> I return to Warsaw with them, and shall exert all my feeble abilities to stay the hand of destruction. A great deal of excitement (unnecessary in my opinion) has been created through apprehension that the Mormons had massacred Capt. Singleton's Company, as well as Gov. Ford and his escort, on hearing of the death of their prophet. If those apprehensions are realized in the remotest degree, no power on earth can prevent an indiscriminate slaughter of the entire population of Nauvoo. After the boat is under way, I shall address the troops, as well as all

23. G. T. M. Davis [Quincy, 6 A.M.] to John Bailhache, 28 June 1844, in *Alton Telegraph*, 6 July 1844. "Dreadful News. Attempt at Rescue—Killing of Joe Smith—Hyrum Smith in the Carthage Jail," *Quincy Whig*, 3 July 1844. This was issued as a reprint of an extra issued on "Friday morning last," the 28th of June. See also Davis, *Authentic Account*, 24 and Josiah B. Conyers, *Brief History of the Leading Causes of the Hancock Mob, 1846*, "certain individuals were dispatched from Carthage and Warsaw to Quincy in order to make a false report, viz., that the attack has been made by the 'Mormons,' and they expected that these two places were then burnt to ashes and Governor Ford and his detachment murdered," quoted in Roberts, *Comprehensive History* 2:290, note 7. The fabricated report is also mentioned by Thomas Ford, *Message of the Governor* [1844], 17, also in Smith, *History of the Church* 7:25–26.

24. Ibid. "Dreadful News . . .," *Quincy Herald*, 28 June 1844.

25. Ibid.

others, assembled on her, with a view of allaying excitement, and preventing, if possible, the shedding of more blood, save in the dernier resort of absolute self-defense.

. . . I will write from Warsaw. I have seen a slip from the office of the "Quincy Whig," which is inaccurate in regard to the particulars of the tragedy. The particulars given in my second letter, you may rely upon.

Yours truly, G. T. M. D.[26]

The news soon spread up and down the river.

*　*　*　*　*

Steamer Dove, June 28, 1844.

Editors Reveille—

Passenger from Bryant's Landing report the deaths of Joe Smith and his brother Hyrum, last evening, by a mob of 200 men, dressed in disguise, with their faces blackened who took them from the jail in Carthage, where they had been confined, and shot them. It is feared that the exasperated followers of the "Prophet" will make an attack upon the town of Carthage, and make a general massacre of the citizens, unless a sufficient force can be raised to defend the place.

The excitement is great and the whole country is rising, while at the same time the Mormons will muster their entire strength.

I have not time to detail all the circumstances as our passengers report them, but these are the most important. The above has been corroborated by a messenger from Carthage, who stood upon the landing at Bryant's.

S. Compton Smith.[27]

*　*　*　*　*

We left Nauvoo about daylight this morning—all was quiet. The Mormons had not heard of the death of the Smiths, as Governor Ford, who was encamped a few miles back, had as is supposed, intercepted the [messengers] from Carthage.

At Warsaw, all was excitement. The women and children were all removed, and an immediate attack was expected from the Mormons.

We met the 'Boreas' just above Quincy, with 300 men armed and equipped for Warsaw, eager for fight.

I send you the "Quincy Herald" printed this morning, containing the particulars of Smith's death.

In haste, yours, &c,

A. J. Stone.

On board Steamboat: St. Croix[28]

*　*　*　*　*

---

26. Ibid. Davis would later claim that he had not heard Roosevelt's remarks. Davis, *Authentic Account*, 27.

27. S. Compton Smith to the editors of the *St. Louis Reveille,* 28 June 1844, in *New Orleans Daily Picayune,* 6 July 1844.

28. A. J. Stone to Flagg, 28 June 1844, in *Cincinnati Daily Enquirer & Message,* 4 July 1844.

A messenger gently knocked on the door of the Nauvoo Mansion room of Joseph Smith's attorney, James W. Woods. Joseph and Hyrum had been murdered in Carthage jail, he was told. A little after daylight, a courier from the governor arrived at the Nauvoo Mansion confirming the news. The governor requested Woods "to restrain the Mormons," and authorized him to "to put the city in a condition to repel any mob, and if possible prevent the Mormons from leaving the city." Woods sought out the wives and mother of the murdered men.[29]

A trumpet sounded across the city, borne by a man riding "an old white horse." Its urgent notes were punctuated with horrible news: "Joseph and Hyram are killed, are shot!" The people began to assemble.[30]

Woods faced ten thousand grief-stricken Saints gathered in the Temple Grove. "Sorrow & gloom was pictured in every countenance and one universal scene of lamentation pervaded the city," Woods would later write. "The agony of the widows & orphan children was inexpressible and utterly beyond description." He pleaded for calm. Six hundred men formed a detail to "prevent any one [not authorized] from leaving or coming into the city." Woods left for Carthage to arrange for an escort to bring the bodies home.[31]

Governor Ford reached Columbus, in Adams County, early Friday morning, "very much exhausted, so much so that he had to be lifted from the carriage." In the course of the night, militia had been congregating throughout the Military Tract. Troops were marching from Schuyler and Brown counties, Ford was informed, with orders reportedly issued by the commander in chief. Their march was immediately countermanded. At Columbus, Captain Abraham Jonas had "raised a company of one hundred men, who were just ready to march." The governor ordered Jonas to postpone his march and "await further orders."[32]

The doors and windows of the Carthage jail had been left open. Lucy Clayton took her sister to the second-floor sitting room. "Everything seemed upset," Eliza recalled, as though people had left in great haste. "There were some Church books on the table and portraits of Joseph and Hyrum's families on the mantelpiece." Their eyes caught sight of the blood formed "in pools on the floor" and "spattered on the walls." Overcome with grief at the loss of their prophet and his brother, they broke down. Eventually the girls managed to gather the personal belongings of Joseph and Hyrum and "placed them together in a trunk that was in the room." Afterwards, Lucy cleaned "the plaster from the floors which was shot from the walls, also the blood that stained the floors." Knowing their lives were no longer safe in Carthage, the remaining Mormon families in Carthage moved back to Nauvoo.[33]

---

29. Woods, Memoirs, in Stiles, *Recollections and Sketches*.
30. Ibid. John S. Fullmer to Wilford Woodruff, 18 October 1881, Martin Collection, Regional Archives, Western Illinois University.
31. Ibid.
32. Mr. Chambers [editor of *the Missouri Republican*] in Quincy, published in the *Dayton Journal and Advertiser*, 16 July 1844. Ford, *Message of the Governor* [1844], 18–19, also in Smith, *History of the Church* 7:28. Abraham Jonas to *Quincy Whig*, 20 July 1844, in *Quincy Whig* 24 July 1844.
33. Eliza Clayton, Reminiscence, in Holzapfel, *Women of Nauvoo*, 132. Madsen, *In their Own Words*, 224–25. Bullock, *Pioneer Camp*, 32, note 25.

"Warsaw, June 28, 1844, 2 p.m. . . . All is quiet . . . all our citizens, comprising either the escort of Gov. Ford, or the members of Capt. Singletons' company, are safe and unharmed," George T. M. Davis wrote to John Bailhache in Alton. He had reached Warsaw on the *Boreas* a few minutes before.

> The three individuals from among the citizens who are wounded, are Mssrs. Wills, Gallaher, and Voorhees. I had a personal interview with Mr. Wills, who informs me that he was shot by Joe Smith, who fired a six barreled revolving pistol in the crowd before he was shot.—There were about a dozen Mormons [sic!] in the room where the Smiths were confined; and the only wonder is, all were not killed . . .
>
> A large portion of the citizens of this place marched to Carthage and back yesterday, a distance of nearly forty miles, over very bad roads, and are consequently wholly unfit for service today. They are now, however, fully relieved and protected by the four companies from Quincy . . .
>
> I return to Quincy on the *Boreas*; and if any thing new is learnt before the *Die Vernon* leaves to-morrow morning, I will write you.
>
> Yours truly, G. T. M. D.[34]

As Woods returned to Nauvoo mid-afternoon, a line of Saints nearly two miles long formed to greet the entourage. The escort consisted of lawyers Woods and Hugh T. Reid, Artois Hamilton, Samuel H. Smith, one of the two remaining Smith brothers, and Willard Richards, the only Mormon not wounded or killed in the attack on the jail. As the "two rude boxes in the wagon, covered by the Indian blanket" containing the bodies of the Generals Smith came into view, a low, anguished moan arose from the streets of the Holy City. A mounted guard from the Nauvoo Legion escorted the boxes.

Recalling the promise in Romans—"Vengeance is mine, saith the Lord, and I will repay"—many of the Saints prayed for God to avenge the blood of the prophets Joseph and Hyrum:

> And now O God wilt though not come out of thy hiding place and avenge the blood of thy servants.—that blood which thou hast so long watched over with a fatherly care—that blood so noble—so generous—so dignified, so heavenly you O Lord will thou not avenge it speedily and bring down vengeance upon the murderers of thy servants that they may be rid from off the earth and that the earth may be cleansed from these scenes, even so O Lord thy will be done. We look to thee for justice. Hear thy people O God of Jacob even so Amen.[35]

Some preferred not to wait for the Lord's intervention. One Nauvoo policeman, a former Danite, solemnly resolved, as he stood by, helpless, watching the

---

34. G. T. M. Davis to John Bailhache, 28 June 1844 [Warsaw, 2:00 p.m.], in *Alton Telegraph* 6 July 1844.

35. Clayton, Nauvoo Journal 2, in Allen, *Trials of Discipleship*, 141. Woods, Memoirs, in Stiles, *Recollections and Sketches*. B. W. Richmond, "The Prophet's Death," *Chicago Times*, 20 November 1875. Daniels, *Correct Account*, 16, notes. "The anti-Mormons knew they had committed a deed that would have justified them [the Mormons] in taking summary vengeance . . . But the course taken by the people of Nauvoo, so entirely different from this, is known to all . . . 'Vengeance is mine, saith the Lord, and I will repay.'" This sentiment is also found in the Book of Mormon, Mormon 3:13–15.

procession, that he "would never let an opportunity slip unimproved of avenging their blood upon the head of the enemies of the Church of Jesus Christ." He later wrote, "And I hope to live to avenge their blood; but if I do not I will teach my children to never cease to try to avenge their blood and then teach their children and children's children to the fourth generation as long as there is one descendant of the murderers upon the earth." Others also demanded vengeance. "The blood of those men and the prayers of the widows and orphans and a suffering community will rise up to the Lord of Sabaoth for vengeance upon those murderers."[36]

The bodies were taken to the dining room of the Nauvoo Mansion where they were washed, dressed, and prepared for viewing. Joseph had five gunshot wounds—in the right breast, in his chest under the heart, in his lower abdomen, on the right side, and on the back of his right hip. One ball had exited at the right shoulder blade. Camphor-soaked cotton was stuffed into each wound to cover the stench of death and help stop drainage from seeping out onto the floor. Joseph and Hyrum were dressed in "fine plain drawers and shirt, white neckerchiefs, white cotton stockings and white shrouds." When the preparations had been completed, the bodies were arranged beneath the west windows of the room.[37]

The families of the deceased were brought in. "Who killed my sons?" Lucy Mack Smith asked. There was no answer. "Why did they kill my sons?" She appeared lost. Emma, too, was disconsolate. "Why, oh God, am I thus afflicted? Why am I a widow and my children orphans?" She approached her beloved Joseph. "Joseph, Joseph, are you dead? Have the assassins shot you?" Hyrum's face was swollen and distorted from his gunshot wound. Mary Fielding confronted the lifeless body of her husband. "O! Hyrum, Hyrum! Have they shot you, my dear Hyrum. Are you dead? O! speak to me my dear husband. I cannot think you are dead, my dear Hyrum!"[38]

Some in Nauvoo could "scarce refrain from expressing aloud their indignation at the Governor and at few words would raise the City in arms & massacre the Cities of Carthage & Warsaw & lay them in ashes." Others counseled calm. "It is wisdom to be quiet."[39]

Orrin Porter Rockwell, longtime companion and personal bodyguard of the prophet, would not be consoled. "They have killed him," he bellowed. "They have killed him. God damn them, they have killed him." Rockwell resisted requests to remain quiet and not cause an uprising. "The murder of the two Smiths was a well digested, and systematically arranged plan," he protested. "Ford knew all about it, and promoted it." As evidence Rockwell offered the fact that "the Governor professed to come to Nauvoo to hunt for counterfeiters and bogus money; but when he came here, spent an hour abusing them on the stump, and left without making any

36. Allen J. Stout, Journal, 19, quoted in Quinn, *Origins of Power*, 151, Van Wagoner and Walker, "The Joseph/Hyrum Smith Funeral Sermon," 3, Schindler, *Orrin Porter Rockwell*, 137, Brooks, *John Doyle Lee*, 208. William Clayton, in Allen, "One Man's Nauvoo," 57, Allen, *Trials of Discipleship*, 142.

37. Smith, *History of the Church* 6:627.

38. David Wells Kilbourne to T. Dent, 29 June 1844, in Hallwas and Launius, *Cultures in Conflict*, 226–28. Dr. B. W. Richmond, "The Prophet's Death," *Chicago Times*, 20 November 1875.

39. Clayton, Nauvoo Journal 2, in Allen, *Trials of Discipleship*, 142.

examination." Rockwell believed "the whole object of this visit was to be at Nauvoo, out of the way, while the murder was perpetrated at Carthage."[40]

Colonel Stephen Markham concurred with Rockwell's view of the affair. "Gov. Ford was privy to the murder," he agreed. "On the morning of the day upon which the two Smiths were shot, [Markham] went to the jail to see them, and on his coming out, he was accosted by the citizens aground the jail, and in the town, with very abusive language, and that several told him before midnight of that day, they meant to have his life, as well as that of the Smiths." Markham reported the threats to the governor, who appeared unconcerned. "It was the whiskey that spoke and not the men," Ford had said.[41]

George T. M. Davis forced his way through the crowd at the Quincy courthouse. "Tell us about Governor Ford!" the people cried. Rumors were circulating that Governor Ford was in some way involved in the murders. Although Davis, a Whig, and Ford, a Democrat, had been "uncompromising political and personal enemies" for many years, Davis assured them that any rumor of complicity on the part of Illinois's chief executive in the assassination of Joseph and Hyrum Smith was completely without foundation.

"No greater precautionary measure for their safety could the governor have taken," Davis said. "To accuse or suspect, in view of such circumstance, that Governor Ford was in any way privy to Joe Smith's death is an insult to our common intelligence." He was insistent. "From facts within my personal knowledge which, under the strictest injunctions of confidence, I am precluded from disclosing, I unhesitatingly avow that I am as confident of the innocence of Governor Ford, as to his having had any previous knowledge or even suspicion of the fate that befell the two Smiths, as I am that I am about to conclude the remarks that I have to submit to you . . . There is nonetheless a silver lining to the cloud that now overshadows us, in the reflection and assurance that in the sudden taking off of two of the vilest religious and moral imposters in the world's history, justice is satisfied and Rome is free!"[42]

Public viewing of the bodies of Joseph and Hyrum was reserved until Saturday. Joseph's wounds continued to drain, the "gory fluid trickled down on the floor and formed in puddles across the room." By noon Hyrum's body was so swollen as to be unrecognizable. Tar, vinegar, and sugar were burned to cover the stench. "Joseph looks very natural except being pale through loss of blood," William Clayton noted as he passed the bodies. "Hyrum does not look so natural."[43]

To prevent the crowds from overwhelming the viewing area, speeches were given in various parts of Nauvoo. The crowd, estimated at between eight and ten thousand,

---

40. Anson Call, "The Life and Record of Anson Call, Commenced in 1839," 27. Davis, *Authentic Account*, 43–44. This view is corroborated by several sources. John Greene, in Smith, *History of the Church* 6:611. Orrin Porter Rockwell affidavit, 14 April 1856, in Smith, *History of the Church* 6:588–89, said that during Ford's Nauvoo speech, Rockwell witnessed a man in Nauvoo declare, "The deed is done before this time." Willam G. Sterrett affidavit, 3 October 1850, in Smith, *History of the Church* 6:589–90.

41. Davis, *Authentic Account*, 43. Jeremiah Willey statement, 13 August 1844, LDS Archives.

42. Davis, *Autobiography*, 87 and 90. The comparison to Rome was used also in the *Nauvoo Expositor*.

43. Dr. B. W. Richmond, "The Prophet's Death," *Chicago Times*, 20 November 1875. Clayton, Nauvoo Journal 2, in Allen, *Trials of Discipleship*, 142.

spread out "in every direction almost as far as the eye could reach." The Saints waited for hours in the sweltering heat to pass by the bodies of their prophet and patriarch. The mourners were addressed by Carthage massacre survivor Williard Richards, Joseph's political secretary William W. Phelps, lawyers Woods and Reid, and bodyguard Stephen Markham. Lawyer Woods "censured Gov. Ford . . . for the careless and guilty part he had acted in not protecting the prisoners" and condemned the whole affair. The people paid their respects until nightfall.[44]

When the viewing was concluded, William W. Phelps read to the Saints from the sixth chapter of Revelation.

> And when he had opened the fifth seal, I saw under the altar, the souls of them that were slain for the word of God. And they cried with a loud voice, saying, How long, O Lord, holy and true, dost thou not judge and avenge our blood on them that dwell on the earth?

Phelps told the assembled faithful that the prophet had declared, the day before his death, that his people should study that chapter. "It was about to be fulfilled," Joseph had said. Phelps preached on that theme.[45]

The viewing rooms were cleared, the bodies of the Mormon prophet and patriarch put in coffins, and hidden in an interior room of the Nauvoo Mansion. Two "rough, outside coffins"—filled with bags of sand—were presented to the people and "carried in solemn procession to the city cemetery." The Saints "chanted and wept around the graves of the leaders whom they really supposed they were burying." The actual bodies were buried by the family in an undisclosed location to prevent them from being dug up and mutilated by anti-Mormons.[46]

Ford established his command headquarters in Quincy. Express riders departed for the seat of war, returning hourly with the latest intelligence. "He is alike afraid to trust either the troops or the citizens about Carthage or Warsaw," one reporter noted.[47]

Despite his role in promoting the conspiracy, Abraham Jonas, of Columbus, who had supplied the press that printed the *Nauvoo Expositor*, was delegated by the governor to head a commission to "visit the Mormons at Nauvoo, to inquire particularly into their situation, and to give them such instructions or orders as may be deemed necessary." If it would serve to defuse the tense situation, Jonas was also given authority to disband the militia troops remaining in Warsaw and Carthage. He headed upriver.[48]

George T. M. Davis was relaxing in the lounge of the Quincy Hotel when Ford entered with some of his Democratic associates. "Davis!" the governor called out,

---

44. Woods, Memoirs, in Stiles, *Recollections and Sketches.*
45. Van Wagoner and Walker, "The Joseph/Hyrum Smith Funeral Sermon."
46. Dr. B. W. Richmond, "The Prophet's Death," *Chicago Times,* 20 November 1875. Davis, *Authentic Account,* 32.
47. Thomas Ford to Abraham Jonas and Hart Fellows, 30 June 1844, in *Times and Seasons,* 1 July 1844, 565. Hart Fellows and Abraham Jonas, 1 July 1844, in *Times and Seasons,* 1 July 1844, 566. Mr. Chambers [editor of *Missouri Republican*] in Quincy, *Dayton Journal and Advertiser,* 16 July 1844.
48. Mr. Chambers [editor of *Missouri Republican*] in Quincy, *Dayton Journal and Advertiser,* 16 July 1844.

grasping the Whig editor's hand and shaking it with obvious gratitude. "I have just been told by some who were present," the governor continued, "that at the public meeting of the people at the Court House yesterday, you, had the moral courage to defend me in your speech . . . I want to express to you publicly here, that I am deeply grateful to you for that manly act of yours toward a political enemy. You are the last man in Illinois from whom I would have expected the vindication for which, my friends tell me, I am indebted to you. I hope would past enmities may hereafter be forgotten."

"Governor Ford," Davis replied, "I do not consider you are under any obligation to me whatever, for what I said yesterday in your defense as the Chief executive of this State. I was only shielding the people of Illinois, and you as its Governor, from what I believed to be the basest of calumnies."[49]

Davis excused himself and arranged for his return to Alton the next day.

---

49. Davis, *Autobiography*, 90–91.

Chapter Fifteen

The Kingdom Delayed

The council [of Fifty] consider it best for all the traveling elders to stop preaching politics—preach the gospel with double energy, and bring as many to the knowledge of the truth as possible. The great event of 1844, so long anticipated, has arrived, without a parallel since the birth of Adam.

Willard Richards to Brigham Young, June 30,1844[1]

Nauvoo remained in mourning. Following the imagined and real burials of Joseph and Hyrum a young barrel maker named William Daniels, armed with letters of introduction to "the leading men of Nauvoo," entered the Holy City. Daniels sought out Willard Richards, one of the two Carthage survivors. He told the Mormon elder he had experienced a vision and reported that three days after the murder of Joseph Smith the martyred prophet appeared to him in a dream and took him "up into a high mountain." As Daniels slipped in the shifting soil, "Joseph would reach out his hand and lift [him] along." At the summit Daniels was seated. Joseph gave him a "glass of clear cold water . . . placed his hands upon [his] head, prayed to the Lord, blessed [him] and departed." Following this epiphany Daniels was determined to tell all he knew about the murders. He had been forced to join the Warsaw militia, he claimed, and was at the jail when the crime was committed. Embarrassed and ashamed by his involvement, Daniels sought redemption.

Richards wasn't interested. Daniels's knowledge "would be of no particular use" to the Mormons at that time, Richards told him. He should "wait for the proper officers of the State to move forward in the matter."[2]

Daniels stayed in Nauvoo for several days and swore out an affidavit before a justice of the peace on the Fourth of July. There was no Independence Day celebration in Nauvoo. "Instead of celebrating with splendor and joy," William Clayton wrote in his journal, "we celebrate" the nation's "down-fall with grief and mourn for the loss of our prophet & Patriarch & pray to God to avenge their blood speedily."[3]

---

1. Willard Richards to Brigham Young, 30 June 1844, in Smith, *History of the Church* 6:147–48.
2. Daniels, *Correct Account*, 17–18.
3. William Daniels, affidavit, 4 July 1844, in Smith, *History of the Church* 7:162–63. Clayton, Nauvoo Journal 2, in Allen, *Trials of Discipleship*, 152. See also James C. Snow, "When the news arrived of his death the people were disappointed and the shock was universally felt. Some of the most influential

Days later William Daniels went to Quincy and met with Governor Ford, informing him what he knew of the affair. Ford told Daniels he would likely be one of the key witnesses for the prosecution in the case. Within a few weeks Daniels returned to Nauvoo and was baptized into the Mormon church. His conversion was opportunistic at best. He intended to publish his story as a book and hoped to make some money along the way. Lyman O. Littlefield, an apprentice in John Taylor's printing establishment, helped the aspiring author with the necessary "filling" to make the story sell. An artistic rendering of the Carthage massacre was completed by a local sign painter. Visitors were charged to view the bloody scene, complete with a dramatic light from heaven, which, it was claimed, had frozen the gunmen in place after they shot the prophet.[4]

Lucien Woodworth, the former Council of Fifty ambassador to the Republic of Texas, wrote to President Sam Houston in early July. Woodworth included copies of the Book of Mormon, Doctrine and Covenants, and July 1 issue of *Times and Seasons.*. In *Times and Seasons* Houston would find, Woodworth said, "correct statements concerning the murder of Generals Joseph and Hyrum Smith in Carthage jail on the 27th ult. by a mob of 150–200, painted and disguised men." Woodworth explained that the names of the men involved "are well known, but the Governor Ford as yet has taken no action to bring them to justice."

According to reports, some of the men engaged in the murder had "already started for Texas," Woodworth noted. The prospect of having enemies as neighbors in their proposed Mormon kingdom within the Republic of Texas, however, did not "discourage the members in the leest, but they feel more dispared then ever to carry out Gen Smiths views in <u>all things</u>."

Woodworth reminded Houston of their earlier negotiations. "Recent occurrences has prevented my making the propositions desired. If you still consider the plan practicable, communicate and a reply shall be forthcoming." He would never hear from the General. Texas had signed a secret treaty of annexation with the United States in April. With the Mormons no longer vital to the Texan strategy for survival, the much-anticipated political Kingdom of God would have to wait a while longer.[5]

Newspapers throughout the U.S. brought forth more lurid details of the murders. It wasn't until the middle of July, more than two weeks after the massacre, when the eastern Saints came to fully realize that the unthinkable had occurred. Joseph and Hyrum were no more. There would be no nominating convention in Baltimore presenting Joseph's name to the nation. The hope for political salvation through a national government headed by a prophet of God was lost.

Political rallies continued on schedule throughout the eastern states until traveling electioneers received official word of Joseph's death. Some gatherings erupted in violence. "According to what we hear in this country about the 'Mormons' in the

---

men immediately predicted the downfall of the nation because they looked lamely on and sang lullaby-baby. JAMES C. SNOW." Dated City of Joseph [Nauvoo], November 17th, 1845, in Smith, *History of the Church* 7: 527.

4. Smith, *History of the Church* 7:168.

5. Lucien Woodworth to Sam Houston, 11 July 1844, LDS Archives. Durning transcription. See also Bitton, "Mormons in Texas," 9, note 6 and Willard Richards to George Miller [undated], LDS Archives, cited in Godfrey, "Causes of Conflict," 70. Smith, *History of the Church* 7:249.

west," Brigham Young wrote to Willard Richards from Salem, Massachusetts, on July 8, "I should suppose that there is an election about to take place, or the Prophet had offered himself for some office in the United States: for of all the howlings of devils and devil's whelps, this season cannot be beat . . ." Brigham was optimistic. "The prevailing opinion is, that [Joseph Smith] is the smartest man in the Union, and the people are afraid of his smartness. Some will vote for him for the novelty of the thing, and some to see what a Prophet will do at the head of government . . . You might ask what we think about Brother Joseph's getting the election this year? You know all about it. We shall do all we can and leave the event with God—the God of heaven will do just as he pleases about it." Rumor of the deaths of Joseph and Hyrum reached him the next day. Confirmation came a week later, in a letter written from Boston by Wilford Woodruff, signed, "Yours in the kingdom of God." Brigham would arrive back in Nauvoo on August 6, a day after the summer elections.[6]

Press reports of Joseph's death soon reached Kentucky, where John D. Lee was preaching and electioneering. Could it be true? "A personage whose face shone as lightning stood before me and bid my fears depart," Lee wrote in his journal in early July, recording an unusual vision he had experienced. The heavenly being told him his work in behalf of the Lord was accepted, just as were the labors of the "12 and 70 that were sent out by the Son of God," Jesus Christ. "They supposed that their labors were lost when their leader was taken and crucified instead of being crowned King (temporal) of that nation as they fondly expected." The heavenly messenger reassured him:

> So it is with you—instead of electing your leader the chief magistrate of this nation they have martyred him in prison—which has hastened his exaltation to the executive chair over this generation—so now return home in peace and there wait your endowment from on high as did the disciples at Jerusalem, for this circumstance is parallel to that.[7]

Tear-stained letters from Nauvoo certified the horrible news. Public meetings in Philadelphia, Boston, and elsewhere attempted to comfort the bereaved Saints. Their jobs over, the once determined political missionaries began the long sorrowful trek back to Nauvoo. When John D. Lee received confirmation of the deaths of Joseph and Hyrum, he was overwhelmed. "[T]he feeling of grief and anguish operated so powerful upon my natural affections as to destroy the strength of mind and rendered it almost impossible for me to fill my appointments—some of which I disappointed." Lee penned his final diary entry as he reached Nauvoo. He noted simply, "End of Mission."[8]

Even with the majority of the Twelve Apostles and many of the Council of Fifty still in the east promoting Joseph's presidential bid, the remaining Nauvoo leadership

---

6. Brigham Young to Willard Richards, 8 July 1844, in Smith, *History of the Church* 7:209–11. See also Brigham Young, Manuscript History, 170–71 [16 July 1844]. Wilford Woodruff to Brigham Young and Orson Pratt, 16 July 1844, in Smith, *History of the Church* 7:194.
7. John D. Lee, Diary No. 4, quoted in Brooks, *John Doyle Lee*, 61.
8. Ibid., quoted in Brooks, *John Doyle Lee*, 61–62.

turned its attention to selecting Joseph Smith's successor. "The greatest danger that no[w] threatens us is dissensions and strifes amongst the Church," William Clayton observed. Several claimants would eventually come forward. Chief among the possible successors to Joseph Smith was William Marks, the Nauvoo stake president. On the evening of July 4 a council met at Marks's home. A number of the brethren agreed that "brother Marks['s] place [was] to be appointed president & Trustee in Trust" of the church "and this accords with Emma's feelings."[9]

Many in Nauvoo, however, wanted to wait until the traveling Quorum of the Twelve had returned home. Emma objected. Due to the pressing business arising out of the settling of Joseph Smith's estate (his personal business transactions were hopelessly tangled with the affairs of the church), she felt a trustee should be appointed immediately. There was considerable concern over the possible appointment of Marks, however, who agreed "with [William] Law & Emma in opposition to Joseph & the quorum," on the issue of polygamy. They feared that their "spiritual blessings be destroyed inasmuch as [Marks] is not favorable to the most important matter [i.e. plural marriage]." Marks would be removed as stake president in October and leave Nauvoo in the spring of 1845.[10]

"The Trustee must of necessity be the first president of the Church," others argued, and "Joseph has said that if he and Hyrum were taken away Samuel H. Smith would be his successor." Following Samuel, the next logical choice to lead the church was Joseph's other surviving brother, William. Neither man would ever get the chance. Samuel died at the end of July. William remained in the east and continued his work promoting Joseph's political principles after taking over the editorship of *The Prophet* in late June.[11]

Sidney Rigdon, Joseph's vice presidential running mate and counselor in the First Presidency of the church, was also prepared to succeed the slain prophet. Rigdon returned to Nauvoo on August 3. His proposal to be made a "Trustee-in-trust" for the church, although supported by Emma and William Marks, met with considerable opposition.

Brigham Young returned to Nauvoo three days after Rigdon, had a larger following, and actively sought Sidney's removal. Brigham's authoritative position as president of the Quorum of the Twelve, together with his unwavering support of polygamy and his superb ability as an organizer, ensured his ultimate success. Rigdon was excommunicated in early September. He shortly afterwards left Nauvoo and returned to Pittsburgh, where he would establish his own church.

Following a long period of *de facto* rule as the head of the Quorum of the Twelve Apostles, Brigham Young was sustained as president of the Church of Jesus Christ of Latter-day Saints in late 1847 at Winter Quarters, Nebraska, almost two years after departing Nauvoo. About half of the Nauvoo Saints followed Young to Utah, where his movement was fortified by a growing number of converts from the British Isles.

Emma Smith, Joseph Smith's first wife, having rejected polygamy and Brigham Young's leadership, remained in Nauvoo. Several splinter organizations were formed

---

9. Clayton, Nauvoo Journal 2 [4 and 6 July 1844], in Clayton, *Intimate Chronicle*, 137.

10. Ibid., [12 July 1844], in Clayton, *Intimate Chronicle*, 138, Clayton, *Writings*, 32.

11. Ibid.

Brigham Young at Nauvoo, ca. 1845. At the time he was president of the Quorum of the Twelve Apostles. Courtesy of the Church Archives, the Church of Jesus Christ of Latter-day Saints.

out of the communities of Saints left behind. One of the most successful was the True Church of Jesus Christ of Latter-day Saints, formed by James J. Strang, an early claimant to succeed Joseph Smith. Strang gathered his followers in Voree, Wisconsin Territory. For a time, William Smith, Joseph's only surviving brother, and Lucy Mack Smith, Joseph Smith's mother, advocated Strang's claims as the prophet's true successor. Strang also attracted such prominent Nauvoo Mormons as George Miller and William Marks. Dr. John C. Bennett joined the Strangite movement for a time, and suggested moving Joseph and Hyrum's remains to Voree. After Strang's assassination in 1856, several thousand of his followers formed the nucleus of The Reorganized Church of Jesus Christ of Latter-day Saints. Founded at Amboy, Illinois, in 1860, the Reorganized movement denounced polygamy as an innovation introduced by Brigham Young, and, during the second half of the nineteenth century, remained the Utah Mormons' chief rival as the authentic successor to the church established by Joseph Smith. Today they are known as the Community of Christ rather than RLDS.

But even before the fragmentation of the Mormon movement in the months and years following the death of Joseph Smith, the most immediate problem was identifying and prosecuting the men engaged in the assault on Carthage jail, most of whom had returned to their normal lives as farmers, merchants, editors, and county officials.

Chapter Sixteen

"Bound by common guilt and danger to commit almost any act to save them from infamy"

Anxious to return to their homes in Carthage and Warsaw, the Old Citizens of Hancock County slogged through the muddy roads rendered nearly impassable by the overflowing banks of the Mississippi River.[1] The high water mark had been reached on June 27, nearly a week before. That was the day the settlers abandoned their homes, fleeing the anticipated invasion by Nauvoo's twelve thousand outraged Mormons, who were expected to burn Carthage and Warsaw to the ground in retaliation for the murder of their leaders. The returning citizens found their homesteads intact. An uneasy calm prevailed amidst the prospect of continued violence.[2]

Within days of the event, the Carthage conspiracy nearly collapsed under the press of its own weight. To begin with, the anti-Mormons could not agree on what public face to put on the murders. When members of the Warsaw Committee returned from their exhausting propaganda campaign, they were outraged to read the *Warsaw Signal Extra* of June 29. The Carthage incident had been reported under "Events of the Week."

> About four o'clock P.M., a company of about one hundred armed men, marched to the jail in Carthage, and demanded the prisoners. A rush was made on the guards, who fired, but hurt nobody. They were immediately secured, and the men rushed up stairs to the room of the prisoners. For about two minutes the discharge of fire arms within the jail was very rapid. Finally, Joe Smith raised the *window, exclaimed "Oh my God," and threw himself out. He fell heavily on the ground, and was soon dispatched. Hiram was shot in the jail. There were two other prisoners, Dr. Richards, who we learn was not hurt, and J. Taylor, editor of the Nauvoo Neighbor, who received five balls, in his arms and legs. Immediately on the work being done, the men fled . . .
>
> *the prisoners were not in cells, but in the private room of the jailor, the windows of which were not barred.[3]

---

1. Minor R. Deming to [his parents] 22 December 1844, Deming Papers, Illinois Historical Survey, Urbana (infamy quote).
2. Clayton, Nauvoo Journal 2, in Allen, *Trials of Discipleship*, 152–53.
3. "Events of the Week," *Warsaw Signal Extra*, 29 June 1844.

Runners sent to Quincy, St. Louis, and elsewhere along the Mississippi told a very different story, namely that the deaths were caused by the Mormons themselves when they attempted to deliver their prophet and his brother from the confines of Carthage jail. The militia had no choice, the messengers said, but to shoot the escaping prisoners.

One Warsaw Committee member charged that "Sharp ought to have sworn" to the fabrication; instead, Sharp had "told the truth in his paper." This unauthorized disclosure would make it much more difficult to hide the involvement of the Warsaw militia and Thomas Ford's collusion in the affair.[4]

Sharp never apologized for his indiscretion; his motivation for publishing the true circumstances surrounding the murders would forever remain unclear. It is possible that he recognized, given the large number of witnesses, that the main facts in the case were bound to be publicly disclosed perhaps even in court. He simply chose not to wait. As the weeks wore on, and no arrest warrants were issued, Sharp became even bolder in his public statements and went so far as to justify the killings of the Mormon leaders as a military-style "summary execution" that had been decided upon days before the actual event. Those familiar with military law would have understood Sharp's statement as applying to situations in which prisoners under arrest could be dispatched if it was determined they might flee or otherwise escape justice. Few in the county would disagree with him.[5]

"My dear Friends," Onias C. Skinner wrote to attorneys Calvin A. Warren and Almeron Wheat of Quincy on July 8. Skinner, a Carthage lawyer, was aide-de-camp to Brigadier General Deming and master in chancery of the Carthage Circuit Court, two positions which afforded him unparalleled access to valuable intelligence. Skinner was one of the men who had served on a Carthage Committee delegation to Governor Ford before the arrest of Joseph and Hyrum, and was a prosecuting attorney during the hearings in Carthage the day prior to their deaths. Skinner (who would move to Quincy in December) informed his associates that he couldn't leave Hancock County for some time. "I took a trip to the country the other day," he said, "and found some of the Mormons well pleased that the Smiths were gone; others were sullen as 'grim visaged death.'" He warned his colleagues to be very careful in their efforts to influence the coming elections. Warren and Wheat were both Democrats, confederates of Governor Ford, whose military headquarters were being maintained in Quincy. Skinner was an independent member of the political coalition opposed to the Mormons and moved easily between the Whig and Democratic camps. "We must move cautiously with an honest cry to the August election," Skinner cautioned. "But no intriguing with us." The previous weeks had seen enough intrigue to last several lifetimes. Still, a critical election was just weeks away and had to be won. Just who

4. Minor R. Deming to Thomas Ford, 3 July 1844, in "Grand Discovery," *Warsaw Signal*, 4 September 1844.

5. [Thomas Sharp editorial] *Warsaw Signal*, 10 July 1844, quoted in Bitton, *Martyrdom Remembered*, 58, note 9. I would like to thank Gordon C. Thomasson for pointing out the significance of this statement. Similarly, Davis, *Authentic Account*, 17, noted, "They were determined the Smiths should not escape summary punishment." George Rockwell to Thomas H. Rockwell, 3 August 1844, believed that those opposed to Joseph Smith were obligated to "execute justice." (Hallwas and Launius, *Cultures in Conflict*, 237).

would win was not yet certain.[6]

Joseph Smith's followers, although factionalized over the succession question and polygamy, remained a potent political force that had to be confronted and manipulated. The impending August election would select state and local officials as well as determine who would serve as representatives to the U.S. Congress in 1844–45. It was widely viewed as a litmus test for the November presidential vote.

Whom would the Mormons support? The answer depended upon who was thought to be behind the assassination of their prophet and patriarch. If the governor was implicated, then the Mormons were likely to go with Whig candidates. If the Whigs were charged with being behind the crime, Mormon support for the Democrats would be strengthened.

Many Mormons accused the Missourians of backing the conspiracy. The Avery "kidnap" drama was still fresh in many minds and highlighted the ever-present danger lurking just across the Mississippi River. Certainly, the Missourians had reason to continue hounding the Latter-day Saints. Governor Boggs's 1838 "extermination order" was still in effect. (It would take until 1976 for Missouri to rescind the edict.) And, it was widely believed that Joseph Smith was behind an 1842 murder attempt against Boggs. The Mormons could also point to the large numbers of volunteer gunmen seen crossing the Mississippi just hours before (and after) the assassination.

The Mormons firmly believed that Illinois's Democratic governor was in league with the assassins. Evidence for his involvement was common knowledge. When Ford departed for Nauvoo around noon on the June 27, it was argued, he knew full well what would occur. If that was not so, why hadn't he brought Joseph with him to Nauvoo, as promised? And how was it that Ford understood the significance of the alarm guns and was so quick to depart from Nauvoo after his derogatory speech?

The existence of a Missouri-backed Democratic conspiracy was proclaimed from the very moment the news of Joseph and Hyrum's demise arrived in Nauvoo. The near-universal condemnation of the governor, and by implication the Democrats of Illinois and Missouri, meant that the Mormon leadership at Nauvoo for all intents and purposes overlooked the Whigs as possible suspects in the murders. It was a blind spot the partisans of Henry Clay would use to great advantage.[7]

"All is perfect peace at Nauvoo," Carthage survivor Willard Richards wrote to Abraham Jonas on July 10. Jonas was a noted Illinois Whig and past grand master of the Illinois Masonic Lodge. It was Jonas who had made Joseph a Mason at sight in 1842, and it was he who stood up for the Nauvoo Lodge when the Illinois Grand Lodge withdrew its charter. The Mormons, Richards told Jonas, were "calmly waiting the fulfilment of Governor Ford's pledge to redeem the land from blood by legal process. You can do much to allay the excitement of the country in your travels, and the friends of peace will appreciate your labors." Richards thanked Jonas for his "endeavors for the promotion of truth and justice." He was referring to Jonas's travels throughout the Military Tract on behalf of the governor. A week or so earlier

---

6. Onias C. Skinner [Carthage] to Calvin A. Warren and Almeron Wheat [Quincy], 8 July 1844, Wilford C. Wood Collection.

7. See, for example, John Hardy [Boston] to *The Prophet,* 26 July 1844, in *The Prophet,* 3 August 1844: "Governor Ford was one of the main wire-pullers of the damnable deed."

Jonas had delivered an abrasive speech to the people of Warsaw—given onshore while keeping a small skiff close at hand just in case the inhabitants rushed him.

Jonas would have found Willard Richards's words doubly ironic, as they were unknowingly addressed to the man who provided the press used to print the *Nauvoo Expositor,* thereby precipitating the downfall of the Mormon prophet. Additionally, Richards did not know that Jonas, on the evening of June 27—under the guise of a Quincy Whig political meeting—had organized a band of Adams County militiamen in preparation for a planned march against Nauvoo the day after the murders. Jonas was careful to do nothing that would disabuse the Mormons of their trust in him. After all, at the time Jonas was running for a seat in Illinois's Fourteenth General Assembly and doubtless hoped to parlay his own Mormon support into a Latter-day Saint vote for Henry Clay in November. In one more seemingly effortless maneuver, Jonas winningly fulfilled his duties to the governor, the Mormons, and to his party. Whig involvement in the Carthage conspiracy would remain safe from Mormon cries for vengeance.[8]

Outside of Nauvoo, the coalition of Whigs and Democrats engaged in the conspiracy strained confidences and traditional allegiances. Some were bound to talk. A few did.

When Governor Ford departed Carthage for Nauvoo at noon on June 27 he left Brigadier General Minor Deming in charge at the county seat. Ford fully expected that Deming would make a valiant effort to protect the Smiths from harm; indeed, the Brigadier General was one of the few militia officers who did *not* know Ford and the Greys were accomplices in the plot to murder the Smiths. And, if Deming lost his life in the process of protecting the Smiths, Ford would have conveniently (and without personal risk) rid himself of one more annoyance.

Deming had become a thorn in the side of the governor and the anti-Mormon coalition even before the fatal assault on the jail. It should be recalled that when Deming showed the Mormon prisoners the proper honor to be accorded officers in the state militia, the Carthage Greys turned against him. Deming also became a target simply because he knew too much.

It was Deming, who, "long before breakfast" on the morning of June 27, had informed his commander in chief (the governor), "that there was going to be an attempt made to rescue the Smiths out of jail and visit summary punishment upon them." Deming was reliably informed that "*it was the Whigs* that intended to do it." Anxious to protect the Whigs (who were shielding him from discovery as well), Ford dismissed this damning intelligence and would later deny that Deming ever made such a statement.[9]

In his largely autobiographical *History of Illinois,* completed in 1846, Ford also misrepresented Deming's actions that fateful afternoon. "General Deming, who was

---

8. Willard Richards to Abraham Jonas, 10 July 1844, in Smith, *History of the Church* 7:175–76. "The Mormon Excitement," *Quincy Whig* 10 July 1844. Mr. Chambers [editor of the *Missouri Republican*], in *Dayton Journal and Advertiser,* 16 July 1844, and "Mr. Jonas, Whig candidate for State Senate, will address the people, at the Court House in Quincy on Thursday evening," *Quincy Whig* 26 June 1844.
9. G. T. M. Davis to Thomas Ford, 9 August 1844, in *Illinois State Register,* 8 November 1844.

left in command," Ford wrote, "being deserted by some of his troops, and perceiving the arrangement with the others, and having no force upon which he could rely, for fear of his life retired from the village." Ford's motivation for maligning Deming no doubt was to place blame for the murders at least partially on the Brigadier General's shoulders. At the same time, Ford inadvertently acknowledged that the murders were not the result of a spontaneous uprising of disbanded militiamen, as was commonly reported, but the culmination of an "arrangement" earlier entered into. That Ford knew more than he let on is further confirmed by his own admission (again in his *History*) that on the afternoon of June 27 when Colonel Buckmaster warned him of a planned attack on the jail, Ford said he "entertained no suspicion of such an attack; at any rate, none before the next day in the afternoon." Ford obviously knew about the conspiracy to murder the Mormon leaders; the onslaught simply occurred earlier than he had expected.[10]

Furthermore, contrary to Ford's rendering of Brigadier General Deming's supposed fainthearted withdrawal from Carthage, the truth of the matter was that Deming fully expected to leave for Quincy on the afternoon of June 27 in order to attend the funeral of his brother Edwin, who had been killed by lightning earlier in the week. After putting his troops under the command of a junior officer, Deming returned to his home to prepare for his departure. He was told of the killings a short time after they occurred.[11]

Deming's response to the murders is more revealing than Ford's attempt to disparage his character. Deming was one of only a handful of non-Mormon residents of Hancock County who considered the killing of Joseph Smith to be "a ferocious and fiendish murder." In his search for the truth surrounding the assassination, Deming discovered that the guards posted at the jail had loaded their guns with blank cartridges, firm evidence pointing to complicity on the part of the Carthage and Warsaw troops.[12]

Newspaperman George T. M. Davis, the chief Illinois Whig leader shielding Ford from public exposure, sought to limit the potentially harmful effects of Deming's intelligence. Davis, like Ford, unwittingly confirms Deming's story. "I have hitherto said but little in regard to Gen. Deming," Davis wrote in a widely circulated account of the assassination. "My reason for this is, I had no confidence whatever in him, from the attempts which I knew he was constantly making while I remained in Carthage." Davis's remarks refer to the morning of June 27; he left town with Governor Ford around noon that day and never returned to the county seat. Davis was apprehensive because Deming had attempted "to give this unfortunate affair a political turn, and to impress upon the minds of his superiors, that the Whigs were the prime movers through the whole of it. And as he had not succeeded in making any body believe

---

10. Thomas Ford to G. T. M. Davis 26 August 1844, in *Illinois State Register*, 8 November 1844. Ford, *History of Illinois*, in Smith, *History of the Church* 7:22.

11. Minor R. Deming to Stephen Deming, 26 June 1844, Deming Papers, Illinois Historical Survey, Urbana.

12. Arthur B. Deming, *Naked Truths About Mormonism*, 1888 (1.1), Introduction. M. R. Deming to [his parents] 1 July 1844, Illinois Historical Survey, Urbana. Minor R. Deming to Thomas Ford, 3 July 1844, in "Grand Discovery," *Warsaw Signal* 4 September 1844.

his silly, foolish story, had failed in what I regarded a dishonorable scheme for selfish purposes." Davis never tells his readers what he believed Deming's ulterior motive to be. And, of course, Davis fails to reveal his own motivation for protecting the governor, a sworn political enemy. As we shall see, their alliance would be short-lived.[13]

A week after the Carthage massacre, Deming informed the governor that he knew his own life was in danger. "The mob subsequent to their butchering the prisoners took a vote to murder myself and others, those who would not sustain them." Unaware that Thomas Ford himself was a conspirator in the affair, Deming cautioned him that threats of Mormon vengeance also continued to circulate, on account of the governor's "strident" Nauvoo speech and claims that he was a party to the murders. "It is necessary for the honor of the State and the vindication of your character that the truth in this matter should be fully known." While certainly desirous of having his character restored, Ford had no wish to open a full investigation into the circumstances surrounding the deaths.[14]

Deming's devotion to principle, together with his law and order approach to justice, led the Mormons to support his candidacy for Hancock County sheriff in the August elections. In late August the newly elected sheriff wrote to his family in the east. Matters in Hancock County were still unsettled, Deming informed them. "The exterminators are of the two, more fanatical than the Mormons and less regardful of the law," he wrote. "They threaten death of all who have enough daring or humanity to oppose them . . . The Mormon question since the murder of the Smiths has become political and the venum [sic] of party spirit breathes in detraction. There were some 2 or 300 engaged in the murder and they with their friends and alliance of the Whig party in the county, who mean to sustain and protect the murderers, make a strong party that by threats, violence & desperation aim at supremacy above the law and justice." Deming's moral stand against the Whig alliance would eventually cost him his life.[15]

Press coverage of the murders was hampered by poor communication. And yet, it, too, quickly turned political. Each party accused the other of provoking the Carthage incident. As late as the Fourth of July, Springfield's Whig newspaper, the *Sangamo Journal*, reported it was "unable to state anything very definite in relation to affairs at Nauvoo" and the surrounding countryside. "Rumor says . . . that on Thursday of last week Joe Smith, Hyram Smith, and Dr. Richards were shot by a mob [at] Carthage." The Whig editor was skeptical about how the governor could have "placed them in a situation where they would be murdered. The rumor is too preposterous for belief."

The Democratic *Illinois State Register* lost no time in responding. "The *Journal* of yesterday, in that dastardly spirit for which its controllers are remarkable, intimates that Gov. Ford received Jos. Smith and Hir. Smith as prisoners, pledged himself for their protection, and 'then placed them in a situation where they would

---

13. Davis, *Authentic Account*, 29.
14. Minor R. Deming to Thomas Ford, 3 July 1844, in "Grand Discovery," *Warsaw Signal* 4 September 1844.
15. Minor R. Deming to [his parents] 22 August 1844, Illinois Historical Survey, Urbana, quoted in Hallwas and Launius, *Cultures in Conflict*, 271.

be murdered!'" The *Journal* article was all partisan politics, insisted the *Register*.

> What opinion will the public form of a party, whose leading editor feigns disbelief in the murder of the Smiths, for the purpose of stabbing indirectly the honor of the State, through the bosom of its Chief Magistrate? and this, too, for a party purpose, as is plainly manifest on the face of the dastardly article itself—that purpose being to induce the Mormons to vote with the Whigs. To obtain their votes, the Journal indirectly invents an infamous lie, which lie stabs the public faith, and blackens the honor of the State.

Major Edward D. Baker, an Illinois Whig running for U.S. Congress to replace John J. Hardin, had just arrived in Springfield. "We hope the Major has not suffered his personal difficulties with the Governor to poison his mind so far as to communicate the substance of the article which appears in the *Journal*, to its editor," the *Register* continued. "An editor who would make such a charge, would not be too good to blacken his face and join the band of midnight assassins who murdered Smith."[16]

In the northern part of the state, the Democratic *Galena Sentinel* and the Whig *Upper Mississippian* were likewise engaged in political combat. The *Sentinel* struck the first blow:

> Since the foul murder of the Smiths by the Anti-Mormons, many of the Whig electioneers are boasting that Sweet [a Whig] will beat Hoge [the Democratic incumbent] in the Congressional District. A gentleman who was at Camp meeting last Sunday heard them endeavoring to make capitol even on the Sabbath, out of this foul stain on our State! It would appear that the leaders of the Whig party, by their letters printed, first agitated the question which has resulted so lawlessly—all for political effect and are doing their best to implicate Gov. Ford as conniving in the murders.

Thomas Gregg, assistant editor of the *Upper Mississippian*, responded with relish. "It has seldom been our fortune to notice a meaner and more reckless attempt to make political capital, than is displayed in the above," he replied. Gregg reminded the editor of the *Sentinel* that *he* had been a citizen of Hancock County "long before the Mormons settled in it, and know a thousand times more about her local affairs." Gregg knew more than he would ever tell. Gregg was in regular communication with the Nauvoo dissidents; his brother James first carried the news of the Carthage murders to Warsaw; his brother-in-law, Frank Worrell, was in charge of the guard at the time of the assault. And, Gregg's support for Henry Clay was widely known.

Gregg pronounced the charge against the Whigs "a vile slander!" At the same time he readily acknowledged that "the best men of both parties [Whig and Democrat] . . . have been for years steadily endeavoring to check the mad ambition, and slay the reckless career, of the Mormon leader. And had their laudable endeavor been seconded as they deserved to be . . . the melancholy tragedy would have never taken

---

16. "The Mormon Difficulties," *Sangamo Journal*, 4 July 1844. "Assassination of Joseph Smith," *Illinois State Register*, 5 July 1844.

place." Gregg pressed on by insisting that "the idea that the Whigs charge Gov. Ford with conniving at the murders, is just so much stupid flammery." Gregg's closing words turned the table on the Democrats. "Let such politicians as the editor of the *Sentinel* hold their peace about these Mormon difficulties. Their conduct brought these disasters upon us. It is they who have brought this stain upon our State and her institutions."[17]

For the most part, newspapers outside of Illinois simply reproduced articles originally written from Nauvoo, Warsaw, Quincy, St. Louis, and Alton, supplying little commentary beyond condemnation of the affair. Some even applauded the action. A Tennessee Whig editor exclaimed, "Smith was killed, as he should have been. THREE CHEERS to the brave company who shot him to pieces!"[18]

One of the few editors to acknowledge the role Joseph Smith's presidential bid played in his untimely death was William Ogden Niles, Baltimore publisher of the independent *Niles' National Register*. "Alas for human greatness!" his editorial began. "One of the nominated candidates for the next presidency is already a lifeless corpse." He offered no sympathy, expressed no remorse, no condemnation of the perpetrators.

Niles pointed immediately to Joseph's political activism, introducing the topic with a mocking portrayal of the Mormon prophet. "Even the sanctity of his high profession as a prophet and a leader, could not preserve him, though performing almost miracles, in deluding thousands to his mystical faith, and detaining them in unaccountable subservience to his will."

Mormonism, in Niles' view, perverted the example of righteousness initiated by the Savior. "Notwithstanding the flagrant deviation of [Joseph Smith's] course from that designated by the meek and lowly pattern [of Jesus Christ] whom he professed to be imitating and serving, who so often and emphatically declared to his disciples, 'My kingdom is not of this world.'"

Joseph Smith's political goals, on the other hand, were incredibly ambitious, as the prophet "evidently aspired to a full share [of] the kingdoms of this wor[l]d," Niles wrote, "as far, and as fast as he could grasp hold of them . . . Joseph unquestionably indulged some faint hope of extending his rapidly accumulated power, from Nauvoo, to the extremities of the Union, and dreamed even of expanding those limits far beyond what they now are circumscribed to." Joseph's plans were well known. "His expose of what he would do if elected president of the United States, his letters to the several candidates, and his nomination by conventions at Boston and elsewhere, evince that he was determined to make a demonstration for the Capitol and dictatorship."

The prophet-candidate was brought down, Niles suggested, by the one force he could not control, the press. "Joseph made an attempt . . . like other sovereigns, to regulate the public press, in his dominions . . . Joseph adopted his own method of

---

17. "The Mormons-Galena Sentinel," *Upper Mississippian*, 20 July 1844.
18. William G. Brownlow, *Jonesborough [Kentucky] Whig*, 24 July 1844, reprinted in *Warsaw Signal*, 10 February 1845. Quoted in Swinton, *American Prophet*, 18. This is an example of what Thomas Ford referred to when he wrote, "The whig press in every part of the United States came to their assistance." (Ford, *History of Illinois*, in Smith, *History of the Church* 7:46)

regulating the press, a summary process, and conclusive . . . It was a dangerous nerve to touch, as Joseph soon ascertained."

Now that the Mormon prophet was dead, Niles's main concern was the recent influx of European converts to Nauvoo, "who, if we are not mistaken, will, most of them, as citizens of Illinois, exercise the privilege of voting on the presidential question, without regard to the U. States naturalization laws." Niles recognized that securing the Mormon vote (naturalized or not) in the November election remained a priority for Whig and Democrat alike.[19]

An editorial that originally appeared in a Cincinnati paper was copied by Horace Greeley's *New York Tribune*. Joseph Smith's death, the article asserted, "seems to have been made legally by the guard resisting his forcible attempt to escape, but the popular action against the Mormons will be represented as persecution. The worst part of the Mormon affair we have ever seen, is the atrocious grant by the Illinois Legislature (as we believe for political purposes) of special charters to Nauvoo City and the Nauvoo Legion . . . The difficulty in Illinois and Missouri is in singling the Mormons out as a body to be favored or persecuted according to the political interests or popular prejudices of the day." Incredibly, the Whig editor was capable of passing from murder to the larger political question in less time than it takes to gasp for breath! Furthermore, the Warsaw Committee's distorted version of Carthage events was alive and well.[20]

James Gordon Bennett, Democratic editor of the *New York Herald*, concurred with the views advanced by the *Tribune*. It was "political feeling," he wrote, that "entered largely into the popular excitement in that region against the Mormons." Bennett then took his claims one step further than most editors were willing to put into print. He laid the conspiracy at the feet of the Whigs, who, he said, "feared . . . that the Nauvoo people would give material aid to Polk. This affords another and most melancholy illustration of the pernicious, demoralizing, brutalizing influence of the party presses," (of which the *Herald* was one!), "which are daily inflaming the passions of the people by the vilest and most incendiary tirades against their respective opponents." Bennett plainly attributed the Carthage tragedy to the political machinations of the Illinois Whig party, which feared the potential impact of the Mormons voting Democratic in the November election.[21]

Back in Illinois, Whig newspaperman G. T. M. Davis presented his impressions of recent events in Hancock County in a series of on-the-spot letters and editorials published in the *Alton Telegraph*. In early July he informed his readers that he had just returned to Alton following a ten-day visit to Carthage, Warsaw, Nauvoo, and Quincy "amid the scenes of excitement which existed previous and subsequent to the fatal termination of the Smiths' earthly career." He was preparing a history of the Mormon war.[22]

As a participant-observer with the unprecedented ability to move between opposing camps in the conflict, Davis's reporting had an immediacy no other journalist

---

19. "The Mormon Tragedy," *Niles' National Register*, 13 July 1844.
20. "The Mormon Excitement," *New York Tribune*, 11 July 1844, copied from the *Cincinnati Chronicle*.
21. James Arlington Bennet editorial from the *New York Herald*, copied by *The Prophet* 13 July 1844.
22. "Let Him that is Without Sin Cast the First Stone," *Alton Telegraph*, 13 July 1844.

could match. His sources included everyday Mormons, members of Nauvoo's secretive Council of Fifty, leaders of the Carthage and Warsaw Anti-Mormon Committees, the local and state militia, and, of course, the governor.

Davis completed his history in early July. The work would appear in pamphlet form as *An Authentic Account of the Massacre of Joseph Smith, the Mormon Prophet, and Hyrum Smith, his brother, together with a brief history of the rise and progress of Mormonism, and all the circumstances which led to their death.* Copies of the booklet were sent to American Whig leaders, including Horace Greeley and Henry Clay.[23]

More than anything else, Davis's tract was a propaganda piece. Davis assured his readers, somewhat disingenuously, that his motivation for writing the work was "Actuated by no spirit of partisanship, with either the one side or the other, we were a calm and dispassionate observer, and determined to give the whole facts to the people in an impartial and authentic manner." At the end of his small treatise, Davis again avows that he had "endeavored to do justice to all parties, and to place their situations fairly before the public . . . This I have done honestly and fearlessly."[24]

Contrary to his repeated protestations of impartiality, Davis early on reveals his animosity towards the Mormons. "The founders of the Mormon faith . . . admitted on all hands to be of all absurdities the most absurd . . . imposing their delusions . . . practicing their impositions . . . the chief of imposters, JOE SMITH THE PROPHET." Davis justified the killing of Joseph and Hyrum as ridding the earth of "two as wickedly depraved men, as ever disgraced the human family." Impartial and fair he was not.[25]

As a Whig supporter of Henry Clay, Davis was obligated to do all he could to ensure a Whig victory in November. His efforts to do so occasionally bordered on the extreme. Davis certainly never disguised his support for the men engaged in the extralegal murders. John Bailhache, senior editor of the *Alton Telegraph*, disagreed with Davis's claims that "the press has been too harsh, in its denunciations of the recent outrage" and that the "ruthless assassins of the Mormon leaders" had an excuse for their drastic actions in the redress of their grievances. "A just sense of our responsibility to the public, would not permit us to say less," Bailhache concluded, "and the intelligent reader, being now in possession of the views of our respected associate, as well as of our own, we submit the whole matter to his better judgement."

The editorial disagreement between Bailhache and Davis was not to be construed as applying to "National politics," however. Baihache insisted: "There is not, it is believed, one single point, however unimportant, on which [we] differ; and such is also the case with our State affairs. In other things, each one is left free to express his own sentiments, subject to a notice of dissent from the other, when thought expedient, as is done in the present number." Somehow the two men, at least in print, were

---

23. Greeley's copy of the Davis pamphlet is in the Beineke Rare Book and Manuscript Library, Yale University. It is inscribed, "Horace Greely [sic] Esq. New York with the respect of the Author Alton Ill Aug 21 1844." Henry Clay's receipt of Davis's pamphlet is acknowledged in Henry Clay to G. T. M. Davis 31 August 1844, in *Papers of Henry Clay* 10:107–8.

24. "Let Him That is Without Sin Cast the First Stone," *Alton Telegraph*, 13 July 1844. Davis, *Authentic Account*, 47.

25. Davis, *Authentic Account*, 3.

capable of separating Joseph Smith's murder from his political threat to the Whig cause. The separation was more cosmetic than real.[26]

For the "intelligent reader" of the day, to borrow Bailhache's phrase, the most unusual aspect of Davis's pamphlet would have been its unyielding support of Illinois Democratic governor Thomas Ford. The two men were, by all accounts, uncompromising personal and political enemies. Davis's protection of the governor was governed by one fear, the betrayal and public identification of the men engaged in the murders. Indeed, *Authentic Account* was one of the chief propaganda tools used by the Whigs to shield the participants from discovery. And, later that year, the document would be distributed in the Illinois legislature as part of the ultimately successful Whig effort to repeal the Nauvoo Charter.

After reviewing "all the material facts connected with the riot at Nauvoo, the death of its authors, and the subsequent occurrences up to the 3d of July," Davis proposed to "notice one or two objections made to the course of the Executive of Illinois, giving his own reasons for that course." The most serious charge against Governor Ford was that he had promised Joseph and Hyrum Smith protection if they surrendered to state authorities. Davis argued that the governor's assurance, "was a gratuitous verbal pledge given to the Mormon committee who visited Carthage, and subsequently repeated to the Smiths, after they reached that place, and not made by them previous, a condition of such surrender . . . I maintain, therefore, that the pledge did not extend to their personal safety, upon their surrender, on any other charge, than the one preferred against them for riot." The protection did not apply when the men were rearrested for treason, Davis asserted. The argument rested on a legal technicality, but the governor had kept his original pledge—according to Davis, at least. He neglected to mention that, two days after the murders, the governor reaffirmed that he had indeed pledged to protect the Smiths from harm.

It was also submitted by some, Davis acknowledged, that the governor, knowing he could not protect the imprisoned leaders, ". . . should have opened the prison doors, and allowed them to escape." Davis disagreed. "Had he done this, nothing could have prevented [the Governor's] impeachment and conviction." The men were jailed on a charge of treason, "a charge of the most serious character known to our laws." The governor had acted properly in keeping them in jail because, "The punishment, upon conviction, being death, the accused could not be bailed." (When it came to the treatment of the men accused of the murders, this legal point would be conveniently disregarded.)

Furthermore, Davis discounted the claim that "Gov. Ford knew the feelings of the Carthage Greys, towards the Smiths." The evidence usually cited to support that position was the Grey "revolt" on the morning of June 25, when Joseph and Hyrum were paraded before the troops. "But such is not the case," Davis countered. The enmity "was directed towards Gen. Deming." Davis concluded: "There is nothing that has been disclosed," (which in itself says a great deal), "which would have led Gov. Ford to suppose, that the guard he placed at the jail would prove recreant to their trust, and become accomplices in the destruction of the prisoners." Based upon the

---

26. "The Recent Tragedy," *Alton Telegraph*, 13 July 1844. [hand] *Alton Telegraph*, 13 July 1844.

evidence presented in his *Authentic Account* Davis found no wrong in the Democratic governor's dealings with the Mormons.[27]

At the time Davis penned his unqualified support for the governor the summer elections were nearly a month away. Just days before the August election a letter from the governor, chastising the people of Warsaw and blaming them for much of the unrest in Hancock County, was sent (inadvertently, it was later claimed) to the people of Nauvoo. In the days leading up the election more than one stump speaker warned that if the Mormons did not vote Democratic the governor would withdraw his protection and support. It was the summer of 1843 all over again.[28]

Sidney Rigdon, who had recently returned to Nauvoo from Pittsburgh upon hearing of the murders, insisted that the Mormons of Nauvoo exercise their constitutional right. Although many Latter-day Saints were inclined not to vote—the governor had in fact recommended to the Mormon leadership that the Saints abstain from attending the polls altogether—it was believed they had little choice. To begin with, their opponents were running on an "anti-Mormon ticket." The Mormons were compelled to vote in self-defense. Furthermore, Rigdon argued, "if they did not vote the report would go abroad and be believed throughout the world, that the Mormons had dispersed and abandoned their religion; and that their city had been deserted and broken up; and these reports would seem to be sanctioned by the fact that no votes had been given in Nauvoo." The message to the world had to be clear and it had to be unified.[29]

The election for representatives to the U.S. Congress took place on August 5. In Illinois' Sixth District, Democrat Joseph P. Hoge received 76 percent of the vote in Hancock County. His overall margin of victory was 52 percent; 45 percent of the vote went to the Whig candidate, and 3 percent to the Liberty party.[30]

Not surprisingly, Horace Greeley's *Clay Tribune* reporting of the August election results was headed "The Mormon District in Illinois." It minced no words. "Hoge, the Loco elected to Congress from the 6th district of Illinois, must be considered the Representative of the Mormons. Hancock County, where Nauvoo, the Mormon city is situated, gave Hoge a majority of 1357. In the remainder of the District . . . the Whig candidate, Sweet, had a majority of 473." In a effort to cover-up Whig involvement in the murder of Joseph Smith, and with a faint hope of recovering the Mormon vote, the *Clay Tribune* stressed that "the Mormons were told (falsely) that [Whig candidate] Sweet was their bitterest enemy, and had endeavored to justify the mob that had killed their Prophet." On the contrary, in this the Mormons had been correctly informed.[31]

Another report, also in the *Clay Tribune*, conceded,

27. Davis, *Authentic Account*, 32–35.

28. Nauvoo Correspondent to *New York Tribune*, 3 August 1844, in *Clay Tribune*, 24 August 1844. Anonymous [Burlington, Iowa] to S. M. Bartlett [editor, *Quincy Whig*], 4 August 1844, in *Quincy Whig*, 7 August 1844.

29. Thomas Ford to G. T. M. Davis, 26 August 1844, in *Illinois State Register*, 8 November 1844. See Joseph M. Cole to Willard Richards, 5 August 1844, in cited in Godfrey, "Causes of Conflict," 70–71.

30. Pease, *Illinois Election Returns*, 149.

31. "The Mormon District in Illinois," *Clay Tribune*, 31 August 1844.

the State [of Illinois] is Loco-Foco, by about the same majority as the State Election in 1840 . . . They may do better now, but for the present the State may be set down as decidedly Loco. The new Congressional Delegation stands . . . V. Stephen A. Douglass, by a small majority[;] VI. Joseph P. Hoge, over M. P. Sweet, Whig[;] VII. Edward D. Baker, Whig, over John Calhoun[.] All Locos elected, but Mr. Baker, who takes the place of Hon John J. Hardin, [who had] declined [to run]. The Whigs hoped to beat Douglass and Hoge; but Douglass is said to be re-elected by 250, while Hoge is saved by the great Mormon vote cast unanimously for him. The vote of Nauvoo stands, Hoge 1275, Sweet twenty! So Mormonism goes the whole hog for Polk, Texas & Co. So we will call Illinois a Polk state until the Whigs carry it for Clay.

Edward D. Baker would now replace John J. Hardin as the only Illinois Whig to serve in the U.S. Congress.[32]

Hardin had recently returned to his home in Jacksonville. On August 5 (the day of the election), Governor Ford requested that Hardin, a Brigadier General in the state militia, oversee matters in Hancock County while he (Ford) attended a National Democratic Convention in Nashville. Ford planned to be gone for two weeks and thought it proper to "leave some person in charge of the affairs in Hancock County until my return." Ford warned Hardin that he should be "careful not to adventure any action in a military capacity unless you are well persuaded that you will be sustained thoroughly by the officers and men under your command."[33]

This move highlighted Ford's own difficulties. Ford himself was vulnerable and had become an assassination target. He had unsuccessfully requested the use of U.S. Army troops from Missouri to keep the peace while the accused assassins were rounded up and arrested. When that effort failed, Ford had to rely on the Whigs for assistance.

Hardin, as Henry Clay's stepnephew, was an ardent Whig. While serving in Congress from 1843–44, Hardin was responsible for overseeing Clay's presidential campaign in Illinois. He was present (together with G. T. M. Davis) at the Baltimore nominating convention in May and supplied the first poetic verses dedicated to the Clay-Frelinghuysen ticket. Ford's appointment of Hardin, therefore, reflected an unmistakable erosion in the Democratic governor's base of power. Ford himself admitted that he found it necessary to put his trust in political opponents in order to maintain military discipline in Hancock county, "that which [his] own political friends, with two or three exceptions, were slow to do."[34]

Days after the election, G. T. M. Davis attended the land sales office in Quincy. While there Davis spoke with "some fifteen or twenty citizens of Hancock" who informed him that Governor Ford, just previous to his departure for Tennessee, "had prepared a list of names to be presented to the Grand Jury, with a list of witnesses to procure their indictment and conviction." If the governor went forward with his proposed actions against the murderers of the Smith brothers, the anti-Mormons assured Davis "they would show beyond doubt, that [Ford] knew all about it."

---

32. "Illinois," *Clay Tribune*, 24 August 1844.
33. Thomas Ford to John J. Hardin, 5 August 1844, Hardin Papers, Chicago Historical Society.
34. Ford, *History of Illinois*, in Smith, *History of the Church* 7:46.

On August 9, Davis wrote a confidential letter to the governor. He began by referring to their unusual political arrangement, which had been forged during the fateful days of late June. "You are well aware of the relation I bear towards you in regard to the late Mormon difficulties, and the position I have occupied before the public. You cannot be otherwise than satisfied that from the previous relations existing between us, my motives could not have been otherwise than pure in sustaining you in the course you had taken." Davis reminded Ford that he had been "assailed privately as well as publicly" by many of his "political friends, and the enmity of some of them has not been appeased to this day."

Even with those difficulties, Davis was still in a position to support him, he said, but only "if proof is not adduced to show that you have been influenced by political motives." Davis made reference to Ford's recent letter to the people of Warsaw, which was at least partially responsible for the Mormon's Democratic vote on August 5.

More critical to their common cause was the simple fact that damning intelligence about the governor's involvement in the affair was continuing to surface. Colonel Buckmaster had reported to Colonel March and to "one or two other" citizens of Alton (which no doubt would have included G. T. M. Davis) that "on your way to Nauvoo, you and [Buckmaster] talked the matter over, and both agreed that the Smiths would be killed during your absence, and that it was his suggestion to you, to leave the wagons a few miles out of Nauvoo, so that you and your escort could get as far out of the way," before news of the killing could reach Nauvoo. "If this statement of Buckmaster's is correct," Davis warned him, "your implication in the matter is fixed."

Davis applied even more pressure. How could the governor indict Hancock County men, he asked, if evidence could be brought forward to prove his own involvement? Testimony came from Thomas Sharp, editor of the *Warsaw Signal.* Davis had spoken with the editor just the day before, who informed him "that on the morning of the day the Smiths were killed, he called upon you at your room and told you that the people intended to take the law into their own hands, and that you replied to him, they must not do it, or attempt it, while you was at Carthage, that you had come there to sustain the law, not to witness its violation."

Further, there was additional testimony that "two different individuals, heard Col. Deming on the same morning long before breakfast, state to you that there was going to be an attempt made to rescue the Smiths out of jail and visit summary punishment upon them, *but that it was the Whigs* that intended to do it." (Emphasis in the original.) Davis cautioned Ford that there was a good deal more evidence that implicated him even further.

"Now my only object in writing to you, is that of a desire to see you sustained before the public in this unfortunate affair. And the best way I can serve you is to state to you facts within my knowledge, that you may act with a full view of all the circumstances before you." The "full view" would have included the simple fact that Davis had no desire for the indictments to be put forward. No one knew what the conspirators would admit to under oath.

"What possible good can grow out of a renewal of excitement in Hancock county?" Davis queried. "If indictments are gotten up against these men, and attempts are made to arrest them, a scene of bloodshed and massacre will ensue, unequaled during the existence of this republic." No matter that Davis's claims were greatly ex-aggerated; he knew that Ford would not want to add such an episode to his already dismal record as governor.[35]

Following his return to Springfield from Nashville in late August, Ford wrote a detailed response to Davis's charges. Upon the recommendation of his Democratic political advisors, however, Ford's reply was never sent. The secret correspondence would not be leaked to the Illinois press until after the November presidential election.[36]

---

35. G. T. M. Davis to Thomas Ford, 9 August 1844, in *Illinois State Register*, 8 November 1844.

36. Ibid. Thomas Ford to G. T. M. Davis, 26 August 1844, in *Illinois State Register*, 8 November 1844.

Chapter Seventeen

Wolf Hunts

"I did not help to kill Joe Smith, for I did not go to the jail with those who killed him."

Thomas Sharp, *Warsaw Signal*, September 25, 1844[1]

E VEN IN THE FACE OF possible public exposure and the threat of impeachment proceedings by the Whigs in the Illinois legislature, Democratic governor Thomas Ford had little choice but to move forward with his proposed indictments against the men accused of murdering the Smith brothers. Events in Hancock County were rapidly escalating out of control.

In mid-September, flyers were distributed throughout the Military Tract inviting all armed men to participate in a "wolf hunt" scheduled to take place near Warsaw on the 26th and 27th of the month. The proposed wolf hunt was a common practice at the time used to rid the prairie of roving predators. This wolf hunt, however, was aimed at attacking Nauvoo and ridding Hancock County of the Mormons. When Ford was informed of this plan to harass the Latter-day Saints, he "thought it to be most advisable to call on some influential persons to raise 600 or 700 troops in this section of country." The task would not be an easy one. Ford had been accused by the Whigs of having "used up" Abraham Jonas's political capital in the weeks following the murders. Under such circumstances, few men with political aspirations would willingly come to his aid. Ford had little recourse now but to request the help, once again, of General John J. Hardin. "I have endeavored my dear Sir," Ford wrote to Hardin, "with all the ingenuity in my power to keep this whole matter free from politics." Ford promised that his entreaty for Hardin's services would be kept "a strict confidence between us."[2]

Within days nearly five hundred Illinois volunteers from nine counties surrounding Hancock were placed under the command of Brigadier-General John J.

---

1. "Postscript," *Warsaw Signal*, 25 September 1844.
2. Smith, *History of the Church* 7:xxvii, xxix, 45, 270, 276 ("wolf hunts"). Thomas Ford to John J. Hardin, 18 September 1844 [second letter] (troops quote). Edward D. Baker to John J. Hardin, 18 September 1844. Thomas Ford to John J. Hardin, 18 September 1844 [first letter] (confidence quote). Hardin Papers, Chicago Historical Society.

Hardin. He was assisted by fellow Whig Major Edward D. Baker. The men gathered their forces and marched towards Nauvoo.

Impatient at the waiting game being played by the governor, the first writs against the men thought to be responsible for the murders of Joseph Smith were issued by Nauvoo's municipal court even before Hardin and his troops reached the Holy City. John Taylor, now almost fully recovered from his wounds, swore out an affidavit in which he asserted that he "had good reasons to believe and does believe that Levy Williams [and] Thomas C. Sharpe——have been and were guilty of committing said criminal act." Because the Quincy militia refused to accompany him to Warsaw without direct orders from the governor, Sheriff Minor Deming was unsuccessful in his attempt to arrest the two men. When Sharp and Williams learned that the writs were returnable at Nauvoo, they fled across the Mississippi and set up an encampment in Alexandria, Missouri.[3]

Nauvoo's municipal court issued another writ for Joseph H. Jackson, also believed by the Mormons to be a participant in the murders. A non-Mormon, Jackson was a one-time associate of Joseph Smith (later linked with the Nauvoo dissidents) and author of an anti-Mormon tract published in Warsaw. Jackson, too, fled the state.

Additional Nauvoo writs were issued for Mormon dissidents William Law (Joseph Smith's former counselor), his brother Wilson Law, Doctor Robert Foster, Charles A. Foster, and "one of the Higbees." The five men, none of whom were in Carthage at the time of the murders, had settled in Hampton, Illinois, following the tragedy. They eluded capture by slipping away from the arresting officers at night, taking a boat "up to Port Byron, went on board of a boat in the morning, came down to Hampton, where the officers had remained, [and] came off the boat as [the arresting officers] went on." The dissidents were yet at large.[4]

On September 28, General Hardin (accompanied by Thomas Ford) inspected the Nauvoo Legion. Many of the local officers paraded without weapons of any kind, a pointed reminder to the governor that he had disarmed the Mormon militia just prior to the Carthage massacre.

Departing Nauvoo following the military exercises, Ford prepared a force to invade Missouri and capture Sharp, Williams, and Jackson. Major Edward D. Baker was promoted to the rank of colonel to give him greater authority during his negotiations with the fugitives.

"Our little force arrived at that place," a mile above Warsaw, about noon on September 28, Ford would later write. "That night we were to cross to Missouri at Churchville [now Alexandria], and seize the accused there encamped with a number of their friends." Sometime during the afternoon, Colonel Baker "visited the hostile encampment, and on his return refused to participate in the expedition, and advised all his [Whig] friends against joining it." Ford knew he was powerless to force the

---

3.   "An order to all sheriffs, coroners and constables in Illinois," 21 September 1844. Signed by Aaron Johnson, Justice of the Peace, PLW, Documents, 246. See also Smith, *History of the Church* 7:275.

4.   *Upper Mississippian*, 5 October 1844. Law, Nauvoo Diary [27 June 1844], in Cook, *William Law*, 60. Law's final entry is dated 28 June 1844, followed by his views regarding Joseph Smith's dissolute moral character.

issue. "There was no authority for compelling the men to invade a neighboring state," Ford observed, "and for this cause, much to the vexation of myself and several others, the matter fell through."[5]

Colonel Baker had been successful, however, in using his influence with the men (as well as the governor) and "partly arranged the terms for the accused to surrender." The conditions were unusual for men accused of a capital offense. Williams and Sharp "were to be taken to Quincy for examination under a military guard; the attorney for the people was to be advised to admit them to bail, and they were to be entitled to a continuance of their trial at the next court at Carthage." Ford wrote to the Mormons at Nauvoo: "Williams and Sharp have surrendered and will be sent to Quincy for trial. Jackson has not come over and is so very sick that we could do nothing with him if we had him. It will be necessary to get all the witnesses down as soon as possible."[6]

On October 2, Williams and Sharp's defense counsel agreed to enter a recognizance. Williams and Sharp were to be freed on a nominal bail. Unlike the earlier case of the Smith brothers at Carthage, the phrasing of the new document made it amply clear that the accused refused to admit to any guilt in the affair. The wording was emphatic and uncompromising.

> In appearing & entering into recognizance to appear to answer to any charge preferred against them, they do not make or intend to make any admission of probable cause to bind them over; but that it is done to save time, delay in consequence of the absence of witnesses, and for this reason only . . . in entering into said recognizance, [they] do so under a protestation of their entire innocence of their offence with which they are charged . . . but enter into said recognizance for no purpose whatever, than that above expressed.[7]

Edward D. Baker and O. H. Browning, regarded as among the best lawyers and Whig politicians in the state, signed the document for the defendants. There could be no doubt that the Whigs were not only behind the murders but were also fully committed to protecting the men directly involved in the assassination conspiracy.[8]

---

5.   Edward D. Baker commission signed by Thomas Ford, 28 September 1844 Illinois State Archives, Springfield, cited by Braden, "The Public Career of Edward Dickinson Baker," note 58, 86–87. The "Illinois Volunteers in the Mormon War," 36, records that Baker was mustered on the 24th of September and discharged from duty on the 29th, for a total of six days of service. Ford, *History of Illinois*, in Smith, *History of the Church* 7:47. "Gov. Ford's Agreement," 30 September 1844, Hardin Papers, Chicago Historical Society.

6.   Ford, *History of Illinois*, in Smith, *History of the Church* 7:47. "Gov. Ford's Agreement," 30 September 1844, Hardin Papers, Chicago Historical Society. Thomas Ford to [Brigham Young], 30 September 1844, in Roberts, *Comprehensive History* 2:313–14. See also *Nauvoo Neighbor* 2 October 1844.

7.   Recognizance, Quincy, Illinois, 2 October 1844, Mormon Collection, Chicago Historical Society, microfilm, Regional Archives, Western Illinois University. A partial transcript can be found in Hill and Oaks, *Carthage Conspiracy*, 41. See also "Gov. Ford's Agreement," 30 September 1844, Hardin Papers, Chicago Historical Society. The state was represented by A. P. Bledsoe and Thompson Camplin.

8.   Gregg, *History of Hancock County*, 327. Hill and Oaks, *Carthage Conspiracy*, 41.

Except for some difficulties with the state's attorney at Quincy, which ultimately were resolved to his satisfaction, Baker's job was finished. The newly elected congressman could now depart for the nation's capital knowing that the work of defending Sharp and Williams was left in the able hands of Orville Hickman Browning. As subsequent events would prove, collusion between the two sides in the case did not end with the release of Sharp and Williams.[9]

Browning's selection as the chief attorney for the defense would have been unexpected and perhaps even mystifying to the Mormons. Born in 1806 in Cynthiana, Harrison County, Kentucky, O. H. Browning was admitted to the Kentucky bar in 1831 and shortly thereafter moved to Quincy, Illinois, where he established a law practice in the Land Office Hotel. In those early years the town was small, with fewer than four hundred inhabitants.

Browning was elected to the Illinois Senate in 1836, where he met another young lawyer from Kentucky, Abraham Lincoln. The two Whigs became trusted friends; Browning's wife was Lincoln's personal confidant. When Lincoln visited Quincy he sometimes stayed with Orville's cousin, gunsmith Jonathan Browning, as Orville's house was too small to accommodate guests. In the early 1840s the gunsmith joined the Mormon church and moved to Nauvoo.[10]

O. H. Browning's interest in the Latter-day Saints began several years before his cousin's conversion. In the winter of 1838–39, Browning witnessed the expulsion of the Mormons from Missouri and their initial welcome by the citizens of Quincy. He became acquainted with Joseph Smith after the prophet's arrival in Quincy following his escape from Liberty jail in early 1839.

Browning served as one of Joseph's defense attorneys during an extradition attempt by Missouri in 1841. Although Joseph Smith was set free on a legal technicality, the prophet never forgot Browning's eloquent plea in his behalf. It was the memory of this episode that likely prompted Joseph's final request for Browning's services on June 27, 1844. This time, however, Joseph's request went unheeded.

The circuit court at Carthage opened on October 21 and would last through the 25th. The grand jury "composed exclusively of men who were not Mormons" inquired into the death of Joseph Smith. A list of nearly sixty individuals for possible indictment in the crime was presented to the body.[11]

William Daniels and Benjamin Brackenbury came forward as eyewitnesses. Daniels, newly baptized into the Mormon church, had earlier submitted (before his

9. Oaks and Hill, *Carthage Conspiracy*.

10. Browning and Gentry, *John M. Browning*, 16.

11. *Nauvoo Neighbor*, 6 November 1844, quoted in Oaks and Hill, *Carthage Conspiracy*, 60, note 7. Several efforts have been made to compile a listing of the men involved in the assault on the Carthage jail. Each is problematic. The earliest surviving list is that of William Clayton's Nauvoo Journal 2 [28 June 1844], in Clayton, *Intimate Chronicle*, 135–36, which makes no distinction between the men thought to have been involved in the conspiracy and those who were present at the jail. Sheriff Jacob Backenstos's list of "Those active in the massacre at Carthage" was compiled (contrary to many published assertions) in 1846 (Lundwall, *Fate of the Persecutors*, 269–71, Smith, *History of the Church* 7:142–45, Journal History, 29 June 1844, 2). Willard Richards also attempted to compile a "Listing of the mob at Carthage," (Lundwall, *Fate of the Persecutors*, 271, Smith, *History of the Church* 7:146. Journal History, 29 June 1844, 2). The date of his compilation is uncertain. Richards incorrectly places several of the Nauvoo dissidents at the scene.

conversion) an affidavit to a justice of the peace in Nauvoo. His testimony on the Fourth of July was straightforward and without embellishment. It read, in part, "That your said affiant saw Joseph Smith leap from the window of the jail, and that one of the company picked him up and placed him against the well curb and several shot him, Col. Williams exclaiming, 'Shoot him!' and further your affiant saith not."[12]

His October testimony was more detailed. Daniels testified that Warsaw militia leaders Jacob C. Davis, William N. Grover, and Mark Aldrich "the night before the Smiths were killed" selected twenty men to "go and kill Joseph and Hiram Smith in jail." And when the troops were disbanded by Colonel Levi Williams around noon on June 27, some of the men returned to their homes, "but most of them went on toward Carthage."[13] When they were within four miles of the town a messenger from the Carthage Greys came out bearing a letter signed, "Carthage Grays." Aldrich read it to the men. "Now is a delightful time to kill the Smiths," it said. "The governor is gone to Nauvoo, and there is nobody in Carthage, but what can be depended upon."[14]

Daniels testified that when the men reached Carthage, "Col Williams came up from another direction to the men and told them to go into the jail, for the guard wouldn't hurt them. They then seized the guard and held them, and others rushed into the jail." Daniels further testified that after Joseph fell from the window Colonel Williams ordered the men to "shoot the God d——d scoundrel (or rascal)." Smith was propped up against the well curb by a member of the mob. "They then shot him."[15]

Daniels identified several of the men who had stormed the jail. "I saw a number come out of the jail — these were wounded. One man they called John Mills [Wills] was shot in the right arm in the wrist, he said he had shot Hiram Smith—and Joe had shot him. A man called William Voras was wounded in the left shoulder. A man the name of Gallagher was grazed on the side of the face. I saw a man the name of Allen, a cooper, shooting with [the] others."[16]

Daniels admitted that he had been offered a bribe of "$2,500 if I would leave the state so as not to testify against the men who killed the Smiths — $1,500 in money and $1,000 in real estate in New York. This was made me in Quincy. I do not expect to receive any remuneration for coming here to give testimony. I have never been offered anything to come and testify against the men who killed the Smiths." It was soon rumored that the Mormons had offered Daniels $1,000 to testify against Sharp.[17]

Benjamin Brackenbury, a non-Mormon youth of Nauvoo who drove the militia baggage wagon from Warsaw to Golden Point, confirmed much of Daniels' story. Brackenbury testified that immediately after the murders of Joseph and Hyrum,

12. William Daniels affidavit, 4 July 1844, in Smith, *History of the Church* 7:162.
13. William Daniels, October 1844 grand jury testimony, P13, F41, Community of Christ Archives. See also Hosea Stout, Diary [24 October 1845], in Stout, *On the Mormon Frontier* 1:6.
14. William Daniels, October 1844 grand jury testimony, P13, F41, Community of Christ Archives. In 1892, an individual known as Old Man Brooks recalled that he "saw the last bullet shot into the old boy." (Lundwall, *Fate of the Persecutors*, 293).
15. William Daniels, October 1844 grand jury testimony, P13, F41, Community of Christ Archives.
16. Ibid.
17. Ibid. [R. T.] Madison [Plymouth, Ill] to Thomas Sharp, 27 October 1844, Thomas Coke Sharp Papers, LDS Archives.

A number came from the Jail and got into the wagon, among whom was Grover, Mills, Voras, Gallagher and 2 of the Chittendens. Grover said they had killed the Smiths, and Joe struck him twice with his fist. Mills, Voras and Gallagher were wounded. Went on a piece and told them I could not haul so many, some got out, left five in wagon. Sharp came up and said the Smiths were both dead, for he had hold of one since the men left the jail. I went on to Warsaw. I knew it was Col. Williams I saw at the Jail horseback, and cannot be mistaken, for I knew him whilst I was stopped near the jail. Jacob Davis and some others drove past towards the Jail and the same ones returned to Warsaw with us.

Brackenbury's main weakness as a witness was his fondness for the bottle. "I drank liquor that day," he admitted, "whenever I felt like it. Do not know that I was drunk, but drank enough to feel pretty well." (In fact, whiskey had been provided to the men that day, "to make them brave.")[18]

Even with potentially tainted corroborative testimony, the grand jury handed down its indictments. In all, nine men were charged with the murders: Levi Williams, Colonel, Fifty-ninth Regiment Illinois militia; Mark Aldrich, Major, Warsaw Independent Battalion; William N. Grover, Captain, Warsaw Cadets; Jacob C. Davis, Captain, Warsaw Rifle Company; John Wills, militiaman, wounded; William Voras, militiaman, wounded; Gallagher, militiaman, wounded; Allen, militiaman; and Thomas Sharp, anti-Mormon editor of *Warsaw Signal*. The case file was labeled *Levi Williams et al*, recognition that, with the exception of Thomas Sharp, the writs were directed at members of the Warsaw militia. Williams was the highest-ranking officer charged with participation in the crime.

Once the grand jury had determined who would be held accountable for the murders (and more important for those actually involved in the killing, who would *not*), the Mormons were pleased that the state was finally taking some action in the matter. And, the anti-Mormons were relieved that more men were not implicated by what they regarded as perjured testimony. After all, how much could a wagon driver and an eleventh-hour conscript possibly know about the larger conspiracy?

Attachments and subpoenas were issued for witnesses in the case. On account of supposedly poor conditions at the Carthage jail the defendants were "discharged until [the] time of trial," scheduled for the following May. With a delay that could only have been intentional, the June 27, 1844, inquest "upon the bodies of Joseph and Hyrum Smith" (signed by a dozen men who were potential witnesses in the case) was filed in the Carthage courthouse only *after* the October grand jury had concluded its main business. The prosecution would never get the upper hand.[19]

---

18. Benjamin Brackenberry [as given], October 1844 grand jury testimony, P13, f41, Community of Christ Archives. Brackenberry also said, "[Afterwards] Sharp came up and said the Smiths were both dead, for he had hold of one since the men left the jail." Jeremiah Willey statement, 13 August 1844, LDS Archives. Oaks and Hill, *Carthage Conspiracy*, 46–63.

19. People vs. Levi Williams . . ., Indictment for murder of Joseph Smith and Hyrum Smith, 26 October 1844, in Hancock County, Illinois, Courthouse, Record Book D:207. See also Golding, "A Research Aid," 139–41, and "Indictments," *Warsaw Signal* 30 October 1844. Inquest upon the bodies of Joseph and Hyrum Smith, 27 June 1844, in Lundwall, *Fate of the Persecutors*, 276–77. According to the published versions of the inquest it was filed either October 23 or October 25, 1844, and was

On November 1, the Democratic *Illinois State Register* reviewed the recent grand jury actions in Hancock County. " ... This anti-Mormon jury has had the honesty to indict both Mormons [for the destruction of the *Expositor*] and anti-Mormons [for the murder of Joseph Smith] for alleged violations of law," it noted. The editor reminded his readers "that the Whig papers of Illinois said that nothing would be done with those men for this outrage." The same issue of the *Register* published "Mr. Clay's [1843] Letter to the Mormons." Both articles were written with the intent of distancing the Mormons from the Whig cause. The presidential election was only four days away.[20]

---

apparently not available to the grand jury during its October deliberations. See also *Deseret Evening News*, 12 September 1890, in Journal History, 28 June 1844, 9, and Bernauer, "Still 'Side by Side'," 2, note 4.

20. "Another Mormon Outrage," *Illinois State Register*, 1 November 1844. "Mr. Clay's Letter to the Mormons," *Illinois State Register*, 1 November 1844.

Chapter Eighteen

The Campaign Continues

I would rather have the dead body of the Prophet than some men who are alive and I would rather have the clothes of the Prophet stuffed with straw for president of the United States than any man whose name is now before the nation as a candidate, for the straw would not do any harm.

Brigham Young, August 18, 1844[1]

I dreamed of speaking before a large congregation on the policy of the nation and the policy of our religion. I said that Joseph the Prophet had laid the foundation, and we would have to carry out his measures. Joseph was present [in the dream], and heard all I said and sanctioned it.

Heber C. Kimball, August 5, 1844[2]

JOSEPH SMITH'S PRESIDENTIAL CAMPAIGN DID not end with his death. If there was at first some uncertainty about the political course the Saints were to take now that the prophet Joseph was no longer at the helm, indecision was shortly replaced by a renewed sense of purpose. The Mormons were to fall behind the candidate who most closely adhered to the principles and policies advocated by the slain Mormon leader. Joseph and Hyrum's younger brother William had already taken over the editorship of *The Prophet* in New York City on June 29, before word of their murders reached the east. William would remain as editor through November 16, 1844, relinquishing his position at *The Prophet* only after the presidential question had been decided.[3]

The July 13 issue of *The Prophet* proclaimed, enthusiastically, "This is the day on which the Convention of the True Jeffersonians will assemble at Baltimore, several of the Delegates have passed through our city from different parts of the Union. Will not 'Michael the Great Prince' [a reference to Jesus Christ as a deliverer] soon 'stand

---

1. Smith, *History of the Church* 7:256 [18 August 1844]. I would like to thank Gordon C. Thomasson for bringing this passage to my attention. RSW
2. Ibid., 7:228 [5 August 1844].
3. Crawley, *Descriptive Bibliography*, 254–57.

up for his people?'" Hours before the convention was to take place, word arrived that their candidate was no more.[4]

The Prophet responded to the deaths of Joseph and Hyrum with a simple acknowledgment on the 13th. Subsequent black-bordered issues collected articles on the murder of the prophet and his brother and published the "Correspondence between General Joseph Smith and the Hon. Henry Clay," including the full text of Joseph's acerbic May 13 letter to the Kentucky senator. With most of the electioneers safely back in Nauvoo, Joseph's campaign now became an offensive waged in the columns of church-sponsored newspapers.

The first issue of the *Times and Seasons* following Brigham Young's return to Nauvoo appeared on August 15. It contained an important message for all Latter-day Saints, "in Nauvoo and all the World," signed by Brigham Young as president of the Quorum of the Twelve Apostles. He acknowledged that even without a prophet, the Mormon people still had apostles to guide and direct them. This was the time for millions throughout the earth to hear the gospel message, "awake to its truths and obey its precepts; and the kingdoms of this world will become the kingdoms of our Lord and of his Christ." He then warns that "As rulers and people have taken counsel together against the Lord, and against his anointed, and have murdered him who would have reformed and saved the nation, it is not wisdom for the saints to have anything to do with politics, voting, or president-making, at present." He presented several reasons for staying out of the political arena. All of the lawmakers and politicians were corrupt, he said, and had refused to "redress wrong or restore right, liberty or law." The Saints were to find a candidate who, "if elected, will carry out the enlarged principles, universal freedom, and equal rights and protection, expressed in the views of our beloved Prophet and martyr, General Joseph Smith." That man had not yet been found.

An editorial (most likely written by John Taylor) published in the *Times and Seasons* extended Brigham Young's message. The piece was called "The Next President." The writer was unflinching in his assertion. "*Our* candidate for this high office," he wrote, "has been butchered in cold blood . . . to prevent him from being elected." And yet, "the murderers [are] running at large with impunity." Pointing the finger at neighboring Missouri, "as we are not [radical] abolitionists and will not go against one half of the interests of the Nation—what shall we do as honest and consistent men?" There was only one answer.

> Shall we honor the "views of the powers and policy of the government," as published by the now *martyred Gen. Joseph Smith*? WE WILL. Therefore let every man of our faith be left free to choose and act for himself, but as a people we will honor the opinions and wisdom of our martyred General; and, as a matter of propriety, we cannot vote for, or support a candidate for the presidency, till we find a man who will pledge himself to carry out *Gen. Smith's views of the power and policy of the*

---

4. *The Prophet,* 13 July 1844. We have been unable to find record of minutes for the July 13 meeting, presumably because it never took place. Several newspapers reported that the Saints would make "no movement on the presidential question." ("Important," *Quincy Whig* 7 August 1844.) Similarly, Leonard, *Nauvoo,* 465.

government as he published them. Patriotism and integrity demand this course from every true Latter day Saint. *Unus pro omnium.*[5]

The Prophet accepted the revised charge and embarked on its own campaign to further the cause. From the start, the New York City paper was conciliatory towards the Democrats. It was decidedly anti-Whig. The paper began with an overview of New York's "political press" and observed that, "the Whig papers of this city have teamed with abuse—which lies that even the Devil would blush to own, about our motives, designs, and movements, as a body . . . insomuch that we can scarcely pick up a paper advocating the claims of Henry Clay, but we find lies about the Mormons. It is a fact worthy of note, that no such abuse has appeared in the papers of the Democratic Party."[6]

Later articles in *The Prophet* promoted the annexation of Texas and the Oregon country, and proposed that the Saints close rank behind Colonel James K. Polk, "as he is the only candidate before the people that is pledged to carry out any of the views of the late General Smith."[7]

One of the chief difficulties facing the editors of *The Prophet* was how to reconcile the commonly held belief that Democrats were behind the murders of Joseph and Hyrum with their proposed support for a Democratic presidential candidate. They did so by renouncing party politics and not political principles:

> We must say we have been and are still Democrats; firm supporters of Jeffersonian principles, "free trade and sailors rights;" in these principles we ever shall remain. Principle, is our Motto, & not party; it is said that the Mormons will vote for Polk perchance they may; they will vote just as they please. We will not be made tools of by any party. We "go whole hog" for Jeffersonian Democracy, and we would advise Democratic Editors and Whig Editors to cease the publication of lies about the Mormons. We are a party distinct from either, and are governed by principles, not men, and if Mr. Polk has the right principles we go for him, or if Mr. Clay is governed by the proper principles, we go for him, and them of their party go to hell where they belong.[8]

Other articles in *The Prophet* returned to the matter of responsibility for the murders at Carthage and once again attempted to minimize the party question.

---

5. "The Mormon Massacre," *The Prophet*, 13 July 1844. *The Prophet* of 20 and 27 July contained black borders to mourn the loss of their leaders. Both issues collected newspaper articles and correspondence regarding the Carthage incident. "Correspondence between General Joseph Smith and the Hon. Henry Clay," *The Prophet*, 27 July 1844. "An Epistle of the Twelve to the Church of Jesus Christ of Latter-day Saints, in Nauvoo and all the World," 15 August 1844, in *Times and Seasons* 15 August 1844. "The Next President," *Times and Seasons* 15 August 1844.

6. "The Political Press," *The Prophet* 24 August 1844.

7. "Texas and Oregon," *The Prophet* 31 August 1844. "Our Politics," *The Prophet* 8 September 1844. The first article even claimed that if Joseph Smith had known that James K. Polk was to be the Democratic nominee, Joseph would never have put his hat into the ring, as his main goal was to prevent Martin van Buren from being re-elected. This is clearly ex-post-facto reasoning on the part of *The Prophet's* editors. This view is also expressed in "Our Political Course," *The Prophet* 28 September 1844.

8. "To our Brethren and Friends," *The Prophet* 14 September 1844. The article concluded that the true republican ideal was the protection of religious freedoms.

In relation to our remarks on politics, we do not wish to be understood as charging upon any particular party the murder of our brethren. As far as [Democratic] Governor Ford is concerned, in relation to the late mob violence [at Carthage], in not bringing the murderers to justice, we do not look upon as a specimen of democracy. That there should be "wolves in sheep's clothing" in political as well as religious parties, we do not think it strange . . . Let us try it once more—the canvass is near at hand, and soon it will be known who is to be honoured with the highest office in the gift of the people. Remember little Van is not in the field—true democracy is the same, let men do what they please—good principles cannot change, whatever men may do. Mr. POLK is the MAN. He has never been tried—let us try him. What say ye? [9]

A final political editorial, "The Consequence of one Vote," was published in *The Prophet* on October 19, two weeks before the national election. It returned to its earlier practice of blasting the party of Henry Clay:

What would be the result should Whiggery obtain the ascendancy? Why, repetitions of the scenes in Missouri and Carthage jail, for already have they united with the party whose greatest deed has been the destruction of Catholic churches, and already have they, in Philadelphia, elected to Congress a man who stands accused before a Grand Jury for riot and treason. Brethren, will you give countenance to such an unholy alliance? If no, vote for Jas. K. Polk and Geo. M. Dallas.[10]

Henry Clay was defeated by James K. Polk on November 5. Nationally, the vote was extremely close. Polk attracted 49.6 percent of the popular vote (1,337,243), while Clay trailed slightly behind at 48.1 percent (1,299,062). The troublesome Liberty Party siphoned off 2.3 percent of the electorate (62,300 votes). Clay carried eleven states to gain 105 electors, while Polk won fifteen, putting his electoral vote total at 170, well above the 138 needed to decide the election. In Illinois, 54 percent of the voters went for "Polk and expansion."

Hancock County and the Mormons voted overwhelmingly Democratic (1,399 to 747). Not all of the Nauvoo Saints were comfortable with the decision to support Polk, however. "Today was the Presidential election and the brethren all concluded to vote for Polk and Dallas for President and Vice president of the United States," Hosea Stout wrote in his diary. He pondered the bloody fate of Joseph Smith, "the man we had elected as man of our choice for president of the United States," the person the Saints believed was "the means to pursue to avoid a disunion and overthrow of our Government." Although Joseph was no more, to Stout and others the prophet's "voice seemed yet to sound in the air, teaching this nation the way they might be saved." Stout had approached the election "with little confidence," given that he "could but vote for those, who, if they had not approved of the murder of our own candidate had remained silent" following his assassination.[11]

---

9. "Our Course in Politics," *The Prophet* 21 September 1844.
10. "The Consequence of One Vote," *The Prophet* 19 October 1844.
11. Hosea Stout, *Diary*, 2:8–9 [5 November 1844].

Six thousand votes in the state of New York spelled defeat for Henry Clay. Like much of the nation, New York voters posted a slim Democratic majority of only 1.2 percent. Its thirty-six electoral votes ensured James K. Polk's victory. In the New York race, 237,588 of the voters chose Polk. Clay received 232,482 votes. The Liberty Party garnered 15,812. As more than one presidential scholar has noted, "if New York alone had gone Whig, Clay would have been elected."[12]

Did the anti-Whig campaign waged by *The Prophet* have any impact on New York voters? Was Clay's defeat solely due to the influence of the Liberty Party, or had the Mormons tipped the scales? Brigham Young attributed the Democratic victory to the efforts of his Mormon political editors in the east. To David Rogers, a New York City artist who had painted Joseph and Hyrum's portrait during a visit to Nauvoo in 1842, and one of *The Prophet*'s chief contributors, he wrote, "we hasten to express to you our entire approbation of your course in the late presidential Election. Indeed the Stand which you took—which you boldly and successfully maintained, gives us many pleasing reflections. The Democratic banner floats again triumphant over our Country. God grant that it ever may."[13]

The next issue of *The Prophet* echoed Brigham Young's words, going so far as to assert that the Mormons now held "the balance of power" between the two great parties in American politics:

> "Our Political Interest"
> Since the first organization of this church, on the 6th of April, 1830 we have had to contend incessantly with the Political, and Religious world . . . At the ballot box have we been courted for our support, and after freely given, they have as freely given us the lash; but the two parties (whigery and democracy,) must remember that that day has gone by, they who hold the balance of power are no longer to be treated with contempt . . . As yet we have never supported a candidate for the Presidency but what has been elected, nor never will.
>
> *The Prophet* (New York City) December 21, 1844

George T. M. Davis was stunned. He couldn't accept the fact that his bold efforts to control the Mormon vote had failed so miserably. "For the last three weeks I have suffered mentally more than human tongue can describe," he wrote to John J. Hardin on November 24. "Suffered, that Mr. Clay should be sacrificed by a ruthless band of foreigners." William Ogden Niles's prediction that Mormon converts recently arrived from England would "exercise the privilege of voting on the presidential question, without regard to the U. States naturalization laws" had come to pass. Even Davis had warned Clay about the potentially negative impact of the Mormon "foreign vote" on the presidential election. Following the disastrous effects of his Raleigh Letter opposing annexation, however, the Kentucky senator remained silent on the immigration issue.

---

12. Durham, *Joseph Smith, Prophet-Statesman*, 203–5.

13. Brigham Young to David Rogers, 5 December 1844, Mormon Collection, Beineke Library, Yale University. Transcription courtesy Will Bagley. Rogers was initially opposed to the Democrats. See David Rogers to Brigham Young, August 1844, LDS Archives, cited in Godfrey, "Causes of Conflict," 71. On Rogers, see Crowley, *Descriptive Bibliography*, 236.

"You know my ardent temperament," Davis continued in his letter to Hardin, "and how enthusiastically I was attached to Mr. Clay. His success I never for a moment doubted, and his defeat, has unmanned me." Davis's response to the undoing of the Kentucky senator was repeated in countless Whig editorial offices, sitting rooms, and correspondence throughout the Union, with Clay himself nearly destroyed by the catastrophe.[14]

In Springfield a movement was underway to repeal the Nauvoo charter. As part of that effort, G. T. M. Davis distributed copies of his *Authentic Account* to politicians in the state capital.[15]

Mormon representative Almon W. Babbitt (Joseph's former legal counsel and a member of the Council of Fifty) came forward and delivered two impassioned speeches against the repeal of the Nauvoo charter. Although a Latter-day Saint, Babbitt was a sometime collaborator in the conspiracy against Joseph Smith. Just the day before the assault on the jail, he refused a request from the prophet to serve as his legal representative. "You are too late," Babbitt chided, "I am already engaged on the other side." Now that the plight of his people had once again reached a crisis point, Babbitt stepped forward with the strongest indictment he could muster.[16]

His first Springfield oration concluded, "If the privileges of the Nauvoo charter are too extensive, if it grants power exceptionable, repeal those provisions, and leave them in possession of their just rights." Governor Ford, in his address to the state legislature detailing recent events in the "Mormon War," agreed that the Nauvoo charter should be revised, not repealed.[17]

Babbitt's second speech before the Illinois legislature was even more impassioned. "The destruction of a press in Nauvoo was sounded as the token of alarm to awaken the people to a sense of apparent danger from 'Mormon' violence," Babbitt charged. A Mormon press in Missouri had been destroyed years before. "Why was it not trumpeted to the ends of the earth—made the subject of public investigation, and visited by the work of legislative condemnation? Presses have been destroyed in our own state, and passed unnoticed by the public." Babbitt reminded the legislators of the 1837 Lovejoy incident, in which the press of Elijah P. Lovejoy had been broken up by antiabolitionists in Alton, Illinois. Lovejoy himself was later murdered. "Mr. Speaker, why are these invidious distinctions made?

"Disguise it as we may, make such imputations as we please, charge it upon this or upon that, it is but the base and unhallowed spirit of religious intolerance, and the workings of unsatisfied political ambition." This "unsatisfied political ambition" led to the establishment of the *Nauvoo Expositor* in the city of Nauvoo, itself a provocative act. This was not the work of the Mormon dissidents acting alone. "The press in Nauvoo," Babbitt informed the legislature, "was established for political purposes by the Whigs." With its destruction came an excuse to move forcibly against the

---

14. G. T. M. Davis to John J. Hardin, 24 November 1844, Hardin Papers, Chicago Historical Society. Leslie Combs to J. P. Phoenix, 20 November 1844, University of Kentucky Archives. Horace Greeley "wore himself down to such an extent that he broke out with a rash of boils at the close of the [1844] campaign." (Van Deusen, *Horace Greeley*, 95.)

15. A. L. Babbitt to Brigham Young, 19 December 1844, in Journal History, 19 December 1844, 1.

16. Smith, *History of the Church* 6:600. The original source for Babbitt's remark has not been traced.

17. Oaks and Hill, *Carthage Conspiracy*. Ford, *Message*.

Mormon presence in Hancock County. "Mr. Speaker, why this continued opposition? Why are we brought up here to be the object of vindictive legislation, when the very cause of all complaint is removed? It was Joseph Smith the Prophet of the 'Mormon' people who was alleged to be the sole cause of all difficulties. He is no more—they have wreaked their vengeance upon his head—they have murdered him. And must it now be, as in olden times, because the fathers have eaten sour grapes the children's teeth are set on edge?" Babbitt's revelation about the Whig plot and heartfelt plea on behalf of his people had no effect.[18]

On January 17, 1845, the Illinois Senate voted unanimously to repeal the Nauvoo Charter. The House followed shortly. Weeks after selecting a new head of the entire nation, the citizens of Nauvoo found themselves without a government of their own. Brigham Young was disheartened at the turn of events. "The nation has severed us from them in every respect and made us a distinct nation, just as much as the Lamanites [Native Americans]," he said, "and it is my prayer that we may soon find a place where we can have a home and live in peace according to the Law of God."[19]

The trial of the accused assassins of Joseph Smith began in Carthage on May 20, 1845. O. H. Browning had assembled a top-notch legal defense team, which included William A. Richardson, Onias C. Skinner, Calvin A. Warren, and Archibald Williams. All were residents of Quincy. Browning and Williams were Clay Whigs. Richardson and Warren were Democrats. Skinner was an independent. Almeron Wheat, Warren's law partner, took careful notes of the proceedings. Mormon recorder James D. Watt remained in the courtroom during the entire trial, making a verbatim transcript of the trial in his own shorthand and regularly passing the encrypted pages to couriers who rushed them back to Nauvoo.[20]

The lawyers and defendants assembled in the Carthage courthouse were well acquainted with each other. The prosecution was headed by Josiah Lamborn, a former law partner of Edward D. Baker, the man most responsible for freeing Sharp and Williams from custody the previous fall. On the defense team was Archibald Williams, a member of the state's Whig Central Committee. He was the brother of Wesley Williams, an anti-Mormon militiaman from Carthage. (Wesley's was the first signature affixed to the June 27, 1844, coroner's inquest on the bodies of Joseph and Hyrum. He was never called as a witness in the case.) Colonel Levi Williams, one of the defendants, was cousin to both Wesley and Archibald. These familial and professional relationships were never called into question.[21]

The actual murderers were still at large. Edward Bonney, a former non-Mormon member of Joseph Smith's Council of Fifty, sometime counterfeiter and government agent, was investigating another set of murders at the time of the opening of the trial in Carthage. He inquired of a Mr. Agard, who lived in Adams County just south of the Hancock County line, where it was known some of the gunmen had fled following the assault on the Carthage jail nearly a year earlier. John C. Elliott, one of the men who had shot the Mormon prophet, was among those in hiding.

18. Roberts, *Comprehensive History* 2:484–85.
19. Ibid., 2:487.
20. Oaks and Hill, *Carthage Conspiracy*.
21. See, for example, Edward D. Baker Papers, Illinois Historical Society, Springfield.

"My name is Agard," the man offered as he opened the door.

"The sheriff of your county directed me to call on you," Bonney said.

"Oh! I suppose I know your business," Agard replied. "You are in pursuit of the murderers of Jo Smith. Well, well, I suppose I must go with you."

"That is not my business," Bonney corrected him.[22]

Even with it known that the actual perpetrators of the horrific crime were not in custody, the mock trial proceeded on schedule. "The evidence for the prosecution has been very positive and to the point nominally," one newspaper reporter covering the trial acknowledged, "but never were witnesses more thoroughly ridiculed in the cross-examination. So completely and effectually were they discredited, that the Prosecution Attorney felt himself obliged to declare three of them perjured scoundrels."[23]

Only incompetence or deliberate collusion on the part of the prosecutor and the defense team would have caused the state's attorney to avoid asking even the most basic questions of a witness. And yet just such "oversights" occurred repeatedly throughout the trial. The testimony of Franklin Worrell is among the most telling.

On Saturday morning, May 24, 1845, the fifth day of the trial, Lieutenant Worrell, of the Carthage Greys, was called to the stand as a witness for the prosecution. He "was on guard near the jail" he admitted, and "saw Smith killed." There were between one and two hundred there, Worrell recalled, "they did not stay more than two or three minutes." The men first came up in front of the jail and then "made a rush for the door." Worrell didn't know how many went in, and claimed he "did not know any of them that came up there." All was confusion, he said, "there was a great crowd as thick as this court room, their pieces were going off all the time and so much noise and smoke that I could not see or hear anything that was said or done." Worrell and the guard "were pushed out of the way," he said, and "forced back about fifty feet."[24]

The prosecution continued its questioning:

Q: Did you see any of these five men there? [The prosecutor was referring to Levi Williams, Thomas Sharp, Jacob C. Davis, Mark Aldrich, and William N. Grover, all present and seated in the courtroom.]

A: I did not . . .

Q: Did any stop to examine his body?

A: No.

Q: Did you see Smith when he died?

A: I did.

Q: How long did he live after he fell?

A: Not to exceed a minute after he struck the ground.

Q: Did you see him hanging in the window?

A: I did not.

---

22. Bonney, *Banditti of the Prairies*, 40–41. Similarly, Irene Hascall Pomery [to her parents], 2 June 1845, "I delayed in writing on account of the trial of the murderers at Carthage. It is thought the murderers are at liberty." (Hascall and Pomeroy, "Letters of a Proselyte," 61).

23. *Burlington Hawkeye*, 5 June 1845, quoted in Oaks and Hill, *Carthage Conspiracy*, 174.

24. Franklin Worrell, 24 May 1845 trial testimony, LDS Archives. Compare Sharp, *Trial*, 4.

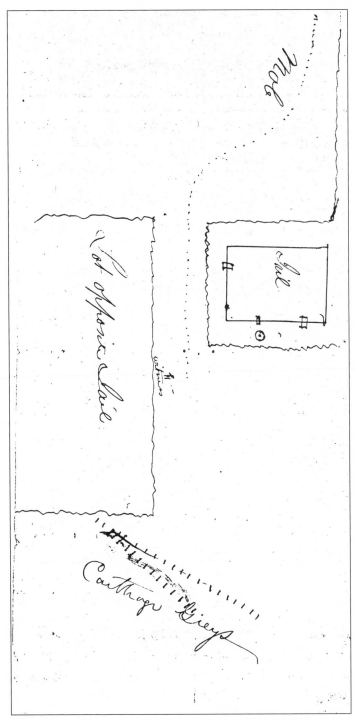

Sketch of the environs of the Carthage jail. Produced during 1845 trial of the accused assassins of Joseph Smith for O. H. Browning. The note "witness" in center presumably refers to William Daniels. Library-Archives, Community of Christ, Independence, Missouri. Reproduction by Office of Graphics Arts.

Q: You saw him die?

A: I did.

[The prosecution carefully avoided the question as to whether or not Joseph Smith was shot after he fell from the window.]

Q: You are acquainted with almost every body in the County, I suppose?

[Worrell was a dry-goods merchant in Carthage and the assistant postmaster.]

A: I am acquainted with about one third.

Q: And there was between one hundred to one hundred and fifty people there and you did not know a single one.

A: No. There was such a hurry I could not tell who was there.

[Worrell's inability to identify even one person at the jail would be used to distinct advantage in O. C. Skinner's closing, where he argued that the assault was conducted by men from Missouri and not Illinois.]

That afternoon the prosecuting attorney recalled Lieutenant Worrell to the stand, "to ask him questions that were before omitted." Lawyer Browning objected. He opposed to any new questioning and reviewed the law upon the subject, "which lasted some time." The court gave the prosecution the privilege of reopening the questioning, but only "with strict injunctions, upon the witness not to answer any questions that would implicate himself."

Q: Mr. Worrell, do you know, if the Carthage Grays, that evening, loaded their guns, with blank cartridge?

["You need not answer that question!" Browning and Richardson called out.]

A: I will not answer that question. I know nothing about the Carthage Grays, only the six men I had to do with.

[He was never asked their names.]

Q: Well, do those six men load their guns with blank cartridge that evening?

A: I will not answer it.

Q: Let it go to the country then in that way, that he would not answer the question for fear of implicating himself.

Worrell was retired as a witness.[25]

The judge withdrew the testimony of William Daniels from consideration by the jury. Just weeks before the trial was set to begin, Daniels's expanded account of the Carthage massacre appeared in booklet form, issued from John Taylor's press in Nauvoo. The miraculous story of a light from heaven that protected Joseph's body from mutilation was added by Littlefield to make the story appeal to the Latter-day Saint market, now served to discredit Daniels's entire testimony. Benjamin Brackenbury's testimony was also stricken from the record. The state's case was effectively shattered.[26]

---

25. Franklin Worrell, 24 May 1845 trial testimony, typescript, Wilford C. Wood Collection; Watt transcript, LDS Archives, 17–19, 26. John Hay later commented, "It would be difficult to imagine anything cooler than this quiet perjury to screen a murder." (Hay, "The Mormon Prophet's Tragedy," 669, 675). Hay's apt words became a chapter title, "Quiet Perjury to Screen a Murder," in Oaks and Hill, *Carthage Conspiracy*, 120.

The trial concluded on May 30, 1845. The jury deliberated for two and a half hours and found the defendants not guilty of the murder of Joseph Smith. The men were free to return to their homes and families. When news of the verdict reached Nauvoo, Brigham Young noted, wryly, that the result was "as we had anticipated."[27]

The trial of Hyrum's assassins, set to begin on June 24, was "dismissed for want of prosecution" when the state's lawyers failed to present themselves in court. The defendants were discharged.[28]

That same afternoon, Minor R. Deming confided in a hurried letter to his brother Stephen that "I have within the last half hour killed a man." The previous December, Deming, as Hancock County sheriff, had attempted to arrest Democratic state legislator Jacob C. Davis. (Significantly, Deming chose to ignore the legal papers allowing the indicted men to remain at large.) Almost immediately the state legislature passed a special decree, "that no member shall be subjected to any process, whether civil or criminal, during the session of the Senate." Disappointed, Deming returned to Carthage empty-handed.[29]

Upon the expectation that Governor Ford would order an election for his replacement "before [his] resignation should take effect," Deming had retired as Hancock County sheriff in June. This latest transgression was not forgotten by the anti-Mormons, however, and the moment was now right for their own form of retributive justice.[30]

The individual minor Deming had killed was Dr. Samuel Marshall, county clerk, a local man of considerable influence and physical stature. Marshall had approached Deming at the courthouse just as the trial for Hyrum Smith's accused assassins was set to begin and "assailed [him] in a fit of passion." Nearly overcome by his superior strength, Deming shot the man with a "pepperbox revolver." Deming was arrested (he was no longer under the protective cloak of an official capacity), and assigned a $5,000 bail. Deming believed the entire incident was a setup, a "party question," nothing more, as the men who testified at his hearing were the very ones who stood "guard at the jail" the day Joseph Smith was shot. Unfortunately, another man had died.[31]

Throughout the late summer and early fall, Deming's already frail health worsened. His case would never come to trial. After being confined to Carthage jail for several months, on September 10, 1845, Deming succumbed to "congestive fever" and died "within twenty feet of where the Mormon prophet was shot." With his passing, Hancock County's only conciliatory voice was silenced. "When the intelligence of [Deming's] death reached Warsaw," Deming's wife wrote to his family in the East, "the mobocrats threw up their hats and shouted as if they had gained a political

26. Oaks and Hill, *Carthage Conspiracy*, 172–73, 190, note 95. The imprint reads, "Published by John Taylor, for the Proprietor."

27. Smith, *History of the Church* 7:420.

28. Oaks and Hill, *Carthage Conspiracy*, 191.

29. M. R. Deming to [parents] 22 December 1844, Deming Papers, Illinois Historical Survey, Urbana. *Illinois State Register*, 31 January 1845. *Reports Made to the Senate and House of Representatives of the State of Illinois* (1844), 2. Hampshire, 262, note 20. Daniels, *Correct Account*, 22.

30. M. R. Deming to General Ewing, 17 July 1845, Deming Papers, Illinois Historical Survey, Urbana.

31. M. R. Deming to Stephen Deming, 24 June 1845, Deming Papers, Illinois Historical Survey, Urbana.

triumph." Which indeed they had. Deming was buried in the Quincy cemetery next to his brother. An armed escort of fifty to one hundred Mormon militiamen accompanied his family to Nauvoo.[32]

O. H. Browning chaired the Resolutions Committee at the Carthage Convention held in early October 1845, the second gathering of a body that first met in Quincy in late September. Archibald Williams served on the Resolutions Committee; Abraham Jonas was on the Military Committee. The purpose of the meetings was to counter the Mormon claim of persecuted innocence. Browning's turnabout on the Mormon question could not have been more profound. One of Browning's resolutions proclaimed: "We utterly repudiate the impudent assertion so often and so constantly put forth by the Mormons, that they are persecuted for righteousness' sake. We do not believe them to be a persecuted people." Browning also presented a declaration before the convention, that the circuit court "be requested not to hold a Court in Hancock county, this fall; as . . . such Court could not be holden without producing collision between the Mormons and Anti-Mormons, and renewing the excitement and disturbances which have recently afflicted" the county. Both resolutions were adopted enthusiastically.[33]

On orders from Governor Ford, General John J. Hardin arrived in Hancock in late September and took command of local military forces. After protracted negotiations, the Saints finally agreed to leave Illinois. In early 1846 the great exodus began, with Brigham Young and his Nauvoo Saints headed to a land of refuge in the West, beyond the borders of the United States. The City of Joseph was soon nearly deserted.

---

32. "Death of Minor R. Deming," *Warsaw Signal*, 17 September 1845. A. B. Deming to [Stephen Deming?] 28 September 1845, Deming Papers, Illinois Historical Survey, Urbana. A. B. Deming to Nathan Seely [undated], Deming Papers, Illinois Historical Survey, Urbana. Arthur B. Deming, *Naked Truths About Mormonism* 1.1, 1888, Introduction (shot quote).

33. "The Proceedings of the Carthage Convention," edited version in Hallwas and Launius, *Cultures in Conflict*, 304–9. Quotations from 305 and 308. Originally published in Josiah B. Conyers, *A Brief History of the Leading Causes of the Hancock Mob*, 17–21.

Chapter Nineteen

"To avenge the blood that stains the walls of Carthage jail"

Every one who had passed through their endowments, in the Temple [at Nauvoo], were placed under the most sacred obligations to avenge the blood of the Prophet, whenever an opportunity offered, and to teach their children to do the same, thus making the entire Mormon people sworn and avowed enemies of the American nation.

John D. Lee and W. W. Bishop, *Confessions* (1877)[1]

Prayers for vengeance upon the murderers of Joseph and Hyrum Smith were heard from the moment the horrible news reached Nauvoo. Within days of the event *Times and Seasons* published a lengthy poetic eulogy by one of Joseph's plural wives, Eliza R. Snow. It had a correspondingly long title: "The Assassination of Generals Joseph and Hyrum Smith, First Presidents of the Church of Jesus Christ of Latter-day Saints, Who were Massacred by a Mob, In Carthage, Hancock County, Ill., on the 27th of June, 1844." Eliza expressed the inconsolable loss felt by many Latter-day Saints:

> For never, since the Son of God was slain,
> Has blood so noble flow'd from human vein,
> As that which now on God for vengeance calls
> From "freedom's" ground—from Carthage prison walls!
> Oh, Illinois! Thy soil has drunk the blood
> Of Prophets, martyr'd for the truth of God.
> Once-lov'd America! what can atone
> For the pure blood of innocence thou [ha]'st sown?[2]

Her words were prefaced by the prophetic passage on vengeance from the Book of Revelation, the same verses used by W. W. Phelps in his Joseph Smith funeral oration two days earlier.[3]

---

1. Lee, *Confessions*, 160.
2. Eliza R. Snow, "The Assassination of General Joseph Smith and Hyrum Smith . . .," *Times and Seasons* 12, 575 (1 July 1844). Snow, *Poems*, 142–45.
3. The August 1, 1844, issue of *Times and Seasons* included a hymn by W. W. Phelps, "Praise to the

When he was sufficiently recovered from his wounds, John Taylor wrote an article on the "Martyrdom of Joseph Smith the Prophet, and his brother, Hyrum Smith the Patriarch," first published in the August 1844 printing of the Doctrine and Covenants. Modern LDS editions of the D&C list it as Section 135. The main section of his account declared the simple truth (for Mormons) that Joseph and Hyrum were victims of persecuted innocence, and that their deaths, like those of other martyrs, required vengeance. The italicized portions are in the original:

> They were innocent of any crime, as that had often been proved before, and were only confined in jail by the conspiracy of traitors and wicked men; and their *innocent blood* on the floor of Carthage jail is a broad seal affixed to "Mormonism" that cannot be rejected by any court on earth, and their *innocent blood* on the escutcheon of the State of Illinois, with the broken faith of the State as pledged by the governor, is a witness to the truth of the everlasting gospel that all the world cannot impeach; and their *innocent blood* on the banner of liberty, and on the *magna charta* [Constitution] of the United States, is an ambassador for the religion of Jesus Christ . . . and their *innocent blood*, with the innocent blood of all the martyrs under the altar that John saw, will cry unto the Lord of Hosts till he avenges that blood on the earth. Amen.[4]

The reference to John the Revelator in the last line constitutes the operative LDS definition of the "innocent blood" of martyrs—it is the blood of one who had been cleansed of the sins of this generation, a witness to the gospel of Jesus Christ who died for his beliefs—which requires retribution in kind, a principle known as blood atonement.[5]

In the days leading up the May 1845 trial of the accused assassins, Latter-day Saints were warned in the pages of the *Nauvoo Neighbor* that "Until the blood of Joseph and Hyrum Smith have been atoned for by hanging, shooting, or slaying in some manner, every person engaged in the cowardly assassination, no Latter day Saint should give himself up to the law." Voices calling for vengeance cried even louder when the men accused of assassinating the prophet were acquitted. As the verdict was entered, William Clayton remarked that "the whole state of Illinois has made itself guilty of shedding the blood of the Prophets by acquitting those who committed the horrid deed, and it is now left to God to take vengeance in His own way in His own time."[6]

Man," dedicated to the memory of Joseph Smith, a hymn with clear references to blood atonement, which continues to be sung in Latter-day Saint congregations to this day.

4. Doctrine and Covenants 135.

5. Smith and Evans, *Blood Atonement*. Roberts, *Comprehensive History* 4:126–37.

6. See McConkie, *Mormon Doctrine*, 821. Significantly, McConkie writes that "men are forbidden to execute vengeance upon their fellow men, unless by revelation (acting in the capacity of the Lord's agents) they are sent forth to do his appointed will. (D & C 98:23–48)." John Taylor, in *Nauvoo Neighbor*, 23 April 1845, quoted in Oaks and Hill, *Carthage Conspiracy*, 71. William Clayton, Temple History, in Allen, *Trials*, 142, Clayton, *Intimate Chronicle*, 543. For additional statements concerning the obligation to avenge the deaths of Joseph and Hyrum, see *Writings of Early Latter-day Saints*, Infobases Collectors Library CD-ROM.

On June 27, 1845, the first anniversary of the deaths of Joseph and Hyrum, Carthage survivors John Taylor and Willard Richards met with other members of the Council of the Twelve, who "thanked the Lord that they were not in Carthage jail," and prayed "that God would avenge the murders of Joseph & Hyrum." That same day Brigham Young, president of the Quorum of the Twelve Apostles and de facto leader of the church, wrote that "we consider that it belongs to God & his people to avenge the blood [of his] servants. We did not expect that the laws of the land would do it."[7]

Months later, in September of 1845, the Council of the Twelve once again "offered up prayers that the Lord would preserve his servants and deliver those who had been active in the mob that killed Joseph and Hyrum into our hands that they might receive their deserts." These weren't the only pleas made by the Twelve. Heber C. Kimball recorded that "ever since Joseph's death" he and "seven to twelve persons who had met together every day to pray . . . have covenanted, and never will rest . . . until those men who killed Joseph & Hyrum have been wiped out of the earth." In the same journal entry (of December 21, 1845), Kimball expressed concern that "the Twelve would have to leave [Nauvoo] shortly, for a charge of treason would be brought against them for swearing to avenge the blood of the anointed ones, and some are prone to reveal it." What had begun as a simple prayer uttered by the faithful had now become an oath and a promise to exact retribution on the murderers.[8]

When the Nauvoo temple became fully operational in early 1846, the Oath of Vengeance was institutionalized as part of the endowment ritual. The earliest published version of the ceremony, dating to 1847, describes the experiences of a husband and wife at Nauvoo as they received their own endowments shortly after the temple was completed.

> We are now conducted into another secret room, in the centre of which is an altar with three books on it—the Bible, Book of Mormon, and Doctrine and Covenants, (or Joseph's Revelations.) We are required to kneel at this altar, where we have an oath administered to us to this effect; that we will avenge the blood of Joseph Smith on this nation, and teach our children the same. They tell us that the nation has winked at the abuse and persecution of the Mormons, and the murder of the Prophet in particular; Therefore the Lord is displeased with the nation, and means to destroy it.[9]

Another account of the Oath of Vengeance was recorded by William Smith, Joseph Smith's youngest brother and a vocal opponent of Brigham Young. Published

7. Willard Richards, Diary [27 June 1845], Rathbone transcription, LDS Archives. Also cited in Quinn, *Origins of Power*, 179. Brigham Young to Wilford Woodruff, 27 June 1845, quoted in Hill, *Quest for Refuge*, 171.

8. Clayton, Nauvoo Journal 4 [19 September 1845], in Clayton, *Writings*, 74, quoted in Hill, *Quest for Refuge*, 175. Heber C. Kimball, Diary [21 December 1845], quoted in Buerger, "The Development of the Mormon Temple Endowment Ceremony," 53 and Tanner, *Evolution of the Mormon Temple Ceremony*, 25.

9. McGee [Van Deusen], *The Mormon Endowment*, 9, photostatic reprint in Tanner, *Evolution of the Mormon Temple Ceremony*, 161.

in 1849 as part of his "Remonstrance [to the U.S. Congress] . . . against the Admission of Deseret [Utah] into the Union," Smith provides the earliest record of the precise wording of what he called "The Oath." Smith bolstered his argument that the Brighamites were guilty of treason against the United States by claiming that the Oath of Vengeance, administered after the endowment portion of the ceremony, was sworn to by "1,500 Salt Lake Mormons . . . in the temple of God at Nauvoo." Smith's estimate was far too low. In fact, some 5,200 Latter-day Saints were endowed in the Nauvoo temple prior to the 1846 exodus; each would have sworn to this obligation.

> You do solemnly swear in the presence of Almighty God, his holy angels, and these witnesses, that you will avenge the blood of Joseph Smith on this nation, and teach your children; and that you will from this time henceforth and forever begin and carry out hostilities against this nation, and to keep the same intent a profound secret now and forever. So help you God.[10]

While it is acknowledged that these early descriptions of the Oath of Vengeance at Nauvoo are taken from sources unfriendly to the followers of Brigham Young, both agree in essential points with the endowment ceremony as practiced in Utah until 1927, when the oath was removed from Mormon temple ritual. Furthermore, slight differences in the wording of the Nauvoo oath and the later Utah version are to be expected; the temple ceremony wasn't formally written down until 1877 (with the completion of the St. George temple) and not fully standardized until the 1920s.[11]

The presence of an Oath of Vengeance in the Nauvoo endowment ceremony is additionally confirmed by a meeting of the LDS First Presidency held in Salt Lake City on December 6, 1889. During the previous several weeks church leaders had met together to consider "the propriety of putting further testimony in [U.S.] Court, more fully explaining the instructions to pray for the avenging the blood of the prophets in the Endowments." Apostle George Q. Cannon recalled that he

> understood when he had his endowments in Nauvoo that he took an oath against the murderers of the Prophet Joseph as well as other prophets, and if he had ever met any of these who had taken a hand in the massacre he would undoubtedly have attempted to avenge the blood of the martyrs. The Prophet [Joseph] charged Stephen Markham to avenge his blood should he be slain: after the Prophet's death Bro. Markham attempted to tell this to an assembly of the Saints [in Nauvoo], but Willard Richards pulled him down from the stand, as he feared the effect on the enraged people.[12]

10. Smith, *Remonstrance of William Smith.* While B. H. Roberts (*Comprehensive History* 3, Ch. 89) does not deny the presence of a "treasonable oath to avenge the blood of Joseph Smith upon the nation of the United States" in the Mormon temple endowment ceremony, he sidesteps the issue with his remark that "just how the hostility was to 'begin forthwith,' and at the same time be kept a profound secret, does not appear." See also Buerger, "The Fulness of the Priesthood," 25. Buerger, "The Development of the Mormon Temple Endowment Ceremony," 49 and 58 [table].

11. Beurger, *Mysteries of Godliness.*

12. Abraham H. Cannon, Journal [6 December 1889], 205–6, photostatic reproduction of original in Tanner, *Evolution of the Mormon Temple Ceremony,* 27.

How many individuals became targets of Mormon vengeance will never be known for certain. In the early 1880s, for example, Wilford Woodruff composed a list of four hundred "enemies of the church." The First Presidency and Council of the Twelve met together in the Salt Lake City temple and conducted a "prayer of damnation" against these enemies. How many actually lost their lives as a consequence of the Oath of Vengeance can only be guessed at.[13]

* * * * *

John C. Elliott was the gunman who shot the fatal bullet into the breast of the prophet Joseph. During his time in Illinois, Elliott demonstrated an almost uncanny ability to elude justice. In the winter of 1843, he was arrested (and later escaped from jail) for the kidnap of Daniel Avery. The Carthage court subsequently dismissed the complaint against Elliott and reduced the charge to "false imprisonment," with the defendant "ordered to go free without delay."

In the summer of 1844, Elliott served as an honorary captain in the Hancock County militia, led the men who stormed the jail at Carthage, and could be easily identified as one of the four men who shot the prophet. Yet he was passed over for indictment ("with impartiality that seems too convenient") during grand jury deliberations. His name appears nowhere in the surviving militia rosters. And within days of the conclusion of the October 1844 grand jury proceedings, Elliott was working as an officer of the peace under Sheriff Minor C. Deming, the chief law enforcer in Hancock County. It is hard to imagine that Elliott's choice of employment, with the man most devoted in putting the murderers behind bars, was anything but a deliberate move to gain valuable intelligence about Deming's possible actions against the anti-Mormons. True to form, Elliott remained close to the action and seemed to almost relish the challenge presented by Mormon efforts to prosecute him.[14]

In early February 1845, Elliott rode into Nauvoo and "put up with William Marks," the former Nauvoo stake president who had been dropped from the Council

---

13. Woodruff, *Journals* 7:547 [28 January 1880]. See *Revelations in Addition to Those Found in the LDS Edition of the Doctrine and Covenants*, Wilford Woodruff, 26 January 1880, "Concerns the Indignation of the Lord Upon the Wicked." [New Mormon Studies CD-ROM] See also Staker, "Waiting for World's End: Wilford Woodruff and David Koresh," 4 [19 January 1881] and *Waiting for World's End*, xvii. For an earlier reference see Woodruff, *Journals* 3:378 [18 October 1848].

14. Oaks and Hill, *Carthage Conspiracy*, 81 (impartiality quote). There are, regrettably, no original muster lists from the period of the actual conflict in late June of 1844. Surviving militia rosters, virtually all of which were compiled months after the events in question for purposes of determining soldier pay, include only those men who requested payment from the state for their services. These are preserved in the Illinois State Archives and the Chicago Historical Society. A useful guide to the former is *Illinois Volunteers in the Mormon War*. On Elliott note also "The People of the State of Illinois vs. Joseph McCoy, Wm. Middleton, William Clark, John Elliott, Levi Willis, and John Williams, Indict for false imprisonment," Hancock County (Illinois) Court Records, D, 198. See also Roberts, *Comprehensive History* 2:322, note 7. Return, 25 October 1844 [Hancock County Courthouse, Carthage]. John C. Elliott served as deputy sheriff under Minor R. Deming, sheriff of Hancock County. Elliott also worked as a clerk during the August election. He was paid $1.00 for his services. *Hancock County Commissioners*, Vol. 4, 1843–1847, 139, September Term 1844. Transcript, Illinois State Archives, Springfield. Later, Elliott was "allowed the sum of Eleven dollars" for services during the November election. *Hancock County Commissioners*, Vol. 4, 1843–1847, 173, 21 November 1844. Transcript, Illinois State Archives, Springfield.

of Fifty days earlier. For several months Elliott had served as constable and deputy sheriff, and frequently visited the Saint's city on official business. On this occasion he was in Nauvoo to serve several summonses. After he had concluded his business, Elliott prepared to leave on the morning of February 11. As he was departing, two men stepped out of a "cellar-pit by the side of the road," where a large group of diggers were working. Armed with sharpened spades, the men caught Elliott's horse by the bridle.

"You are our prisoner!" they called out. Elliott asked the charge. "For the murder of the Smiths." Elliott requested that they first accompany him to Mr. Marks, in order to put up his horse. On their way to William Marks's home, an officer approached Elliott, read a formal writ, and took him into custody on a charge of murder. Word soon spread that Elliott had been "suspected as a spy." Elliott responded that had suffered from a "severe toothache for several days, and wore a large woolen comfort" to protect his face from the cold, "which was my only disguise." William Marks notified several Warsaw lawyers of Elliott's predicament, a move that further estranged Marks from the Nauvoo hierarchy.[15]

"Elliott was *now* acting in 'the full tide of successful experiment,' as a Deputy Sheriff of Hancock county," one Mormon observer remarked. "We are ignorant how he crept into the Sheriffality, to thus sting the sensibilities of honest men, tear open an 'old sore' to bleed before a wondering world."[16]

The hearing was reported in the pages of the *Nauvoo Neighbor*. John Scott, the man who had filed the original complaint against Elliott, admitted that "he knew nothing personally" about Elliott's involvement in the June murders, "but sufficient upon which to found an affidavit of arrest." Scott stood aside.

Daniel Avery, the Mormon farmer kidnapped by Elliott in late 1843, was called to the stand.

Q: Did you ever hear him threaten the lives of Joseph and Hyrum Smith?
A: . . . Mr. Elliott declared he was ready at any time, at a moment's warning, to assist the Missourians, or any body else, to take their lives. He said Joe Smith, (as he called him,) was a d——d villain, and that he would take his life. If I know any thing of the nature of a covenant, they certainly entered into a covenant that night to take the life of not only Joseph and Hyrum Smith, but of all the leading men of the church. Said they: We have got one d——d Mormon (meaning myself), but this was just a commencement, for we will not cease our exertions until we have got them all . . .
Q: Do you know the date on which the murder of Joseph and Hyrum Smith was committed?
A: They were murdered on the 27th of June 1844, some six or seven months after they had covenanted to take their lives.

15. "To the Public," *Warsaw Signal*, 19 February 1845. Hosea Stout, Diary, 12 February 1845, in Brooks, *On the Mormon Frontier* 1:20–21.

16. "Arrest of Elliott," *Nauvoo Neighbor* 19 February 1845. See "Examination of John C. Elliott," *Nauvoo Neighbor*, 19 February 1845. Minutes were taken by "L. O. L.," Lyman O. Littlefield, the collaborator with William Daniels on *Correct Account*. Another version of the testimony can be found in "Arrest and Commitment of J. C. Elliott," *Warsaw Signal*, 19 February 1845. See also Nauvoo Civil and Criminal Dockett Book, The People v. John C. Eliout [sic], 11 February 1845, Mormon Collection, Chicago Historical Society.

Benjamin Brackenbury, a wagon driver during the assault on the jail, next testified.

Q: Do you know anything about Mr. Elliott's being engaged in the murder of Joseph and Hyrum Smith?

A: . . . I saw the company that followed up the ravine, come out of the woods, go to the jail, and soon after returned to where I was placed. When they came up, I heard them say: We killed Joe Smith.

Q: Was Mr. Elliott in the company that followed up the ravine?

A: He was.

Q: How do you know it was Mr. Elliott?

A: I had seen him before and I knew him well when I saw him. He had on the same undercoat that he has on now or one just like it.

Q: Was Mr. Elliott painted?

A: He was not.

Q: Was Mr. Elliott in the company that returned from the jail?

A: He was.

Q: Was he armed?

A: He was. He had arms like Col. Williams' company.

Q: Was Col. Williams in that company?

A: He was.

Q: Did you hear any gun fired at the jail while that company was there?

A: I heard four or five guns fired.

John C. Burns was called to the stand.

Q: Mr. Burns, what do you know about Mr. Elliott's being connected in the murder of Joseph and Hyrum Smith?

A: I cannot say that I know much of anything about it.

Q: Has Mr. Elliott made any admissions to you, at any time, that he was engaged in the murder?

A: The [United States] Marshal of Iowa and Mr. Elliott were at my house soon after the murder was committed. I was explaining to the Marshal the manner of Joseph Smith's death, as I had understood it. I told him that in all probability he was dead when he fell from the window, or was killed by the fall. I told him that but two balls entered his body. But Mr. Elliott immediately interrupted me by saying: I *know* you are mistaken, placing great emphasis on the word *know*. I *know* (said he) he was not dead when he fell from the window, and I *know* he was shot with four or five balls. He also said something about his attempting to clamber up against the well-curb, but what he said about it I do not distinctly remember. He stated that he had left Illinois to evade the service of a writ which he expected had been or would be issued against him for that murder. His manner caused the Marshal to remark to me afterwards: that man knows something about that murder.[17]

---

17. John Scott testimony, 12 February 1845, in *Nauvoo Neighbor*, 19 February 1845. Daniel Avery testimony, 12 February 1845, in *Nauvoo Neighbor*, 19 February 1845. Benjamin Brackenberry [as

The prosecution rested.

In the face of overwhelming testimony of Elliott's involvement in the June 27 murders, his lawyers threatened "that the blood of more of [the Mormons'] best men would be shed if the prisoner was committed for trial." Undeterred by the threat of violence, the judge delivered his decision. "Every exertion by the prisoner to clear himself from the charge, has signally failed and gone to strengthen the evidence for the State . . . enough has been proven here, to-day, to fix very, very strongly upon the prisoner the certainty of guilt." Court was adjourned.[18]

Sheriff Deming escorted Elliott to the Carthage jail. He wouldn't remain a prisoner for long. "I deem it proper to say," Elliott wrote in a public statement after he had escaped from custody, "that I did not consider it safe for myself or the jailor's family, to remain in the Stone House for three months, and I think all will concur in the opinion, that it was prudent to decline the General's proffered hospitality. I shall remain in the county until Court, and then shall be in Carthage. If the Grand Jury find aught against me, I shall be there to answer. J. C. ELLIOTT." Within two weeks, while serving as Warsaw constable under anti-Mormon George R. Rockwell, Elliott was again arrested by Sheriff Deming. Released on a writ of habeas corpus, Elliott fled into Adams County. He never returned to Carthage.[19]

In the spring of 1845, Mormon author Lyman O. Littlefield observed that "Not one solitary person has ever seen the inside the walls of a jail for that murder, with the exception of John C. Elliott, who was arrested and examined in Nauvoo, and committed for trial before the Circuit Court; and he did not remain in jail but a very short time." Despite the fact that there was more testimony about his involvement in the actual murder of Joseph Smith than any other single individual—he had the unfortunate habit of bragging about his exploits—Elliott's name was scarcely mentioned during the 1845 trial of the accused assassins.[20]

Frank Worrell, captain of the guard when John C. Elliott and his selectmen stormed the jail, became one of the first casualties of Mormon vengeance. In early 1844, Worrell was engaged to marry Ann Lawton. "My own dear Ann," the Carthage storekeeper and assistant postmaster wrote to his intended. "I have this evening been to church," he said, "opened the Nauvoo Mail—and made up the Eastern & Warsaw Mail; have just this moment closed my shutters and locked the door—and now am

reported] testimony, 12 February 1845, in *Nauvoo Neighbor*, 19 February 1845. John C. Burns testimony, 12 February 1845, in *Nauvoo Neighbor*, 19 February 1845. Minor R. Deming was called as a witness for the defense. His testimony was unexceptional.

18. Esquire Backman's closing arguments, 12 February 1845, in *Nauvoo Neighbor*, 19 February 1845.
19. "Arrest and Commitment of J. C. Elliott," *Warsaw Signal*, 19 February 1845. Added to the end of the main article is the comment: "*Thursday Afternoon.*—Elliott we learn has given the Brethren leg bail.—Good!" "To the Public," *Warsaw Signal*, 19 February 1845. "Re-Capture of J. C. Elliott," *Warsaw Signal*, 12 March 1845.
20. Daniels, *Correct Account*, 22, and Littlefield, *The Martyrs*, 86. Elliott is mentioned only twice during the 1845 trial of the accused assassins of Joseph Smith. Benjamin Brackenbury admits to having provided testimony during "Elliott's trial at Nauvoo." (Sharp, *Trial*, 25) William Smith (not the brother of the prophet), testified that he did not recall whether or not Brackenbury had stated "anything before the Grand Jury about Elliott; my impression is that he did not." (Sharp, *Trial*, 26). At no point in the proceedings did Elliott become a part of the prosecution's case, either as a witness or possible defendant.

entirely alone (I could see no lights when at the door around the square) while the goodly inhabitants of this burg, slumber, I with pleasure sit down to scrawl a few lines, to my own dear Ann about I dont know what." Ann was living in Warsaw with her sister and brother-in-law, publisher Thomas Gregg. "Give my love to Mrs. Gregg and many a kiss—retain one for yourself. [signed] Frank." They were married on February 22, 1844. A son was born to the couple in late autumn.[21]

After the 1845 trial, Worrell continued to ride with a Carthage company to "reconnoitre the country, and then to return to devise ways and means for their own safety, and the security of their property." Rumor had it he was also involved in occasional burnings of Mormon barns and haystacks.[22] On the morning of September 16, 1845, Lieutenant Worrell left his wife and child for another reconnaissance. He gave her a kiss and said he would return before nightfall. He told Ann not to fear, that "he would not fight the Mormons." She spent the day anticipating his safe return. Ann's sister (wife of editor Thomas Gregg) had heard that Frank had been wounded that afternoon but could not bear to convey the horrible news. Finally, a young boy was sent to Carthage with a bag of grain for the mill. Inside the sack was a letter to "Mrs. W." telling what had happened. In shock she read the missive, "stained with the blood of her husband." He was dead. Mormon enforcer and former Danite Orrin Porter Rockwell, acting on orders from Mormon sympathizer Sheriff Backenstos, had fired the fatal shot.[23]

That evening one Nauvoo Saint wrote in her journal, "To day Porter Rockwell Shot [blank in manuscript] as they ware pursuing mr. Backenstos on the parrarie near the rail road. Ther was about 30, this one was at the hed. He helped to concot the plan to slay Joseph and Hirum; he was at the Jail at the murder." Another Mormon wrote, "Wednesday 17th . . . We learned this morning that the person killed yesterday was Frank Worrell, the person who stood at the jail door when Joseph and Hyrum were killed beckoning the mob and urging them on." Underlying the wording of each entry was a belief in retributive justice.[24]

Backenstos and Rockwell were tried for Worrell's murder. Both men would be acquitted. The requirements of Mormon vengeance had been fulfilled.[25]

Jonathan Dunham, a general in the Nauvoo Legion, also became a casualty of Mormon vengeance, although in an unexpected way. There is evidence that on the day of his death Joseph Smith sent a request (perhaps through Stephen Markham) to General Dunham with orders to call out the Nauvoo Legion and rescue him from Carthage jail. Dunham ignored the command and kept the correspondence secret.

21. Franklin Worrell to Ann Lawton [undated, "Carthage, 11 oclock Sunday eve" February 1844], Lawton Papers, Regional Archives, Western Illinois University. Franklin Worrell to Ann Lawton [undated, "Carthage Friday morn," postmark Carthage, Illinois, 21 February 1844], Lawton Papers, Regional Archives, Western Illinois University. Archbold, *A Book for the Married and Single*, 42–44.

22. Archbold, *A Book for the Married and Single*, 42.

23. Ibid., 43–44.

24. "Murder of one of our best men. To Arms! To Arms!" *Warsaw Signal*, 17 September 1845. Zina Diantha Huntington Jacobs, "All Things Move . . ." Clayton, Nauvoo Journal 4 [17 September 1845], in Clayton, *Writings*, 74.

25. "Trial of J. B. Backenstos, Esq . . . for the Murder of Franklin Worrell," *Illinois State Register*, 19 December 1845.

"And while they were in jail," former Danite Allen Stout wrote in his journal, "Brother Joseph wrote an official order to Jonathan Dunham to bring the Legion and preserve him from being killed, but Dunham did not let a single man or mortal know that he had received such orders, and we were kept in the city under arms, not knowing but all was well, until the mob came and forced the prison."[26]

Months later the letter was discovered in the streets of Nauvoo (Dunham had apparently dropped it) and its contents revealed. As the truth became known, Dunham was effectively banished by the Saints. (His induction into the Council of Fifty by Brigham Young was likely a ruse.) Shortly thereafter Dunham was sent on a mission to the West where he reportedly succumbed to a fever or dysentery. Others said he died by his own hand, unable to bear any longer the shame of betraying the prophet's trust. Some believed Dunham was killed by his companion, an Indian by the name of Lewis Dana, a Freemason and a fellow member of the Council of Fifty, commissioned by Brigham Young to sacrifice Dunham's life as atonement for his unpardonable sin. Unfortunately, Joseph's letter to Dunham is no longer in existence to confirm the story. In the 1980s, Mormon document dealer Mark Hofmann concocted a modern forgery of the order. Considered genuine at the time, it was published in the collected writings of Joseph Smith.[27]

William N. Daniels was another casualty of the Carthage massacre. Daniels had been an involuntary member of the disbanded Warsaw militia (or so he claimed) when it stormed the Carthage jail. His testimony before Governor Thomas Ford and the October grand jury was the single most important source for indictments against Levi Williams, Thomas Sharp, and the other men accused of the crime. Shortly afterwards, Daniels converted to Mormonism and moved to Nauvoo. "Nauvoo," Daniels wrote in late 1844, "is considered by my friends the only place where my life would be secure, and agreeably to their counsel, I sent for my family, and made that beautiful and flourishing city the place of my future residence." Together with L. O. Littlefield, himself a Mormon writer of some ability, Daniels composed an account of the massacre. It was published, first, without their consent, in Thomas Sharp's *Warsaw Signal* in late 1844, and again, in booklet form, just weeks before the 1845 trial of the assassins.[28]

The embellishments added by Daniels and Littlefield to make the story sell were sufficiently incredible for the court to discredit his entire testimony and led to the acquittal of the men accused of the crime. Both sides had reason to want Daniels out of the way, and, appropriately enough, there are two conflicting accounts of how he "disappeared."

---

26. Allen Stout, Journal, Trevor Fisher transcription, cited in Sillito and Roberts, *Salamander*, 547–48. See also Jones, *Martyrdom*, 91.

27. Stenhouse, *Rocky Mountain Saints*, 164, note. Quinn, *Origins of Power*, 179 and 529. Clayton, Nauvoo Journal 4 [9 September 1845], in Clayton, *Writings*, 72. Jessee, *Personal Writings of Joseph Smith*, 616–17. Sillitoe and Roberts, *Salamander*, 547–48. Turley, *Victims*.

28. "A Complete Latter-Day History of the Murder of Joseph and Hyrum Smith, At the Carthage Jail, on the 27th day of June, 1844. By Scape-Gallows Daniels," *Warsaw Signal*, 25 December 1844. Daniels, *Correct Account*. See Crawley, *Descriptive Bibliography of the Mormon Church*, 298–301, for a bibliographic description of this work.

In 1846, Joseph Smith's only surviving brother William (by then estranged from Brigham Young) related that "after the court was over; some of Brigham's guard was heard to say that it was best to save Daniel's soul while he was in the faith . . . [and put him] where he can tell no lies, or recall his former statement." Littlefield, who used large portions of their jointaccount in his own writings, recalled that "the where-abouts of Mr. Daniels had been unknown to the writer since 1846. It is not at all unlikely that some of the parties implicated in the tragedy at Carthage assassinated him for exposing them. They swore they would do so." Daniels was never heard from again.[29]

* * * * *

The Mormon call for vengeance extended beyond the walls of the temple. Throughout the nineteenth century Mormon patriarchal blessings frequently ad-monished individual Saints to fulfill their sacred duty: "Thou shalt dwell upon the earth to see thy Savior coming in the clouds of heaven," read one 1856 blessing given to a Utah Mormon, "and be numbered with those who will avenge the blood of the prophets and Joseph."[30]

In mid-1857, Illinois congressman Stephen A. Douglas accused the Utah Mor-mons of being "bound by horrid oaths and terrible penalties, to recognize and main-tain the authority of Brigham Young." These were harsh words from a man who had been friendly to the Latter-day Saints during their Nauvoo sojourn. Douglas now considered Mormonism a "loathsome, disgusting ulcer," which had to be "cut out." Like many other eastern politicians Douglas believed that Brigham Young should be removed as governor of the Utah Territory and a U.S. military force dispatched to maintain order there. In a show of defiance against the United States government, Brigham Young ordered the California trails to be closed and forbade the Saints to have any business dealings with emigrant parties. Mormonism once again found itself under siege.[31]

One of the worst tragedies in the history of the settlement of the American West occurred just three months after Douglas's condemnatory speech. In September of 1857 an Arkansas wagon train—consisting of forty men, thirty women, and sev-enty children—passed through southern Utah en route to California. Shortly before their arrival in the territory, word had reached Salt Lake City that the beloved Mor-mon apostle Parley P. Pratt had been killed in Arkansas by the estranged husband of

29. Hosea Stout, Diary, 1:6, note 11.

30. Patriarch Isaac Morley blessing of Leonard Elsworth Harrington, 29 February 1856. Leonard Har-rington, Journal, Utah State Historical Society, published in Infobases Collectors Library CD-ROM. See also Patriarch Elisha H. Groves blessing of William Horne Dame, 20 February 1854, in Brooks, *John Doyle Lee*, 209. Patriarch Isaac Morley blessing of Philip Klingensmith, 28 May 1857. "Thou shalt yet be numbered with the sons of Zion in avenging the blood of Brother Joseph for thy and thy spirit can never be satisfied until the wicked are subdued." Klingensmith was one of the prin-cipals in the Mountain Meadows Massacre. See Poll, "History and Faith: Reflections of a Mormon Historian," 95, Bates, "Patriarchal Blessings," 9–14, Bates, "Thematic Changes in Blessings," 21 on "avenging the blood of the prophets."

31. Stephen A. Douglas, quoted in Roberts, *Comprehensive History*, 2:184–89. For same imagery, see James H. Carleton to W. W. Mackall 25 May 1859, in Carleton, *The Mountain Meadows Massacre*, 39.

Pratt's twelfth polygamous wife. It would later be reported that some in the Arkansas emigrant company had poisoned a local well, boasted of participating in anti-Mormon riots in Missouri and Illinois, and claimed they had the gun that "killed Old Joe Smith." Unlikely as some of those stories were, the end result was that on September 11, 1857, a group of Mormon militiamen headed by John D. Lee (a spiritual son of Brigham Young) aided by local Indians murdered more than 120 men, women, and children at a staging point known as Mountain Meadows. The bodies of the victims were buried unceremoniously in shallow unmarked graves. More than a dozen surviving children, most of them too young to remember the names of their parents, were distributed among Mormon families in the area. The possessions of the emigrants, which included nearly six hundred head of cattle, three dozen wagons, and thousands of dollars in gold coins, eventually ended up in Mormon hands. Some of their belongings even found their way to the Tithing Office in Salt Lake City.[32]

Deflecting blame for the tragedy away from the Latter-day Saints, Brigham Young claimed that Indians were entirely responsible for the murders. An oath of silence prevented the Mormon militiamen from telling even their wives what had gone on at Mountain Meadows. The Mormon temple covenant was taken literally and became a justification for the massacre, some of the participants claiming "Josephs blood had got to be Avenged." Another wrote that "they had been privileged to keep a part of their covenant to avenge the blood of the prophets."[33]

U.S. Army officer James Carleton, sent to investigate the crime more than a year after the massacre, was overwhelmed and disgusted by the presence of tattered clothing, strands of women's hair, and bones still scattered across the landscape at Mountain Meadows, many dug up out of their pit graves by coyotes and other wild scavengers. Carleton had the human remains reburied under a rock cairn topped by a commemorative wooden cross, inscribed with a New Testament passage from Romans: "Vengeance is mine, I will repay saith the Lord." The words were intended to serve both as a comfort to the souls of those who had been murdered at Mountain Meadows and a warning to the men Carleton rightly believed were ultimately responsible for the tragedy and cover-up, namely, followers of the Mormon prophet Brigham Young and possibly even Brigham Young himself.[34]

When President Young visited the killing ground for the first time in 1861, he "corrected" the wording of the inscription by exclaiming, "Vengeance is mine, saith the Lord, and I *have* repaid!" The cross was taken down and the stone cairn destroyed. Any acknowledgement of wrongdoing on the part of the church was out of the question. There would be no admission of Mormon guilt.[35]

John D. Lee, Council of Fifty member under Brigham Young and an 1844 political missionary for Joseph Smith, was made a scapegoat in the affair. Following two

---

32. Bagley, *Blood of the Prophets*, 117 (gun quote). See also Brooks, *Mountain Meadows Massacre*. Van Wagoner and Walker, *A Book of Mormons*, 158.

33. Dimick Huntington, Journal, 1857 [20 September 1857] (Joseph quote), quoted in Bagley, *Blood of the Prophets*, 170. Lee, *Mormonism Unveiled*, 247–50 (privileged quote). Bagley, *Blood of the Prophets*, 158.

34. James H. Carleton to W. W. Mackall 25 May 1859. (Carleton, *The Mountain Meadows Massacre*, 35).

35. Roberts, *Comprehensive History* 4:176, note 24, citing Stenhouse, *Rocky Mountain Saints*, 453. Woodruff, *Journals* 5:577 [25 May 1860] differs slightly from Stenhouse, although the message remains the same: "President Young said it should be Vengeance is mine and I have taken a little."

trials Lee was executed by firing squad in 1877 for his part in the atrocity, the only person ever to be punished for the crime. (In Utah the firing squad as a preferred form of execution remains in force to this day, a relic of the Mormon doctrine of blood atonement, although there is an active movement to do away with the archaic practice.) Lee explained that "I believed I was obeying *orders*, and acting for the good of the Church, and in strict conformity with the oaths that we have all taken to avenge the blood of the Prophets. You must either sustain the people for what they have done, or you must release us from the oaths and obligations that we have taken." It would be another fifty years before the Oath of Vengeance was removed from the Mormon temple ceremony.[36]

Three years after Mountain Meadows, the American republic witnessed the outbreak of the Civil War. That catastrophe was interpreted by many Latter-day Saints as a direct consequence of the 1844 Carthage incident. Brigham Young called the Civil War, "a visitation from heaven because they have killed the prophet of God, Joseph Smith, Jr."[37]

Eliza R. Snow, one of Joseph's plural wives who subsequently married Brigham Young ("for time"), was the preeminent Mormon woman of letters in the nineteenth century. In 1862, she composed a poem about the destiny of the nation in light of the war raging in the American Republic to the east:

> Its fate is fixed—its destiny
> Is sealed—its end is sure to come;
> Why use the wealth of poesy
> To urge a nation to its doom?
> [...]
> It must be so, to avenge the blood
> That stains the walls of Carthage jail.[38]

Mormon predictions to the contrary notwithstanding, the United States survived the Civil War.

U.S. government pressure on the church continued to mount through the second half of the nineteenth century. In 1889, President Wilford Woodruff issued an official declaration in which he asserted that "this Church does not claim to be an independent, temporal kingdom of God, or to be an imperium in imperio aiming to overthrow the United States or any other civil government."[39] A year later the church officially suspended the practice of polygamy; both moves were calculated to prevent the breakup of the church and the confiscation of its assets.

Utah achieved statehood in 1896. In 1903, objections were raised over the right of Mormon apostle Reed Smoot to take his elected seat in the U.S. Senate. The

---

36. Lee, *Mormonism Unveiled*, 253.
37. Hirschon, *Lion of the Lord*, 259. Brigham Young's comments were published in *The New York Times*, 8 November 1863. The LDS belief that the American nation was to atone for the murders of Joseph and Hyrum was frequently expressed in public settings throughout the nineteenth century. See, for example, Heber C. Kimball (*Journal of Discourses* 5:253), Orson Hyde (*Journal of Discourses* 6:154), F. D. Richards (*Journal of Discourses* 26:345). All are quoted in Tanner, *Evolution of the Mormon Temple Ceremony*, 23. See also Wilford Woodruff, Journal 5:616 [31 December 1861].
38. Eliza R. Snow in 1861, in *New York Times*, 20 January 1862, quoted in Hirschon, *Lion of the Lord*, 259.
39. "Official Declaration," 12 December 1889, quoted in Hansen, "Metamorphosis," 230–31.

protest was mounted because of lingering concerns about Mormon allegiance to the government of the United States. "It is claimed Mr. Smoot has taken an oath as an apostle of the Mormon Church which is of such a nature as to render him incompetent to hold the office of Senator."[40]

Hearings were held in Washington, D.C. In response to a question as to whether he had pledged to "never cease to importune high heaven to avenge the blood of the prophets upon this Nation," Senator Smoot replied:

> I did not, nor was there anything said about avenging the blood of the prophets or anything else on this Nation or on this Government. There was nothing said about avenging the blood of Joseph Smith, Jr., the prophet. And it seems strange that such a thing should be spoken of, because the endowments have never changed, as I understand it; it has been so testified, and that Joseph Smith, Jr., himself was the founder of the endowments. It would be very strange, indeed, to have such an oath to avenge his death when he was alive.

Several more times Senator Smoot was asked about the Oath of Vengeance. Each time his reply was the same.

> Q: But I understand you to say positively that there was nothing at all in the ceremony about avenging the blood of the martyrs or prophets?
>
> A: I said so. . .
>
> Q: Is there anything in the ceremony about avenging the blood of the martyrs or the martyrs?
>
> A: No; there is not.[41]

Transcripts of the hearings were widely distributed, bringing unwelcome public attention to the doctrines and practices of the Church of Jesus Christ of Latter-day Saints. Given the seriousness of the charge (and for most Mormons, the sacred character of the obligation), official acknowledgment of the Oath of Vengeance proved impossible. In much the same way that Joseph Smith denied the practice of plural marriage, LDS church officials never publicly admitted the presence of an Oath of Vengeance in the Mormon endowment ritual. "These charges," levied against Senator Smoot, one prominent Mormon asserted, "were, as every Latter-day Saint knows, based in the deepest falsehood."[42]

After three years of intense debate, Smoot was eventually confirmed and served in the U.S. Senate until 1933, remembered in Utah to this day for his "unimpeachable honesty, loyalty, dedication, service and patriotism."[43]

---

40. *Proceedings Before the Committee on Privileges and Elections of the United States,* quoted in Tanner, *Evolution of the Mormon Temple Ceremony,* 24.

41. *Testimony of Important Witnesses,* 4 and 44.

42. Joseph Fielding Smith, *The Life of Joseph F. Smith,* Ch. 39 (Infobases Collectors Library CD-ROM). The charges levied against Smoot included the claims that "there was a union of church and state in Utah [that] 'Mormons' who were endowed in the Temple took an oath of vengeance against the United States." Smith's protest notwithstanding, both accusations were justified.

43. Current (2002) wording of the Reed Smoot Award, Provo, Utah.

Between 1921 and 1927, Salt Lake temple president George F. Richards, a descendant of Carthage witness Willard Richards, was given the task of simplifying and standardizing the temple ceremony for the church. Several justifications were put forward for eliminating the Oath of Vengeance. One stake president felt that since "this prayer has been answered" it was "no longer necessary." Others argued that "the language was harsh" and "offensive to the young people." On February 15, 1927, Richards wrote an official letter to all temple presidents. His directive was simple: "Omit from the prayer in the circle all references to avenging the blood of the Prophets." He added that the temple presidents should also "Omit from the ordinance and lecture all reference to retribution."[44]

For Utah Mormons "Carthage" became a code word for persecuted innocence and a call for vengeance against any opponents of the Latter-day Saints. Through the first quarter of the twentieth century, Carthage remained forcefully imprinted on the consciousness of all temple-going Mormons, accomplished through the complex and intensely personalized endowment ritual, reinforced as one returned to perform vicarious "temple work" for deceased ancestors, a practice initiated in the 1870s. The quest for vengeance became even more widely dispersed in the Utah tradition of written patriarchal blessings, issued to all worthy and desiring church members, intended to be read, contemplated, and fulfilled.

The simple fact that the Carthage survivors—John Taylor and Willard Richards—followed Brigham Young to Utah and remained as living reminders of the Carthage incident, meant that firsthand knowledge of the martyrdom was perpetuated much longer for Latter-day Saints in the West than for the eastern churches devoted to the prophet Joseph. The Reorganized Church (today known as the Community of Christ), for example, failed to develop an elaborate martyrdom mythology, in part because by rejecting Brigham Young and polygamy they also abandoned Mormon temple ritual.

---

44. Edward H. Snow, quoted in Beurger, "Mormon Temple Endowment," 55 (answered quote). St. George Temple Minutes, 19 June 1924, quoted in Beurger, "Mormon Temple Endowment," 55 (harsh quote). Darter, *Celestial Marriage*, 60, quoted in Tanner, *The Changing World of Mormonism*, 533 (offensive quote). George F. Richards to the president of the St. George Temple, 15 February 1927, quoted in Buerger, *Mysteries of Godliness*, 140 and Bergera, "Secretary to the Senator," 41, note 29.

Chapter Twenty

How Wide the Conspiracy?

J OSEPH SMITH UTTERED THE FIRST four words of the Masonic distress cry as he fell from the second story window of Carthage jail. Yet none of the Masons in the mob surrounding the jail made any effort to come to his aid. That circumstance gave rise to the suspicion that there was a Masonic conspiracy to take his life, a claim voiced privately and in public by Joseph Smith's successor, Brigham Young.

Brigham Young's Masonic Plot

By the spring of 1844, Freemasonry had become a vital part of social and ritual life in Nauvoo. Joseph Smith firmly believed there was "similarity of priesthood in Masonry" and that Freemasonry had been "taken from the [ancient] priesthood but has become degenerated." Masonic symbols, gestures, and penalties were reflected in the newly revealed Mormon temple ritual. Almost every church leader was a Mason and nearly two-thirds of all Freemasons in Illinois were Latter-day Saints. With the deaths of two of the most prominent Mormon Freemasons, however, the privileged position of the craft among Latter-day Saints took a drastic fall from which it never recovered.[1]

The *Times and Seasons* issue of July 15, 1844, contained an editorial headed, "The Murder." Its purpose was not to present a descriptive account of the Carthage incident (that had been done earlier in the month), but to put before the world once again the Mormon cry of persecuted innocence and to present Joseph and Hyrum as true martyrs for the cause of God. The editorial condemned the Freemasons for not preventing the murders when it was within their power to do so. Joseph had given the Masonic sign of distress when hanging in the window of the jail and yet none had come to his aid. This was not the first time Joseph had used his Masonic ties in order to extricate himself from a difficult situation. Following the prophet's June 1843 arrest at Dixon, for example, a correspondent wrote from Nauvoo that "today, Joseph was brought home in triumph, having suffered a few days' imprisonment in an old barn; from which he escaped, I am told, by giving some Masonic sign, before his friends arrived."[2] Joseph's experience at Carthage, however, ended, not in triumph, but tragedy. The *Times and Seasons* editorial of July 15, 1844, read, in part,

---

1. Heber C. Kimball to Parley P. Pratt, 17 June 1842, in Kimball, *Heber C. Kimball*, 85. See Literski, *Method Infinite.*
2. Charlotte Haven to her parents, 2 July 1843, in Haven, "A Girls Letters from Nauvoo," 634.

Leaving religion out of the case, where is the lover of his country, and his posterity, that does not condemn such an outrageous murder, and will not lend all his powers, energies and influence to bring the offenders to justice and judgment? Eve[n], that these two innocent men were confined in jail for a supposed crime, deprived of any weapons to defend themselves [sic!]: had the pledged faith of the State of Illinois, by Gov. Ford, for their protection, and were then shot to death, while, with uplifted hands they gave such signs of distress as would have commanded the interposition and benevolence of Savages or Pagans. They were both Masons in good standing. Ye brethren of "the mystic tie" what think ye! Where is our good Master Joseph and Hyrum? Is there a pagan, heathen, or savage nation on the globe that would not be moved on this great occasion, as the trees of the forest are moved by a mighty wind? Joseph's last exclamation was "O Lord my God!"

Readers of the Mormon newspaper, most of whom were members of the Nauvoo Lodge, would have readily understood the Masonic references in this passage. The "uplifted hands" was the Masonic distress signal, known to all indoctrinated Freemasons, here called "brethren of the mystic tie." Any Mason witnessing such a sign, especially when supplemented by the words, "O Lord, my God, is there no help for the widow's son?" was, by their sacred oath, required to offer assistance. The unwillingness of the Masons in the mob to come to Joseph and Hyrum's aid branded them as even less than pagans, heathens, or savages, all unbelievers in Christ. Joseph Smith's unheeded Masonic distress cry would echo throughout the Mormon and Masonic community for decades to come.[3]

There is little evidence that the Illinois Freemasons, as a body, were behind the murders of Joseph and Hyrum Smith. Furthermore, the Carthage and Warsaw Lodges had their charters recalled by the Illinois Grand Lodge as a consequence of the involvement of lodge members in illegal activities surrounding the Carthage incident, as well as their subsequent efforts to use the Craft to protect individuals from prosecution. (Significantly, though, the Quincy Lodge was not censured for its anti-Mormon stance.) It is true, nonetheless, that several of the men indicted for Joseph Smith's murder attempted to benefit from the Masonic pledge of mutual protection in the months leading up to the 1845 trial.

Local Masonic lodges in Carthage and Warsaw were first organized at the very time the Nauvoo Mormon lodges were being placed under suspension. Hancock Lodge No. 20, in Carthage, was established under dispensation in 1842; its charter was granted the following year. Wesley Williams (brother of Archibald and cousin of Colonel Levi Williams) was one of its original members. The 1844 return for the Carthage Lodge lists Wesley Williams, Robert F. Smith, and Onias C. Skinner as Master Masons. All three men were active in the anti-Mormon movement.

The founding Worshipful Master of Warsaw Lodge No. 21 was Abraham I. Chittenden; their first meeting was held in early 1843. Among those who served with Chittenden were Mark Aldrich, treasurer, and Henry Stephens, secretary. Again, all three men were noted anti-Mormons. Following the October grand jury

3.   Hogan, *Mormonism and Freemasonry*, 303. Compton, *In Sacred Loneliness, 108.* Wyl, *Mormon Portraits*, 154. Lee, *Mormonism Unveiled*, 153.

proceedings, Thomas Sharp and Levi Williams were initiated into the Warsaw Lodge. Jacob C. Davis and William H. Roosevelt were raised to the Master Mason degree. The "Chittenden boys" (William W. and E. F. Chittenden), both mentioned in October grand jury testimony, became Master Masons in January of 1845. George Rockwell was raised in late February; Levi Williams in March.[4]

The Mormons at Nauvoo watched the Masonic activity in Warsaw with no small interest. Orson Hyde addressed the high priests of Nauvoo in late April 1845. "I may be regarded as a treasonable, blasphemous character," he said, "but I wanted to express my feelings. I want those murderers to know that their lies cannot always shield them; that although they join the *fraternity of brethren*," that is, the Freemasons, "to save them from the just penalty of their crime, this cunning resort cannot rescue them from punishment. But it may possibly postpone it, and give it a chance to stand on interest till the Saints judge the world." The Mormon political Kingdom of God was yet at hand. Punishment of the murderers would come at last.[5]

Although the Grand Lodge of Illinois was not pleased with the activities of its Hancock County brethren, there would be no official condemnation of the murders of Joseph and Hyrum Smith, two of the most prominent Mormon Freemasons. Nonetheless, the charter of the Carthage Lodge was surrendered in late 1844 "on account of [the] Mormon difficulties." It would not be rechartered until 1856. The Warsaw Lodge likewise lost its charter. Following the acquittal of Sharp, Williams, Davis, Aldrich, and Grover in 1845, however, the Grand Lodge received the Warsaw Lodge once again into its "affectionate confidence." The justification for accepting the Warsaw Lodge was that "although the lodge erred, and greatly erred" by allowing the men to join the lodge (or become Master Masons) while under indictment, "the error was an error of the head and not of the heart . . . the men have been since tried by the laws of their country by a jury of their peers and acquitted."[6]

Abraham Jonas, once Illinois's most venerated Past Grand Master, also fell out of favor. Columbus Lodge No. 6 filed no returns in 1844 or 1845. In 1846 his lodge surrendered its charter. As a past grand master, Jonas was never officially censured for his role in the Carthage conspiracy but would remain forever relegated to the background of Illinois Masonic affairs.[7]

William Gano Goforth was less fortunate. Following his Masonic "work" in the clandestine Nauvoo Lodge in the spring of 1844, Goforth was censured by the Illinois Grand Lodge and expelled from the fraternity. Goforth joined the Mormon church at Nauvoo in early 1845 (he was baptized by Brigham Young), and followed the new prophet to Utah.[8]

In August 1860, Brigham Young, then in Salt Lake City, made a claim extending the charges of the 1844 *Times and Seasons* editorial. Brigham Young met with John Taylor, one of the two Carthage survivors, and several other members of the

---

4. Carr, *Freemasonry and Nauvoo*, 32.
5. Hyde, *Speech*, 6.
6. Carr, *Freemasonry and Nauvoo*, 35.
7. Hogan, "Abraham Jonas."
8. See Carr, *Freemasonry and Nauvoo*, 28, Turnbull, 133. Hogan, "Strange Case."

Quorum of the Twelve Apostles. Wilford Woodruff recorded President Young's comments on this occasion:

> President Young said the people of the United States had sought our destruction and they had used every Exertion to perfe[c]t it. They have worked through the masonic institution to perfect it. Joseph & Hyrum Smith were Master Masons and they were put to death by masons or through there instigation and he gave the sign of distress & he was shot by masons while in the act. And there were delegates from the various lodges in the Union to see that he was put to death. I hope to live to see the day when I can have power to make them do right. They have got the blood of the prophets upon their heads & they have got to meet it.[9]

Three separate claims are here being made about Masonic involvement in the Carthage conspiracy. First, that Joseph and Hyrum were "put to death by Masons or through their instigation." Second, that Joseph "was shot by Masons while in the act" of giving the Masonic distress sign. Third, and most important, Brigham Young asserted that "there were delegates from the various lodges in the Union to see that he was put to death." In other words, Brigham Young apparently believed there was a national Masonic conspiracy to take Joseph Smith's life. Brigham Young's final point, an obligation to avenge the "blood of the Prophets," was the subject of the previous chapter.

However emphatic and authoritative his words may appear on the surface, Brigham Young's 1860 statement is not evidence for a national Masonic conspiracy to murder Joseph Smith. At the time Brigham Young made his assertions, rumors were surfacing that an attempt would be made to establish a gentile Masonic lodge in Utah, to "try to get an influence with some here to lay a plan to try to murder me [Brigham Young] & the [other] leaders of the Church." The Masonic threat was again in the air.

Nonetheless, it is true that Brigham Young had known for some time that representatives from throughout the Union met in Carthage on the night of June 26, 1844, (the day prior to the assassination of Joseph and Hyrum) and condemned the two incarcerated Smith brothers to death.[10]

Carthage survivor Willard Richards died in 1854. His demise dealt a severe blow to the compilers of the Joseph Smith history. Requests were made of all remaining Carthage witnesses to record their observations in writing and forward them to the Church Historian's Office in Salt Lake City. One of the respondents was one of Joseph Smith's bodyguards, Stephen Markham, who in June of 1856 wrote a lengthy statement detailing events surrounding the final days of the prophet. Markham described the June 26, 1844, meeting of the Carthage Committee of Safety at the Hamilton Hotel, noting, "There were delegates in the meeting from every state in the Union except three." Markham made no reference to Freemasons.[11]

9. Woodruff, *Journals* 5:482 [19 August 1860].
10. Woodruff, *Journals* 5:483 [19 August 1860]. In all published histories known to the authors the meeting has been placed erroneously on the morning of the 27th of June. (See note 13, below.)
11. Black, *Who's Who in the Doctrine and Covenants*, 241–44. Stephen Markham to Wilford Woodruff, 20 June 1856, LDS Archives. See also Journal History, 27 June 1844, 1. Smith, *History of the Church* 6:605–6.

Brigham Young used Markham's manuscript account (or the version published in the *Deseret News* as part of the Joseph Smith history) at least twice in public discourses delivered before the Saints in Utah. On February 10, 1860, several months before the aforementioned August meeting, President Young asked whether America's national leaders knew of the plan to murder Joseph Smith. "Were they aware of it at the seat of government?" Without citing specific evidence, he answered in the affirmative. "I have no doubt," he said, "they as well knew the plans for destroying the Prophet as did those in Carthage or in Warsaw, Illinois. It was planned by some of the leading men of the nation. I have said here once before, to the astonishment of many of our own countrymen, that there was a delegate from each State in the nation when Joseph was killed. These delegates held their council." In 1867, Brigham Young would again assert, "The mob that collected at Carthage, Illinois, to commit that deed of blood contained a delegation representing every state in the Union. Each has received its blood stain." Brigham's numerical misrepresentation ("every state in the Union") was no doubt affected to heighten the rhetorical impact of his remarks.[12]

John Taylor, badly injured in the assault on the jail, also responded to a request from the Church Historian's Office for information about the martyrdom. Taylor's version of events was completed in August 1856, in consultation with George A. Smith, while the two men were in the eastern United States. They worked together for more than a month, composing "entirely from memory, as we are without documents," other than Ford's *History of Illinois*. Taylor responded to assertions about a larger movement to murder the prophet, more than likely prompted by Markham's letter which had been received by the Church Historian's Office in June. The underlined passages (added by the authors) stress the caution that John Taylor exercised in assigning blame for the assassination.

> It was rumored that a strong political party, numbering in its ranks many of the prominent men of the nation, were engaged in a plot for the overthrow of Joseph Smith, and that the Governor was of the party, and Sharp, Williams, Captain Smith and others were his accomplices, but whether this was the case or not I do not know. It is very certain that a strong political feeling existed against Joseph Smith, and I have reasons to believe that his letters to Henry Clay, were made use of by political parties opposed to Henry Clay, and were the means of that statesman's defeat. Yet, if such a combination as the one referred to existed, I am not apprised of it.

Taylor intimates ("I have reasons to believe") he had information concerning Clay's 1844 presidential bid beyond that generally reported. In all likelihood Taylor's source was Dr. John Bernhisel, another Carthage witness and Council of Fifty member, who in 1850 was a newly seated territorial representative from Deseret. In early 1850 Bernhisel wrote to Brigham Young of his introductory visits to Washington politicians. Henry Clay, he reported, though cordial, was "still writhing under the

---

12. Brigham Young, 10 February 1860, in *Journal of Discourses* 8:320–21, quoted in Lundwall, *Fate of the Persecutors*, 327. Brigham Young, 17 August 1867, in *Journal of Discourses* 12:121, quoted in Lundwall, *Fate of the Persecutors*, 271–72.

infliction of a certain letter addressed to him by Pres. Joseph Smith in 1844," which had soundly condemned the elder statesman. Dr. Bernhisel was in Washington, D.C., at the time Smith and Taylor were writing and served as a valued resource for information concerning Joseph Smith's last days. Taylor's remark, and Bernhisel's confirmation, is one more indicator of the long-term impact of Joseph Smith's 1844 presidential campaign. There is no suggestion that Taylor suspected Henry Clay (perhaps the most prominent Freemason in the United States at the time) of being behind the assassination of Joseph and Hyrum. Furthermore, Taylor does not identify the "strong political party" rumored to be behind the prophet's death. Of the men mentioned in Taylor's account, Governor Ford was a Democrat, Thomas Sharp was nominally Whig although effectively nonpartisan, while Levi Williams was a longtime supporter of Whig leader Henry Clay.[13]

Based upon the comments of John Taylor and Brigham Young, there was apparently no material evidence available to the First Presidency of the church concerning a nationwide Masonic plot to murder Joseph Smith. Brigham Young simply inserted Freemasons into his 1860 equation in order to strengthen his case against allowing the formation of a non-Mormon Masonic lodge in the Territory of Utah and discourage the growth of Gentile settlements in the region. Significantly, though, this conclusion does not diminish Stephen Markham's statement that national representatives met at the Hamilton Hotel the night before the assault on Carthage jail, a point returned to in the final section of this chapter.

The Four Men at the Well

Brigham Young's second claim, that Joseph Smith was "shot by Masons," also requires clarification. Dallin H. Oaks and Marvin Hill (whose pivotal study, *The Carthage Conspiracy: The Trial of the Accused Assassins of Joseph Smith*, was first published in 1975 and is still in print today) were unable to identify the men directly responsible for the murders. Not long after the volume was published, Dallin Oaks admitted that the book was an "incomplete history because we do not know who pulled the trigger or who participated in the murders." Indeed, the two main surviving lists of the Carthage mob were compiled long after the event and were greatly influenced by

---

13. George A. Smith to Brigham Young, 19 September 1856, quoted in Jesse, "Return to Carthage," 13. Their admission to a lack of documentary sources is especially significant. John Taylor, in Smith, *History of the Church* 7:116.Thomas Ford's *History of Illinois* simply states that "a council of officers convened on the morning of the 27th of June." (Ford, *History of Illinois*, in Smith, *History of the Church*, 7:16) Ford makes no mention of the secret tribunal he participated in at Hamilton Hotel in Carthage the evening before. Initially, *Times & Seasons* 5.12 (1 July 1844), 562–63 simply refers to "another consultation of the officers" on the morning of the 27th. Consequently, the tribunal, together with the Dr. Wall Southwick-Stephen Markham interchange, has been conflated with the "council of officers" and placed in the morning of the 27th in the Joseph Smith History (Journal History, 27 June 1844, 1) and in Smith, *History of the Church* 6:605–6. The erroneous chronology has been perpetuated in Leonard, *Nauvoo*, 388. A comment at the end of Markham's 20 June 1856 letter to Wilford Woodruff concerning the secret tribunal, that "nothing more particularly passed through the day," could refer only to the 26th of June and could not apply to the 27th. (See also Roberts, *Comprehensive History* 2:275 and Smith, *History of the Church* 7:16.) Jesse, "Return to Carthage," 14 is uncertain about the significance of the discrepancy between the Joseph Smith History and Markham versions. John H. Bernhisel to Brigham Young, 21 March 1850, in Journal History, 21 March 1850, 2–6.

the grand jury indictments of the fall and events leading up to the 1845 trial of the accused assassins.[14]

Another reason the chief gunmen have not been identified with any degree of certainty is that the individuals actually engaged in the shooting deliberately obscured their identities; with one possible exception, they were not among those indicted for the crime. Furthermore, there were no surviving Mormon witnesses to record Joseph Smith's demise. In the late afternoon of June 27, 1844, there were four Mormons in the upper room of the Carthage jail—Joseph Smith and his brother Hyrum, both of whom were killed, John Taylor, who was badly wounded and rolled under the bed to protect himself, and Willard Richards, who survived nearly unscathed save for a cut on his ear. Although Richards was the only Mormon left standing at the conclusion of the firefight, he was not in a position to have witnessed Joseph's final moments.

Richards's journal provides insight into the extent of his personal knowledge regarding what took place at shortly after five P.M. on June 27, 1844:

> All [of us] sprang against the door. The balls whistled up the stairway and in an instant one came through the door. Joseph, Taylor, and Richards sprang to the left and Hyrum back in front of the door. [He] snapped his pistol, when a ball struck him in the left side of his nose. [He] fell back on the floor saying, "I am a dead man." Joseph discharged his 6 shooters in the entry reaching round the door casing. Discharges continued [to] come in the room. 6 shooter missed fired 2 or 3 times. Taylor sprang to leap from the east window [and] was shot in the window.[15]

The entry stops abruptly mid-scene. From this point Taylor responds to being shot by rolling under the bed, bleeding but alive. Joseph, still in the room, heads for the window. The panel door is forced open by the assailants, trapping Richards in the corner of the room. While this action providentially saved his life, it also prevented him from witnessing what was taking place in the courtyard. This is in accord with the physical layout of the room and is confirmed by Dr. Barnes, the physician who attended John Taylor's wounds. According to Barnes, Richards "stood next to the hinges of the door . . . so when they [the mob] crowded the door open it shut him up against the wall and he stood there and did not move till the affair was all over."[16]

---

14. Sheriff Jacob Backenstos's list of "Those active in the massacre at Carthage" was compiled (contrary to many published assertions) in 1846 (Lundwall, *Fate of the Persecutors*, 269–71, Smith, *History of the Church* 7:142–45, Journal History, 29 June 1844, 2). Willard Richards also attempted to compile a "Listing of the mob at Carthage," (Lundwall, *Fate of the Persecutors*, 271, Smith, *History of the Church* 7:146, Journal History, 29 June 1844, 2). The date of his compilation is uncertain. Richards incorrectly places several of the Nauvoo dissidents at the scene.

15. Willard Richards, Journal, 27 June 1844, quoted in *Old Mormon Nauvoo*, 190.

16. Thomas Barnes to Miranda Barnes Haskett, 6 November 1897, in Mulder and Mortensen, *Among the Mormons*, 151. Huntress, *Murder*, 152–53. Lundwall, *Fate of the Persecutors*, 220–23. Davis, *Authentic Account*, concurs: "Dr. Richards, who was also in the same room with the deceased, escaped uninjured, by retreating at the first onset behind the door, and against the wall." (p. 23) For an illustration of the interior of the jail showing Richards behind the door, see C. A. A. Christensen's 1890 painting, "The Blood of the Martyrs is the Seed of the Church," BYU Art Museum.

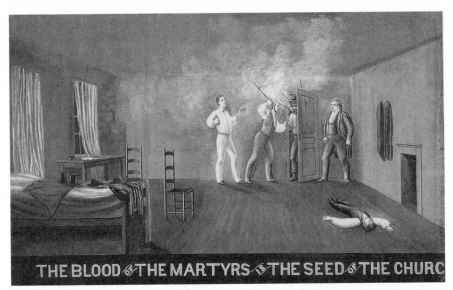

THE BLOOD ᛫THE MARTYRS ᛫THE SEED ᛫THE CHURC

Interior of Carthage Jail, by C. C. A. Christensen, ca. 1890. In this late rendition, Joseph is shown holding a set of scriptures rather than the "pepper box" pistol that had been smuggled in to him hours before the onslaught. John Taylor attempts to keep the intruders out with a cane. Willard Richards waits behind the door. The men's coats hang beside the fireplace. The inscription comes from Tertullian, a second- to third-century Christian author. The phrase is used frequently in Latter-day Saint rhetoric. Courtesy of Brigham Young University Museum of Art. All rights reserved.

Willard Richards's semi-official recital of that fateful day in June, called "Two Minutes in Jail," appeared in the *Nauvoo Neighbor* for July 24, 1844, and was reprinted in the August 1 issue of *Times and Seasons*. The relevant section reads:

> Joseph attempted as the last resort, to leap the same window from whence Mr. Taylor [nearly] fell, when two balls pierced him from the door, and one entered his right breast from without, and he fell outward exclaiming, "O Lord my God!" As his feet went out of the window my head went in, the balls whistling all around. He fell on his left side a dead man. At this instant the cry was raised, "He's leaped the window," and the mob on the stairs ran out. I withdrew from the window, thinking it of no use to leap out on a hundred bayonets, then around Gen. Smith's body.[17]

In this version of events, Richards presents himself as taking a more active role during the prophet's final moments than was actually the case. Indeed, it is difficult to envision how the wounded prophet could have fallen out of the window at the same time the corpulent Richards pulled himself back inside, all the while remaining unharmed.[18]

---

17. See also Willard Richards to Brigham Young, 30 June 1844, in Smith, *History of the Church* 7:147. Note Willard Richards to Reuben Hedlock, 9 July 1844, LDS Archives, Turley, *Selected Collections*, 1.31, in which he acknowledges that Joseph was shot after he fell from the window.
18. Compare John Taylor's version, in Taylor, *Witness*, 92 and Smith, *History of the Church* 7:105.

Richards's mention of Joseph's distinctive injuries is more significant. More than likely Richards's description (and chronology) of the wounds is based upon a post-mortem examination of the body of Joseph Smith, not his actual experience at the jail. On June 30, for instance, Richards wrote to Brigham Young, then still in the east, about Joseph's murder. He described Joseph's wounds: "Joseph received four bullets, one in right collar bone, one in right breast, and two others in his back, he leaped from the east window of the front room, and was dead in an instant." For Richards, then, Joseph Smith was killed as he sat on the window ledge preparing to jump to the ground below. In time this would become the standard LDS view of the murder; the fatal act would be provided with additional moral force by asserting that Joseph's jump from the window was a deliberate attempt on his part to draw attention away from the other men in the room.[19]

In any event, it was the bullet that struck Joseph in the right breast that delivered the fatal injury. The indictment prepared by United States Attorney William Elliott for the October 1844 term of Hancock County Circuit Court described Joseph's mortal wound, "in and upon the right breast of him the said Joseph Smith a little below the right pap of him the said Joseph Smith one mortal wound of the depth of six inches and of the breadth of one inch of which said mortal wound he the said Joseph Smith, then and there instantly died." One of the witnesses at the 1845 trial similarly testified that he "examined [Joseph's] wounds. He was shot in the right breast, abdomen and left shoulder. Shot a little below the right pap . . . The wound in the breast was mortal, think it was made with a rifle ball."[20]

In all probability, Joseph Smith was shot no more than once—in the thigh—while he remained in the upper room of the jail. His remaining wounds were inflicted by a four-man firing squad. The shot in his right breast, which would have proved fatal, was fired by John C. Elliott (no relation to U.S. Attorney Elliott), known to the Mormons of Nauvoo as a Warsaw-area schoolteacher. No one suspected that Elliott, infamous for his part in the December 1843 kidnapping of Daniel Avery, was an undercover deputy United States marshal from Ohio. Overlooked as a primary suspect during the grand jury proceedings in the fall of 1844 and seldom mentioned during the 1845 trial, Elliott's role in the murder of Joseph Smith has gone almost unnoticed by later writers.

Through the early 1840s, John C. Elliott worked as a woodcutter contracting with landowners to harvest timber on unimproved land near Hamilton on the Great Miami River north of Cincinnati, Ohio. From 1842–43 he helped Cincinnatian Jacob Burnet settle a major logging claim in Burnet's favor, leaving him indebted to the young Butler County woodsman. Burnet's bond to John C. was reinforced by the fact that Elliott's

---

19. John Taylor's account in Doctrine and Covenants 135 has Joseph Smith shot in the window and falling dead to the ground below and then shot again after he was already a lifeless corpse. Gordon B. Hinckley's *Truth Restored* (written before he was sustained as president of the church in 1995), indicates, "With bullets bursting through the door, Joseph sprang to the window. Three bullets struck him almost simultaneously, two coming from the door and one from the window. Dying, he fell from the open window, exclaiming, 'O Lord, my God!'" (78–79). A similar view is presented in *Fulness of Times*, 283.

20. William Elliott indictment, October 1844, LDS Archives. Jonas Hobart 1845 trial testimony (Sharp, *Trial*, 2).

uncle, the Reverend Arthur W. Elliott, had been a major contributor to William Henry Harrison's presidential campaign of 1840. (Burnet was Harrison's campaign manager.) By mid-1843, however, the younger Elliott was unemployed; his bankruptcy claim (on a debt of $15.38) had been denied. Desperate for work, Elliott's appointment as a deputy United States marshal was probably made at his uncle's request.[21]

In mid-November of 1843, Elliott departed Hamilton by flatboat, caught a steamer in Cincinnati, and disembarked at the Warsaw dock a week later. (Is it coincidence that Elliott departed Ohio shortly after Henry Clay received Joseph Smith's presidential inquiry?) Elliott boarded with Schrench Freeman of Green Plains, "about four miles and a half south of Warsaw." His physical appearance was singular. Elliott

> looked to be a man of some twenty six or eight years; nearly five feet eight inches tall; stoutly built, and athletic. He had on a jeans coat, with large pearl buttons, which was united at the upper part of his breast in a careless manner. The pants were taken from casinett [sic] and were considerably tattered. This dress was covered by an overcoat, cut from a green Mackinaw blanket. When he doffed his white nutria hat, it disclosed a prominent forehead and a rather disordered head of black hair. His countenance was dark; his eyes were hazel and sunk to a considerable depth in his head, over which jutted out his heavy dark eyebrows, which a continual scowl knit closely together, giving him at once a savage and heartless look . . . he flourished a pearl handled dirk knife, which he plied with considerable dexterity in the cavity of his ample mouth, which filled the office of a tooth-pick.[22]

To make his sudden arrival in Green Plains appear less conspicuous, Elliott posed as a schoolmaster, no easy task for a woodsman more at home in the wilderness than among civil society. Although many suspected his occupation was hardly that of a teacher (more likely, "teaching the young . . . how to shoot," said one), Elliott's ties to Jacob Burnet, Hamilton, Ohio, and the 1844 Whig presidential race were never revealed publicly during his Illinois sojourn.[23]

---

21. Cone, *Biographical and Historical Sketches*, 184. John C. Elliott's 1842 deposition makes it clear that Elliott was personally acquainted with the Cincinnati businessman: "In August or Sept 1840 I called on Jacob Burnet to leace a part of the land spoken of and he replied that he had given the land to his sun William." The details of the trial of Jacob Burnet vs. Hall and Lee are in Butler County Chancery Record, Vol. 8, 366–70 [June Term 1843]. John C. Elliott is not mentioned in the summary. All Butler County (Ohio) Records Center. "Rev. A. W. Elliott," *Hamilton Telegraph*, 14 September 1848. *A History and Biographical Cyclopedia of Butler County, Ohio*, 365. Heizer, *Hamilton in the Making*, 307–8. "Application of John C. Elliott for the benefit of Insolvency," 23 December 1842. (Butler County (Ohio) Records Center). See also Butler County Common Pleas Record, 20.394 [1842]. Case was "dismissed at the costs of the said applicant." Deputy appointments were chiefly the result of the political spoils system. Note also Henry Clay to John Woods, 17 August 1842, quoted in *Papers of Henry Clay* 9:760, and John McLean's 1847 case, in which he permitted deputy U.S. marshals to cross state lines (Calhoun, *The Lawmen*, 62). Elliott's presence in Illinois would not have been that unusual.

22. Elliott's actual arrival in Warsaw and his precise mode of transportation is not recorded. His description is from "Examination of John C. Elliott," *Nauvoo Neighbor*, 19 February 1845.

23. "Kidnapping," *Times and Seasons*, 1 November 1843 [sic, for 20 December 1843] (shoot quote). On Elliott as a schoolmaster, see also Woodruff, *Journal*, 18 December 1843. Daniel Avery affidavit, in Smith, *History of the Church* 6:145–46.

Elliott's account of his involvement in the murder of Joseph Smith was preserved by an acquaintance, Stephen D. Cone, a Hamilton, Ohio, newspaperman and local historian. Cone included Elliott's remarkable life story in his 1896 volume of biographical sketches of prominent individuals with ties to southwest Ohio. As if to ensure it would not be missed by even casual readers, Elliott's entry is by far the longest, sandwiched between the lives of Ohio's governors and congressmen.

Cone recorded that Elliott, as a deputy U.S. marshal, had responded to a "secret national call" to kill the Mormon leader after Smith withdrew support for existing political parties and "asserted that the government was to be conducted by Joe Smith, as the servant of God." Prior to his departure from Ohio, Elliott was provided with a large bore long rifle made by a local Butler County gunsmith.

On the day of the attack, Elliott said he was "one of the advance assailants," who, after overpowering the guard, entered the jail. Cone reported that "Joe Smith attempted to escape by jumping from the second story window and fell against the curb of an old fashioned well . . . while in a sitting position, the conspirators dispatched him with four rifle balls through the body. The rifle that John C. Elliott carried . . . was the largest bore in the attacking party. Upon examination of Smith's body it was found that John C. Elliott had fired the fatal shot." Elliott took the gun with him when he returned to Ohio in 1850. The rifle remained in the possession of a Hamilton, Ohio, family through the late 1890s. It has since disappeared.[24]

Elliott's highly placed political connections, together with his considerable native ability, enabled him to elude justice. Elliott remained in hiding for several years following the Carthage incident and only returned to his home near Hamilton, Ohio, in late 1849. During the 1850s Elliott served as Butler County deputy sheriff, Hamilton City marshal, and a deputy U.S. marshal for Ohio's Southern District. It was in this last capacity that Elliott became one of the principal defendants in a fugitive slave case brought before the United States Supreme Court in 1857. At the outbreak of the Civil War, forty-four-year-old Elliott enlisted as a private in the Ohio Volunteers. Plagued by poor health throughout his military service, he died of a ruptured blood vessel during a company wrestling match in Taylorsville, Kentucky.[25]

It remains unclear as to why Elliott—a backwoodsman from Hamilton, Ohio—would have been chosen to spearhead the assassination of the Mormon prophet in western Illinois. Certainly there were other men "perfectly devoid of fear" who would have served just as well. One potentially important fact in this regard is that Laomi Rigdon, brother of Mormon leader Sidney Rigdon, was a prominent physician from Hamilton, Ohio, and, moreover, a noted southwest Ohio Whig. (See Chapter One.) Furthermore, Anthony Howard Dunlevy, of Lebanon, Ohio, a legal partner of Supreme Court justice (and presidential hopeful) John McLean as well as Laomi and Sidney Rigdon's brother-in-law, was in Hancock County at the time of Joseph Smith's murder. Dunlevy's presence in Illinois in June of 1844 makes absolutely no sense unless it had something to do with the demise of the Mormon prophet.

---

24. Cone, *Biographical and Historical Sketches*, 184–85, 188.
25. The case is reviewed in Prince, "Rescue Case of 1857." Calhoun, *The Lawmen*, 82–84. Campbell, *The Slave Catchers*, 161–64.

It should also be noted that Elliott was not the only person engaged in the murders at Carthage with ties to southwest Ohio. Late in life Warsaw militiaman William Chittenden, one of the "Chittenden boys" and an advance assailant at the jail, admitted he "was present when Smith, the Mormon prophet, was killed. He knew the men who fired the fatal shots—there were four of them." The young Chittenden, coincidentally, was born and raised in Oxford, Ohio, where his father, Abraham, was the founding master of the Oxford Masonic Lodge. Oxford was just five miles from Darrtown, the boyhood home of John C. Elliott. Both would have been about 16–17 years old when the Chittenden family moved to the Illinois frontier in 1833. It is possible the two men knew each other as youths and renewed their acquaintance in Warsaw. True to the oath of silence sworn by the assailants, Chittenden named no names.[26]

At least two of the other men in the four-man firing squad can be identified with certainty. James Belton, a member of the Warsaw Rifle Company under Captain Jacob C. Davis, left Illinois shortly after the murder of Joseph Smith and made his home in Mount Airy, North Carolina. In 1898, when he was near death, Belton called a Methodist pastor to his bedside. "There is something I want to tell you, something I have had on my conscience a long time," he said. "I am going to die, and I want to make a full confession before I pass on." Significantly, Belton presents the identical scenario as put forward by Elliott and Cone, namely that the same men who entered the jail also formed the four-man firing squad near the well curb and were responsible for Joseph Smith's death.

Belton admitted that he and "three other men murdered Joseph Smith in Carthage, Ill., in 1844." About a dozen men met in Carthage the night before, he said, and "pledged that they would neither eat nor sleep until Smith was dead." They had planned to murder Smith in jail, "but somehow the man escaped by jumping through a window . . . the blow stunned him so he lay on the ground until the four men," including Belton, "ran around to where he was." Once in position, the men shot the prophet propped against the well curb.[27]

William Vorhees was the third gunman at the well. Like Elliott and Belton, Vorhees participated in the initial assault on the jail but was wounded in the shoulder by Joseph Smith during the altercation on the second-story landing. Shortly after the murders Jeremiah Willey, a Mormon resident of Warsaw (who lived "on Mr. Pinchback's Farm," where the Warsaw militiamen regrouped following their assault on the jail) was told that Vorhees "shot [Joseph Smith] from outside of the prison." After Joseph fell from the window, Vorhees turned the prophet over, cursed, and struck him as he lay against the well curb. "Vorus then left him," the informant said,

---

26. Gregg, *History of Hancock County*, 659.

27. "Man Who Helped Kill Mormon Head In 1844 Confessed in Mount Airy," *Mount Airy News*, 24 February 1927. This account concludes, somewhat inaccurately, "and one of the number shot him through the head and killed him." An abbreviated version of Belton's account consonant with the traditional LDS view of the murder relates that "as the Mormon leader leaped out of a window, [the mob] riddled his body with bullets." ("Death Bed Story Reveals Murderer of Prophet," *Deseret News*, 18 February 1927 and "Anachronisms, Et Cetera," *Saints' Herald*, 5 October 1946, 19). Belton's militia service record can be found with Militia records, Chicago Historical Society. Lundwall, *Fate of the Persecutors*, 305–6, contains a mythical rendering of Belton's later life.

after which "there were more guns fired at him." Vorhees later received a "fine suit of broad cloth" from the people of Green Plains and Warsaw "for [his] bravery." This version of events is confirmed by William Daniels's July 4 affidavit and his grand jury testimony of October 1844 (before his account was "amplified" by Lyman O. Little-field), in which he recalled that when Joseph "fell near the well" one of the men "went and raised him up" and cursed the prophet. "They then shot him."[28]

The identity of the fourth gunman is less certain. Two possible candidates stand out. One was Jacob C. Davis (mentioned above), a Democratic state legislator and captain of the Warsaw Rifle Company. Although Davis later claimed he had "finished" Joseph Smith, it is not certain if his remark was intended to refer to his personal involvement or simply to the actions of the men under his command (i.e. Belton).[29] Certainly Davis's position as the leader of a rifle company presupposes considerable skill with firearms. He would have been a logical choice to ensure that the job was done. If Davis was indeed one of the four gunmen at the well (and this is by no means certain), he was the only one who joined the Masonic fraternity; Davis was raised to the Master Mason degree following his indictment by the October 1844 grand jury.[30]

Another candidate for the fourth man at the well is William N. Grover, captain of the Warsaw Cadets. Like Davis, he was indicted for the murder of Joseph Smith in the fall of 1844. During the 1845 trial, a witness (whose testimony would later be thrown out of court) claimed that Grover had said "he had killed Old Jo." With the charges against Davis and Grover dropped for "lack of legal evidence," the likelihood of establishing with any degree of certainty which of the two was indeed the fourth gunman at the well remains problematic.[31]

Furthermore, as part of the effort to protect the men in the firing squad from discovery, several conspirators and their associates—before the 1845 trial, in perjured trial testimony, and even decades later—were insistent in their claims that Joseph Smith was not shot after he fell from the window. Others argued that if he was shot by the well, the "semi-barbarous" Missourians were to blame.[32]

G. T. M. Davis, for example, wrote the following account of Joseph Smith's last moments in his July 1844 pamphlet *An Authentic Account of the Massacre of Joseph Smith*:

> Upon reaching the window and throwing aside the curtain, and perceiving unexpectedly, a large armed force in disguise at the end of the building, upon the ground, he exclaimed, "Oh! My God," when a number of muskets were, with the rapidity of

---

28. William Daniels, October 1844 grand jury testimony, P13, f41, Community of Christ, Archives (wounded in shoulder). Jeremiah Willey statement reporting a conversation with Henry Mathias on 27 June 1844, 13 August 1844. Each of these accounts provides a slightly different rendition of what Vorhees said to Joseph as he lay by the well. See also Turley, *Victims*.

29. Eliza Jane Graham, 1845 trial testimony (Sharp, *Trial*, 20).

30. On Jacob C. Davis, see Eliza Jane Graham, 1845 trial testimony (Sharp, *Trial*, 18–21). George Walker, 1845 trial testimony, said he "heard [Davis] say, he'd be d——d if he was going to kill men confined in prison." (Sharp, *Trial*, 4). Which Davis is to be believed?

31. Hill and Oaks, *Carthage Conspiracy*, 147. On dropping of charges, 173.

32. Hay, "The Mormon Prophet's Tragedy," 676.

thought, discharged at the unfortunate wretch, five or six of which took effect. He fell head forward to the earth, and was dead, as I am informed by one who examined him immediately on falling, when he struck the ground. He was wounded in the breast by five or six different shots, either of which would, in all human probability, have proved fatal.

Later in the booklet Davis taunted his readers. "The expectations of the public, may possibly, anticipate a disclosure of the names of the persons connected with the destruction of the Smiths, and the extent to which the citizens, generally, were privy to the affair. To say that I do not know *any* who participated in the attack, would not be true. But the circumstances under which I came in possession of that knowledge, were of that nature, that no inducement on earth, could prompt, *or coerce* me, to divulge their names."[33]

During the 1845 trial, Thomas Dixon testified for the prosecution that he "did not see [Joseph] set up by the well curb. He set himself up. Did not see any strange miraculous light, or four men shoot Smith, or any one paralyzed." Similarly, Thomas R. Griffiths, who years later discovered the June 27, 1844, coroner's inquest, recalled that he "was eighteen years old when the Smiths were killed, and witnessed the tragedy, he being a member of the old Carthage Greys. He says Smith was not shot at after he fell from the jail window."[34]

One of the most influential articles on the murder of the Mormon prophet was written more than two decades after the event by John Hay, the son of Charles Hay, Warsaw militia surgeon and former Kentucky neighbor of Henry Clay. The younger Hay, who served as secretary to Abraham Lincoln and later became his biographer, was just seven years old at the time of Joseph Smith's death. Following a visit to his hometown of Warsaw in 1869, where he interviewed some of the surviving assailants and examined trial documents in the Carthage courthouse, Hay composed his own version of events surrounding the death of the first Mormon prophet for the Boston literary magazine *The Atlantic Monthly.* Called "The Mormon Prophet's Tragedy," Hay's description of Joseph's final moments includes the scene at the well. "With his last dying energies he gathered himself up, and leaned in a sitting posture against the rude stone well-curb." In place of the selectmen from the Warsaw militia, however, Hay inserts a "squad of Missourians who were standing by the fence." These men "leveled their pieces at him, and, before they could see him again for the smoke they made, Joe Smith was dead." Hay's critical substitution of actors in this drama (keeping in mind that his effort was more on the level of popular literature than serious history) effectively deflected blame away from the actual participants in the assault on the jail, many of whom at the time of his writing were still living in Hancock County. Hay's account also served to reinforce the popularly held belief that the Missourians were the prime movers behind the conspiracy to murder the Mormon prophet.[35]

---

33. Davis, *Authentic Account,* 23.
34. Thomas Dixon, 1845 trial testimony (Sharp, *Trial,* 18). "Coroner's Jury Verdict in Murder of Joseph Smith," [unknown newspaper] 2–6–58.
35. John Hay, "The Mormon Prophet's Tragedy," *The Atlantic Monthly* 24 (1869):676. Hay apparently follows O. C. Skinner's closing arguments at the 1845 trial, in which the latter claimed, "The fact that

In 1886 Jason H. Sherman, then an attorney in upstate New York, published his reminiscences. An acknowledged participant in the attack on Carthage jail, Sherman stressed, "But it is not true, as was sometimes reported, that his assailants leaned his body up against the curb and made it a target. * * *" (Asterisks, signifying missing words, are in the original.) Likewise, in 1890 Hancock historian Thomas Gregg (the same individual who in 1844 was campaigning for Henry Clay in Rock Island, Illinois,) disputed the claim that a firing squad shot the prophet as he was propped up by the well curb. "This, from reliable information, we believe was not the case." Gregg's unnamed source was identified only by his initials, J. H. S., "a highly intelligent gentleman who was a resident of Carthage at that time and well-known in the county." That man was, of course, Jason H. Sherman. Even in their old age Sherman and Gregg were intent upon keeping the identity of the assailants a secret.[36]

At the end of the century, by which time most of the participants had passed away, the scene at the well could go unmentioned. William R. Hamilton, son of Artois Hamilton (the proprietor of Carthage's main hotel), perhaps the youngest member of the Carthage Greys in 1844, and one of the last surviving eyewitnesses, concluded a 1902 recounting of events at Carthage with these telling words: "There are many facts and names of persons connected with that tragedy, which are now lost to the world—where it seems best to let them remain." Hamilton's account of the assassination makes no mention of a firing squad.[37]

Clay's Men

"There is more truth whispered 'round Hal,
than your philosophy ever dreamed of."

appended to "The Murders at Carthage,"
Nauvoo Neighbor, October 30, 1844[38]

"The Murders at Carthage" reported on the October indictments of nine Hancock County men for the deaths of Joseph and Hyrum Smith the previous June. The cryptic epigram appended to the notice is a reference to Henry Clay, who, following his successful negotiations for the Treaty of Ghent in 1814, became popularly known as Prince Hal, named after a character in Shakespeare's play Henry IV.

The unimaginable "truth" alluded to in this verse was recognition that Joseph Smith's assassination was looked upon favorably by Clay and his political managers. Numerous editorials in the Mormon press chastised Henry Clay (and the Whigs generally) for not condemning the Carthage affair and insisting that the men

neither of them [Franklin Worrell and two other witnesses] saw one person among them he knew is the clearest proof that they were not the Warsaw troops but others and strangers in the county," in other words, Missourians. (29 May 1845, Wilford C. Wood Collection, trial transcript, 96).

36. Published in the *Ithaca Daily Journal* 26 April 1886, quoted in Marsh, "Mormons in Hancock County," 52–53, Gregg, *Prophet of Palmyra*, 278–80, Scofield, *History of Hancock County*, 84–87, Hallwas and Launius, *Cultures in Conflict*, 228–31. Gregg, *The Prophet of Palmyra*, 284.

37. William R. Hamilton to Foster Walker, 24 December 1902, Martin Collection, Regional Archives, Western Illinois University.

38. "The Murders at Carthage," *Nauvoo Neighbor*, 30 October 1844.

responsible be brought to justice. Notably, Clay himself never publicly commented on the death of his fellow presidential candidate, nor did he offer condolences to the Saints on their loss. Clay's silence meant that he was willing to throw away the Mormon vote and with it the potential to carry the state of Illinois for the Whigs. With the presidential election just days away, this article strikes once more at the Whig leader, reminding its readers that the Latter-day Saints had little reason to trust Clay's leadership and should support instead the Democratic candidate, James K. Polk.

Although some knew that the conspiracy to murder Joseph Smith went beyond the local level, few individuals, in Hancock County or elsewhere, had the whole picture. John C. Elliott, the main shooter at Carthage jail, for example, acknowledged that he went to western Illinois from Ohio in response to a "secret national call." While it is likely that he knew who was responsible, Elliott failed to name the men behind the appeal. Joseph Smith's bodyguard, Stephen Markham, recalled that when he broke up the secret tribunal being held at the Hamilton Hotel in Carthage the night before Joseph's murder, the minutes book revealed "there were delegates in the meeting from every state in the Union except three." Since the volume was in his possession only for a short time, Markham does not supply a list of those present. On the day of the assault, Hancock County Sheriff Minor R. Deming warned the governor that the Whigs were planning to take the life of Joseph Smith while he remained in jail. In the weeks following the assassination, Deming continued to insist (both privately and in public) that the Whigs were also behind the cover-up and protection of those engaged in the murder. Some months later, Mormon Almon C. Babbitt informed the Illinois legislature that the press used to publish the *Nauvoo Expositor* had been "established for political purposes by the Whigs." Perhaps fearing possible repercussions if they spoke more freely, neither informant named names.

Because the men engaged in the conspiracy to murder Joseph Smith were careful to destroy any written documentation that might tie them to the crime, the task becomes that of identifying what significant linkages existed between the men involved in the murder of Joseph Smith and the Whig hierarchy in Illinois. The sociogram on the following page clarifies these relationships.

The sociogram highlights the fact that the major Illinois players engaged in the assassination conspiracy and cover-up—Abraham Jonas, Orville Hickman Browning, G. T. M. Davis, and John J. Hardin—had direct ties to Henry Clay as well as the Mormon leadership at Nauvoo, and were among Henry Clay's chief political managers in the Illinois campaign.

Joseph Smith–*Abraham Jonas*–Henry Clay

Beginning with his rise to the position of grand master of the Kentucky Lodge in the 1820s and continuing through to his election to the Illinois state legislature in 1842, Abraham Jonas maintained a long-standing personal and political relationship with Henry Clay. Jonas was responsible for the successful establishment of a Mormon Masonic Lodge at Nauvoo and made Joseph Smith and Sidney Rigdon "masons at sight." Three potential links to the murder conspiracy have been identified:

Link 1   Jonas was a member of the Whig Central Committee for Illinois's Fifth District.

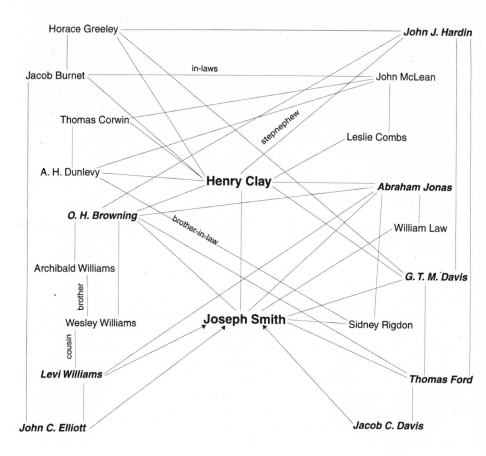

Link 2:   Jonas supplied the Nauvoo dissidents with the press used to print the *Expositor*. The publication and subsequent destruction of the *Expositor* press led directly to Joseph Smith's death less than three weeks later.

Link 3:   Jonas was delegated by Governor Thomas Ford to act as a liaison with the Mormons at Nauvoo following the murders.

Joseph Smith–*Orville Hickman Browning*–Henry Clay

O. H. Browning had a lengthy personal and professional relationship with Joseph Smith, John J. Hardin, and Archibald and Wesley Williams, cousins of militia leader Colonel Levi Williams. Browning's cousin, Jonathan Browning, converted to Mormonism and became a prominent Nauvoo (and later Utah) gunsmith. At least four significant links have been identified:

Link 1:   O. H. Browning targeted the Latter-day Saints as a potential Whig political asset and promoted efforts to obtain the Mormon vote for Henry Clay.

Link 2:   O. H. Browning met secretly with Henry Clay in late July 1844.

Link 3:   O. H. Browning (together with E. D. Baker) was responsible for ensuring that Levi Williams and Thomas Sharp were released from custody, even though the two men were charged with murder.

Link 4:   O. H. Browning represented the men accused of the murder of Joseph Smith.

Browning reportedly withdrew his candidacy in the 1844 U.S. Senate race on account of poor health. Shortly after the murders of Joseph and Hyrum Smith, Browning departed (in late June or early July) for the Blue Lick Salt Springs of northern Kentucky in order to recuperate from his illness and remained there through early August. How much Browning's Kentucky sojourn was for health reasons (the weeklong journey from Illinois to Kentucky would have been perilous in itself) and how much was because of politics is hard to say. Certainly both objectives came into play.

While in Kentucky, Browning did his best to keep his presence from becoming public knowledge. Local newspapers, eager for news about the Mormon War, made no mention of his return. Furthermore, Browning's presence at political rallies would have strengthened Henry Clay's claims that he could win Illinois in November, yet Browning declined all invitations to address Whig gatherings.

Henry Clay visited the Blue Lick Springs, about a day's journey northward from his Ashland estate near Lexington, in late July. The two men spoke privately for three hours. At the conclusion of the interview Browning wrote to his wife, Eliza, who had stayed behind in Illinois. "Mr. Clay, arrived here last evening," Browning informed her on July 24. "I was introduced to him this morning. We took a walk after breakfast, and had a conversation of three hours. I was never more charmed with a man. So plain, so unaffectedly kind, so dignified, so unaustentatious, so simple in his manners and conversation, that he is irresistably fascinating. When I was introduced to him he said, 'Ah Mr. Browning, I am very happy to meet you. You are of Quincy, Ills. You were the Whig candidate for Congress there last year. I think you are the brother in law of Capt O'Bannon.'" Clay, Browning marveled, "seemed to know as much about me as an old acquaintance." Browning promised to visit Clay again the following week before returning to Illinois.

Precisely what the two Whigs discussed during their private meetings in July of 1844 is not known. With the exception of Browning's letter to his wife, what written evidence there once was, if any, has long since disappeared. There can be no doubt, however, that the two men spoke about politics and the upcoming presidential election. At the very end of his July 1844 letter to Eliza, Browning commented that "the whigs are thoroughly awake in this state, and there is no doubt about Judge Owsley's [August] election [to Kentucky's governorship], tho his majority will not be as great as Mr. Clay's [in November]." How much Henry Clay knew about the Illinois conspiracy to murder Joseph Smith can only be guessed at. It is certain, at the very least, that Clay was well informed of political events transpiring on the Illinois frontier. Browning's comments during his visit to Kentucky are sufficient evidence of this, not to mention Clay's decades-long friendship with Abraham Jonas, the part played by Clay's stepnephew John J. Hardin in his 1844 presidential campaign, and Clay's comment to Joseph Smith (in late 1843) that he had "viewed with lively interest the progress of the Latter-day Saints."[39]

Furthermore, Clay's response to his receipt of G. T. M. Davis's *An Authentic Account of the Murder of Joseph Smith* offers confirmation that he followed Davis's advice that the Whigs should "pass the Mormons by *sub silentio*" to the letter. Clay marked his return correspondence to Davis "Private" and wrote simply, "I received your favor." Clay had no desire to be linked with or even comment on the Mormon murders.[40]

Joseph Smith–*George T. M. Davis*–Henry Clay

Davis was Henry Clay's legal representative in Alton, Illinois, and a regular correspondent of John J. Hardin. At least four significant links can be identified:

Link 1:   Davis managed the Illinois Whig newspaper campaign aimed at convincing Joseph Smith (and his followers) to vote Whig in the upcoming presidential election.

Link 2:   Davis attended the Whig National Convention in Baltimore in May 1844, where he met with Horace Greeley and other national Whig leaders.

Link 3:   Davis participated in a secret meeting of national political delegates at the Hamilton Hotel in Carthage, Illinois, on the night of June 26, 1844.

Link 4:   Davis wrote his *Authentic Account* in an effort to disprove claims of Whig involvement in the murder of Joseph Smith, as well as to absolve Democratic

39. O. H. Browning to Eliza Browning, 24 July 1844, Illinois Historical Survey, Urbana. Henry Clay to Joseph Smith, 15 November 1843, in Hopkins and Hargreaves, *Papers of Henry Clay* 9:890–91. Smith, *History of the Church* 6:376.

40. Henry Clay ["Private"] to G. T. M. Davis, 31 August 1844, in Hopkins and Hargreaves, *Papers of Henry Clay* 10:107. G. T. M. Davis to John J. Hardin, 29 December 1843, Hardin Papers, Chicago Historical Society. Significantly, Clay's response to Davis would indicate that Davis wanted Clay to make a public statement on the naturalization issue, although apparently not to the Mormon question directly.

governor Ford of any complicity in the affair. Copies of the booklet were sent to Henry Clay and Horace Greeley, among others.

Joseph Smith–*John J. Hardin*–Henry Clay

Hardin was Henry Clay's stepnephew. Hardin and Henry Clay's brother, Porter Clay, both resided in Jacksonville, Illinois.

Link 1:   As the only Illinois Whig in the U.S. Congress from 1843 to 1845, Hardin organized and oversaw Henry Clay's Illinois campaign.

Link 2:   Hardin was present at the 1844 national Whig convention in Baltimore.

Link 3:   Hardin was partly responsible for ensuring that Levi Williams and Thomas Sharp were released from custody even though the two men were charged with Joseph Smith's murder.

Link 4:   Hardin was delegated by Governor Thomas Ford to oversee military operations in Hancock County in the fall of 1844 and to negotiate the Mormon departure from the state in 1846.

Below the state-level managers were the local operatives, men who were directly engaged on the ground. Of that group, John C. Elliott and Levi Williams were by far the most important. Colonel Levi Williams orchestrated the main assault on the Carthage jail, and undercover Deputy U. S. Marshal Elliott was the leader of the men who actually stormed the jail and was at the head of the four-man firing squad that shot the Mormon prophet. Each drew upon the resources of Hancock County's Anti-Mormon Party and the local militia organization. As far as is known at present, neither had a personal relationship with Henry Clay, although together they had significant ties to Illinois and Ohio Whig leaders:

Levi Williams–Abraham Jonas–Henry Clay

Levi Williams–Wesley Williams–O. H. Browning-Henry Clay

John C. Elliott–Jacob Burnet–Henry Clay

John C. Elliott–Levi Williams–Abraham Jonas–Henry Clay

From the perspective provided by these documented linkages, the initial decision to assassinate Joseph Smith was more than likely made by Whig political managers in Illinois, quite possibly at the suggestion of Abraham Jonas, O. H. Browning, or G. T. M. Davis. To what extent national Whig leaders, such as John J. Hardin, Jacob Burnet, or Henry Clay were aware of the Illinois plot to assassinate Joseph Smith remains an open question.

The sociogram does not assist in answering some additional questions about certain key players within the conspiracy. For example, based on available evidence, only two Democrats with state-level connections—Governor Thomas Ford and legislator Jacob C. Davis—are identified as having significant roles in the murders. It is quite likely that other prominent Democrats also assisted in the plan to kill Joseph Smith. For example, what did Thomas Benton, a Democrat from

Missouri and longtime Mormon opponent, have to do with the murder? Did Stephen A. Douglas, one-time friend of Joseph Smith, take an active part in the conspiracy? Their involvement, although suspected, remains unclear.[41]

What was Sidney Rigdon's contribution to the assassination plot? Rigdon certainly had a motive (recall Joseph Smith's infatuation with his daughter, Nancy) and he had opportunity. Rigdon was in a position to view the goings-on at Nauvoo at close range, and had all the necessary ties to the anti-Mormons of Hancock County as well as the Whig leadership in Ohio. (Keep in mind that Rigdon's brother-in-law, Anthony Howard Dunlevy, was a legal partner of Judge John McLean, then presiding over the U.S. Circuit Court in Springfield, and was himself present in Hancock County at the time Joseph Smith was murdered.) Not to mention that Rigdon was Joseph Smith's vice-presidential running mate. The disturbing fact that there is no record of Rigdon ever having made a campaign speech in support of Joseph Smith is telling. Barring the discovery of implicating documentation, however, Rigdon's place in the larger drama must remain somewhere left of center stage. It cannot be forgotten than Rigdon's mental health was very poor during this period, and the likelihood that he would be trusted with an insider's knowledge of (and involvement in) the grand conspiracy is quite small.

Due to a lack of confirming documentary evidence, some potentially critical players are not included in the sociogram. What of Dr. William Gano Goforth, the Clay Whig who attended the state political convention in Nauvoo and later joined the Mormon church? Or William H. Roosevelt, the Warsaw Whig (and scion of the New York Roosevelt family) who was instrumental in spreading false rumors about the assault on the jail? Who were their primary contacts within the Whig organization? And what about Sylvester Emmons, non-Mormon editor of the *Nauvoo Expositor*? What was his relationship, if any, to the larger conspiracy?

And then there is the matter of Dr. Wall Southwick, who is perhaps the most enigmatic character in this entire drama. When "Dr. Southwick" first makes his appearance in our story he presents himself as the forlorn survivor of a steamboat collision, bereft of money and possessions. He writes to the prophet Joseph for assistance from Centerville, Kentucky, a few short miles from Henry Clay's Ashland estate. Once in Illinois Southwick actively promotes Joseph Smith's plans to establish a Mormon kingdom in Texas, gains valuable intelligence about military preparations against the Mormons, and becomes on intimate terms with Governor Ford. Southwick is present at the star chamber meeting in Carthage the night before the murders, retrieves the secretary's minutes book detailing the proceedings (it was never passed on to Stephen Markham as promised), and in the weeks following attempts to quash William Daniel's implicating testimony with the offer of a large cash bribe. Southwick then simply disappears. Since his name appears nowhere in the U.S. census records for 1840 or 1850 and is absent from available Southwick genealogies, it is

---

41. In 1846 Douglas wrote to John J. Hardin, who had already left for the Mexican War, "Let [Mormons] leave in peace." Stephen A. Douglas to John J. Hardin, 2 May 1846, Hardin Papers, Chicago Historical Society, quoted in Cox, *Hardin*, 145. William Law recalled that Douglas was present at least one of the Hancock County anti-Mormon meetings in June of 1844. (Interview, in Cook, *William Law*, 126). This has not been confirmed.

uncertain if "Wall Southwick" is the name of an actual person. Was he, like John C. Elliott, working undercover? If so, for whom was he working? And what became of the incriminating and potentially explosive minutes book?[42]

In the end, the question confronting the reader of *Junius and Joseph* is whether the murder of the Mormon prophet Joseph Smith was simply the outcome of circumstances and events that led inexorably and inevitably to his death or if his assassination was the result of an active conspiracy that extended well beyond the state of Illinois. The presence of undercover Deputy U.S. Marshal John C. Elliott at Carthage, together with the political meeting at the Hamilton Hotel in Carthage the night before the murders, attended by representatives from nearly every state in the Union, supports the view that Joseph Smith's murder *was* a premeditated action motivated by forces (and individuals) far beyond the western Illinois prairie. Even so, the extent to which national political leaders (both Whig and Democrat) were directly engaged in the Carthage affair may never be known for certain.

---

42. On Southwick, see Van Wagenen, *The Texas Republic*, 47, 49, 50, 73, 97, note 40. Wall Southwick to Joseph Smith, 1 June 1844, in *Warsaw Signal*, 31 July 1844. Stephen Markham to Wilford Woodruff, 20 June 1856, LDS Archives. On Southwick's offer of a bribe to Daniels to "clear out," see Daniels's cross-examination during the 1845 trial, in Sharp, *Trial*, 12-13.

Epilogue

Two Endings

The Republican Ascendancy

BY LATE NOVEMBER 1844, PLANS were underway to organize a new political party to oppose the rising power of the Democrats. A meeting was scheduled for St. Louis in the spring anticipating the formation of an "American Republican Party" to replace the fragmented Whig organization. G. T. M. Davis violently disagreed with the strategy and remained unrepentantly Whig. "The great and important question now is, what are we as a party to do?" He wrote to John J. Hardin in Washington, D.C., requesting the congressman exert political pressure where it was most needed. "Our friends need checking and a few letters from prominent men in whom they have confidence, would prevent their taking steps which in the end may prove destructive of us as a party." Whatever assistance Hardin could give Davis to prevent the disintegration of the Whig party would be short-lived.[1]

One of the first challenges to President James K. Polk's new administration was conflict over the admission of Texas into the Union. With a standing American army of only 5,500 men, thousands of soldiers were desperately needed to support Texan claims of independence from Mexico. In May of 1846, three months after the beginning of the Mormon exodus from Nauvoo, John J. Hardin became the first Illinoisan to volunteer and was commissioned a colonel in the U.S. Army. Hardin marched his Illinois Volunteers into the bloodbath of the Mexican-American War and on February 23, 1847, scarcely a month after celebrating his thirty-seventh birthday, was killed at the Battle of Buena Vista. Hardin was just one year younger than the Mormon prophet Joseph when he lost his life to the Carthage assassins.[2]

G. T. M. Davis organized Illinois volunteers from the Alton area and served as an aide-de-camp to General Winfield Scott during his triumphal entry into Mexico City. Following his return to the U.S. in 1847, Davis distanced himself from national politics and died in 1888 after a long and prosperous business career.

Still unable to fully comprehend his disastrous defeat of 1844, and unsuccessful in his final effort to secure the Whig presidential nomination in 1848, Henry Clay died in mid-1852 at the age of seventy-five. He passed away in Washington, D.C., and was laid in state in the rotunda of the capitol, mourned as sorrowfully as any elected

---

1. G. T. M. Davis to John J. Hardin, 24 November 1844, Hardin Papers, Chicago Historical Society.
2. Cox, "Hardin," 187.

president. Jacob Burnet died a year later (at the age of eighty-three) at his home in Cincinnati, best remembered as one of the authors of Ohio's first constitution.

A gathering of Illinois politicians was held at Bloomington on May 29, 1856, to "keep the party of this state under the control of moderate men, and conservative influences." The event marked the formation of the Illinois Republican Party. Archibald Williams was called as temporary chair. Abraham Jonas was present as a delegate. O. H. Browning was on the Committee of Resolutions, where he drafted the state's conservative Republican platform and advocated the nomination of U.S. Supreme Court Judge John McLean as the national Republican nominee for president.[3]

McLean would never achieve his lifelong dream of sitting in the presidential chair. At the June 1856 National Republican Convention held in Philadelphia, Justice McLean was defeated for the Republican nomination by Western explorer John C. Fremont. The Mormons in the distant Territory of Utah were not forgotten. The Republican platform advocated "the right and imperative duty of Congress to prohibit in the Territories those twin relics of barbarism — Polygamy and Slavery."[4]

Four years later, in 1860, O. H. Browning (again together with Abraham Jonas) played a leading role in promoting Abraham Lincoln's ultimately successful Republican bid for president of the U.S. Browning was appointed U.S. senator from Illinois in 1861, to fill the seat vacated by the untimely death of Stephen A. Douglas. Browning assisted Lincoln with his First Inaugural Address and became known as "Lincoln's mouthpiece" in the Senate. Not a candidate for election in 1863, Browning's senate seat was taken by William A. Richardson, a Democratic co-counsel at the 1845 trial of the accused assassins of Joseph Smith. Following his retirement, Browning remained in the nation's capital, where he conducted a successful legal practice. It was then that he became entangled in another presidential murder conspiracy.[5]

* * * * *

Washington, D.C., April 14, 1865. It was Good Friday. General Robert E. Lee of the Confederacy had surrendered at Appomattox Courthouse five days earlier. The Civil War that had raged for more than four years was finally over. Still, the former senator from Illinois was impatient. There were important matters to discuss. After an hour of waiting, Browning was informed that following dinner the president had gone to the theatre without coming up to his room. Browning returned to his house on the Hill and retired for the evening.

The bell at Senator Browning's home rang some time after 11 P.M. There was horrible news. "The President . . . had just been assassinated . . . at Ford's Theatre," Browning wrote in his journal late that night:

> The [U.S.] Marshal W H Lamon [Lemon] has several times within the last two months told me that he believed the President would be assassinated, but I had no fear whatever that such an event would occur . . . It is one of the most stupendous

---

3. Baxter, *Browning*, 85–86.
4. Neely, *Abraham Lincoln Encyclopedia*, 38.
5. Baxter, *Browning*, passim.

crimes that has ever been committed, and I pray God that all the guilty parties may
be ferreted out and brought to condign punishment . . . It must, necessarily, greatly
inflame and exasperate the minds of the people, and, I fear lead to attempts at summary vengeance upon those among us who had been suspected of sympathy with
the rebellion.

The reader of this diary entry must wonder if, as he wrote those impassioned
lines, Browning's thoughts lingered, maybe only for a moment, on the roles he played
in Joseph Smith's political assassination twenty-one years earlier. If so, Browning
never revealed himself.

President Lincoln died at 7:20 the next morning. The body was brought to the
White House shortly after breakfast. "The corpse was laid in the room on the North
side in the second story, opposite Mrs. Lincoln's room," Browning recorded. "His
eyes were both very much protruded—the right one most—and very black and puffy
underneath. No other disfiguration. The skull was opened . . . and the ball removed.
It was a Derringer ball, much flattened on both sides . . . He never had a moments
consciousness after he was shot."[6]

✶ ✶ ✶ ✶ ✶

Browning's unfinished business with the president of the United States concerned
shipments of Southern contraband cotton by Mrs. Lincoln's half-sister, widow of
Benjamin Hardin Helm. In addition, Browning secretly assisted in the defense of two
men implicated in the Lincoln assassination, Dr. Samuel Mudd and Samuel Arnold,
close associates of John Wilkes Booth. Both men were given life sentences.[7]

By his own admission, Browning's sympathies were with the rebellion. He became disaffected with the politics of the Lincoln administration as early as 1862,
opposed Lincoln's Emancipation Proclamation of 1863, and at least twice made efforts to get the president to change it. In Browning's view, slavery was best left to the
exclusive control of individual states and Congress had no power to prohibit it. In
order to understand his opposition, it is significant that Browning was vice president
of the Illinois branch of Henry Clay's American Colonization Society in 1845, the
very time he was serving as defense counsel for the men accused of the murder of
Joseph Smith. Browning remained a supporter of the ACS through the 1860s. He had
"no doubt of the abstract injustice of slavery," Browning wrote in 1854, yet "whilst
the negroes remain in the country, the good of whites & blacks is alike consulted
by preserving the present relations between them." In 1861, Browning proposed to
Lincoln that the U.S. "subjugate the south, establish a black republic, and then place
a protectorate over it." Browning revealed his frustration at Lincoln's administration
to a correspondent in 1864, admitting that he had "never . . . been able to persuade
myself that he [Lincoln] was big enough for his position."[8]

---

6. O. H. Browning, *Diary* 2:18–19 [14 April 1865], 20 [15 April 1865].
7. O. H. Browning, *Diary*, passim. John Wilkes Booth (1838–1865) had a brother named Junius
    Brutus Booth, Jr. (1821–1883). The actors were named in honor of their father Junius Brutus Booth
    (1796–1852), the famed English reformer (John Wilkes) and his unidentified defender (Junius).
8. Neely, *Abraham Lincoln Encyclopedia*, 39.

Browning was appointed secretary of the interior by President Andrew Johnson in 1866, a post he held through the end of Johnson's administration. Just prior to leaving office in early 1869, Johnson pardoned Dr. Samuel Mudd and released Samuel Arnold from custody. Perhaps Browning had succeeded in freeing the two Samuels after all.[9]

Mormonism Transformed?

> *The highest folly that disgraces the United States is that truth and holiness, which combined and practiced, compose religion, should not be mixed with power and policy, which is the essence of government.*

> *Times and Seasons* (Nauvoo), 1844[10]

> *[T]he Church of Jesus Christ of Latter-day Saints holds to the doctrine of the separation of church and state; the non-interference of church authority in political matters; and the absolute freedom and independence of the individual in the performance of his political duties.*

> LDS First Presidency message, 1907[11]

Without question, the martyrdom of Joseph and Hyrum Smith was one of the most significant transitional moments in the early history of the Church of Jesus Christ of Latter-day Saints. Although the oft-repeated claim that Joseph Smith was killed for his religion is true, contrary to popular Mormon belief he was not a victim of "persecuted innocence." Joseph's attempt to establish a Mormon theocratic state in America, described in his own words as a *theo*democracy—"where God and the people hold the power to conduct the affairs of men in righteousness"—was inextricably tied to his belief that he was called to be God's instrument and fulfill the apocalyptic prophecy of Daniel. This visionary path, which led him to run for the U.S. presidency, brought him into direct conflict with American republican political ideals, and ultimately resulted in his assassination. It was left to Brigham Young to establish the Kingdom of God in Utah, beyond the confines of the United States.

The unimaginable loss of the first Mormon prophet cried out for a mythic interpretation that could be made sense of by Latter-day Saints as they went about their daily lives of faithful service. On one level, the martyrdom became the supreme example of the willingness of the early Saints to sacrifice everything for their belief. By a curious inversion, the martyrdom (for nineteenth-century Mormons, at least) also became a symbol of God's protection of the faithful, evidence that He was actively involved in the welfare of His people.

---

9. Chamless, *Lincoln's Assassins.* Browning, *Diary* 2:27, 34.
10. "A Word to the Wise," *Times and Seasons,* 5.11 [1 June 1844], 552, quoted in Banks, "Role of Journalism," 277. Joseph Smith's 1844 letter to Henry Clay was published in the same issue.
11. *Conference Report,* April 1907, 14.

William Daniels (the young apparently unwilling Warsaw militiaman who later converted to Mormonism) interpreted the scene at the well just after Joseph was shot by a firing squad—when one of the mob reportedly attempted to sever Joseph's head from his body but was prevented from doing so by a blinding light from heaven—as the hand of God protecting Joseph's body from mutilation. It was this passage from Daniels's 1845 pamphlet (written, it will be recalled, together with Mormon Lyman O. Littlefield) which led to the court throwing out his entire testimony during the trial of the accused assassins of Joseph Smith, thereby unintentionally assisting in the acquittal of the men held responsible for murdering the first Mormon prophet. Daniels's original version:

> [A member of the mob] gathered a bowie knife for the purpose of severing [Joseph's] head from his body. He raised the knife and was in the attitude of striking, when a light, so sudden and powerful, burst from the heavens upon the bloody scene, (passing its vivid chain between Joseph and his murderers,) that they were struck with terrified awe and filled with consternation. This light, in its appearance and potency, baffles all powers of description. The arm of the ruffian, that held the knife, fell powerless; the muskets of the four, who fired, fell to the ground, and all stood like marble statues, not having the power to move a single limb of their bodies.[12]

Daniels wrote, no doubt with Littlefield's assistance, that "the light that had flashed over the fallen body of the martyr, was in its appearance so strange, and in its effects so miraculous, and so unlike anything I had ever before witnessed, that I could not help but receive it as a convincing testimony sent from God, that Joseph Smith was a Prophet of the Most High God." The light was reproduced in a woodcut engraving in Daniels's booklet and included in a painting displayed in Nauvoo for months afterwards.[13] (see p. 277)

Despite its unintended consequence of freeing the accused murderers from prison, the mythical "light from heaven" episode soon became a vital part of Mormon folklore. The impact of the "light" was so strong that it required the active intervention of a conservative LDS historian-editor to excise the dramatic episode from the pages of official Mormon history and popular consciousness.

The light was featured in an 1851 color lithograph of the "Martyrdom of Joseph and Hiram Smith" dedicated to Orson Hyde, an apostle, Freemason, and Council of Fifty member. Initially published in New York City, the print was available in several different sizes. In the 1851 print a light from heaven breaks through the clouds. At the same time a dramatic figure (dressed in top hat and tails) steps forward with his right arm uplifted. The mobster standing over the body of the now lifeless prophet, face blackened with wet gunpowder, knife raised, looks up at the stranger with wide open eyes, full of fear and unable to move. The four-man firing squad stands to one side, resting almost casually against their long rifles, apparently unaffected by the miraculous apparition.

---

12. Daniels, *Correct Account*, 15.
13. Ibid., 19. Hosea Stout, Diary [10 April 1845], in Stout, *On the Mormon Frontier*, 45. Oaks and Hill, *Carthage Conspiracy*, 135. See also Daniels's testimony during the 1845 trial (Sharp, *Trial*, 6–13).

Illustration from William N. Daniels, *A Correct Account*. Numbers indicate original captions from Daniels: [1] "The Carthage Greys"; [2] Colonel Levi Williams; [3] "The four ruffians who shot Gen. Joseph Smith"; [4] "The well-curb"; [5] "The flash of light"; [6] "Elder Richards at the window of the jail from which Gen. Smith fell"; [7] "Gen. Smith after he was shot"; [8] Ruffian with knife; [9] "The door leading to the entry, through which the murderers entered"; [10] Captain Robert F. Smith; [11] "The mob"; [12] "The point of wood which the mob entered when going to the jail."

Not surprisingly, Orson Hyde incorporated Daniels's story of a heavenly light into a discourse he delivered at the Tabernacle in Salt Lake City on January 3, 1858:

> Did Joseph Smith overcome, even unto death? Yes. Was God with him? Yes, he was. When they were about to cut off his head, behold, the power of the Almighty came down, and the men stood as it were like marble statues: they could not move, but stood there like Lot's wife—not pillars of salt, but pillars of petrified corruption. The power of the Almighty came down with the vivid glare of lightning's flash, and they had no power to take his head off. Was God with him? Yes. Was his death glorious? Yes.[14]

For Apostle Hyde, the story of the four gunmen at the well was evidence that the miracles documented in the Old Testament had parallels in his own day; God had exercised his will and interceded in the death of the prophet Joseph. Hyde's imagery was also transformed into a widely propagated Mormon myth that the men engaged in the Carthage conspiracy suffered horrible and agonizing deaths.[15]

---

14. Orson Hyde, 3 January 1858, in *Journal of Discourses* 6:154.
15. Oaks and Hill, *Carthage Conspiracy*, 217–221.

Exterior of Carthage Jail, by C. C. A. Christensen, ca. 1890. Courtesy of Brigham Young University Museum of Art. All rights reserved.

By the 1890s the story of the light from heaven was firmly entrenched in Mormon popular culture. Artist C. C. A. Christensen included an 8'x10' rendering of the scene on canvas as part of a traveling panorama of Mormon history which unfolded before large audiences throughout Utah. Christiansen's dramatic depiction of the scene at the well focuses the viewer's attention on the knife-wielding mobster, nearly lifted from the ground as he fights against the heavenly radiance. Joseph's lifeless body lies nearby. The four-man firing squad is no longer to be seen, the marksmen are now blended into the crowd of bystanders and militiamen.[16]

Daniels's account also impacted the writing of Mormon history. Two LDS periodicals, the *Deseret News* (in Salt Lake City) and the *Latter-Day Saints' Millennial Star* (in England), published the church-sponsored "History of Joseph Smith" in the 1850s and early 1860s. Much of the Daniels/Littlefield language was incorporated into the official LDS version of the story. Following Joseph's fall from the window of the jail, a ruffian

> set Joseph against the south side of the well curb, which was situated a few feet from the jail, when Col. Levi Williams ordered four men to shoot him. They stood about eight feet from the curb, and fired simultaneously . . . The ruffian who set him against the well curb now gathered a bowie-knife for the purpose of severing his head from his body. He raised the knife, and was in the attitude of striking, when a light, so sudden and powerful, burst from the heavens upon the bloody scene (passing its vivid chain between Joseph and his murderers), that they were struck

---

16. Most of his paintings are currently at the BYU Museum of Art. Dillenberger, "Mormonism and American Religious Art," 187–200.

with terror. This light, in its appearance and potency, baffles all powers of description. The arm of the ruffian that held the knife fell powerless, the muskets of the four who fired fell to the ground, and they all stood like marble statues, not having the power to move a single limb of their bodies.[17]

When the "History of Joseph Smith" was first published in book form in starting 1902 as the *History of the Church of Jesus Christ of Latter-day Saints,* the editor, Brigham H. Roberts, deleted nearly an entire column of text, beginning with the passage following Joseph's words at the window, "O Lord, my God!" and ending just before "Dr. Richards' escape was miraculous." With a single editorial stroke the scene at the well—the firing squad, the knife-wielding mobster and the divine light—was removed from Mormon history.[18]

B. H. Roberts, a general authority in the LDS Church and assistant church historian, justified his editorial decision because to his mind the "History of Joseph Smith" as earlier published relied too heavily upon Daniels's account, its acceptance and use more than likely influenced by the fact that the booklet was published by John Taylor's printing establishment at Nauvoo and listed as an official church publication for 1845. Roberts was especially concerned because "this whole fabric of myth and legend," often attached to the death of the first Mormon prophet, "has, unfortunately, found its way into some of our otherwise acceptable church works, and still more unfortunately had entered into the beliefs of many Latter-day Saints." Roberts further argued that "the story of Daniels is incredible, not because it involves incidents that would be set down as 'miraculous,' but because the story is all out of harmony with what in the nature of things would happen under the circumstances, and the incidents he details are too numerous, too complicated, too deliberate, and would have occupied too much time to be crowded into the space within which necessarily they must have happened, if they happened at all."[19]

Roberts's blanket statement ("if they happened at all"), while casting appropriate doubt on the impact of the heavenly light, also (and without cause) brings into question the firing squad that faced Joseph as he was propped against the well curb. Thus, while Roberts properly removed a significant example of mythologizing from the life of the first Mormon prophet, his rejection of the scene at the well eliminated any need to identify the four men who shot the fatal bullets into the body of Joseph Smith. The publication of the seven-volume *History of the Church* and Roberts's own *Comprehensive History* (in six volumes) effectively banished from the Mormon collective memory the final moments of Joseph Smith's life. Most often, Joseph Smith's history has been rewritten to make it consonant with Willard Richards's 1844 account, so that the Mormon prophet was hit by bullets from the doorway and courtyard as he sat inside the second-story window of the jail and was dead when he fell to the ground below. Today few Latter-day Saints remember the four gunmen at the well.[20]

---

17. *Millennial Star* 24, 486–87. See Searle, "Authorship," 112–13 for chart showing publication history.
18. Smith, *History of the Church* 6:618. Also Lynne, *True and Descriptive,* 10.
19. Roberts, *Comprehensive History* 2:332–33 and 325, note 14, also quoted in Turley, *Victims,* 12.
20. It should be noted, however, that Roberts, *Comprehensive History* 2:286, acknowledges, "There seems to be conclusive evidence that the Prophet was fired upon as he lay on the ground beside the

The death of Joseph Smith also impacted official Latter-day Saint doctrines and beliefs, especially those related to political Mormonism. The return of Jesus Christ to rule over his earthly kingdom, in 1844 thought to be "at the doors," was delayed indefinitely. The practical effect of this dampening of millennialist expectations was that the narrow time frame envisioned by the early Latter-day Saints was extended into an uncertain future. Consequently, by the end of the nineteenth century, establishing the political Kingdom of God was no longer a vital objective for Utah Mormons. The church and the kingdom became virtually indistinguishable, with Daniel's overpowering vision of the stone cut from the mountain without hands transformed into a simple metaphor for the spread of the gospel message throughout the earth. The literal end of the Mormon political Kingdom of God came in 1945, marked by the passing of LDS President Heber J. Grant, last surviving member of the Council of Fifty.[21]

The legacy of the Nauvoo bloc vote lingered for decades, so much so that extreme measures had to be taken to encourage political pluralism among the Latter-day Saints. During the 1890s, for example, Mormon households in Utah were designated as Republican or Democrat according to whether they were east or west of main street or where congregants sat during church services (one side of the aisle was Republican, the other Democrat). The constitutional separation of

---

old well curb that stood under the window from which he leaped." By his silence on the issue, Roberts does not allow for the presence of a firing squad, citing as evidence only the conflated account of the event written by John Taylor and today known as Doctrine and Covenants, Section 135, verse 1: "They were both shot after they were dead, in a brutal manner, and both received four balls." By referencing Taylor, Roberts reinforces the mistaken idea that Joseph was shot while hanging in the window and was dead when he fell to the ground below. A similar position is taken by several recent writers, including Leonard, *Nauvoo*, 393 (caption), 395, 725, note 49. Leonard, however, discounts the notion that Joseph was shot after he fell. Note as well, Bushman and Bushman, *Building the Kingdom*. Their Fig. 3, a later nineteenth-century popular illustration of the murder, depicts Joseph Smith shot firing-squad style while propped up against the well. The caption for the figure is unrelated to what is portrayed in the illustration: "On June 27, 1844, Joseph Smith was shot in the upstairs window of a jail in Carthage, Illinois, and fell to the ground below." Perhaps uncertain what to make of the various "authoritative" accounts, Remini, *Joseph Smith*, 174, has the prophet shot both in the upper room of the jail and later by a firing squad, which is closer to what has been reconstructed here.

21. Norman, "How Long, O Lord?" Elder Melvin J. Ballard, in the April 1917 Conference of the Church of Jesus Christ of Latter-day Saints, alludes to this change in LDS thinking about the Kingdom of God: "When the Lord spoke to the Prophet Joseph Smith, he cut a stone out of the mountains without hands . . . that stone that would roll forth and fill the whole earth." Elder Ballard stressed that "the kingdom of God, unlike the kingdoms of this world, which are political, the kingdom of God is spiritual, it is religious . . . and I feel that in the two important matters, the establishment of the United States of America among the nations of the earth and the establishment of the Church of Jesus Christ again in the earth, is the fulfillment of that wonderful prophecy. These shall go forth as twin images, and not as competitors, one helping and sustaining the other." (*Conference Report*, April 1917, 123) Today, most LDS authors promote the "spiritual" view of the Kingdom of God.

In a later speech, given at the April 1930 General Conference, Melvin J. Ballard solidifies this transition in LDS thought: "This is the age of the separation of the Church and the state. Yes, there will come a time when it shall be united again, but not under any earthly man . . . Yes, this is the beginning of the realization of Daniel's dream . . . I believe that when he [Christ] comes to rule and reign there will be a union of Church and state under him who right it is to rule and reign. But never has that right been given to a mortal man." (*Conference Report*, April 1930, 157)

church and state, in 1844 considered nonsensical folly, became, by 1907, official church policy.[22]

The stated position of the Church of Jesus Christ of Latter-day Saints remains that of political noninvolvement. On the eve of the 2004 American presidential election (which proved even less predictable in its outcome than the 1844 contest), the First Presidency of the church sent a letter to all bishops and branch presidents to be read to local congregations during their Sunday services: "The Church reaffirms its long-standing policy of neutrality regarding political parties, political platforms, [and] candidates for political office . . . Church leaders and members should avoid statements or conduct that may be interpreted as Church endorsement of any political party, political platform, or candidate." While it might appear that the Church of Jesus Christ of Latter-day Saints has successfully adapted to the American ideal of the separation of church and state, one LDS scholar recently noted that "faithful Latter-day Saints familiar with the millennial prophecy of their faith [continue to] anticipate the eventual revitalization of the Council of Fifty and the political Kingdom of God." For them it is not a matter of *if*, but *when* the prophecy of Daniel will be fulfilled.[23]

Plural marriage formed the central core of Mormon ideas about eternal progression for Joseph Smith and his immediate successors. Church leaders were unrepentant in their support of the principle; indeed, the Latter-day Saints would not easily give up what they believed to be a God-given commandment. In the second half of the nineteenth century, the practice of polygamy among the Utah Mormons became the subject of national debate and punitive legislative action. John Taylor succeeded Brigham Young as president of the Church of Jesus Christ of Latter-day Saints in 1880. The last two years of Taylor's life were spent in "retirement," a seclusion forced upon the leaders of the church in order to avoid prosecution under the United States antipolygamy laws. In acknowledging his passing in 1887, church officials announced that "President Taylor escaped the death which the assassins of Carthage jail assigned." With his death, Taylor once again became a martyr. "In Utah was finished what Carthage began!"[24]

President Wilford Woodruff's 1890 manifesto officially discontinued polygamy as a practice among Latter-day Saints. In the wake of that decision, the modern church (more than a century later) must still contend with tens of thousands of "fundamentalist Mormons" throughout the intermountain West who practice

---

22. *Conference Report*, April 1907, 14.

23. Office of the First Presidency to General Authorities et al., 21 July 2004 ("Members Encouraged to Exercise the Right to Vote/Reaffirmation of the Church's Policy of Political Neutrality"). Damon Cann, (revitalization quote). www.sinc.sunysb.edu/stu/dcann/fifty.htm (accessed 30 December 2004). In a review of J. Keith Melville, *Highlights in Mormon Political History* (Provo: Brigham Young University Press, 1967), Jan Shipps remarked that "Dr. Melville reveals, almost inadvertently, but as plainly has anyone ever has, that there simply was no separation of church and state in early Mormon society and thought." ("Short Notices," *Dialogue* 3.4:104.) Bushman and Bushman, *Building the Kingdom*, in a caption to a photograph (Fig. 4) of LDS Church President Brigham Young, shown with his Masonic pin composed of compass, square, and the letter "G" prominently displayed, note, "Brigham Young became the dominant figure in Utah's political and church governments. He was not concerned about the separation of church and state."

24. Hardy, *Solemn Covenant*. Roberts, *Comprehensive History* 6:188 (Carthage quote).

polygamy illegally and without the blessing of the current LDS hierarchy. Fundamentalists argue that the 1890 manifesto was a political ploy in order to comply nominally with the laws of the United States and avoid the confiscation of the church's assets. They point out that the declaration was not presented as a revelation and further note that plural marriages continued to be solemnized by church leaders (chiefly in Canada and Mexico) for more than a decade after 1890. Furthermore, the doctrine of plural marriage has never been repudiated by the church. In fact, Joseph Smith's 1843 revelation affirming polygamy as a divine principle continues to be taught to LDS congregations. Precisely when (and how) "the principle" will be re-established by the church—either in this life or the next—remains a matter of continuing speculation.[25]

Mormon-Masonic tensions, first exposed at Nauvoo, remain close to the surface even today. In 1878, the Grand Master of the Utah Lodge stated unequivocally, "Such a wound as you gave Masonry in Nauvoo is not easily healed, and no Latter-day Saint is, or can become a member of our Order in this jurisdiction." (The "wound" referred to was the practice adopted by the Nauvoo Lodge of advancing men before they were properly prepared and inducting more than one individual at a time.) It was only in 1984 that Utah Freemasons allowed Mormons to join the fraternity.[26]

From the LDS perspective, Masons are to be blamed for not preserving the life of the prophet Joseph when he displayed the Masonic hailing sign and uttered the first four words of the phrase, "O Lord my God, is there no help for the widow's son?" Furthermore, many LDS apologists, instead of accepting the most likely explanation—that Joseph Smith took from whatever source was available when he founded the endowment ceremony—continue to argue that Joseph Smith would not have borrowed from an "apostate" practice and refuse to acknowledge even the most undeniable connections between Masonic ritual and the Mormon endowment. In order to eliminate obvious reminders of LDS indebtedness to Freemasonry, the Mormon temple ceremony has been systematically purged (most recently in 1990) of Masonic phraseology, tokens, signs, and gestures.[27]

The deliberate eradication of Masonic symbols within Mormonism continues. The Nauvoo temple, destroyed by arson and storm in the mid-nineteenth century, has been rebuilt on its original site. The structure was rededicated on the afternoon of Thursday, June 27, 2002, the 158th anniversary (to the very day and close to the hour) of Joseph Smith's death. It is a working temple, where saving ordinances for both the living and the dead are performed by recommend-holding Latter-day Saints. The interior of the reconstructed temple has been modified to accommodate the requirements of modern temple work. (Interestingly, the use of the Masonic term "work" to

---

25. One current LDS practice that presupposes the continued acceptance of the doctrine of plural marriage without actively practicing "the principle" is the fact that LDS men sealed to a first wife who is then separated through death or divorce can remarry and be sealed to a second wife "for time and eternity" without the sealing to his first wife having been revoked. This practice is a form of serial polygamy. Women, on the other hand, are not allowed the privilege of being sealed to more than one man at a time.

26. Joseph M. Orr, Grand Lodge Communication, 1878, quoted in Cook, "A Review of Factors," 76–78, 81.

27. These changes have been discussed at length on numerous Internet sites. See Tanner, *Evolution*.

refer to the activities taking place in the temple continues, although in recent years "temple worship" has gained in popularity.)

With one notable exception, the exterior of the building is historically accurate. The original tower was surmounted by a weather vane, consisting of a horizontal flying angel and the classic Masonic emblems of a compass and square. In common with nearly all other modern Latter-day Saint temples, the spire of the reconstructed Nauvoo temple consists instead of a three-dimensional gilt fiberglass sculpture of a standing figure of the angel Moroni, the heavenly messenger who delivered the Book of Mormon to Joseph Smith.

With the demise of the original Nauvoo Moroni, and the latest modification of Mormon temple ritual, only two explicitly Masonic symbols continue to play a central role in the lives of millions of temple-going Latter-day Saints. The compass and square are embroidered as ritual emblems on the temple garment worn by all endowed Mormons. Viewed as reminders of the virtues of righteous living in obedience to God's commandments, these markings are among the last remaining symbolic ties to Joseph Smith's great Masonic experiment at Nauvoo.[28]

The 2002 rebuilding and dedication of the Nauvoo temple has transformed the sleepy western Illinois community into a thriving tourist town. More than 331,000 visitors toured the temple during the six weeks prior to its dedication. Beginning on June 27, 2002, church president Gordon B. Hinckley presided over thirteen dedicatory sessions, attended by some 18,000 recommend-holding Latter-day Saints, broadcast live to congregations around the world.

For Mormonism's faithful, Carthage jail has also become a site of pilgrimage, a place of reflective contemplation. During the weeks leading up to the 2002 Nauvoo temple dedication, seasonal visitation almost doubled to nearly 3,000 visitors per day. Used as a county jail until 1866, the building remained in private hands until 1903, when it was purchased by the church. Since that time the structure has been restored to its original 1844 condition. The grounds around the jail have been transformed into a welcome area and park featuring oversized sculptures of Joseph and Hyrum. The official story of "the martyrdom" is presented by missionary guides, which, together with a video and walking tour of the jail, serve to reinforce Mormonism's legacy as a persecuted religious tradition. Despite the importance of Carthage for the history of the church, June 27 has not become a universal day of remembrance for the Mormon faith. That honor is reserved for the 24th of July Pioneer Day celebrations commemorating the 1847 arrival of Brigham Young and the Saints in the Valley of the Great Salt Lake.

In April 2004, the state of Illinois expressed "official regret" for its part in the 1844 murder of Joseph Smith and the forced expulsion of the Latter-day Saints from the state. This belated gesture was accepted graciously by the current LDS leadership in Salt Lake City, a member of the First Presidency commenting that "those days are

---

28. The cover of the official LDS Church publication, the *Ensign*, for December 2001 (issue 31.12) features a painting of the Nauvoo temple depicted with the original horizontal weather vane, "Winter Fun in Nauvoo, 1845–46," by Glen S. Hopkinson, 1998. The latest (2002) exhibition installation in the Museum of Church History and Art in Salt Lake City removed the compass and square from Weeks's drawing of the original Nauvoo temple spire. ("Angel Makeover.")

long gone and far behind us." While viewed by many Mormons as providing closure on a painful period in their history, the Illinois apology is also a powerful reminder that Joseph's cry of "persecuted innocence" continues to resonate up to the present time.[29]

With nearly 12 million members worldwide, more than half of whom live outside of the continental United States and speak a first language other than English, The Church of Jesus Christ of Latter-day Saints has entered a new stage of institutional growth and image transformation. Through a methodical public relations campaign, a careful re-visioning of its foundational narratives, and a newly restructured missionary program, America's most distinctive indigenous religion has made it plain the church today wishes to be regarded as a conservative Christian movement, although a Christian faith with a difference—one having a living prophet to guide and direct the affairs of His church, belief in the Bible ("as far as it is translated correctly") and in the Book of Mormon, since 1981 subtitled 'Another Testament of Jesus Christ'.

As a result of this mainstreaming process, a number of uniquely Mormon doctrinal teachings—on such diverse topics as polygamy, the political Kingdom of God, and eternal progression (that God was once a man and than men can become gods)—have been downplayed in recent years to become Mormonism's "shelf doctrines," beliefs no longer preached openly from the pulpit but which remain at the core of LDS theology. Not surprisingly, longtime students of Mormonism have witnessed a growing dissonance between the Church's official pronouncements (meant to be accepted by new members, the media as well as the general public) and the more complex "operative reality" of Latter-day Saint belief and practice. In the year 2004 as in 1844, the future of Mormonism remains a serious question: What will be the end of things?[30]

---

29. "State offers official regret for persecutions," *Daily Herald* (Provo, UT), 8 April 2004.

30. The notion of "shelf doctrines" has a long history within Mormonism. Significantly, one of the earliest uses of the term relates to the concept of eternal progression expressed in a couplet revealed to Elder Lorenzo Snow in 1840: "As man now is, God once was. As God now is, man may be." Brigham Young, then president of the Quorum of the Twelve, reportedly said, "Brother Snow, that is a new doctrine. if true, it has been revealed to you for your own private information, and will be taught in due time by the Prophet of the Church. till then I advise you to lay it upon the shelf and say no more about it." (Whitney, "Lives of our leaders . . . Lorenzo Snow," 4, quoted in Spencer J. Condie, *Heroes of the Restoration* in *Infobases Collectors Library* CD-ROM.) A former LDS missionary recalled that when LDS General Authority Elder Henry B. Eyring spoke at the mission home in Salt Lake City during the 1970s, Eyring "said that he put the questions he couldn't answer in a box, put the box on a shelf, and intended to ask the Lord about them later." (Anonymous, "My Story by Dr. Jazz," [www.exmormon.org].) Most recently, Robert J. Millett, former dean of Religious Education at Brigham Young University, admitted that "we have what some call 'shelf doctrines'—things we put aside for the time being." (Wright, "A Reporter at Large," 51.) The Snow couplet and attendant doctrine, actively taught in the church from 1844 through the mid-1990s, have been once again placed back on the shelf. For an overview of some of the many LDS statements supporting the belief and current efforts to downplay Mormon distinctiveness, see Ostling, *Mormon America*, especially 421–22 for the official church response to the *Time* interview, and the chapter "How God Came to be God," 295–314. The new LDS Church website, www.mormon.org, is "conspicuously silent on the doctrine of eternal progression." ("New Website Takes Missionary Work into Cyberspace," 76.) See also Sears, "Theology and Christology Through the lens of a Little Couplet."

Biographical Profiles

Clay's Men: The Whig Campaign for Illinois in 1844

John J. Hardin—cousin of Mary Todd Lincoln and stepnephew of Kentuckian Henry Clay—was the only Illinois Whig serving in U.S. Congress from 1843–45. Because of his position, Hardin became the lead architect in the Kentucky senator's crusade to claim Illinois as a Whig state in the 1844 presidential race. The chief political organizers and operatives comprising the informal organization known as Henry Clay's "secret committee" associated with the Illinois campaign are listed below. Notes are provided for information not included in the main text.

John Bailhache (1787–1857). Alton, Illinois, publisher of *Alton Telegraph and Democratic Review*, a Whig newspaper. Associate of Henry Clay and G. T. M. Davis. Freemason.

Edward D. Baker (1811–1861). Springfield, Illinois, attorney; U.S. congressman in 1845. Assigned as district delegate to 1844 Whig nominating convention in Baltimore (did not attend). Illinois militia leader. Associate of Abraham Lincoln, John J. Hardin, and O. H. Browning. Baker negotiated favorable terms of surrender for Levi Williams (Anti-Mormon Party) and Thomas Sharp (Anti-Mormon Party) in the murder of Joseph Smith (LDS Council of Fifty). Served in U.S. Congress between March 4, 1845, (although he did not formally take his seat until December 1, 1845) and January 15, 1847.

Orville Hickman Browning (1806–1881). Quincy, Illinois, attorney. Associate of Abraham Lincoln, Henry Clay, John J. Hardin, Edward D. Baker, Abraham Jonas, Archibald Williams, Wesley Williams (Anti-Mormon Party), Onias C. Skinner (Anti-Mormon Party), and Joseph Smith (LDS Council of Fifty). Cousin of Mormon gunsmith Jonathan Browning. Chief defense counsel for men accused of Joseph Smith's murder. (see p. 53)

Jacob Burnet (1770–1853). Cincinnati, Ohio, attorney and businessman. William Henry Harrison's political manager in 1840; political manager (and in-law) of John McLean in the 1844 presidential campaign. Associate of Henry Clay, John C. Elliott, and former associate of William Goforth, grandfather of William Gano Goforth. Freemason. (see p. 32)

Henry Clay (1777–1852). Lexington, Kentucky, attorney and politician. Whig presidential hopeful in 1844. Former U.S. senator and Grand Master of Kentucky Masonic Lodge. Brother of Porter Clay, who married widowed mother of John J. Hardin, and lived in Jacksonville, Illinois, in the 1840s. (see p. 31)

Leslie Combs (1793–1881). Lexington, Kentucky, military hero. Businessman and Freemason. Longtime friend and political adviser to Henry Clay. Gave political speeches throughout the U.S. in support of Clay during campaign of 1844. Instrumental in bringing John McLean into the Clay camp. In 1845 Combs's supporters warned Brigham Young (LDS Council of Fifty) that the Mormons shouldn't attempt to settle in California.[1]

Thomas Corwin (1794–1865). Lebanon, Ohio, attorney and Freemason. Former Ohio governor (1840–42) and U.S. congressman. Lost 1842 gubernatorial re-election bid due to strength of Liberty Party. Associate of Henry Clay, Anthony Howard Dunlevy, and John McLean. Freemason.

George T. M. Davis (1810–1888). Alton, Illinois, attorney and Whig editor of the *Alton Telegraph and Democratic Review* together with John Bailhache. State senatorial delegate to 1844 Whig nominating convention in Baltimore. Associate of Illinois governor Thomas Ford (1800–1850), Henry Clay, Edward D. Baker, Horace Greeley, John J. Hardin, George Rockwell (Anti-Mormon Party), Onias C. Skinner (Anti-Mormon Party), and William Marks (LDS Council of Fifty). Regulated Whig press coverage of Joseph Smith's assassination and protected Democratic governor Thomas Ford from accusations of collusion in the murder. (see p. 66)

Anthony Howard Dunlevy (1793–1881). Lebanon, Ohio, attorney. Brother-in-law of Sidney Rigdon (LDS Council of Fifty). Associate of Henry Clay, Thomas Corwin, and John McLean. Was in neighborhood of Nauvoo, Illinois, at the time of Joseph Smith's assassination.

John C. Elliott (1816–1861). Hamilton, Ohio, Deputy U.S. Marshal. Former woodsman. Associate of Jacob Burnet, Abraham Jonas, Edson Whitney (Anti-Mormon Party), Levi Williams (Anti-Mormon Party), and William Marks (LDS Council of Fifty). Secret Whig agent posing as a schoolteacher in Illinois; principal in 1843 Avery kidnap. Led assault on Carthage jail; fired fatal bullet that killed Joseph Smith.

William Gano Goforth (1795–1847). Belleville, Illinois, physician. Secret Whig delegate to Nauvoo state convention in spring of 1844; made several unsuccessful attempts to bring Mormons into Clay camp. Associate of Joseph Smith, Sidney Rigdon (LDS Council of Fifty), Robert D. Foster (Nauvoo Dissidents), and William Law (Nauvoo Dissidents). Freemason.

Horace Greeley (1811–1872). New York City political manager and publisher of *New York Tribune*, *Clay Tribune*, and *The Junius Tracts*. Associate of Henry Clay, John J. Hardin, and G. T. M. Davis. (see p. 30)

Thomas Gregg (1808–1892). Warsaw, Illinois, newspaper publisher of *Warsaw Message*. Whig political editor of *Upper Mississippian* (Rock Island) during 1844 campaign. Clay Club organizer. Brother-in-law of Frank Worrell (Anti-Mormon Party) and associate of Francis Higbee (Nauvoo Dissidents). (see p. 50)

John J. Hardin (1810–1847). Jacksonville, Illinois, attorney; U.S. congressman; step-nephew of Henry Clay. Served in U.S. Congress between March 4, 1843, and March 3, 1845. Associate of Illinois governor Thomas Ford, O. H. Browning,

1. Backwoodsman [Palmyra, Missouri] to [Brigham Young] 22 October 1845 (Leslie Combs warning) (Smith, *History of the Church*, 7:499).

Edward D. Baker, George T. M. Davis, Horace Greeley, Anson G. Henry, and Abraham Jonas. (see p. 37)

Anson G. Henry (1804–1865). Springfield, Illinois, attorney. State Whig Central Committee chairman; oversaw organization of local Clay Clubs. Associate of Abraham Lincoln, Henry Clay, and John J. Hardin.

Abraham Jonas (1801–1864). Columbus, Illinois, attorney; on Whig Central Committee for Illinois's Fifth District. Associate of Abraham Lincoln, Henry Clay, John J. Hardin, O. H. Browning, Levi Williams (Anti-Mormon Party), Joseph Smith (LDS Council of Fifty), Sidney Rigdon (LDS Council of Fifty), Willard Richards (LDS Council of Fifty), and Illinois governor Thomas Ford. Freemason; former grand master of Kentucky and Illinois Lodges. Supplied printing press to Nauvoo dissidents. (see p. 58)

John McLean (1785–1861). Cincinnati, Ohio, U.S. Supreme Court judge and Whig presidential hopeful. Associate of Jacob Burnet, Thomas Corwin, Anthony Howard Dunlevy, and G. T. M. Davis. Was in Springfield, Illinois, presiding over U.S. Circuit Court during arrest and murder of Joseph Smith in June of 1844. (see p. 28)

Archibald Williams (1801–1863). Quincy, Illinois, attorney. President, Illinois Whig State Central Committee; Chair of Whig Central Committee for Illinois's Fifth District. Associate of O. H. Browning and Abraham Jonas. Brother of Wesley Williams (Anti-Mormon Party); cousin of Levi Williams (Anti-Mormon Party). Defense counsel for men accused of Joseph Smith's murder.

Joseph Smith's Political Kingdom of God: Council of Fifty, 1844–1845

The secretive Council of Fifty was formed in the spring of 1844 to manage Joseph Smith's presidential campaign and establish the political Kingdom of God on the earth. Distinct from the Church of Jesus Christ of Latter-day Saints (it included non-Mormons in its ranks), this body continued to influence Mormon political ideology through the 1880s. Never formally disbanded, the Council of Fifty technically ceased to exist with the death of its last surviving member, LDS President Heber J. Grant, in 1945.

Only individuals mentioned in the body of the text are listed here. Church affiliation, additional offices, and special assignments are given in brackets, followed by additional biographical information. With the exception of Joseph Smith, Willard Richards, and William Clayton, numerical ranking is by age. Members dropped by Brigham Young following Joseph Smith's death are prefaced by an asterisk (*); members added by Brigham Young in 1845 are prefaced by two asterisks (**). All LDS are residents of Nauvoo, Illinois.

Joseph Smith, Jr., Standing chairman, no. 1 (1805–1844). Ordained Prophet, Priest, and King within the Kingdom of God, April 11, 1844. [LDS; President of the Church of Jesus Christ of Latter-day Saints; president, Anointed Quorum; Mayor of Nauvoo; Chief Justice of the Peace; Freemason; initiated Danite; Lieutenant General, Nauvoo Legion; polygamist.] Murdered at Carthage jail, June 27, 1844. (see pp. ii, 15, 43)

Willard Richards, Recorder of Kingdom (1804–1854). [LDS; Apostle; Major, Nauvoo Legion; Anointed Quorum; Freemason; polygamist; unranked by age.] Slightly wounded at Carthage jail, June 27, 1844. (see p. 86)

William Clayton, Clerk of Kingdom (1814–1879). [LDS; Anointed Quorum; Freemason; polygamist; unranked by age.] In Nauvoo at the time of the martyrdom. His sister, Lucy, was living with the Stigall family at the Carthage jail at time of Joseph Smith's assassination. (see p. 39)

Members:

Almon W. Babbitt, no. 44 (1813–1856). [LDS; Anointed Quorum; proposed ambassador to France; attorney to Joseph Smith.] Possessed of a volatile and unpredictable temperament, Babbitt was frequently reprimanded by church authorities. In league with the Nauvoo dissidents during the spring of 1844, he was one of the few Latter-day Saints who recognized that the *Nauvoo Expositor* was "established for political purposes by the Whigs."

John M. Bernhisel, no. 21 (1799–1881). [LDS; Anointed Quorum; central campaign committee for Joseph Smith's presidential bid.] Physician.

*Edward Bonney, no. 34 (1807–1864). [Non-LDS; Freemason; aide-de-camp, Nauvoo Legion.] Counterfeiter and detective. One of Joseph Smith's intended defense witnesses during trial for destruction of *Expositor* press. In Nauvoo at time of Joseph Smith's death. Dropped in late 1844 or early 1845.

*Uriah Brown, no. 5 (1785–   ). [Non-LDS; Rushville, Illinois, inventor; chairman of state nominating convention at Nauvoo.] Dropped February 4, 1845.

**Lewis Dana, no. 33 (1804–   ). [LDS; Native American; Oneida tribe; Freemason.] Admitted March 1, 1845. Companion of Jonathan Dunham during an assigned journey out West.

**Jonathan Dunham, no. 25 (1800–1845). [LDS; former Danite; Major General, Nauvoo Legion; Freemason.] Admitted March 1, 1845. Disregarded request by Joseph Smith to call out the Nauvoo Legion and rescue the prophet from Carthage jail. Later sent on Western mission from which he did not return.

Jedediah M. Grant, no. 48 (1816–1846). [LDS; Freemason; political missionary.] In Nauvoo during murder of Joseph Smith.

John P. Greene, no. 12 (1793–1844). [LDS; former Danite; Nauvoo City Marshal; Anointed Quorum; Freemason.] Destroyed *Expositor* press set up by Nauvoo dissidents.

*David S. Hollister, no. 36 (1808–1858). [LDS; Freemason; national delegate.] Possibly dropped after December 25, 1846.

Orson Hyde, no. 30 (1805–1878). [LDS; Apostle; former Danite opponent; Nauvoo City Council; Anointed Quorum; Freemason; Ambassador to Washington, D.C.; national delegate; polygamist.]

Heber C. Kimball, no. 25 (1801–1868). [LDS; Apostle; Anointed Quorum; Freemason; national delegate; polygamist.]

**John D. Lee, no. 48 (1812–1877). [LDS; former Danite; Freemason; polygamist. Political missionary to Kentucky.] Admitted March 1, 1845 (?).

*William Marks, no. 10 (1792–1872). [LDS, Nauvoo Stake President; Anointed Quorum; Freemason; polygamy opponent; associate of John C. Elliott (Clay's Men).] Dropped February 4, 1845.

*George Miller, no. 13 (1794–1856). [LDS; Anointed Quorum; Freemason; Brigadier General, Nauvoo Legion; political missionary.] Dropped after December 26, 1846. Excommunicated December 3, 1848.

William W. Phelps, no. 8 (1792–1872). [LDS; Anointed Quorum; Freemason; political writer; on Joseph Smith's presidential campaign central committee.]

Parley P. Pratt, no. 33 (1807–1857). [LDS; Apostle; former Danite; Anointed Quorum; Freemason; political missionary; polygamist.]

*Sidney Rigdon, no. 11 (1793–1876). [LDS; First Counselor in LDS First Presidency; former LDS First Presidency liaison to Missouri Danites; Anointed Quorum; Freemason; Joseph Smith's U.S. vicepresidential running mate; polygamy opponent; brother-in-law of Anthony Howard Dunlevy (Clay's Men); father-in-law of George W. Robinson (Anti-Mormon Party); proposed to be made Trustee-in-Trust for the church following Joseph Smith's death.] Excommunicated September 8, 1844. Dropped from Council of Fifty, February 4, 1845. (see p. 17)

Orrin Porter Rockwell, no. 47 (1813–1878). [LDS; former Danite; Freemason; Joseph Smith bodyguard.] Accused in attempted murder of former Missouri governor Lilburn W. Boggs; assisted in destruction of *Nauvoo Expositor* press. Killed Franklin Worrell (Anti-Mormon Party), September 16, 1845.

George Albert Smith, no. 49 (1817–1875). [LDS; Apostle; former Danite; Major, Nauvoo Legion; Anointed Quorum; Freemason; political missionary.]

Hyrum Smith, no. 23 (1800–1844). [LDS; Church Patriarch; former Danite; Brevet Major General, Nauvoo Legion; Anointed Quorum; Freemason; polygamist.] Murdered with his brother Joseph Smith, at Carthage jail, June 27, 1844. (see p. 43)

*William Smith, no. 41 (1811–1893). [LDS; Apostle; Major, Nauvoo Legion; Anointed Quorum; Freemason; appointed church Patriarch following death of his brother Hyrum; editor of *The Prophet* (New York City) through end of 1844.] Dropped from Council of Fifty after September 9, 1845. Excommunicated October 12, 1845. Published early exposé of Mormon temple Oath of Vengeance.

Erastus Snow, no. 51 (1818–1888). [LDS; Freemason; political missionary to Vermont; polygamist.]

John Taylor, no. 37 (1808–1887). [LDS; Apostle; Colonel, Nauvoo Legion; Anointed Quorum; Freemason; polygamist.] Editor of *Nauvoo Neighbor* and *Times and Seasons* newspapers. Badly wounded at Carthage jail, June 27, 1844. (see p. 45)

**Theodore Turley, no. 26 (1800–1872). [LDS; Lieutenant-Colonel, Nauvoo Legion; Freemason; polygamist.] Admitted March 1, 1845. Gunsmith and counterfeiter.

*Lyman Wight, no. 16 (1796–1858). [LDS; Apostle; former Danite; Brevet Major General, Nauvoo Legion; Anointed Quorum.] Dropped February 4, 1845. In 1845, took a group of Saints to Texas in order to fulfill Joseph Smith's charge of establishing the Kingdom there. Excommunicated December 3, 1848, after refuting the right of the Quorum of the Twelve to lead the church.

Wilford Woodruff, no. 32 (1807–1898). [LDS; Apostle; Anointed Quorum; Freemason; political missionary.]

*Lucien Woodworth, no. 19 (1797–   ). [LDS; Anointed Quorum; Freemason; secret ambassador to Republic of Texas.] Dropped after 1848.

Brigham Young, no. 24 (1801–1877). [LDS; President, Quorum of the Twelve Apostles; Anointed Quorum; Freemason; polygamist; political missionary; appointed standing chairman February 4, 1845. Anointed and ordained King.] (see pp. 104, 196)

Anti-Mormon Party, Hancock County, Illinois, 1843–1845

Originally founded in 1841, the Anti-Mormon Party was reinvigorated in the fall of 1843 following Hyrum Smith's "political revelation" that the Mormons should vote Democratic. Composed of both Whigs and Democrats, as well as a sprinkling of political independents, the organization was dedicated to checking the rapidly increasing strength of the Mormon electorate in local and state politics. A Central Corresponding Committee (also known as the Committee of Safety) was formed in Carthage, the Hancock County seat. Smaller communities also had corresponding committees. Anti-Mormon representatives from Quincy (Adams County) and Macomb (McDonough County) frequently assisted their Hancock confederates.

William D. Abernethy (–   ). Local Whig organizer from Augusta, Hancock County, Illinois. Associate of John J. Hardin (Clay's Men). Elisor (one of two persons appointed to select the jury) during trial of accused assassins of Joseph Smith.

Mark Aldrich (1801–1874). Warsaw, Illinois, businessman. Freemason; member Warsaw Lodge. Militia leader; Major in command of the Warsaw Independent Battalion composed of Warsaw Cadets (under William N. Grover) and Warsaw Rifle Company (under Jacob C. Davis) attached to the Fifty-ninth Regiment (under Colonel Levi Williams). Son-in-law of Abraham Chittenden. Accused assassin of Joseph Smith.

Walter Bagby (–1846). Carthage, Illinois, tax collector. Member of Carthage Central Committee.

Thomas L. Barnes (1812–1901). Carthage, Illinois, physician. Anti-Mormon leader. Captain, Carthage Militia. Treated John Taylor (LDS Council of Fifty) after assault on jail.

Abraham I. Chittenden (1781–   ). Warsaw, Illinois, farmer. Militia leader. Freemason; founding Worshipful Master, Oxford, Butler County, Ohio Lodge and Warsaw, Hancock County, Illinois Lodge; father-in-law of Mark Aldrich. Warsaw militia camped on his farm prior to assault on Carthage jail.

William W. Chittenden (1818–   ). Son of Abraham Chittenden; member Warsaw militia. Brother-in-law of Mark Aldrich. Together with his brother, Edward F., were known as the "Chittenden boys." Was present during assault on Carthage jail. Later admitted "he knew the men who fired the fatal shots—there were four of them."

Jacob C. Davis (1815–1883). Warsaw, Illinois, attorney. Democratic state representative. Militia leader; Captain of the Warsaw Rifle Company under Major Mark Aldrich. Freemason; member Warsaw Lodge. Accused assassin of Joseph Smith.

William N. Grover (1818–   ). Warsaw, Illinois. Militia leader; Captain, Warsaw Cadets. Treasurer, Hancock County School Board. Associate of Robert D. Foster (Nauvoo Dissidents). Accused assassin of Joseph Smith.

Charles Hay (1801–1884). Warsaw, Illinois, physician. Militia leader and surgeon. Freemason; member Warsaw Lodge. Former Ashland, Kentucky, neighbor of Henry Clay. Charles's son John, who later became Abraham Lincoln's secretary and biographer, wrote a highly influential article on the murder of Joseph Smith called "The Mormon Prophet's Tragedy" for the literary journal *Atlantic Monthly* in 1869. John Hay was seven years old at the time of Joseph Smith's assassination.

George W. Robinson (1814–1878). La Harpe, Illinois. LDS dissident; left the church in 1842. Former Danite. Son-in-law of Sidney Rigdon (LDS Council of Fifty). Chair of La Harpe Anti-Mormon Committee. Reputed associate of John C. Bennett, who reportedly wanted to set Sidney Rigdon up as a "puppet" president of the LDS Church following death of Joseph Smith.

George Rockwell (1815–   ). Warsaw, Illinois, druggist. Militia leader. Freemason; member Warsaw Lodge. Associate of G. T. M. Davis (Clay's Men).

William H. Roosevelt (1806–1865). Warsaw, Illinois, businessman and Whig politician. Freemason; member Warsaw Lodge. Associate of O. H. Browning (Clay's Men). Brother of James J. Roosevelt (1795–1875) of New York City.

Thomas C. Sharp (1818–1894). Warsaw, Illinois, attorney and editor of anti-Mormon *Warsaw Signal*. Promoted bi-partisan efforts to thwart Mormon political designs. Accused assassin of Joseph Smith.

Onias C. Skinner (1817–1877). Carthage, Illinois, attorney and anti-Mormon leader. Freemason; member Hancock (Carthage) Lodge. Political independent. Associate of G. T. M. Davis (Clay's Men) and O. H. Browning (Clay's Men). Prosecuting attorney against Joseph Smith the day before the prophet's death. Defense counsel for men accused of Joseph Smith's murder following his move to Quincy, Illinois, in late 1844.

Robert F. Smith (–   ). Carthage, Illinois, Justice of the Peace. Anti-Mormon leader. Militia leader; Captain, Carthage Greys. Freemason; member Hancock (Carthage) Lodge. Presided over Joseph Smith hearing on charge of riot for destruction of *Nauvoo Expositor*; issued warrant for the Mormon prophet's arrest for treason against the state of Illinois; was in charge of protecting Joseph and Hyrum Smith during their incarceration at Carthage jail.

Edson Whitney (1809–   ). Farmer from Green Plains, Illinois. Local anti-Mormon leader. Associate of John C. Elliott (Clay's Men).

Levi Williams (1794–1860). Farmer from Green Plains, Illinois. Militia leader; Colonel of the Fifty-ninth Regiment of the Illinois Militia. Joined Warsaw Masonic Lodge in 1845. Cousin of Wesley Williams and Archibald Williams (Clay's Men). Associate of Abraham Jonas (Clay's Men) and John C. Elliott (Clay's Men). Coordinated Warsaw militia assault on Carthage jail, June 27, 1844. Accused assassin of Joseph Smith.

Samuel O. Williams (1819–1844). Carthage, Illinois, farmer and sometime clerk of court. Son of Wesley Williams. Militia leader, Carthage Greys. Author of early account of Carthage massacre.

Wesley Williams (1792–1870). Carthage, Illinois, farmer and businessman. Freemason; member Hancock (Carthage) Lodge. Militia leader, Carthage Greys. Brother of Archibald Williams (Clay's Men); cousin of Levi Williams. Associate of O. H. Browning (Clay's Men).

Franklin Worrell (–1845). Carthage, Illinois, dry goods merchant. Assistant postmaster. Lieutenant in Carthage Greys. Brother-in-law of Thomas Gregg (Clay's Men); married Ann Lawton. In charge of guard at Carthage jail during the assault by Warsaw militia on June 27, 1844. Killed by Orrin Porter Rockwell (LDS Council of Fifty) September 16, 1845.

Nauvoo Dissidents: The Men Behind the *Expositor*

As internal resistance mounted to Joseph Smith's doctrinal innovations, such as polygamy and his plans to join church and state, dissidents within the Church of Jesus Christ of Latter-day Saints were systematically excommunicated. A group of "apostates" organized the Reformed Mormon Church in the spring of 1844 and with Whig support executed plans to establish an opposition newspaper in Nauvoo. The *Expositor* saw one issue, of June 7, 1844, before the press was ordered destroyed by Joseph Smith. This action contributed to the death of the Mormon prophet less than three weeks later.

Sylvester Emmons (1808–   ). Non-Mormon editor of *Nauvoo Expositor*. Member Nauvoo City Council; Justice of the Peace; prosecuting attorney against Joseph Smith the day before the prophet's death.

Charles A. Foster (–   ). Non-Mormon brother of Robert D. Foster. Nauvoo correspondent for Horace Greeley's (Clay's Men) *New York Tribune*.

Robert D. Foster (1811–1878). LDS dissident; excommunicated 1844. Physician to LDS church leaders in Nauvoo. Hancock County school commissioner. Polygamy opponent; joined Reformed Mormon Church. Associate of William N. Grover (Anti-Mormon Party).

Chauncey L. Higbee (1821–1884). LDS dissident; excommunicated in 1842.

Francis M. Higbee (1820–   ). LDS dissident, brother of Chauncey L. Higbee. Associate of Thomas Gregg (Clay's Men). Both Higbees were sons of Elias Higbee (1795–1843), who was living in Cincinnati, Ohio, when he joined the LDS Church in 1832.

William Law (1809–1892). LDS dissident; excommunicated April 18, 1844. Counselor to Joseph Smith in LDS First Presidency (1841–1844); dropped from presidency, January 8, 1844. Polygamy opponent. Founded Reformed Mormon Church. Publisher of *Nauvoo Expositor*, printed on press acquired from Abraham Jonas (Clay's Men). Whig sympathizer.

Wilson Law (1807–1877). LDS dissident; excommunicated 1844. Older brother of William Law. Brigadier General of Nauvoo Legion. Publisher of *Nauvoo Expositor*.

Abbreviations

Publications

Journal History	Journal History of The Church of Jesus Christ of Latter-day Saints. Multivolume compilation of documents and daily events, many taken from early church newspapers. Church History Library, Family and Church History Department of The Church of Jesus Christ of Latter-day Saints, Salt Lake City, Utah.
Millennial Star	*Latter-Day Saints' Millennial Star* (Manchester and Liverpool, 1841–46).

Archives and Repositories

BYU Americana	Mormon and Western Americana Collection, L. Tom Perry Special Collections of the Harold B. Lee Library, Brigham Young University, Provo, Utah.
Community of Christ Archives	Library and Archives, Community of Christ (formerly Reorganized Church of Jesus Christ of Latter Day Saints), Independence, Missouri.
LDS Archives	Church Archives and History Library, The Church of Jesus Christ of Latter-day Saints, Salt Lake City, Utah. Joseph Smith Papers. See Turley, *Selected Collections* CD-ROM.
NARA Chicago	National Archives and Records Administration, Great Lakes Region, Chicago, Illinois.

Selected References

The works that have proven most useful for this study are preceded by an asterisk (*). Manuscript sources and early periodical articles are listed in full in the notes. Published diaries and journals are listed by author rather than editor.

A History and Biographical Cyclopedia of Butler County, Ohio, with illustrations and sketches of its representative men and pioneers. Cincinnati: Western Biographical Publishing Company, 1882.

Adams, Charles Francis. "Charles Francis Adams Visits the Mormons in 1844." Ed. Henry Adams, Jr. *Massachusetts Historical Society Proceedings* 68 (1952): 267–300.

Adams, John Quincy. *Memoirs of John Quincy Adams, comprising portions of his diary from 1795 to 1848.* Ed. Charles Francis Adams. Philadelphia: J. B. Lippincott & Co., 1874–77.

Allen, James B. "One Man's Nauvoo: William Clayton's Experience in Mormon Illinois." *Journal of Mormon History* 6 (1979): 37–59.

———. *Trials of Discipleship: The Story of William Clayton, a Mormon.* Urbana: University of Illinois Press, 1987.

———. "Was Joseph Smith a Serious Candidate for President of the United States?" *Ensign* 3 (September 1973): 21–22.

*Allen, James B., Ronald W. Walker, and David J. Whittaker. *Studies in Mormon History, 1830–1997: An Indexed Bibliography.* Urbana: University of Illinois Press, 2000.

Allman, John Lee. "Policing in Mormon Nauvoo." *Illinois Historical Journal* 89 (Summer 1996): 85–98.

Anderson, Richard Lloyd. "Joseph Smith's Prophecies of Martyrdom." *Sidney B. Sperry Symposium.* Provo, UT: Religious Instruction, 1980, 1–14.

"Angel Makeover." *Sunstone* 123 (July 2002): 14.

Archbold, Ann. *A Book for the Married and Single, the grave and the gay: and especially designed for steamboat passengers.* East Plainfield, OH: N. A. Baker, 1850.

Arrington, Leonard J. and Davis Bitton. *The Mormon Experience: A History of the Latter-day Saints.* New York: Alfred A. Knopf, 1979.

Asbury, Henry. *Reminiscences of Quincy, Illinois, containing historical events, anecdotes, matters concerning old settlers and old times, etc.* Quincy, IL: D. Wilcox and Sons, Printers, 1882.

Bachman, Daniel W. 1993. Joseph Smith, a True Martyr. In *Joseph Smith: The Prophet, The Man,* ed. Susan Easton Black and Charles D. Tate, Jr. Provo, UT: Brigham Young University, Religious Studies Center.

*Bagley, Will. *Blood of the Prophets: Brigham Young and the Massacre at Mountain Meadows.* Norman: University of Oklahoma Press, 2002.

Baker, Beverly Jeanne. "The Whigs and the Presidency: National Issues and Campaign Tactics 1840–1848." MA thesis, North Texas State University, 1979.

Baker, LeGrand L. "On to Carthage to Die." *Improvement Era* 72 (June 1969): 10–15.

Banks, Loy Otis. "The Role of Mormon Journalism in the Death of Joseph Smith." *Journalism Quarterly* 27 (Summer 1950): 268–81.

[Barnes, Thomas L.] "Carthage Jail Physician Testifies." *The Pioneer (Sons of Utah Pioneers).* Spring 1954: 47–53.

Barnett, Steven G. "The Canes of the Martyrdom." *BYU Studies* 21 (Spring 1981): 205–11.

Bates, Irene R. "William Smith, 1811–93, Problematic Patriarch." *Dialogue* 16 (Summer 1983): 11–23.

———. "Patriarchal Blessings and the Routinization of Charisma." *Dialogue* 26 (Fall 1993): 1–29.

Baxter, Maurice. *Orville H. Browning: Lincoln's Friend and Critic.* Bloomington: Indiana University Press, 1957.

Beaver, R. Pierce. "The Miami Purchase of John Cleves Symmes." *Ohio State Archaeological and Historical Quarterly* 40 (January 1931): 284–342.

Bentley, Joseph I. "Martyrdom of Joseph and Hyrum Smith." In *Encyclopedia of Mormonism*, ed. Daniel H. Ludlow, 2:860–62. New York: Macmillan, 1992.

Bergera, James Gary. "Secretary to the Senator; Carl A. Badger and the Smoot hearings." *Sunstone* 8 (January/April 1983): 36–41.

Bernauer, Barbara Hands. "Still 'Side by Side': The Final Burial of Joseph and Hyrum Smith." *John Whitmer Historical Association Journal* 11 (1991): 17–33.

———. *Still "Side by Side": The Final Burial of Joseph and Hyrum Smith.*. Parkdale, MO: Arrow Press, 1994.

Biographical Directory of the Texan Conventions and Congresses. Austin, TX: Book Exchange, 1941.

Biographical Review of Hancock County, Illinois. Chicago: Hobart, 1907.

Bishop, W. W. See: Lee, John D.

Bitton, Davis. *The Martyrdom Remembered: A one-hundred-fifty-year perspective on the assassination of Joseph Smith.* Salt Lake City, UT: Aspen Books, 1994.

———. "The Martyrdom of Joseph Smith in Early Mormon Writings." In Launius and Hallwas, *Kingdom on the Mississippi Revisited* (1996): 181–97.

———. "Mormons in Texas: The Ill-fated Lyman Wight Colony, 1844–1858." *Arizona and the West* 11 (Spring 1969): 5–26.

———. *The Martyrdom Remembered: Reactions to the Assassination of the Prophet Joseph Smith.* Salt Lake City, UT: Aspen Books, 1994.

Black, Susan Easton. *Membership of The Church of Jesus Christ of Latter-day Saints, 1830–1848,* 50 vols. Provo, UT: Religious Studies Center, Brigham Young University, 1984–88.

———. *The Tomb of Joseph.* Provo, UT: Foundation for Ancient Research & Mormon Studies, 1997.

Blake, Reed. *24 Hours to Martyrdom.* Salt Lake City, UT: Bookcraft, 1973.

———. *The Carthage Tragedy: The Martyrdom of Joseph Smith.* Provo, UT: LDS Book Publications, 1994.

The Book of Mormon. Translated by Joseph Smith, Jr. 1830. Salt Lake City, UT: The Church of Jesus Christ of Latter-day Saints, 1980.

Bowman, Martha. "The Wyandot Indians of Ohio in the Nineteenth Century." MA thesis, Bowling Green State University, 1965.

Braden, Gayle Anderson. "The Public Career of Edward Dickinson Baker." PhD diss., Vanderbilt University, 1960.

Brodie, Fawn. *No Man Knows My History: The Life of Joseph Smith the Mormon Prophet.* Second ed., rev. and enlarged. New York: Alfred A. Knopf, 1971.

Brooks, Juanita. *John Doyle Lee: Zealot – Pioneer Builder – Scapegoat.* Glendale, CA: Arthur H. Clark, 1962.

———. *The Mountain Meadows Massacre.* Norman: University of Oklahoma Press, 1962, 1970.

Browning, Orville Hickman. *The Diary of Orville Hickman Browning.* Ed. Theodore C. Pease. Collections of the Illinois State Historical Library. Springfield: Illinois State Historical Library, 1925–1933. 2 vols.

Buckley, James Monroe. "The Prophet Joseph and the Patriarch Hyrum Assassinated." *The Christian Advocate* 22 (June 1905): 968–969.

Buckingham, J. H. "Illinois As Lincoln Knew It: A Boston Reporter's Record of a Trip in 1847." In *Papers in Illinois History and Transactions for the Year 1937.* Springfield: Illinois States Historical Society, 1938.

Buerger, David John. "The Development of the Mormon Temple Endowment Ceremony." *Dialogue* 20 (Winter 1987): 33–76.

———. "The Fulness of the Priesthood: The Second Anointing in Latter-day Saint Theology and Practice." *Dialogue* 16 (Spring 1983): 11–44.

———. *Mysteries of Godliness: A History of Mormon Temple Worship.* Salt Lake City, UT: Signature Books, 1994.

Bullock, Thomas. *The Pioneer Camp of the Saints: the 1846 and 1847 Mormon trail journals of Thomas Bullock.* Ed. Will Bagley. Spokane, WA: A. H. Clark, 1997.

Burnet, Jacob. *Speech of Judge Burnett [sic], of Ohio, in the Whig National Convention, giving a brief history of the life of Gen. William Henry Harrison.* Washington, DC: Printed at the Madisonian Office, 1839.

Burton, Richard F. *The City of the Saints and Across the Rocky Mountains to California*. Ed. Fawn M. Brodie. New York: Alfred A. Knopf, 1963. Originally published in 1861, Appendix III contains the earliest publication of "The Martyrdom of Joseph Smith by Apostle John Taylor."

Bush, Lester E., Jr. "Mormonism's Negro Doctrine: An Historical Overview." *Dialogue* 8 (Spring 1973): 11–68.

Bushman, Claudia Lauper and Richard Lyman Bushman. *Building the Kingdom: A History of Mormons in America*. Oxford: Oxford University Press, 1999, 2001.

Calhoun, Frederick S. *The Lawmen: United States Marshals and Their Deputies, 1789–1989*. Washington, DC: Smithsonian Institution Press, 1989.

Calhoun, John C. *The Papers of John C. Calhoun*. Ed. Clyde N. Wilson. University of South Carolina Press, vols. 17–18, 1986, 1990.

Campbell, Stanley W. *The Slave Catchers: Enforcement of the Fugitive Slave Law, 1850–1860*. Chapel Hill: University of North Carolina Press, 1968, 1970.

Carleton, J. H. *The Mountain Meadows Massacre: A Special Report by J. H. Carleton, Bvt. Major U.S.A. Captian 1st Dragoons 1859*. Spokane, WA: Arthur H. Clark, 1995.

Carr, Robin L., Alphonse Cerza, and Robert Barnard. *Freemasonry and Nauvoo, 1839–1846*. Bloomington, IL: Masonic Book Club, 1989.

Cartwright, Peter. *Autobiography of Peter Cartwright: The Backwoods Preacher*. Cincinnati and New York: Cranston and Curts, Hunt and Eaton, 1856.

Cerza, Alphonse. *A Concise History of Freemasonry in Illinois*. Chicago: Grand Lodge of Illinois, 1968.

Chamless, Roy Z., Jr. *Lincoln's Assassins: A Complete Account of Their Capture, Trial, and Punishment*. Jefferson, NC: McFarland & Company, 1990.

Church History in the Fulness of Times: The History of the Church of Jesus Christ of Latter-day Saints. Prepared by the Church Educational System. Salt Lake City, UT: The Church of Jesus Christ of Latter-day Saints, rev. ed. 1993.

Cincinnati: A Guide to the Queen City and Its Neighbors. Cincinnati, OH: Wiesen-hart Press, 1943.

Clayton, John. *Illinois Fact Book and Historical Almanac, 1673–1968*. Carbondale: Southern Illinois University Press, 1970.

Clayton, William. *Clayton's Secret Writings Uncovered*. Comp. Gerald and Sandra Tanner. Salt Lake City, UT: Utah Lighthouse Ministry, 1982. Cited as Clayton, *Writings*.

———. *An Intimate Chronicle: The Journals of William Clayton*. Ed. George D. Smith, 1991. 2nd ed. Salt Lake City, UT: Signature Books in Association with Smith Research Associates, 1995. Cited as Clayton, *Intimate Chronicle*.

Colton, Calvin. *The Junius Tracts*. New York: Greeley & McElrath, 1843–1844. No. 1, The test, or Parties tried by their acts; No. 2, The currency; No. 3, The tariff; No. 4, Life of Henry Clay; No. 5, Political abolition; No. 6, Democracy; No. 7., Labor and capital; No. 8, The public lands; No. 9, Annexation of Texas; No. 10, The tariff triumphant.

Compton, Todd. *In Sacred Loneliness: The Plural Wives of Joseph Smith*. Salt Lake City, UT: Signature Books, 1997.

Cone, Stephen D. *Biographical and Historical Sketches: A Narrative of Hamilton and Its Residents from 1792 to 1896*. Hamilton, OH: Republican Publishing Company, 1896.

Conrad, John B. *History of Grant County Kentucky*. Williamstown, KY.: Grant County Historical Society, 1992.

Conrad, William. *Life and Travels of Elder William Conrad*. Cincinnati, OH: Wrighton & Co., 1876.

Conyers, Josiah B. *A Brief History of the Leading Causes of the Hancock Mob, in the Year 1846*. St. Louis: Cathart & Prescott, 1846.

Cook, Glen A. "A Review of Factors Leading to Tension Between the Church of Jesus Christ of Latter-Day Saints and Freemasonry." *The Philalethes* 48 (August 1995): 76–78, 81.

Cook, Lyndon W. "James Arlington Bennet and the Mormons." *BYU Studies* 19 (Winter 1979): 247–49.

———, ed. *The Revelations of the Prophet Joseph Smith: A Historical and Biographical Commentary of the Doctrine and Covenants*. Provo, UT: Seventies Mission Bookstore, 1981; Salt Lake City, UT: Deseret Book, 1985.

———. "William Law, Nauvoo Dissenter." *BYU Studies* 22 (Winter 1982): 47–72.

*———. *William Law: Biographical Essay, Nauvoo Diary, Correspondence, Interview*. Orem, UT: Grandin Book Company, 1994.

*Cox, Nancy L. "A Life of John Hardin of Illinois 1810–1847," MA Thesis, Miami University, Oxford, Ohio, 1964.

*Crawley, Peter. *A Descriptive Bibliography of the Mormon Church: Volume One 1830–1847*. Provo, UT: Religious Studies Center, Brigham Young University, 1997.

Cummings, Horace. "Conspiracy of Nauvoo." *The Contributor* 5 (April 1884): 251–60.

*Daniels, William M. *A Correct Account of the Murder of the Generals Joseph and Hyrum Smith at Carthage, on the 27th Day of June, 1844*. Nauvoo, IL: John Taylor, 1845. Written together with Lyman O. Littlefield. See: Littlefield, *The Martyrs*.

Darnell, M. B. "The Tragedy at Carthage." *Millennial Star* 56:252. Published as "An Eye Witness to Joseph Smith's Death." In Lundwall, *Fate of the Persecutors*, 212–215.

Darter, Francis M. *Celestial marriage; the sermons that cost Francis M. Darter his membership*. Salt Lake City, UT: By the Author, 1937.

Davidson, Karen Lynn. *Our Latter-day Hymns: The Stories and the Messages*. Salt Lake City, UT: Deseret Book, 1988.

*Davis, George T. M. *An Authentic Account of the Massacre of Joseph Smith, the Mormon Prophet, and Hyrum Smith, His Brother, Together with a Brief History of Rise and Progress of Mormonism, and All the Circumstances Which Led to Their Death*. St. Louis, MO: Chambers and Knapp, 1844.

*———. *Autobiography of the late Col. Geo. T. M. Davis, captain and aide-de-camp Scott's army of invasion (Mexico), from posthumous papers. Pub. by his legal representatives*. New York: Jenkins and McCowan, 1891.

Deseret News. Salt Lake City, UT: 1850–.

Dickens, Charles. *American Notes for General Circulation*. London: Chapman and Hall, 1842.

Dillenberger, Jane. "Mormonism and American Religious Art." In *Reflections on Mormonism : Judaeo-Christian parallels : papers delivered at the Religious Studies Center symposium, Brigham Young University, March 10–11, 1978*, ed., with an introductory essay, by Truman G. Madsen, 187–200.

The Doctrine and Covenants of The Church of Jesus Christ of Latter-day Saints. Salt Lake City, UT: The Church of Jesus Christ of Latter-day Saints, 1980.

Driggs, Howard R. "Visits to Carthage." *Juvenile Instructor* 46 (June 1911): 319–24.

Durham, G. Homer. *Joseph Smith: Prophet-Statesman*. Salt Lake City: Bookcraft, 1944.

———. "Joseph Smith and the Political World." *Improvement Era* 55 (October 1952): 712–713, 746–751.

———. "Joseph Smith's Statecraft." *Improvement Era* 45 (December 1942): 782–783, 823–826.

Durning, Bonnie Means. "A History of the Mormon Church in Texas, 1843–1906." MA thesis, East Texas State College, 1964.

Ehat, Andrew F. "'It Seems Like Heaven Began on Earth': Joseph Smith and the Constitution of the Kingdom of God." *BYU Studies* 20 (Spring 1980): 253–79.

Ellsworth, Paul D. "Mobocracy and the Rule of Law: American Press Reaction to the Murder of Joseph Smith." *BYU Studies* 20 (Fall 1979): 71–82.

English, Thomas Dunn. *1844, or the Power of the "S. F." a tale, developing the secret action of parties during the presidential campaign of 1844*. New York: Burgess, Stringer, 1847. Fiction.

Esplin, Ronald K. "Life in Nauvoo, June 1844: Vilate Kimball's Martyrdom Letters." *BYU Studies* 19 (winter 1979): 231–40.

Ferguson, James Carroll. "The Whig Party in Illinois and Indiana, 1844–1854." MS thesis, Illinois State University, 1964.

Fielding, Joseph. "'They Might Have Known That He Was Not a Fallen Prophet'—The Nauvoo Journal of Joseph Fielding." Trans. and ed. Andrew F. Ehat, *BYU Studies* 19 (Winter 1979): 133–66. Cited as Fielding, Nauvoo Journal.

Firmage, Edwin Brown and Richard Collin Mangrum. *Zion in the Courts: A Legal History of the Church of Jesus Christ of Latter-day Saints, 1830–1900*. Urbana: University of Illinois Press, 1988.

Fisk, William L. "John Bailhache: A British Editor in Early Ohio." *The Ohio Historical Quarterly* 67 (April 1958): 140–47.

Flake, Chad J., ed. *A Mormon Bibliography, 1830–1930: Books, Pamphlets, Periodicals, and Broadsides Relating to the First Century of Mormonism*. Salt Lake City, UT: University of Utah Press, 1978.

*Flanders, Robert B. *Nauvoo: Kingdom on the Mississippi*. Urbana: University of Illinois Press, 1965.

———. "The Kingdom of God in Illinois: Politics in Utopia." *Dialogue* 5 (Spring 1970): 26–36.

*Ford, Thomas. *Message from the Governor, in Relation to the Disturbances in Hancock County, December 21, 1844*. Springfield, IL.: Walters & Webers, Public Printers, 1844. Much of this text was incorporated verbatim into Ford's *History*.

*———. *A History of Illinois from its Commencement as a State in 1818 to 1847*. Chicago: S. C. Griggs and Co., 1854. Portions published in Smith, *History of the Church* 7: 1–51.

*———. *A History of Illinois from its Commencement as a State in 1818 to 1847*. 2 vols. Ed. Milo Milton Quaife. Chicago: Lakeside Press, R. R. Donnelley & Sons Co., 1945–1946.

Ford, Worthington. "The Campaign of 1844." *Proceedings of the American Antiquarian Society* 20 (October 1909): 106–126.

Fullmer, John S. *Assassination of Joseph and Hyrum Smith, the prophet and the patriarch of the Church of Jesus Christ of Latter-day Saints* . . . Liverpool, England: F. D. Richards, 1855.

Gardner, Hamilton. "The Nauvoo legion, 1840–1845: A Unique Military Organization." *Journal of the Illinois State Historical Society* 54 (Summer 1961): 181–97.

Garr, Arnold K. 1995. Joseph Smith: Candidate for President of the United States. In *Regional Studies in Latter-day Saint Church History*, ed. H. Dean Garrett, 151–68. Provo, UT: Brigham Young University, Department of Church History and Doctrine.

Gayler, George R. "Governor Ford and the Death of Joseph and Hyrum Smith." *Journal of the Illinois State Historical Society* 50 (winter 1957): 391–411.

———. "The Mormons and Politics in Illinois: 1839–1844." *Journal of the Illinois State Historical Society* 49 (Spring 1956): 48–66.

———. "The Expositor Affair: Prelude to the Downfall of Joseph Smith." *The Northwest Missouri State College Studies* 25 (February 1961): 3–15.

Gentry, Jeffery S. "Joseph Smith—religious prophet and secular politician." BYU student paper, 1994. BYU-Americana.

Gentry, Leland H. "The Danite Band of 1838." *BYU Studies* 14 (Summer 1974): 421–50.

Givens, George W. *In Old Nauvoo: Everyday Life in the City of Joseph*. Salt Lake City, UT: Deseret Book, 1990.

Givens, Teryl L. *The Viper on the Hearth: Mormons, Myths, and the Construction of Heresy*. New York: Oxford University Press, 1997.

Gibbons, Francis M. *Joseph Smith: Martyr, Prophet of God*. Salt Lake City, UT: Deseret Book, 1977.

Gibbons, Ted. *Like a Lamb to the Slaughter: The Nauvoo Expositor: Traitors & Treachery*. Orem, UT: Keepsake, 1990. Republished as *The Road to Carthage: Conspiracy and Betrayal*, 2002.

———. *I Witnessed the Carthage Massacre: The Testimony of Willard Richards*. Orem, UT: Keepsake, 1988. Republished as *Sealing the Testimony: An Eyewitness Account of the Martyrdom*, 2002.

Glazer, Walter. *Cincinnati in 1840: the social and functional organization of an urban community during the pre-Civil War period*. Columbus: Ohio State University Press, 1999.

Godfrey, Kenneth W. "Non-Mormon Views of the Martyrdom: A Look at Some Early Published Accounts." *John Whitmer Historical Association Journal* 7 (1987): 12–20.

———. 1993. Remembering the Deaths of Joseph and Hyrum Smith. In *Joseph Smith: The Prophet, the Man*, ed. Susan Easton Black and Charles D. Tate, Jr., 301–315. Provo, UT: Brigham Young University, Religious Studies Center.

———. "The Road to Carthage Led West." *Brigham Young University Studies* 8 (Winter 1968): 204–215.

*———. "Causes of Mormon–Non-Mormon Conflict in Hancock County, Illinois, 1839–1846," PhD diss., Brigham Young University, 1967.

Golding, Robyn Pearl. "A Research Aid to the Original Legal Records of Latter-Day Saint Leaders in Hancock County, Illinois, 1839–1847." MA project, Western Illinois University, 1993.

Gooch, John [printed for Freeman Nickerson]. *Death of the prophets Joseph and Hyram [sic] Smith: who were murdered while in prison at Carthage, on the 27th day of June, A.D. 1844*. Boston: Printed by John Gooch, Minot's Building, Spring Lane, corner Devonshire Street, 1844.

Graham, Bruce L. "The Presidential Campaign of Joseph Smith, Jr., 1844." MA thesis, Lamar University, 1976.

*Gregg, Thomas. *The History of Hancock County, Illinois*. Chicago: Charles C. Chapman, 1880.

———. *Portrait and Biographical Record of Hancock County*. Chicago: Lake City, 1890.

———. *The Prophet of Palmyra: Mormonism reviewed and examined in the life, character, and career of its founder, from "Cumorah Hill" to Carthage Jail and the desert. Together with a complete history of the Mormon era in Illinois, and an exhaustive investigation of the "Spalding manuscript" theory of the origin of the Book of Mormon*. New York: J. B. Alden, 1890.

Gunderson, Robert G. *The Log-Cabin Campaign*. Westport, CT: Greenwood Press, [1977] c1957.

Hack, Gwendolyn Kelley. *A Genealogical History of the Dunlevy Family; Don-Levi, Donlevy, Dunleavy, Dunlavey, Dunlevey, etc*. Columbus, OH: Evans Printing Co., 1901.

Hallwas, John E. *Thomas Gregg: Early Illinois Journalist and Author.* Macomb: Western Illinois University, 1983.

*Hallwas, John E. and Roger D. Launius, eds. *Cultures in Conflict: A Documentary History of the Mormon War in Illinois.* Logan: Utah State University Press, 1995.

Hamilton, Marshall. "Thomas Sharp's Turning Point: Birth of an Anti-Mormon." *Sunstone* 13 (October 1989): 16–22.

*Hampshire, Annette P. *Mormonism in Conflict: The Nauvoo Years.* New York: Edwin Mellen Press, 1985.

———. "Thomas Sharp and Anti-Mormon Sentiment in Illinois." *Journal of the Illinois State Historical Society* 72 (May 1979): 82–100.

———. "The Triumph of Mobocracy in Hancock County, 1844–1846." *Western Illinois Regional Studies* 5 (Spring 1982): 17–37.

Hansen, Klaus. "Joseph Smith and the Political Kingdom of God." *The American West* 5 (September 1968): 20–24, 63.

———. "The Metamorphosis of the Kingdom of God: Toward a Reinterpretation of Mormon History." *Dialogue* 1 (Autumn 1966): 63–83.

———. "The Political Kingdom of God as a Cause for Mormon-Gentile Conflict." *BYU Studies* 2 (Spring-Summer 1960): 241–60.

———. "The Political Kingdom of God as a Cause of Mormon-Gentile Conflict," In Launius and Hallwas, *Kingdom on the Mississippi Revisited* (1996), 62–71.

*———. *Quest for Empire: The Political Kingdom of God and the Council of Fifty in Mormon History.* East Lansing: Michigan State University Press, 1967; reprinted, Lincoln: University of Nebraska Press, 1974.

Hardy, B. Carmon. *Solemn Covenant: The Mormon Polygamous Passage.* Urbana: University of Illinois Press, 1992.

Hardin, John. *Speech of Mr. J. J. Hardin of Illinois Reviewing the Principles of James K. Polk and the Leaders of Modern Democracy, House of representatives, June 3, 1844.*

Hascall, U. B. and I. H. Pomeroy. "Letters of a Proselyte: The Hascall-Pomeroy Correspondence." *Utah Historical Quarterly* 25 (January–October 1957).

Hathaway, James T. *Incidents in the Campaign of 1844.* New Haven, CT: Press of J. T. Hathaway, 1905.

Haven, Charlotte. "A Girl's Letters from Nauvoo." *The Overland Monthly* 16 (December 1890): 616–638.

Hay, John. "The Mormon Prophet's Tragedy." *Atlantic Monthly* (December 1869): 671–678. See: Orson F. Whitney, for LDS response.

Haynes, John E. "Politics in 1844, Being a choice selection of the most important points contended for during the campaign..."Concord, NH: May 1, 1845. Note: a scrapbook containing newspaper clippings of the campaign from May 1–December 1, 1844. North Carolina Room, University of North Carolina Library, Chapel Hill. See: Robert S. Lambert, "Presidential Campaign of 1844." 108–110.

Haynes, Sam W. and Christopher Morris, eds. *Manifest Destiny and Empire[:] American Antebellum Expansionism.* College Station: Texas A&M University Press, 1997.

Heizer, Alta Harvey. *Hamilton in the Making.* Oxford, OH: Mississippi Valley Press, 1941.

Hickman, Martin B., "The Political Legacy of Joseph Smith." *Dialogue: A Journal of Mormon Thought* 3 (Autumn 1968): 22–27.

Hicks, Michael. "'Strains Which Will Not Soon Be Allowed to Die . . .': 'The Stranger' and Carthage Jail." *BYU Studies* 23 (Fall 1983): 389–400.

Hietala, Thomas R. *Manifest Design: Anxious Aggrandizement in Late Jacksonian America.* Ithaca: Cornell University Press, 1985.

Hill, Donna. *Joseph Smith: The First Mormon.* Garden City, NY: Doubleday, 1977.

Hill, Marvin S. "The Manipulation of History." *Dialogue* 5 (Autumn 1970): 96–99.

———. *Quest for Refuge: The Mormon Flight from American Pluralism.* Salt Lake City, UT: Signature Books, 1989.

Hinckley, Gordon B. *Heroes of the Restoration.* Salt Lake City, UT: Bookcraft, 1997.

Hirschon, Stanley P. *Lion of the Lord: A Biography of Brigham Young.* New York: Alfred A. Knopf, 1969.

Hobby, A. M. *Life and Times of David G. Burnet, First President of the Republic of Texas.* Galveston: Galveston News, 1871.

Hoffman, Mark W. "The Prophet for President," *TAMS Journal* 20.4 (August 1980): 150–52. Fantasy Joseph Smith token.

Hogan, Mervin B. *The Dedication of the Nauvoo Masonic Temple and the Strange Question of Dr. Goforth.* Salt Lake City, UT: By the Author, 1983.

————. *The Erection and Dedication of the Nauvoo Masonic Temple.* Salt Lake City, UT: By the Author, 1976.

————. *The Explosive Rupture Between the Grand Lodge of Illinois and the Mormon Lodges of Illinois and Iowa in 1843.* Salt Lake City: By the Author, 1976.

————. *The Founding Minutes of Nauvoo Lodge.* Des Moines, Iowa: Research Lodge Number 2, A. F. & A. M.,1971.

————. *Freemasonry and Civil Confrontation on the Illinois Frontier.* Salt Lake City, UT: By the Author, 1981.

————. *Freemasonry and the Lynching at Carthage Jail.* Salt Lake City, UT: By the Author, 1981.

*————. *Grand Master Abraham Jonas of Illinois.* Salt Lake City, UT: By the Author, 1983.

————. "Henry Clay, Joseph Smith, and the Presidency." *Royal Arch Mason* (Winter 1986): 229–234.

————. *The Involvement of John Cook Bennett with Mormonism and Freemasonry at Nauvoo.* Salt Lake City, UT: By the Author, 1983.

————. *James Adams and the Founding of the Grand Lodge of Illinois.* Salt Lake City, UT: By the Author, 1983.

————. *Mormon Masonry in Illinois Reviewed by a "Grand Master."* Salt Lake City, UT: By the Author, 1984.

*————. *Mormonism and Freemasonry: The Illinois Episode.* Salt Lake City, UT: Campus Graphics, 1980. Reprint of 267–326 from Volume Two of *Little Masonic Library.* Richmond, VA: Macoy Publishing and Masonic Supply, 1977.

————. *The Official Minutes of the Nauvoo Lodge U. D.* Des Moines, IA: Research Lodge No. 2, 1974.

Holt, Edgar Allan. *Party Politics in Ohio, 1840–1850.* Columbus, OH: F. J. Heer Printing Company, 1930.

Holzapfel, Richard Neitzel and Jeni Broberg Holzapfel. *Women of Nauvoo.* Salt Lake City, UT: Bookcraft, 1992.

Holzapfel, Richard Neitzel and T. Jeffery Cottle. *Old Mormon Nauvoo and Southeastern Iowa: Historic Photographs and Guide.* Santa Ana, CA: Fieldbrook Productions, 1991.

Hopkins, James F., ed. and Mary W. M. Hargreaves, associate ed. *The Papers of Henry Clay.* 11 vols. Lexington: University of Kentucky Press, 1959–1992.

Horton, Thomas. *A History of the rise of the Church of Jesus Christ of Latter Day Saints . . . Also a brief outline of their persecution, and martyrdom of their prophet Joseph Smith, and the appointment of his successor James J. Strang.* Geneva, NY: Gazette Print, 1849.

Hughes, Richard T. and C. Leonard Allen. *Illusions of Innocence: Protestant Primitivism in America, 1630–1875.* Chicago and London: University of Chicago Press, 1988.

Huntington, Zina Diantha. "'All Things Move in Order in the City': The Nauvoo Diary of Zina Diantha Huntington Jacobs." Ed. Maureen U. Beecher. *BYU Studies* (Spring 1979): 285–320.

*Huntress, Keith. *The Murder of an American Prophet: Events and Prejudice Surrounding the Killings of Joseph and Hyrum Smith; Carthage, Illinois, June 27, 1844.* San Francisco: Chandler Publishing , 1960.

————. "Governor Thomas Ford and the Murderers of Joseph Smith." *Dialogue: A Journal of Mormon Thought* 4 (Summer 1969): 41–52.

Hyde, Orson. *Speech of Elder Orson Hyde delivered before the High Priests' Quorum, in Nauvoo, April 27th, 1845, upon the course and conduct of Mr. Sydney Rigdon and upon the merits of his claims to the presidency of the Church of Jesus Christ of Latter-Day Saints.* Liverpool, England: James and Woodburn, 1845.

Illinois Volunteers in the Mormon War: The Disturbances in Hancock County 1844–1846. Palmer, IL: Genie-Logic Enterprises, 1997.

Infobases Collectors Library CD-ROM. Salt Lake City, UT: Infobases, 1998.

Jackson, Joseph H. *The Adventures and Experiences of Joseph H. Jackson: Disclosing the Depths of Mormon Villainy Practiced in Nauvoo.* Warsaw, IL: Printed for the Publisher, 1846.

Jaques, John. *The history of Junius and his works: and a review of the controversy respecting the identity of Junius. With an appendix, containing portraits and sketches by Junius.* London: Bell and Wood, 1843.

Jarvis, Edward. *The Autobiography of Edward Jarvis.* Ed. Rosalba Davico. London: Wellcome Institute for the History of Medicine, 1992.

Jensen, Andrew and Edward Stevenson. *Infancy of the Church . . . A Series of Letters* [to the *Deseret News*]. Salt Lake City, 1889.

Jensen, Richard L. and Richard G. Oman. *C. C. A. Christensen, 1831–1912: Mormon Immigrant Artist.* Salt Lake City, UT: The Church of Jesus Christ of Latter-day Saints, 1984.

Jessee, Dean C., ed. *Personal Writings of Joseph Smith.* Salt Lake City, UT: Deseret Book, 1984.

———. "The Reliability of Joseph Smith's History." *Journal of Mormon History* 3 (976): 23–46.

*———. "Return to Carthage: Writing the History of Joseph Smith's Martyrdom." *Journal of Mormon History* 8 (1981): 3–19.

———. "The Writing of Joseph Smith's History." *Brigham Young University Studies* 11 (Summer 1971): 439–73.

Johnson, Clark V. "The Missouri Redress Petitions: A Reappraisal of Mormon Persecutions in Missouri." *BYU Studies* 26 (Spring 1986): 31–44.

———, ed. *Mormon Redress Petitions: Documents of the 1833–1838 Missouri Conflict.* Provo, UT: Brigham Young University, Religious Studies Center, 1992.

Jolley, Clifton Holt. "The Martyrdom of Joseph Smith: An Archetypal Study." *Utah Historical Quarterly* 44 (Fall 1976): 329–350.

Journal of Discourses. 26 vols. London: Latter-day Saints' Book Depot, 1855–86.

Jones, Dan. "The Martyrdom of Joseph Smith and His Brother Hyrum." *BYU Studies* 24 (Winter 1984): 78–109.

Kimball, Heber C. *On the Potter's Wheel: The Diaries of Heber C. Kimball.* Ed. Stanley B. Kimball. Salt Lake City, UT: Signature Books, 1987.

Kimball, James L., Jr. "The Nauvoo Charter: A Reinterpretation." *Journal of the Illinois Historical Society* 64 (Spring 1971): 66–78.

———. "A Wall to Defend Zion: The Nauvoo Charter, 1840–1845." *BYU Studies* 15 (Summer 1975): 491–97.

*Kimball, Stanley B. *Sources of Mormon History in Illinois, 1839–48: An Annotated Catalog of the Microfilm Collection at Southern Illinois University.* 2nd ed. Carbondale: Southern Illinois University, 1966.

Lambert, Oscar D. *Presidential Politics in the United States, 1841–1844.* Durham, NC: Duke University Press, 1936.

Lambert, Robert S., "The Presidential Campaign of 1844 as Seen Through the Press." MA thesis, University of North Carolina, Chapel Hill, 1947.

*Launius, Roger D., "The Murders in Carthage: Non-Mormon Reports of the Assassination of the Smith Brothers." *The John Whitmer Historical Association Journal* 15 (1995): 17–34.

*Launius, Roger D. and John E. Hallwas, ed. *Kingdom on the Mississippi Revisited: Nauvoo in Mormon History.* Urbana: University of Illinois Press, 1996.

LeBaron, Garn, Jr. "Mormon Fundamentalism and Violence: A Historical Analysis." (1995), www.exmormon.org/violence.htm (Accessed 28 December 2004).

Lee, John D. *A Mormon Chronicle: The Diaries of John D. Lee, 1848–1876.* Ed. Juanita Brooks. San Marin, CA: Huntington Library; Los Angeles: Anderson, Ritchie & Simon, 1955.

Lee, John D. and W. W. Bishop. *Mormonism unveiled; or, The life and confessions of the late Mormon bishop, John D. Lee; (written by himself) embracing the history of Mormonism . . . with an exposition of the secret history, signs, symbols and crimes of the Mormon church. Also the true history of the horrible butchery known as the Mountain Meadows Massacre.* St. Louis, MO: Bryan, Brand, 1877.

Leonard, Glen M., *Nauvoo: A Place of Peace, A People of Promise.* Salt Lake City, UT: Deseret Book, 2002.

LeSueur, Stephen C. *The 1838 Mormon War in Missouri.* Columbia: University of Missouri Press, 1987.

Lincoln, Abraham. Basler, Roy P., ed.. *Collected Works of Abraham Lincoln.* New Brunswick, NJ.: Rutgers University Press, 1953–55.

———. Nicolay, John G., and John Hay, eds. *Complete Works of Abraham Lincoln,* vol. 1. New York: Taney-Thomas, 1894 [1905].

Literski, Nick. *Method Infinite: Freemasonry and the Mormon Restoration.* Draper, UT: Greg Kofford, 2005.

Littlefield, Lyman O. *The Martyrs; A Sketch of the Lives and a Full Account of the Martyrdom of Joseph and Hyrum Smith . . .* Salt Lake City, UT: Juvenile Instructor Office, 1882.

Lundwall, N. B., ed. *The Fate of the Persecutors of the Prophet Joseph Smith.* Salt Lake City, UT: Bookcraft, 1952.

Lyne, T. A. *A True and Descriptive Account of the Assassination of Joseph & Hiram Smith, The Mormon Prophet and Patriarch, at Carthage, Illinois, June 27th, 1844 . . .* New York: C. A. Calhoun, 1844.

Mace, Wandle. Autobiography of Wandle Mace. Typescript.

Madsen, Carol Cornwall. *In Their Own Words: Women and the Story of Nauvoo.* Salt Lake City, UT: Deseret Book, 1994.

Marquardt, H. Michael. *The Joseph Smith Revelations: Text & Commentary.* Salt Lake City, UT: Signature Books, 1999.

Marriages of Adams County, Illinois 1825–1860. (n.p.: Great River Genealogical Society, 1979.)

Marryat, Frederick. *Narrative of the Travels and Adventures of Monsieur Violet in California, Sonora, and Western Texas.* London: Longman's, 1843.

Marsh, Eudocia Baldwin. "Mormons in Hancock County: A Reminiscence." Ed. Douglas L. Wilson and Rodney O. Davis. *Journal of the Illinois State Historical Society* 64 (Spring 1971): 22–65.

May, Dean L. "Still a Puzzle—The Mysterious Place of Mormonism in American Culture." *Sunstone* 118 (April 2001): 82–84.

Mayhew, Henry. *History of the Mormons or, Latter-Day Saints with Memoirs of The Life and Death of Joseph Smith, the "American Mahomet."* Auburn and Buffalo: Miller, Orton & Mulligan, 1854. [Note: this work appeared in multiple editions.]

McConkie, Bruce R. *Mormon Doctrine.* 2nd ed. Salt Lake City, UT: Bookcraft, 1966.

McGee, Mr. and Mrs. [Increase and Maria Van Deusen]. *The Mormon Endowment; A Secret Drama, or Conspiracy, in the Nauvoo Temple, in 1846.* Syracuse, NY: By the Authors, 1847.

McLemee, Scott. "Latter-day Studies: Scholars of Mormonism confront the history of what some call 'the next world religion.'" *The Chronicle of Higher Education,* 22 March 2002, A14–A16

Melville, J. Keith. "Joseph Smith, the Constitution, and Individual Liberties." *BYU Studies* 28 (Spring 1988): 65–74.

Meriwether, Robert L., ed. *The Papers of John C. Calhoun.* Columbia: University of South Carolina Press, 1959–.

Merk, Frederick. *Fruits of Propaganda in the Tyler Administration.* Cambridge, MA: Harvard University Press, 1971.

———. *Slavery and the Annexation of Texas.* New York: Alfred A. Knopf, 1972.

Miller, David E. and Della S. Miller. *Nauvoo: The City of Joseph.* Santa Barbara, CA: Peregrine Smith, 1974.

Miller, George. *Correspondence of Bishop George Miller with the Northern Islander: From His First Acquaintance with Mormonism up to Near the Close of His Life.* Comp. Wingfield Watson. Burlington, WI: the Compiler, 1916. Later included in *A Mormon Bishop and His Son: Fragments of a Diary Kept By G. Miller, Sr., Bishop in the Mormon Church, and Some Records of Incidents in the Life of G. Miller, Jr., Hunter and pathfinder,* ed. H. H. Mills, 1917.

———. "De Tal Palo Tal Astilla." Ed. H. W. Mills. *Publications of the Historical Society of Southern California Annual* 10 (1917): 86–172.

Moeckel, Doug. "Governor Thomas Ford and the Nauvoo Riots." *Illinois History* 47 (April 1994): 66–67.

Morcombe, Joseph E. "Masonry and Mormonism: A Record of Events in Illinois and Iowa Transpiring between the years 1840 and 1846." *New Age* 2 (May, June 1905): 2-part series.

Mulder, William and A. Russell Mortensen. *Among the Mormons: Historic Accounts by Contemporary Observers.* 1958. Reprint, Lincoln: University of Nebraska Press, Bison Books, 1973.

Narrative of the late riotous proceedings against the liberty of the press, in Cincinnati with remarks and historical notices, relating to emancipation : addressed to the people of Ohio. Ohio Anti-Slavery Society. Cincinnati: 1836.

Nauvoo Neighbor (Nauvoo, Illinois, 1843–44).

National Party Conventions, 1831–1992. Washington, DC: Congressional Quarterly, 1992.

Neely, Mark E., Jr. *The Abraham Lincoln Encyclopedia.* New York: McGraw-Hill, 1982.

New Mormon Studies CD-ROM. Salt Lake City, UT: Smith Research Associates, 1998.

"New Website Takes Missionary Work into Cyberspace." *Sunstone* 122 (April 2002): 76

Newell, Linda King and Valeen Tippetts Avery. *Mormon Enigma: Emma Hale Smith, Prophet's Wife, "Elect Lady," Polygamy's Foe, 1804–1879.* Garden City, NY: Doubleday, 1984.

Norman, Keith. "A Kinder, Gentler Mormonism: Moving Beyond the Violence of Our Past." *Sunstone* 14.4 (August 1990): 10–14.

———. "How Long, O Lord? The Delay of the Parousia in Mormonism." *Sunstone* 8 (January–April 1983): 48–58.

Oaks, Dallin H. "The Suppression of the *Nauvoo Expositor*." *Utah Law Review* 9 (Winter 1965): 862–903.

*Oaks, Dallin H. and Marvin S. Hill. *Carthage Conspiracy: The Trial of the Accused Assassins of Joseph Smith*. Champaign-Urbana: University of Illinois Press, 1975.

Oaks, Dallin H. and Joseph I. Bentley. "Joseph Smith and the Legal Process: In the Wake of the Steamboat Nauvoo." *BYU Studies* 19 (Winter 1979): 167–198.

Ostling, Richard and Joan K. Ostling. *Mormon America: the Power and the Promise*. San Francisco: HarperSanFrancisco, 1999.

Otten, Leaun G. and C. Max Caldwell. *Sacred Truths of the Doctrine & Covenants*. Salt Lake City, UT: Deseret Book, 1993.

Partridge, George F. "The Death of a Mormon Dictator: Letters of Massachusetts Mormons, 1843–48." *The New England Quarterly* 9 (December 1936): 583–617.

Past and present of Rock Island County, Ill., containing a history of the county—its cities, towns, etc., a biographical directory of its citizens, war record of its volunteers in the late Rebellion, portraits of early settlers and prominent men . . . Chicago: H. F. Kett, 1877.

Pease, Janet K. *Kentucky County Court Records: Grant-Harrison-Pendleton*. Williamstown, KY: Grant County Historical Society, 1985–.

Pease, Theodore Calvin, ed. *Illinois Election Returns 1818–1848*. Collections of the Illinois State Historical Library, Volume XVIII, Statistical Series, Volume I. Springfield: Illinois State Historical Library, 1923.

Picklesimer, Dorman, Jr. "To Campaign or Not to Campaign: Henry Clay's Speaking Tour through the South." *Filson Club Historical Quarterly* 42 (July 1968): 235–242.

Piercy, Frederick Hawkins. *Route from Liverpool to Great Salt Lake Valley*. Ed. James Linforth. 1855. Reprint, ed. Fawn M. Brodie. Cambridge, MA: Belnap Press of Harvard University Press, 1962.

Poage, George R. *Henry Clay and the Whig Party*. Chapel Hill: University of North Carolina Press, 1936.

Poll, Richard D. "Joseph Smith and the Presidency." *Dialogue* 3 (Autumn 1968): 17–21.

———. *History and Faith: Reflections of a Mormon Historian*. Salt Lake City, UT: Signature Books, 1989.

Pollock, Gordon D. *In Search of Security: The Mormons and the Kingdom of God on Earth, 1830–1844*. Dissertations in Nineteenth-Century American Political and Social History. Garland Publishing, 1989. [1977]

Porter, Larry C. "How Did the U.S. Press React When Joseph and Hyrum were Murdered?" *Ensign* 14 (April 1984): 22–23.

Poulson, Richard C. "Fate of the Persecutors of Joseph Smith: Transmutations of an American Myth." *Dialogue* 11 (Winter 1978): 63–70.

Power, John Carroll. *History of Springfield, Illinois its attractions as a home and advantage for business, manufacturing, etc.* Springfield, IL: Illinois State Journal Print, 1871.

Prince, Benjamin F. "The Rescue Case of 1857." *Ohio Archaeological and Historical Publications* 16 (1907): 292–309.

Proceedings of the Grand Lodge of Kentucky, F. and A. M . . . annual communication. Louisville, The Grand Lodge. Various.

Proceedings of the Most Worshipful Grand Lodge of Ancient Free and Accepted Masons of the State of Illinois. (n.p: n.p, 1840–.) Reprint edition Freeport, IL: Journal Print, 1892. Cited as *Proceedings/Reprint*.

Proceedings Before the Committee on Privileges and Elections of the United States Senate in the Matter of the Protests Against the Right of Hon. Reed Smoot, a Senator from the State of Utah, to hold his Seat. U.S. Senate Document 486 (59th Congress, 1st Session), 4 vols. Plus index. Washington, DC: Government Printing Office, 1906.

The Prophet. New York City: Society for the Diffusion of Truth. 1844–1845.

Quinn, D. Michael. "The Council of Fifty and Its Members, 1844 to 1945." *BYU Studies* 20 (Winter 1980): 163–97.

*———. *The Mormon Hierarchy: Origins of Power*. Salt Lake City, UT: Signature Books, 1994.

———. "The Mormon Succession Crisis of 1844." *BYU Studies* 16 (Winter 1976): 187–233.

Remini, Robert V. *Henry Clay: Statesman for the Union*. New York: W. W. Norton, 1991.

———. *Joseph Smith*. New York: Viking, 2002.

Reynolds, John. *My Own Times: Embracing Also the History of My Life*. Belleville, IL: Printed by B. H. Perryman and H. L. Davison, 1855.

Richardson, William A., Jr. "Many contests for the County Seat of Adams County, Ill." *Journal of the Illinois State Historical Society* 17 (October 1924): 369–380.

Rigdon, Sidney. *Oration Delivered by Mr. S. Rigdon on the 4th of July, 1838, at Far West, Caldwell Co., Missouri*. Far West: Printed at the Journal Office, 1838.

Roberts, Brigham H. *A Comprehensive History of The Church of Jesus Christ of Latter-day Saints, Century One*. 6 vols. Salt Lake City, UT: Deseret News Press, 1930.

———. *The Rise and Fall of Nauvoo*. Salt Lake City, UT: Deseret News, 1900; reprint Salt Lake City, UT: Bookcraft, 1965.

Robertson, Andrew W. *The Language of Democracy: Political Rhetoric in The United States and Britain, 1790–1900*. Ithaca and London: Cornell University Press, 1995.

Robertson, Margaret C. "The Campaign and the Kingdom: The Activities of the Electioneers in Joseph Smith's Presidential Campaign." *BYU Studies* 39.3 (2000): 147–80.

Rugh, Susan Sessions. *Saints and Old Settlers: The Conflict in Hancock County, Illinois, 1840–1846*. The Newberry Papers in Family and Community History. Chicago: Newberry Library, 1991.

Salmela, Kirk Roger. "Illinois whiggery, politics and statesmanship: a study of destiny, dissent, and bitterness in the era of southwestern expansion, 1844–1848," DA thesis, Illinois State University, 1989.

Schindler, Harold. *Orrin Porter Rockwell: Man of God, Son of Thunder*. 1966. 2nd ed. Salt Lake City, UT: University of Utah Press, 1983.

Scofield, Charles J. *History of Hancock County*. Chicago: Munsell, 1921.

Searle, Howard C. "Authorship of the History of Joseph Smith: A Review Essay." *BYU Studies* 21 (Winter 1981): 101–122.

Sears, L. Rex. "Theology and Christology Through the lens of a Little Couplet." *Sunstone* 122 (April 2002): 34–39.

Seller, Charles. 1971. Election of 1844. In *History of American Presidential Elections 1789-1968*, ed. Arthur M. Schlesinger, Jr. 747–861. New York: Chelsea House

Shalhope, Robert. "Republicanism and Early American Historiography," *William and Mary Quarterly* 3a (April 1982):334–56.

[Sharp, Thomas]. *Trial of the Persons Indicted in the Hancock Circuit Court for the Murder of Joseph Smith at the Carthage Jail, on the 27th day of June, 1844*. Warsaw, IL: Warsaw Signal, 1845.

Shipps, Jan. "The Mormons in Politics, 1839–1844." MA thesis, University of Colorado, 1962.

———. "The Mormons in Politics: The First Hundred Years." PhD diss., University of Colorado, 1965.

———. *Sojourner in the Promised Land: Forty years among the Mormons*. Urbana: University of Illinois Press, 2000.

———. "Surveying the Mormon Image Since 1960." *Sunstone* 118 (April 2001): 58–72.

Sillitoe, Linda and Allen Roberts, *Salamander: The Story of the Mormon Forgery Murders*. Salt Lake City, UT: Signature Books, 1988.

Smith, Andrew F. *Saintly Scoundrel: The Life and Times of Dr. John Cook Bennett*. Urbana: University of Illinois Press, 1997.

Smith, Eliza R. Snow. *Biography and Family Record of Lorenzo Snow[:] One of the Twelve Apostles of the Church of Jesus Christ of Latter-day Saints. Written and Compiled by His Sister, Eliza R. Snow Smith*. Salt Lake City, UT: Deseret News, 1884.

Smith, Henry A. *The Day They Martyred the Prophet: A Historical Narrative*. Salt Lake City, UT: Bookcraft, 1963.

Smith, Joseph, Jr. *General Smith's Views on the Powers and Policy of the Government of the United States*. Nauvoo: John Taylor, 1844. Subsequent editions are listed in Crowley, *A Descriptive Bibliography*, items 201, 209, 210, 213, 214, 215, 216, 217, 218, 219, 220.

———. *History of the Church of Jesus Christ of Latter-day Saints*. 7 vols. Salt Lake City, UT: Deseret News, 1902–12, 1932.

———. *Teachings of the Prophet Joseph Smith*. Salt Lake City, UT: Deseret Book, 1977.

———. *The Words of Joseph Smith: The Contemporary Accounts of the Nauvoo Discourses of the Prophet Joseph Smith*. Ed. Andrew F. Ehat and Lyndon W. Cook. Provo, UT: Brigham Young University, Religious Studies Center, 1980.

————. *An American Prophet's Record: The Diaries and Journals of Joseph Smith.* Ed. Scott H. Faulring. Salt Lake City, UT: Signature Books in association with Smith Research Associates, 1989.

*Smith, Joseph Fielding, Jr. and Richard C. Evans. *Blood Atonement and the Origin of Plural Marriage: A Discussion.* Salt Lake City, UT: Deseret News Press, [1905].

Smith, Joseph Fielding. *The Life of Joseph F. Smith.* Salt Lake City, UT: Deseret News Press, 1938.

Smith, Lucy. *Lucy's Book : Critical edition of Lucy Mack Smith's family memoir.* Ed. Lavina Fielding Anderson. Salt Lake City, UT: Signature Books, 2001.

Smith, William, et al. *Remonstrance of William Smith et. al., of Covington, Kentucky: against the admission of Deseret into the Union, December 31, 1849.* Washington, DC: Government Printing Office, 18——. Miscellaneous, 31st Congress, 1st Session, no. 43.

Snow, Eliza R. *Poems. Religious, Historical, and Political.* Liverpool, England: F. D. Richards, 1856.

Staker, Susan. "Waiting for World's End: Wilford Woodruff and David Koresh." *Sunstone* 16 (December 1993): 11–16.

Stenhouse, T. B. H. *The Rocky Mountain Saints.* New York: D. Appleton and Company, 1873.

Stephanson, Anders. *Manifest Destiny: American Expansionism and the Empire of Right.* New York: Hill and Wang, 1995.

Stiles, Edward H. *Recollections and Sketches of Notable Lawyers and Public Men of Early Iowa . . .* Des Moines: Homestead Publishing Company, 1916.

Stout, Hosea. *On the Mormon Frontier: The Diary of Hosea Stout, 1844–1861.* Ed. Juanita Brooks. 2 vols. Salt Lake City, UT: University of Utah Press and Utah State Historical Society, 1964.

Strohm, Isaac, ed. *Speeches of Thomas Corwin: with a sketch of his life.* Dayton, OH: W. F. Comley & Co., 1859.

Sweeney, John, Jr. "A History of the Nauvoo Legion in Illinois." MA thesis, Brigham Young University, 1974.

Swinton, Heidi S. *American Prophet: The Story of Joseph Smith.* Salt Lake City, UT: Shadow Mountain, 1999.

Tanner, Jerald and Sandra Tanner. *The Changing World of Mormonism.* Chicago: Moody Press, 1981.

————. *Evolution of the Mormon Temple Ceremony: 1842–1990.* Salt Lake City, UT: By the Authors, 1990.

Taylor, James W. *"A choice nook of memory": the diary of a Cincinnati law clerk, 1842–1844, James Wickes Taylor.* Ed. James Taylor Dunn. Columbus: Ohio State Archaeological and Historical Society, 1950.

Taylor, John. "The John Taylor Nauvoo Journal." Ed. Dean C. Jesse. *BYU Studies* 23 (Summer 1983): 1–103.

Taylor, Mark H., ed. *Witness to the Martyrdom: John Taylor's Personal Account of the Last Days of the Prophet Joseph Smith.* Salt Lake City, UT: Deseret Book, 1999. See Burton, *The City of the Saints.*

Taylor, Samuel. *Nightfall at Nauvoo.* New York: Macmillan, 1971.

Testimony of Important Witnesses as given in the Proceedings before the Committee on Privileges and Elections of the United States Senate in the Matter of the Protest Against the Right of Hon. Reed Smoot, A Senator for the State of Utah, to Hold His Seat. Salt Lake City, UT: Salt Lake Tribune, 1905.

Thomas, Michael S. "Freemasonry and Mormonism," www.freedomdomain.com/freemasons/mormons01.html (accessed 28 December 2004).

Thompson, Edward George. "A Study of the Political Involvements in the Career of Joseph Smith." MA thesis, Brigham Young University, 1966.

Times and Seasons. Commerce and Nauvoo, Illinois, 1839–46.

Tracy, Shannon M. *In Search of Joseph.* Orem, UT: Kenning House, 1995.

Turley, Richard E. *Victims: The LDS Church and the Mark Hofmann Case.* Urbana and Chicago: University of Illinois Press, 1992.

Turley, Richard E., Jr., ed.. *Selected Collections from the Archives of The Church of Jesus Christ of Latter-day Saints.* Volume 1 (38 CD-ROMs), Volume 2 (36 CD-ROMs). Provo, UT: Brigham Young University Press, 2002.

Turnbull, Everett R. *The Rise and Progress of Freemasonry in Illinois, 1783–1952.* Harrisburg [?], Grand Lodge of Illinois, 1952.

Turner, Wallace. "Henry Clay and the Campaign of 1844." MA thesis, University of Kentucky, 1933.

Van Noord, Roger. *King of Beaver Island: The Life and Assassination of James Jesse Strang.* Urbana: University of Illinois Press, 1988.

Van Orden, Bruce A. "William W. Phelps's Service in Nauvoo as Joseph Smith's Political Clerk." *BYU Studies* 32 (Winter 1991): 1–11.

Van Wagenen, Michael Scott. *The Texas Republic and the Mormon Kingdom of God.* Kingsville, TX: South Texas Regional Studies, 2002.

Van Wagoner, Richard S. and Steven C. Walker. *A Book of Mormons.* Salt Lake City, UT: Signature Books, 1982.

———. "The Joseph/Hyrum Smith Funeral Sermon." *BYU Studies* 23 (Winter 1983): 3–18.

Vetterli, Richard. *Mormonism, Americanism, and Politics.* Salt Lake City: Ensign, 1961.

Walgren, Kent. "James Adams: Early Springfield Mormon and Freemason." *Journal of the Illinois State Historical Society* 75 (Summer 1982): 121–36.

Walle, Dennis F. "The Whig presidential campaign of 1840 in Illinois." M.A. thesis, DePaul University, 1968.

Waller, Elbert. "Some Half-Forgotten Towns in Illinois." *Transactions of the Illinois State Historical Society,* 1927, 65–82.

Warner, Edward Allen. "Mormon Theodemocracy: Theocratic and Democratic Elements in Early Latter-day Saint Ideology, 1827–1846." PhD diss., University of Iowa, 1973.

Warvelle, George William. *A Compendium of Freemasonry in Illinois; embracing a review of the introduction, development and present condition of all rites and degrees; together with biographical sketches of distinguished members of the fraternity.* Chicago: Lewis Publishing Company, 1897.

Weisenburger, Francis P. *The Life of John McLean: A Politician on the United States Supreme Court.* Columbus: The Ohio State University Press, 1937.

———. *The Passing of the Frontier, 1825–1850.* Columbus: Ohio State Archaeological and Historical Society, 1941.

Whitney, Orson F. *Life of Heber C. Kimball.* Salt Lake City, UT: Bookcraft, 1992.

———. "Lives of our leaders—The Apostles: Lorenzo Snow." *Juvenile Instructor* (January 1, 1900).

———. *"The Mormon Prophet's Tragedy": A Review of an Article by the Late John Hay: published originally in the Atlantic Monthly for December, 1869, and republished in the Saints Herald of June 21, 1905.* Salt Lake City, UT: The Deseret News, 1905.

Whitney, Ellen M., comp. *The Black Hawk War, 1831–1832.* Springfield: Illinois State Historical Society, 1970–.

Whittaker, David J. 1990. The Book of Daniel in Early Mormon thought. In *By Study and Also by Faith: Essays in Honor of Hugh W. Nibley on the Occasion of His Eightieth Birthday 27 March 1990.* Volume 1, ed. John M. Lundquist and Stephen D. Ricks, 155–201. Salt Lake City, UT: Deseret Book, 1990.

Wight, Lyman. *An Address by way of an abridged account and journal of my life from February 1844 up to April 1848, with an appeal to the Latter Day Saints.* 1848. Photostatic copy in Jeremy Benton Wight, *The Wild Ram of the Mountain: The Story of Lyman Wight.* [Afton, WY?]: Star Valley Llama, 1996.

Williams, J. D. "The Separation of Church and State in Mormon theory and Practice." *Dialogue* 1.2 (Summer 1966): 30–54. Also published, slightly revised, in *Church and State* 9 (Spring 1967): 238–62.

Winard, Brent L. "The publishers of the Nauvoo Expositor." [1971] BYU-Americana.

Wood, Timothy L. "The Prophet and the Presidency: Mormonism and Politics in Joseph Smith's 1844 Presidential Campaign." *Journal of the Illinois State Historical Society* 93.2 (Summer 2000): 167–93.

Woodruff, Wilford. *Waiting for World's End: The Diaries of Wilford Woodruff.* Ed. Susan Staker. Salt Lake City, UT: Signature Books, 1993.

*———. *Wilford Woodruff's Journals.* Ed. Scott G. Kenney. 9 vols. Midvale, UT: Signature Books, 1985. Also published in *New Mormon Studies* CD-ROM.

Woodworth, Jed. "Josiah Quincy's 1844 Visit with Joseph Smith." *BYU Studies* 39 no. 4 (2000):71–87.

Wright, Lawrence. "A Reporter at Large: Lives of the Saints; At a time when Mormonism is booming, the Church is struggling with a troubled legacy." *The New Yorker* 21 (January 2002): 40–57.

Wyl, W. *Mormon Portraits or the truth about the Mormon Leaders From 1830 to 1886 . . .* Salt Lake City, UT: Tribune Printing and Publishing Company, 1886.

Young, Brigham. *Manuscript History of Brigham Young 1801–1844.* Comp. Elden Jay Watson. Salt Lake City, UT: Smith Secretarial Service, 1968. Comp. from the *Millennial Star* 25–26.

Index

Organizations and religious terms that have specific meaning within Mormonism are marked (LDS).